Conditio Judaica 67
Studien und Quellen zur deutsch-jüdischen Literatur- und Kulturgeschichte

Herausgegeben von Hans Otto Horch
in Verbindung mit Alfred Bodenheimer, Mark H. Gelber und Jakob Hessing

D1724246

Theodor Herzl:
From Europe to Zion

Edited by
Mark H. Gelber
and Vivian Liska

Max Niemeyer Verlag
Tübingen 2007

Gershon Shaked (1929–2006)
in memoriam

Bibliografische Information der Deutschen Nationalbibliothek

Die Deutsche Nationalbibliothek verzeichnet diese Publikation in der Deutschen Nationalbiblio-
grafie; detaillierte bibliografische Daten sind im Internet über *http://dnb.ddb.de* abrufbar.

ISBN 978-3-484-65167-8   ISSN 0941-5866

© Max Niemeyer Verlag, Tübingen 2007
Ein Imprint der Walter de Gruyter GmbH & Co. KG
http://www.niemeyer.de

Contents

Introduction

The one hundredth anniversary of the death of Theodor Herzl (1860–1904) in 2004 was marked by numerous public and scholarly activities in Israel, Europe, and elsewhere internationally. This anniversary provided a timely opportunity to reassess his career, writings, and their reception utilizing a wide range of different approaches and methodologies. There have been fundamental shifts in the way Herzl has been viewed over the course of the last century. There are several reasons which might explain these shifts that go beyond the normal changes and innovations in critical methodologies and analysis during this time period. Following the realization of Herzl's goal, that is, the demonstrable success of political Zionism signalized by the establishment of the State of Israel in 1948, it became clear that Herzl, the utopian visionary and activist, may have been more prescient than many of his contemporary and subsequent antagonists had surmised. It is fair to say that his Zionist writings, for example, *Der Judenstaat* (1896) and *Altneuland* (1902) generated as much controversy and opposition within Jewry as did his political and diplomatic activities, the creation of the World Zionist Organization under his leadership, and the inauguration of what is called in Zionist historiography Congress Zionism. Also, Herzl's understanding of antisemitism was proven, unfortunately, to be quite cogent, not only by the horrific tragedy of the Nazi genocide against European Jewry, but also by the continuation of vicious antisemitism after the Shoah into the 21st century, especially in Europe.

Furthermore, it has become clear on the basis of surveys, population studies, and informed calculations and predictions that the Zionist idea has become in the early 21st century the foremost popular ideology among world Jewry. On one hand, Zionism has proven to be flexible and inclusive enough in order to appropriate sectors of Jewry which historically opposed it. On the other hand, regarding Jewish demographics alone, Zionism appears to have provided the Jewish people with the only social and political framework in which the Jewish population increases yearly on the basis of natural reproduction or the ratio of more live births than deaths. That is, while world Jewry was demographically and geographically transformed by the vicissitudes and dislocations of the Jewish experience in the 20th century, by the end of the 20th century and in the first years of the 21st century, a plurality and perhaps also soon a majority of world Jewry was or would be in fact resident in the Jewish State. There appears to be no general agreement about exact numbers, but the trend is clear and obvious. Furthermore, we submit that the recent, although short-lived, popularity of post-Zionism and the rise of diasporism within Jewry are sure signs of the triumph of Zionism within Jewry at large. How a marginal, minority and in some ways extreme Jewish national movement was able to succeed to this degree within a century and establish its national home as a political state and appropriate large sectors of the Jewish people in different ways, is not easy to explain. But the name of Herzl is ineluctably associated with this historical transformation. As is well known, Herzl, one of the foremost intellectual architects of Zionism and the state idea, predicted with ebullience at the time of the First Zionist Congress in Basel in 1897 that within fifty years, a Jewish State could come into existence. At the time, it appeared by and large to be a totally unrealistic political goal, if not a great folly.

The present volume is comprised of essays which reflect part of the international scholarly and intellectual activity characteristic of the Herzl year in 2004. The core of this collection consists of revised lectures which were delivered at an international conference, »Theodor Herzl, from Europe to Zion,« which was organized by the editors of this volume and the Institute of Jewish Studies at the University of Antwerp. Additional revised lectures given during the Herzl year complement the Antwerp talks. Most of these were delivered at an international conference held in 2004 in Israel, »Theodor Herzl – Then and Now,« organized by Jacob Golomb and Robert S. Wistrich and the Center for Austrian Studies at the Hebrew University in Jerusalem. In effect, Israeli, European, and North American scholars from different disciplines in the humanities and social sciences bring new perspectives to bear on controversial issues which inform the contemporary discussion of Herzl and Zionism. Also new material and analysis is provided regarding unknown or little known aspects of Herzl's reception on stage and on screen. Of course, Herzl is not responsible for the political, social, or cultural problems of the State of Israel. But, the complex reality of the state, embattled as it often is on several fronts at once, appears to loom largely over the scholarly discussions. The failure of the state to achieve peace with the Palestinians and with some of its Arab neighbors is perhaps the most important aspect in this regard, and it seems to be a sub-text in several of the contributions to this volume.

It appears to be in the background of a few essays found in this collection. For example, Robert S. Wistrich, in his article on »Herzl between Myth and Messianism,« attempts to analyze Herzl's Zionism as a secularized messianic movement, maintaining that Zionism ultimately sought a reconciliation between Jewry and the nations of the world. Also, Denis Charbit, in his piece on Herzl's nationalism, situates his analysis broadly within the contemporary scholarly debate regarding the construction of nationalisms. In this context, he seeks to test Herzl's own nationalism against other varieties of nationalist endeavor and identification. In »Theodor Herzl and the Crisis of Jewish Self-

Understanding,« Klaus Hödl discusses the impact of Vienna on Herzl in terms of the way this unique cultural setting with its own nationalities issues exerted certain impact on the specific conversion to Zionism in this case. And, Jacques Kornberg, in his contribution, pinpoints Herzl's Zionism within the larger discussion about the European Enlightenment, as well as within the framework of the debate about Jewish integration and assimilation in Europe. Kornberg's essay poses some questions regarding the possibility of determining the extent to which Herzl's Zionism was European and to what extent it might be Jewish. Thus, Kornberg discusses the possible categorization of Herzl, on one hand, as a Jewish thinker, and, on the other hand, as a European one. Kornberg also raises the issue concerning the positioning of Herzl's proposed Jewish State between Europe and the Orient. In his early Zionist writings, for example in *Der Judenstaat*, Herzl envisioned the Jewish State as a potential barrier for Europe against the barbaric East. In this sense, Zion would assume a protective role on the border between Occident and Orient. However, later on in his career, after he had founded the Zionist Organization, visited in the land of Israel, and come to a deeper understanding of world Jewry and Jewish history, he entertained the idea of the Jewish State in Zion, for example in *Altneuland*, as a bridge between East and West. The Jewish State would thus become a bustling and prosperous transportation and commercial hub, linking East and West, Africa, Asia, and Europe, and it would serve to facilitate cross-cultural transfers. The special role of Africa in Zionist consciousness and Israeli culture, beginning with Herzl's championing of the Uganda plan, is discussed at length by Eitan Bar-Yosef in his contribution to this volume.

Some of the essays in this volume focus on Herzl as a »man of the moment« and his various visual images and their importance for the burgeoning Zionist movement (Michael Berkowitz). Frank Stern investigates these images and their cultural context, as well as their significance as propaganda in early Zionist film. Daniel Hoffman supplies new information concerning Herzl's friendship with Gustav C. Cohen, which in turn sheds light on Herzl's intimate circle of acquaintances and their importance to him, both in terms of male bonding and personal assistance and regarding political and financial support. Benno Wagner, in his contribution, is interested in assessing Herzl's qualities and profile as a leader, while considering the complicating comparative aspects of the perception of him in a leadership role. In order to adumbrate this portrait, Wagner chooses to include in his discussion two very dissimilar counterparts to Herzl: T. G. Masaryk and Franz Kafka. Jacob Golomb considers Herzl as a »Grenzjude,« a marginal Jew, who attempts to negotiate the limits of marginality in his writings, especially in his »Philosophical Tales.« The »Philosophical Tales« are also of great interest in another essay (Vivian Liska) included in this volume, especially to the extent that they reveal and partially conceal subtle dimensions of the tension between Herzl's commitment to his writing (and to his literary career and to his family) as opposed to his commitment to political and diplomatic activity on the stage of world history. This essay and others appear to question the extent to which the Herzl myth was already being constructed by him during his lifetime.

The specific topic of the development of the Herzl myth, its contours, and its various versions in different genres is treated at length (Mark H. Gelber) in more than one contribution to this collection. The reception of Herzl on the stage, for example in plays by Nathan Bistritzki (Gershon Shaked) and George Tabori (Anat Feinberg), also raises the issue of the debunking of that myth or the production of a subversive countermyth, which also poses difficult questions regarding both the heroic image of Herzl and the historical course of Zionism, as it strove to realize the movement's program. At the same time, the theatrical reception of Herzl in Europe and in Zion serves to bring to mind Herzl's own stature as a dramatist. In his essay, »›What Will People Say?‹ Herzl as Author of Comedies,« Bernard Greiner analyzes the manner in which Herzl, following the example of Hugo von Hofmannsthal, attempted to »attain the social« in his light comedies. At the same time, this analysis contributes to our broader understanding of some aspects of the aesthetics of Zionism. Along similar lines, in her contribution Na'ama Rokem utilizes notions of the relationship of the prosaic to prose, derived to a degree from her reading of Hegel, in order to probe the role of literature, especially prose writing, within the process of the revolutionary transformation of Jewish life within Zionism. As a counterpart to the analysis of Herzl, Rokem includes in her paper a section on Haim Nachman Bialik, who is sometimes paired with Herzl. In this connection, Bialik represents the spiritual father, the poetic and cultural inspiration of modern Zionism, while Herzl represents the movement's political father, who inspired its political destiny and diplomatic mission.

*

The editors would like to thank the individual contributors for their scholarly efforts, which led to the realization of this project. Grants from the Research Foundation – Flanders (FWO) and the Flemish Community Department of Education financed the International Herzl conference in Antwerp in 2004. Special thanks are due to the staff of the Institute of Jewish Studies at the University of Antwerp, especially Katrien Vloeberghs and Jan Wolf (†), who has since passed away, for their stellar organization of the Antwerp conference.

Also, the editors are grateful to Jacob Golomb, Robert S. Wistrich, and Alma Lessing of the Center for Austrian Studies at the Hebrew University in Jerusalem, for facilitating the publication of several papers that were delivered at the Herzl Centennial Conference in Israel. A generous grant from the Institute of Jewish Studies at the University of Antwerp made the publication of this volume possible. Regarding the technical process of preparing the essays for publication, the editors would like to thank Hans Otto Horch and Doris Vogel (Aachen) for their advice and assistance.

Unfortunately, Gershon Shaked, one of the contributors to this project and a truly distinguished literary critic and historian, as well as the foremost Israeli scholar of modern Hebrew Literature, passed away before this volume was published. The editors wish to dedicate this volume to his memory: Yehi Zikhro Barukh.

Vivian Liska, Antwerp
Mark H. Gelber, Beer Sheva/Omer

Robert S. Wistrich

Theodor Herzl: Between Myth and Messianism

The First Zionist Congress, which opened in the *grosse Musiksaal* of Basel's elegant municipal casino on August 29, 1897, was a high and solemn occasion attended by 196 delegates from sixteen countries. They had been brought together from four continents by the ancient dream of a return to Zion. The visionary who inspired this founding act, and brilliantly orchestrated the Congress, was an Austro-Hungarian journalist and playwright, Theodor Herzl, whose revolutionary tract, *Der Judenstaat*, had been published eighteen months earlier in Vienna. As he walked to the tribune, he was greeted by several minutes of stormy rejoicing and applause, punctuated by cries of »Long live the King!« The Russian Zionist journalist, Mordechai Ben-Ami, who was present at the proceedings, observed:

> That is no longer the elegant Dr. Herzl of Vienna, it is a royal descendant of David risen from the grave who appears before us in the grandeur and beauty with which legend surrounded him. Everyone is gripped as if a historical miracle had occurred [...] it was as if the Messiah, the son of David, stood before us.[1]

Like most delegates, Ben-Ami was dazzled by Herzl's physical presence – the regal bearing, his dignity and poise, the soft black beard and melancholy eyes – not to mention the impressive *mise-en-scène* of the Congress. Herzl, with his Wagnerian sense of drama, costume, and spectacle, not only succeeded in moving people but made them part of the action – in the words of Ernst Pawel »he had instinctively hit upon the alchemy of mass manipulation and successfully transmuted fantasy into power.«[2] It was no small achievement to have welded together a rather random and motley army of *schnorrers*, beggars, and shmucks (as Herzl unflatteringly described them in his diary) and made them conscious of their historic role as a national assembly of the Jewish people.

On August 24, 1897, just five days before the opening of the Zionist Congress, Herzl described some of the problems of stage-management and maneuvering between the divergent interests he had to contend with, as an egg-dance – »with the eggs invisible.«[3] There were seven eggs he had to balance: the

---

[1] Mordechai Ben-Ami: Erinnerungen an Theodor Herzl. In: Die Welt, 3 July 1914, 692.
[2] Ernst Pawel: The Labyrinth of Exile: A Life of Theodor Herzl. London 1990, 331.
[3] Entry of August 24, 1897, The Diaries of Theodor Herzl. Ed. and trans. by Marvin Lowenthal. London 1958, 220 (hereafter: Abridged Diaries).

Neue Freie Presse, which he could not antagonize for fear of losing his job as its literary editor; the Orthodox Jews; the Modernists; the egg of Austrian patriotism; Turkey; the Sultan; and the Russian government »against whom nothing disagreeable may be said, although the deplorable position of the Russian Jews will have to be mentioned.«[4] Then, there were the Christian denominations, sensitive about the Holy Places, Edmond de Rothschild (who had icely rejected his overtures), the *Hovevei Zion* in Russia who were suspicious of Herzl as a Westernized outsider and unstable adventurer or even a false prophet; at the end of the list came the Palestine settlers, »whose help from Rothschild must not be endangered, *tout en considérant leur misères* [while taking proper account of their troubles].« Nor did Herzl forget the egg of personal differences, of jealousy and envy. Summing up his Herculean task, Herzl concluded with a sentence that captured his own leaderhip style in a nutshell: »I must conduct the movement impersonally, and yet not allow the reins to slip from my hands.«[5]

Despite the tremendous difficulties, Herzl's egg-dance would in fact succeed beyond all expectations. At Basel the spectacular display of Jewish national solidarity certainly caught the imagination of the Jewish world and helped to persuade influential Gentiles that Zionism was a political factor. In Basel a Jewish national assembly was established for the first time in 2000 years, and the foundation stone was laid for what 50 years later would become the sovereign parliament of Israel, the Knesset in Jerusalem. With characteristic self-confidence and even *chutzpa*, Herzl confided in his diaries on September 3, 1897, what must be one of the most astonishing prophecies of modern history:

> If I were to sum up the Congress in a word – which I shall take care not to publish –
> it would be this: At Basle I founded the Jewish State. If I said this out loud today I
> would be greeted by universal laughter. In five years perhaps, and certainly in fifty
> years, everyone will perceive it.[6]

Such a bold prediction could only have been made by a somewhat megalomaniac artist-politician like Herzl, totally convinced of his own providential mission and committed to the inextricable blending of dream and deed in human action. In the very entry where Herzl makes his remarkable »prophecy« he reveals just how important symbols and the aesthetic side of politics were to »imponderables«.[7] He had insisted that the delegates at the First Zionist Congress must have swallow-tails and white ties, and he felt that it had worked out admirably. »Full dress has a way of making most men feel rather stiff. The stiffness induces a measured, deliberate tone – one not so readily come by in light summer suits or travel wear – and I had spared nothing to heighten this tone to

---

4   Entry of August 24, 1897, Abridged Diaries (note 3), 221–222.
5   Ibid., 222.
6   Entry of September 3, 1897, ibid., 224.
7   On the artist in Herzl, see Steven Beller: Herzl's Tannhäuser: The Redemption of
    the Artist as Politician. In: Austrians and Jews in the Twentieth Century: From Franz
    Joseph to Waldheim. Ed. by Robert S. Wistrich. London 1992, 38–57.

the pitch of solemnity.«[8] This attention to formal dress was a vital part of what Herzl saw as his main task of working the people up into the atmosphere of a state and making them feel that they were indeed its National Assembly.

As the »impresario of a national enterprise,« Herzl frequently used his theatrical experience to great effect, observing at one point in his diaries: »actually I am still as ever the dramatist in all this. I take poor, destitute people off the street, dress them in wonderful clothes, and have them perform before the world a marvelous play of mine.«[9]

The dramatist, who had failed as a playwright, now managed to bring the theater into politics, to turn it into a more successful drama, with himself as stage-manager, director and leading actor.[10] The theme of the new play which he was staging was in Peter Loewenberg's words, »the poignant salvation of a people, the plot was one man's vision and sacrifice, which would overcome all odds, the supporting cast was the rulers of the world's nations, and the backdrop was the grim tale of antisemitism and racial persecution in European history.«[11] Only an artist *manqué* who had a rare capacity to pass from the unreal to the real, to mix drama and politics, could have transferred »the enchantment of make-believe staging to the world of diplomacy and political power.«[12]

Carl Schorske, in an influential essay first published thirty years ago, regarded Herzl's aesthetic politics as essentially irrational, part of the *fin-de-siècle* revolt against liberation and an expression of the new mass politics.[13] This is certainly questionable even if we accept the undoubted element of Wagnerian histrionics in Herzl's personality and politics, his readiness to summon up unconscious forces from the deep and his ability to evoke messianic associations. Herzl did admittedly break away from liberal assimilationist assumptions in Central European Jewry (whose credo he had once espoused) but even Schorske admits that his vision of Zion »reincarnated the culture of modern liberal Europe.«[14] Both *Der Judenstaat* and Herzl's utopian novel *Altneuland* bear the unmistakable imprint of European cosmopolitan humanism and exemplify the values of tolerance, *Menschheit* (humanity) and respect for the rights of the individual. However, these values – with which Herzl profoundly identified – were in his view no longer applicable to Jews in an increasingly antisemitic Europe.

---

[8] Entry of September 3, 1897, Abridged Diaries (note 3), 224.

[9] Herzl: Briefe und Tagebücher, vol. 2, 99. On Herzl as an impresario, see Jacques Kornberg: Theodore Herzl: A Re-evaluation. In: Journal of Modern History. Vol. 52, no. 2 (1980), 752.

[10] Peter Loewenberg: Decoding the Past: The Psycho-Historical Approach. Berkeley 1985, 99–135 and Robert S. Wistrich: Theodor Herzl: Zionist Icon, Myth-Maker and Social Utopian. In: The Shaping of Israeli Identity: Myth, Memory and Trauma. Ed. by Robert Wistrich and David Ohana. London 1995, 2–37.

[11] Loewenberg, Decoding the Past (note 10), 117.

[12] Ibid., 117; Wistrich, Theodor Herzl: Zionist Icon (note 10), 16.

[13] Carl E. Schorske: Fin-de-Siècle Vienna. London, New York 1980, 146ff.

[14] Ibid., 173.

One cannot deny to Herzl the prescience of his recognition that the ground was burning under the feet of European Jewry, that a catastrophe of historic dimensions was being prepared – even if he, no more than his contemporaries or successors, could possibly foresee the Holocaust. The events of his own day were at the time no more than warning-signals – the pogroms in Russia, Karl Lueger's antisemitic triumph in *fin-de-siècle* Vienna, the Dreyfus Affair in France – but he read the signs with impressive lucidity. This helps to explain the burning urgency of his Zionist program – the dramatic call for mass emigration, for a new exodus from Europe – and the imperative of finding a »national home« – guaranteed by the Great Powers and under international law.

Indeed, the »visionary« Herzl saw the explosive antisemitic potential, deeply rooted in European society, more realistically than his opponents or most of his followers in the Zionist movement.[15] At the same time, he coolly regarded the antisemitic movements of his time »without fear or hatred,« as a complex reality compounded of the social effects of Jewish emancipation, the ghetto legacy, gentile economic envy, inherited prejudice and religious intolerance, nourished by popular folklore.[16] More daringly, Herzl believed that antisemitism could successfully be channeled for Zionist purposes, that it would become the engine, driving the train towards Zion. His assumption was that *Judennot* (Jewish distress) might be hot enough to push Jews out of Europe, but in a basically liberal world, it would not break »the ultimate bonds of decency.« Arthur Hertzberg has argued that this analysis of antisemitism was paradoxically »one of the great acts of faith in liberalism that was produced by the nineteenth century.«[17] However Herzl very optimistically assumed that the antisemites were ultimately rational in their aims and that the Zionist movement would enable Jews to deal with them on a basis of equality and enlightened self-interest. This was at best the half-truth and at worst it led Zionists into dubious associations with fascists and Jew-baiters at a later period.

Hertzberg has suggested that Herzl's thinking was messianic, even though it was expressed in terms that were entirely secular and political.[18] The point is not so much that Zionism can be viewed historically as the heir of the messianic impulse and of emotions derived from Jewish tradition; more significant is that it was (to quote Hertzberg again) »the most radical attempt in Jewish history to break out of the parochial molds of Jewish life in order to become part of the

---

[15] Israel Eldad: Herzlianiut be-Yamenu, Ma-hi? (What is Herzlianism in Our Times?) In: Ha-Umma 76 (1984), 165–174.

[16] Theodor Herzl: A Solution of the Jewish Question. In: The Jewish Chronicle, January 17, 1896.

[17] Arthur Hertzberg (Ed.): The Zionist Idea: A Historical Analysis and Reader. New York 1973, 50–51. See also Robert S. Wistrich: Antisemitism and the Origins of Jewish Nationalism. In: Midstream. Vol. 28, no. 9 (November 1982), 10–15.

[18] Hertzberg, The Zionist Idea (note 17), 46: »Messianism is the essence of his stance, because he proclaimed the historical inevitability of a Jewish State in a world of peaceful nations.«

general history of man in the modern world.«[19] Zionism, understood in this sense as a *secular messianism*, aimed above all to transform the collective position of the Jews as a people in the gentile world. Whether it looked to enlighten liberalism, integral nationalism or constructive socialism to help it accomplish this end (*within* a Jewish national framework) did not change the fact that Zionism sought a reconciliation of Jewry with the nations of the world, which was thought to be possible once Jews had acquired their own nation-state.

From the Orthodox Jewish religious standpoint, the problem was less the return to Zion (prayers for Jewish restoration to the Holy Land were after all an integral part of Judaism) than the *secular* nature of the movement and its insistence on the primacy of the human effort rather than the divine will. Political Zionism insisted that it was a doctrine of Jewish self-help – that it was not sufficient to return to Zion by prayer alone – deeds were indispensable.[20] David Litwak, the central protagonist of Herzl's *Altneuland* (1902), explains to his guests that with the national rebirth, the Jewish people realized that »they could expect nothing from fantastic miracle workers but everything from their own strength [...] ›*Gesta Dei per Francos,*‹ the French once said – and God's deeds through the Jews' say the truly pious today, those who do not let the partisan Rabbis incite them.«[21]

Herzlian Zionism parted company with the passive track of *Galut* martyrdom and the guilt-ridden beliefs of traditional Jewish messianism. It was not based on any religious belief in the special and miraculous intervention of Divine Providence or faith in a mystical bond with the »Holy Land« or in an ancestral-tribal cult of the »land of the fathers.« Nevertheless, it is difficult to avoid the feeling that Herzl's intense sense of Zionist mission did have some latent messianic features even though he never spoke publicly in this vein. According to the account which he gave to the Hebrew writer, Reuben Brainin, less than a year before his death, Herzl was attracted to the Messiah legends of the Jews from early adolescence. At the age of twelve, he had a »wonderful dream«, which he recounted as follows: »The King-Messiah came, a glorious and majestic old man, took me in his arms and swept off with me on the wings of the wind. On one of the shining clouds we encountered the figure of Moses. The features were familiar to me out of my childhood in the statue by Michelangelo. The Messiah called to Moses: »›It is for this child that I have prayed!‹ And to me he said: ›Go and declare to the Jews that I shall come soon and perform great wonders and great deeds for my people and for the whole world!‹««[22]

Shortly after this dream Herzl reported that he read a popular science book which presented electricity as the new King-Messiah which would liberate the

---

[19] Ibid., 20.
[20] Shmuel Almog: Zionism and History: The Rise of a New Jewish Consciousness. Jerusalem 1987, 58ff.
[21] Herzl: Old-New Land. Trans. by Paula Arnold. Haifa 1960, 83.
[22] Reuben Brainin: Hayyei Herzl (The Life of Herzl). New York 1919, 17–18.

nations and all mankind from servitude. At first he was indignant but then he
began to wonder if electricity might not be the promised redeemer and decided
to become an engineer – a childhood ambition which he never fulfilled. What
is revealing in this dream (which Herzl never publicized) is the strong identification with Moses, with the Exodus from Egypt and also with technological
advances that could totally transform the lives of humanity. It is precisely such
a fusion of tradition and modernity, the idea of a new Jewish exodus and the
Promethean redemption of mankind through the Zionist enterprise, that would
provide the *élan vital* of Herzl's project. The Moses *leitmotif* and the image of
the Messiah would reappear at various intervals in Herzl's Zionist career. In
August 1895 the Chief Rabbi of Vienna, Moritz [Moses] Güdemann, after
listening to Herzl's first sketch of his Zionist plan, remarked to him: »I could
think you were Moses.«[23] Then, as they parted at the Munich railway station,
Güdemann told him with deep fervor, »Remain as you are! Perhaps you are
called of God!«[24] Herzl records only that he »laughingly rejected the comparison« as incongruous. Güdemann would later turn against him and condemn
Zionism as a secularist movement incompatible with historic Judaism.

Another occasion where Herzl found himself compared to Moses was at the
mass meeting in London's East End on July 13, 1896, where he spoke in the
frightful heat.[25] It was that experience that first made Herzl conscious of »how
my own legend is being born,« a process which he himself describes as »perhaps the most interesting thing I am recording in this book.«[26] Soberly, he
recognized that the people were sentimental (»the masses do not see clearly«)
and that they might well have lavished the same affection on a clever dema-
gogue, seducer or impostor. Yet there is more than a biblical echo in his poetic
observation: »A faint mist is beginning to rise and envelop me, and may perhaps become the cloud in which I shall walk.«[27]

Like Moses in Egypt, Herzl had returned to his brethren from the »other
side,« from the dazzling heights of a »refined« Central European culture which
had begun to viciously stereotype and oppress the Jews; like Moses he called
to the oppressors »Let My People Go,« while showing the demoralized Israel-
ites the way from ghetto servitude to freedom, from darkness to light. Like
Moses, too, he would never see the Promised Land.[28] Herzl even thought at
one point of writing a play about the aging Moses who had to face the constant
murmurings and discontent of the people, fight against their slavish characteristics, overcome the revolt of Korah, and then confront the challenge of the
Golden Calf. The play was to be called *Die Tragödie eines Führers, der kein
Verführer ist* (The Tragedy of a Leader who is no Seducer) – a distinction and

---

[23] Entry of August 18, 1895, Abridged Diaries (see note 3), 63.
[24] Ibid., 64.
[25] Ibid., 180.
[26] Ibid., 182.
[27] Ibid.
[28] Entry of November 7, 1902, ibid., 381.

a play on words in German that was indeed important to Herzl. Whenever he had to deal with a new crisis of opposition in his own Zionist ranks, he may well have thought of Moses as his *Leitbild.*

The image of both the Messiah and his shadow, the false Messiah, would accompany Herzl throughout the eight exhausting years of his Zionist leadership. The adulation with which he was often received by the Jewish masses in Eastern Europe, Russia, and the Balkans carried unmistakably messianic overtones, captured in the childhood reminiscences of David Ben-Gurion. In a broadcast on *Kol Israel* (Israel Broadcasting Service) on July 1, 1966, Ben-Gurion recalled that 70 years earlier, when he was about 10 years old, rumors had spread in his native Plonsk in Russian Poland, that the Messiah had arrived – »a tall handsome man – a doctor, no less – Dr. Herzl.« In his recollections, published four years later, the founder of the State of Israel added: »He [Herzl] was a finely featured man whose impressive black beard flowed wide down to his chest. One glimpse of him and I was ready to follow him then and there to the land of my ancestors.«[29] The attraction of Herzl was rooted in more than simply his striking features and his possessing one of the most impressive beards in modern Jewish history! It lay in the receptiveness of East European Jewish youth to his *activist* message, to the idea he embodied – namely that a two-thousand-year dream of the Jewish people was approaching fulfillment. »In such a sense,« Ben-Gurion added, »Herzl was indeed the Messiah since he galvanized the feeling of the youth that Eretz Israel was achievable. He, Herzl, added, however, that it could only come to pass with our own hands.«[30]

The harassed Jews of the Russian Empire were undoubtedly ripe for a redeemer, as Herzl would discover when he visited Vilna in August 1903 and was greeted with impassioned toasts to *Ha-Melekh Herzl* (King Herzl). He described it as an absurdity, »yet it had an uncanny ring in that dark Russian night.«[31] Similar responses came from some of the Sephardic Jews in the Balkans. In March 1895 a communication from Dr. Reuben Bierer in Sophia had enthusiastically informed him that the local Chief Rabbi considered him the Messiah.[32] The same day that he received this letter, Herzl was received by the Reverend William Hechler, a deeply committed Christian Zionist and chaplain to the British Embassy in Vienna. According to Hechler's meticulous calculations based on biblical prophecy and especially the Book of Daniel, Palestine would be restored to the Jews in either 1897 or 1898. Hechler declared the new Zionist movement to be »Biblical«, even though Herzl believed himself to be proceeding rationally.[33] In his *Diaries*, Herzl waxes ironic whenever he evokes Hechler's mystical discourse about the speedy fulfillment of prophecy, though he certainly valued

---

[29] David Ben-Gurion: Recollections. London 1970, 34.
[30] Ibid., 35.
[31] Entry of August 17, 1903, Abridged Diaries (see note 3), 404–405.
[32] Entry of March 10, 1896; ibid., 103–104.
[33] Ibid., 104–106, 123.

his counsel and above all his excellent connections to Imperial Germany, in particular with the Grand Duke of Baden and the Emperor Wilhelm II.

The Reverend Hechler believed that it was God's will that he should be living in Vienna between 1885 and 1910, »in a position which enabled me to bring to the attention of certain people of importance the Messianic vision of the Jewish leader.«[34] Hechler was one of a long line of distinguished British Christians who hoped to see the Jews restored to their historic homeland, a subject on which he had written ever since the Russian pogroms of the early 1880s. His fashionable flat in Vienna's Schillerplatz was overflowing with pictures, maps, temple models, archeological artifacts, and more than a thousand rare Bibles. It was the eccentric Anglican clergyman who most helped Herzl to obtain his long desired audience with the German Kaiser. Herzl never doubted his goodwill but he remained skeptical of Hechler's messianic expectations and publicly avoided any hint that his movement was part of a Providential design.[35]

This caution did not prevent bitter critics of Herzl's Zionism like the satirist Karl Kraus from mocking him as the »King of Zion« in his native Vienna. Stefan Zweig recalled: »When he entered the theater, a handsome bearded personage, grave and compellingly aristocratic in his demeanor, a sibilation arose on all sides: *Der König von Zion*, or ›His Majesty has arrived.‹ This ironic title peered at him through every conversation, through every glance.«[36] Zweig adds that, at the turn of the 20th century, no man was more derided in Vienna (»this sarcastic city«), unless it was Herzl's contemporary and neighbor in the Berggasse, Sigmund Freud.

This scorn for Zionism as a pseudo-messianic movement was commonplace among many Jewish critics of Herzl, whether they were liberal, Reform, socialist or Orthodox. It was also shared to some extent by critics of Herzl within the Zionist movement itself, like Ahad Ha-am, who accused him of having »kindled a false fire« in the people's hearts after the First Zionist Congress. Ahad Ha-am was highly skeptical of the adventurous, fantastic quality of Herzl's dreams, the haste with which he proceeded and the illusory quality of the complete political solution which he proposed. Knowing the disastrous disillusion caused by earlier episodes of this kind in Jewish history, he clearly disapproved of the messianic urgency which he discerned in Herzl's attitude.

Other Russian and Polish-born Zionist leaders were more sympathetic to this visionary side of Herzl. Sokolow praised this prophetic genius, designating it as *ru'ah ha-elohim* (the spirit of God) – and comparing his spiritual pilgrimage from Paris to Jerusalem to that of Paul from Jerusalem to Damascus! Moreover, he added, there was something »apocalyptic« about Herzl's *Juden-*

---

[34] See Hechler's brief comments in: Theodor Herzl: A Memorial. Ed. by Meyer W. Weisgal. New York 1929, 51.

[35] Erwin Rosenberger: Herzl As I Remember Him. New York 1959, 56.

[36] Stefan Zweig: König der Juden. In: Theodor Herzl: A Memorial (note 34), 55.

staat. »Of course there is much fantasy in it; but that, precisely, is its advantage. It is the imaginative power of Messianic vision.«[37]

Some Zionists pointed to parallels between Herzl and earlier would-be Messiahs from the 16th and 17th centuries like Shabbetai Zevi, David Reuveni and Solomon Molcho. From the Zionist viewpoint, such earlier movements, even if they were led by »false Messiahs,« still had a positive aspect if regarded as revivalist movements of »national liberation« seeking to restore the Jewish nation to its ancestral soil.

Even the great Jewish historian Simon Dubnow, despite his ideological opposition to Zionism, believed that there was a messianic element in Herzl's sense of mission and underlined the historical analogy with Molcho. If the latter had returned to his persecuted Jewish brethren from a religious Marranism, Herzl had found his way back from the national Marranism of the 19th century. Both Molcho and Herzl had called for a national restoration, they had sought to free the Land of Israel from Turkish rule and both had negotiated to this end with the German emperor and the Pope in Rome. The exalted 16th century mystic had died in the fires of the Inquisition while Herzl had burned himself out on the altar of his own political struggle.[38]

The Zionist Chief Rabbi of Vienna, Zevi Perez Chajes, understandably preferred the analogy with Moses. Israel's greatest prophet (though raised as an Egyptian Prince and educated at Pharaoh's court) had been chosen by God precisely because he lived in freedom and could therefore imagine and demand complete liberation for the oppressed Jews. So, too, Herzl – as an emancipated individual spared the humiliations of the ghetto milieu and the material suffering of his people – sought the same liberty for his fellow Jews which he already tasted.[39] Shmarya Levin, a leading Russian Zionist, emphasized a different aspect in this popular analogy. Moses and Herzl had both received an alien education so that when the hour of liberation sounded, they would be *believed* by their Jewish brethren. This would not have happened, had they both received a Jewish education, for then their message would have been seen only in the light of tradition, not of rebirth. In moments of crisis, the chosen leader must step forward as a *stranger*, he must come from afar to create an atmosphere of renewed faith.[40]

Jewish artists, too, in their portraits of Herzl, sometimes elevated him to the position of Moses, as the new source of hope for a people scattered in the modern *Mizra'im* of contemporary Europe. The Galician-born Ephraim Moses Lilien, the finest graphic artist of early Zionism, whose life had been trans-

---

[37] Nahum Sokolow: Zionism as a Moral Question. In: ibid., 18.

[38] Simon Dubnow: Weltgeschichte des jüdischen Volkes. Berlin 1929, vol. 10, 338.

[39] M. Rosenfeld: H. P. Chajes, Leben und Werk. Vienna 1933, 159. See also Jacob Allerhand: Messianische Elemente im Denken und Wirken Theodor Herzls. In: Theodor Herzl und das Wien des Fin-de-Siécle. Vienna 1987, 60–75.

[40] Shmarya (Schmarya) Levin: Continuity and Creation. In: Theodor Herzl: A Memorial (note 34), 103.

formed when he heard Herzl speak in Basel, used the leader's face and figure in precisely this sense. In his stained glass window design for the B'nai B'rith in Hamburg, Lilien paid tribute to the great role that he believed Herzl would play in the dreams of the Jewish people and in the fulfillment of ancient prophecy. In his striking design, Lilien shows Herzl standing like Moses on a mount, the Tables of the Law in his hand, in the silent pride of truth and conviction.[41]

An engraving by Boris Schatz, founder of the Bezalel School of Arts in Jerusalem, commemorated the death of Herzl by showing Moses with lifted hand looking across the hills at the land for which he has fought but will never enter. This was only one of the many portraits and likenesses in which Herzl was represented by Jewish artists as a messianic figure and the redeemer of his people.[42] Especially after his death he was canonized in countless photographs, pictures and busts, in engravings, medals and placards. His picture was displayed at every Zionist gathering, his likeness appeared on stamps, as an artistic motive for rugs, as a trademark on Jewish ceremonial objects, household articles, canned milk or even cigarette boxes.

The popular iconization of Herzl represented his unique stature as the »hero« and martyr of the Zionist movement, its founder and prematurely deceased leader. His physiognomy, as Michael Berkowitz has noted, became the personification of Zionism's self-image – one in which modernist, aesthetic and prophetic-messianic motifs coalesced in a glowing mythology. The Herzl portraits looked both backward and forward, they recalled tradition and its messianic hopes but they also portrayed a modern culture-hero:

> His beard and visage placed him squarely in the context of traditional Judaism while his gaze was directed towards the future. His manliness and handsome looks consciously rebuked the antisemitic stereotype of Jewish effeminity and ugliness while his dark complexion and face were perceived and extolled as the perfect face in which the Zionist movement and Jews could take great pride.[43]

Berthold Feiwel, a leading Austrian cultural Zionist and early collaborator of Herzl, evoked the impact of his personality on an entire generation. »In our earliest youth he signified the embodiment of all beauty and greatness. We, the young, had been yearning for a prophet, for a leader. We created him with our longing.«[44] It was indeed the psychological needs of his followers (and of the demoralized Jewish masses) which had provided the source of the Herzl legend, of his messianic aura as the modern savior of the Jewish people. For

---

[41] Lionel S. Reiss: Through Artists' Eyes: The Portraits of Herzl as Revelations of the Man. In: ibid., 111.

[42] M. Narkess: The Arts Portray Herzl. In: ibid., 119–120.

[43] Michael Berkowitz: Art in Zionist Popular Culture and Jewish National Consciousness 1897–1914. In: Studies in Contemporary Jewry 4 (1990), 24–25.

[44] Ibid., 26. The remark was made to the Austrian Jewish poet and dramatist, Richard Beer-Hoffmann, who was an admirer of Herzl and relatively sympathetic to Zionism.

downtrodden Jews in Eastern Europe, his life had become the stuff of popular fantasy (*Volksphantasie*), as Martin Buber already recognized in a eulogy in 1904.[45]

Herzl himself showed cool insight into this mass psychology and considerable interest in the legend of Shabbetai Zevi, the ill-starred predecessor with whom anti-Zionist rabbis and other Jewish opponents enjoyed comparing him. Significantly, in his novel *Altneuland*, an opera about Shabbetai Zevi, the false Messiah, is performed for the visitors to the New Society and the ensuing discussion permits Herzl to formulate some thoughts about the problem of messianic leadership. His hero, David Litwak, seeks to explain why would-be Messiahs and adventurers are able to deceive the people and themselves about their mission:

> I think it was not that the people believed what these charlatans told them, but the other way round – they told them what they wanted to believe. They satisfied a deep longing. That is it. The longing brings forth the Messiah. You must remember what miserable dark ages they were, the times of Sabbatai and his like. Our people were not yet able to gauge their own strength, so they were fascinated by the spell these men cast over them. Only later, at the end of the nineteenth century when all the other civilized nations had already gained their national pride and acted accordingly – only then did our people, the pariah among the nations, realize that they could expect nothing from fantastic miracle-workers, but everything from their own strength.[46]

Herzl was probably not unaware of the possibility that had he lived in an earlier age, he might well have been burned at the stake as a false Messiah. As the self-proclaimed champion of enlightenment, reason and modern science, he was however careful to distance himself from any suggestions that he was proceeding in the footsteps of the Messiah. Yet his diaries testify that from June 1895 (when his Zionist conversion is usually dated) his curiosity and even sense of affinity with Shabbetai Zevi was growing. In March 1896 Herzl recorded the following terse observation:

> The difference between myself and Sabbatai Zvi (the way I imagine him), apart from the difference in the technical means inherent in the times, is that Sabbatai Zvi made himself great so as to be the equal of the great of the earth. I however, find the great small, as small as myself.[47]

---

[45] Buber was critical of Herzl while pointing to his unique role in inaugurating a new era of action in Jewish history. See Buber: Theodor Herzl (1904) and Er und wir (1910). In: Martin Buber: Die jüdische Bewegung: Gesammelte Aufsätze und Ansprachen, 1900–1914. Berlin 1920, 146, 201.

[46] Herzl, Old-New Land (note 21), 82–83

[47] Abridged Diaries (note 3), vol. 3, 960. In July 1895 Herzl had read the novel *Der Jakobsstern* by Ludwig Storch, which dealt with Sabbatai Zvi. See Joseph Nevada: Herzl and Messianism. In: Herzl Year Book 7 (1971), 13–14.

A few months earlier Herzl had been warned by Dr. Joseph Samuel Bloch, editor of the *Österreichische Wochenschrift* (and founder of the first Austrian Jewish self-defense organization) that if he were to present himself as the Messiah, he would have all Jews against him. Rabbi Bloch mentioned various Messiahs in Jewish history, culminating in Shabbetai Zevi, »whose emergence had had fatal consequences for the Jews and who had themselves come to a bad end, either turning their backs on Judaism or committing suicide.« The Messiah, he told Herzl, must remain a veiled, hidden figure. »The moment he takes on actual flesh and blood, he ceases to be the Redeemer. In a word, every Messiah was stricken with blindness and was damned and cursed by the people.«[48]

Others saw the parallel in a more positive light. At a Passover celebration of Unitas, a Jewish student fraternity at the University of Vienna, in March 1896, attended by Herzl, university lecturer Meir Friedmann spoke to him about Shabbetai Zevi and he »winked at me in a way that seemed to say that I ought to become such a Sabbatai. Or did he mean that I already was one?«[49] 1897 was the year of the First Zionist Congress and the ensuing wave of enthusiasm that swept through the Jewish world generated more explicitly messianic emotions. Mordechai Ben-Ami (whom we have already quoted), recalling the mood at the Basel Congress, described the voice of Herzl »as the *shofar* of the Messiah, summoning to the Congress all those who in their hearts were still aware of the ties that bound them to their people.«[50]

In the flood of letters of support and veneration that Herzl received after the Congress, there were many messianic allusions, including some that greeted the Zionist leader as the »anointed of the Lord.« At the synagogue of Sofia, when Herzl stood on the altar platform, unsure how to face the congregation without turning his back to the Holy of Holies, a voice cried out: »It's all right for you to turn your back to the Ark: you are holier than the Torah!«[51] Such response could only have reinforced the fears of the Orthodox Rabbis that Herzl might indeed proclaim himself as the Messiah or act like one. This was indeed a major reason for the bitter opposition of the »Protest Rabbis« in Germany and also of East European *haredi* orthodoxy to his Zionist program. Despite Herzl's strenuous efforts to present his Zionism as purely political, the frequent comparison with Shabbetai Zevi made by Orthodox rabbis was damaging to the cause.[52]

---

[48] Chaim Bloch: Theodor Herzl and Joseph S. Bloch. In: Herzl Year Book 1 (1958), 158. For Bloch's politics and his attitude to Herzl, see Robert S. Wistrich: The Jews of Vienna in the Age of Franz Joseph. Oxford 1989, 270–309.

[49] Entry of March 1896, Abridged Diaries (note 3), vol. 1, 317. See Nedava, Herzl and Messianism (note 47), 16–17.

[50] See Leib Jaffe (Ed.): Herzl ve-ha-Kongress ha-Rishon (Herzl and the First Congress). Jerusalem 1923, 134.

[51] Nedava, Herzl and Messianism (note 47), 19.

[52] Shalom Ben-Horin: Hamishim Shnot Ziyyonut: Max Bodenheimer. Jerusalem 1946, 102–110.

Herzl's visit to Palestine in October 1898 raised another kind of fear in his own mind, that like Shabbetai Zevi over two centuries earlier, he might be arrested by the Turkish authorities. In an entry in his *Diaries* dated October 31, 1898 (the day the German Kaiser consecrated the Church of the Redeemer in the Old City of Jerusalem), Herzl comments on his own visit to the Tower of David: »At the entrance I said to my friends: ›It would be a good idea on the Sultan's part if he had me arrested here‹.« The same entry records his shock at the dilapidated state of Jerusalem and his modernist vision of its future:

> When I remember thee in days to come, O Jerusalem, it will not be with delight. The musty deposits of two thousand years of inhumanity, intolerance, and foulness lie in your reeking alleys. The one man who has been present here all this while, the lovable dreamer of Nazareth, has done nothing but help increase the hate. If Jerusalem is ever ours, and if I were still able to do anything about it, I would begin by cleaning it up. I would clear out everything that is not sacred, set up workers' houses beyond the city, empty and tear down the filthy rat holes, burn all the non-sacred ruins, and put the bazaars elsewhere. Then, retaining as much of the old architectural style as possible, I would build an airy, comfortable, properly sewered, brand new city around the Holy Places.[53]

Herzl was simply appalled by the misery and squalor, the superstition and fanaticism, which he found on all sides and among all the religious denominations. But his visionary eye saw the possibilities of a splendid new Jerusalem being built outside the old city walls, one that could rival Rome itself.

It was indeed to be in Rome, in January 1904, during an interview with King Victor Emmanuel III, that the subject of Shabbetai Zevi came up one final time. The king of Italy told Herzl that one of his more eccentric distant ancestors had conspired with Shabbetai, and then unexpectedly he asked if there were still Jews who expected the Messiah. Herzl's reply is revealing: »Naturally, Your Majesty, among religious circles. In our own, the university-trained and enlightened classes, no such thought exists [...] our movement has a purely national character.« To the king's amusement, Herzl informed him »how in Palestine I had avoided using a white horse or a white ass, so that no one would embarrass me with messianic confusions.«[54]

All the available evidence indicates that Herzl saw himself as a *Realpolitiker* in the mold of Bismarck and the leader of a modern national movement to restore sovereignty and freedom to the Jewish people. His view of the Jewish past was unmistakably secular and instrumental, harking back to examples like the Maccabees, only in so far as they fitted his heroic conception of Zionism and his dream of the new Jew. He envisaged a modern, enlightened Jewish state which would transplant the best of European culture (Viennese opera, German theater, French cafés, English sports) to the Eastern Mediterranean. As a good Central European liberal, he believed in the separation of

---

[53] Entry of October 31,1898, Abridged Diaries (see note 3), 283–284.
[54] Entry of January 23, 1904, ibid., 425–426.

church and state, though he respected Jewish tradition and tried hard to avoid alienating Orthodox rabbis. The core of his activity was clearly political and diplomatic, the effort to secure a legally recognized and binding Charter that would guarantee a national home for the Jews in Palestine. To achieve his end he needed to mobilize and organize what was a completely scattered, disunited, and politically leaderless Jewish people in the Diaspora.

It was Herzl's achievement to give the Jews a national assembly for the first time in two millennia, to create the World Zionist Organization, the Jewish Colonial Trust, the Jewish National Fund, and to tirelessly propagandize for the Zionist cause in his newspaper, *Die Welt*.[55] These were not the actions of a utopian dreamer, a coffee-house *littérateur*, a neurotic self-hating Jew, let alone a »false messiah.« They involved careful planning, organizational skill, diplomatic finesse, great persistence, and unusual leadership qualities.

Zionism was above all an activist doctrine, a movement for the restoration of Jewish honor and independence, a revolt against the traditional passivity of the *Galut* (exile). It was a determined drive for collective dignity and self-respect, predicated on the need for Jews to transform and remake themselves, to awaken from the nightmare of their history and construct the materials for their redemption through their own labor. In that sense, it was a movement both of self-overcoming and auto-emancipation. Herzl's life and example embodied that self-transcendence and the conviction that the road to redemption lay through the *deed*. The Jews, Herzl warned, counted for nothing politically and their paralysis would continue until they created a center for organized political action, one that almost single-handedly provided the groundwork for that momentous transformation – the concrete program, the clarity of goal, the institutions of the movement and the national will for an independent State. The direction which he gave to the Zionist movement enabled it to finally enter the stream of history and ultimately to lay the foundations for the State of Israel.

Herzl was convinced that the Jewish state must come into existence because it fulfilled an objective Jewish need. His understanding of antisemitism had enabled him to foresee that the »Jewish Question« would not disappear but would only be exacerbated over time, eventually making a sovereign Jewish State into a world necessity. At the same time, he envisaged this new society as pluralistic, open, tolerant, and standing at the cutting edge of modern science and technology. The New Exodus of the Jews would in the long run bring not only the salvation of Jewry but also be a light to the Gentiles – an influential part of the irresistible universal movement of material progress and moral improvement.

Herzl's goals have been realized to a remarkable degree in the State of Israel, despite all its problems, its failures, and its flaws. Not surprisingly, there-

---

[55] For the role of *Die Welt* and journalism as Herzl's school for politics, see Robert S. Wistrich: Theodor Herzl: Zwischen Journalismus und Politik. In: Wandlungen und Brüche: Von Herzls »Welt« zur »Illustrierten Neuen Welt« 1897–1997. Ed. by Joanna Nittenberg, Anton Pelinka and Robert S. Wistrich. Vienna 1997, 11–17.

fore, Herzl has traditionally been regarded in Israel as its visionary founder and as the central protagonist in the early, »heroic« phase of Zionism. But even in his own lifetime, despite the tremendous opposition which his program aroused in many Jewish circles, Herzl assumed a messianic halo in the minds of contemporaries. A striking illustration is the eulogy for Herzl given in Jaffa, Palestine after his death in 1904, by Rabbi Abraham Isaac Kook. The man who would eventually become the Chief Rabbi of Eretz Israel under the British Mandate, was, not unexpectedly, ambivalent about Herzl. Yet he awarded him the title »Messiah, son of Joseph,« the fallen redeemer, who had paved the way for a future messianic era. In ancient Jewish tradition, the Messiah ben Joseph was a tragic figure who helps his people towards worldly salvation, but also embodies the inevitability of crisis and defeat. He is in fact a doomed redeemer, whose suffering belongs to the birth pangs of final salvation that can only be brought about by the Messiah ben David. For Rabbi Kook, Herzl and the Zionist movement were »the footsteps of the Messiah,« but it was still a limited »material« messianism, a quest for physical strength, that would inevitably lead to setbacks and crises.

The fight for material improvement was necessary, but it lacked the spiritual dimension, the light of Torah, the knowledge of God.

> Because its preparation is lacking [in the other dimension], the forces are not united [...] until in the end the [Zionist] leader fell victim to the reign of evil and sorrow [...] this man, whom we may consider to have been the harbinger.[56]

In Rabbi Kook's nuanced, dialectical interpretation, Herzl's untimely, early death was tragic testimony to the split between the worldly and the spiritual, the political and the religious sides of the *Judenstaat*. Secular Zionism heralded the worldly salvation of the Jews through national rebirth but it was still a vision borne aloft on clipped wings.[57] Herzlian Zionism was a mixture of light and darkness, not the higher, complete synthesis. As long as adherents of the *Judenstaat* declared that they had nothing to do with religion, Zionism would remain a body without a soul. The task was to broaden »the narrow circle of the late lamented Dr. Herzl's dream, despite all its beauty and strength.« Herzl, as the Messiah ben Joseph, was thereby transmuted by Rabbi Kook into being the necessary forerunner of the true Davidic messianism, with its vision of the »revealed End.«[58]

---

[56] See Abraham Isaac Kook: Ha-Misped bi-Yerushalayim (The Eulogy in Jerusalem). In: Ma'amarei ha-Ra'aya (Articles of Rabbi Abraham Isaac Kook). Jerusalem 1984, 94–99. The quote is from p. 97. For an illuminating discussion of this text see Aviezer Ravitzky: Messianism, Zionism and Jewish Religious Radicalism. Chicago 1996, 99.

[57] Ravitzky, Messianism (note 56), 97–99. On the relationship between secular Zionism and religion, see also Ehud Luz: Parallels Meet: Religion and Nationalism in the Early Zionist Movement, 1882–1914. Philadelphia 1988 and Yosef Salmon: Dat ve-Ziyyonut (Religion and Zionism). Jerusalem 1990.

[58] Ravitzky, Messianism (note 56), 99.

Not only Orthodox Judaism of the national-religious stamp found a way to integrate Herzl as a messianic figure. The great German-Jewish philosopher, Franz Rosenzweig (himself a non-Zionist), favorably compared Herzl in one of his letters to two of his severest Zionist critics, Martin Buber and Ahad Ha-am. »With Herzl alone,« he wrote, »one feels Jewish Antiquity, with Buber and Ahad Ha-am at most the Jewish Middle Ages (Talmud and Kabbalah). Herzl is ›Moses and the Prophets.‹ That he was naïve enough to plan only from the present, out of Jewish distress, that is precisely his greatness [...].«[59]

Herzl's view of his own place in history was more modest and devoid of any hint of mystical or metaphysical messianism. One June 1, 1901, he recorded the following lines in his diaries, which a century later still retain their prophetic resonance:

> If once the Jewish state should come into existence, then everything will seem small and matter-of-course. Perhaps then a fair-minded historian will find that it was after all something that a Jewish journalist without means, in the midst of the deepest degradation of the Jewish people, in a time of the most sickening antisemitism, was able to create a flag out of rag-cloth and a nation out of a foundering rabble – a nation that flocked to this flag with straightened backs.[60]

---

[59] Letter of September, 28, 1916. Franz Rosenzweig: Briefe und Tagebücher. The Hague 1979, vol. 1, 237.

[60] Herzl: Briefe und Tagebücher, vol. 3, 291. My translation.

Denis Charbit

Herzl's Nationalism: Is it Ethnic or Civic?

Both mainstream and revisionist history consider Theodor Herzl the »founding father« of Zionism. The so-called »New Historians« agree with their predecessors about the foundational character of Herzl's *The Jewish State*, which is to Zionism what the *Communist Manifesto* was to the Communist Party. They also admit that through the World Zionist Organization Herzl established the first structured Zionist organization which initiated programs, institutions, a bureaucratic apparatus, a financial arm, a press, and public relations. But it is notable that for one who aspired to be the mainspring of a national movement, Herzl neglected one essential and determining element, or he left it somewhat undeveloped: the Jewish nation.

While at the beginning he had a clear vision of the desired end, a state, the means to that end, the Zionist Organization, and an adequate strategy, that is political Zionist diplomacy, we find little or nothing systematic on the idea of the Jewish nation and, more generally, nationhood. Besides, historiography is, in this respect, discreet. Past and present scholars of Herzl are rather silent on this issue. From Alex Bein to Ernest Pawel, from Jacques Kornberg to Carl E. Schorske, one is left unsatisfied.[1]

Is the »founding father« of the Zionist movement and the Jewish State also the founding father of the modern Jewish nation? What sort of nation did he conceive of in his mind? What do *Der Judenstaat* and *Altneuland* tell us about this subject? Can these works shed light upon his conceptions and representations of nations in general, and of the Jewish nation in particular, in an exhaustive and unequivocal manner? Without seeking to insert Herzl into the contemporary Israeli debate on the nation, we modestly propose to clear the landscape in order to reveal his vision of the nation as it emerges from the elements he disseminated. Also, we will wish to know if, besides his idea of a Jewish State, he had also some specific idea of the Jewish Nation.[2]

---

[1] Cf. Alex Bein: Theodor Herzl, a Biography. Philadelphia: Jewish Publication Society of America 1940; Jacques Kornberg: Theodor Herzl: From Assimilation to Zionism. Bloomington: Indiana University Press 1993; Ernest Pawel: The Labyrinth of Exile: A Life of Theodor Herzl. London: C. Harvill 1990.

[2] Generally, Zionist thinkers devoted more attention to the State than to the Nation. See Ben Halpern: The Idea of the Jewish State. Cambridge/Massachussetts: Harvard University Press 1969.

I   The Herzlian Path to the Jewish Nation

Logically, if Zionism is ordinarily defined as a national movement, this presupposes the existence of a nation. It implies that among the social groups to which humans belong, and among the associations linking human beings beyond the family sphere, there is one expression above all that is stronger than class identity or religious faith, that has directly competed with these for allegiance, and which forms a predominant bond transcending all others: the nation.

Such is the originality and audacity of Zionism that Jews dare to claim as theirs alone this sense of belonging to a nation. By virtue of Zionism, it was no longer necessary for Jews to be grafted within other national configurations that inconveniently maintain their dispersed and minority condition, and physically or culturally might endanger them. Zionism's contribution is of considerable importance in that it proposes another conceptualization of the Jewish collective.

Within the repertoire of principles of social classification by which the Jewish collective is defined, Zionism elevates the nation to a first position to an extent surpassing all other categories of identity and belonging, such as group solidarity, communal ties, and religious tradition. However, we should not be misled by this emerging Zionist consensus, for if we delve into details, we find that the modalities differ from one author to the next, from one trend to another. For some, the nation already exists. For others it has yet to be created. The former have in mind a cultural way of conceiving the nation; the latter substituted or added at the least a political vision of it. The difference may appear essentially rhetorical: in one case the nation must be born; in the other, it must be reborn. But this distinction is not negligible for if there is a rebirth, the enterprise may be thought of as a restoration. If it is a birth, then everything is to be invented anew, everything must be newly constructed. This latter scenario would represent more of a beginning.

It was the same case for the idea of a homeland. Herzl understood it as a great and long-sought aspiration for which the Jewish people had never ceased to yearn, but he admitted that for a part of the Jewish people, this idea »has kept itself alive« and for another part of it, »it has been kept alive by external pressure.«[3]

Thus, a number of questions arise. Generally speaking, why did a dispersed people lacking a majority, its own land, and a State structure, ultimately succeed in achieving these goals? More specifically, concerning Herzl, how did he come to conceive of the idea of a nation in light of his past, as a Jew, as a lawyer, and a playwright, which in no way predisposed him to such a conclusion?

It is clear that Herzl was not an accomplished theorist. He was not embarrassed by adherence to or rejection of various models elaborated by nationalist

---

[3]   Theodor Herzl: The Jewish State (Der Judenstaat). New York: Herzl Press 1989, 88.

thinkers. The majority of them based the legitimacy of national identity on the presence of what they viewed to be objective criteria. However, when applied to Zionism and the Jewish nation, these so-called objective criteria were a source of embarrassment and confusion. Thus Herzl was careful to avoid discussions about them.

Did the Jews have a common history? Two thousand years had elapsed since the dispersion decisively ruptured this identity of fate and history. There were analogous situations, some similarities, strong solidarity, common feelings, and shared troubles, but it was rather difficult or impossible to affirm one unique Jewish destiny from North Africa to America, from Eastern to Western Europe.

Did the Jews possess a common language? Normally, Jews adopted the vernaculars of their host countries. If they sought to maintain internal cohesion by maintaining Jewish languages such as Judeo-German, Judeo-Arab, Judeo-Spanish, etc., none was ever the language of all the Jews but only the privileged attribute of a Jewish local community in relation to the dominant language of the environment. As for Hebrew, Herzl doubted its capacity to develop into a modern language of subtle expression and advanced communication.

Did the Jews reside on a contiguous or common territory? The first objective of Zionism consisted precisely in gathering the dispersed nation onto one land. It seems fitting to have named the movement itself after the place – Zion – where this gathering was to create the much-desired Jewish State. In reality though, there was not yet a common territory – only a common projection of one. But at least there was the desire to possess a territory and, as the East African example illustrates, it is well-known that Herzl did not rule out any territorial possibility as long as it was potentially available: »Let sovereignty be granted us over a portion of the earth's surface that is sufficient for our rightful national requirements; we shall take care of everything else ourselves.«[4]

Were the Jews of one race? Herzl chose not to enter this blind alley. As opposed to Israel Zangwill and other Zionists who supported the principle of a Jewish race, Herzl wrote in his diary on November 19, 1895:

> The racial point of view [is] something I cannot accept, for I merely have to look at him and at myself. All I say is: we are an historical unit, one nation with anthropological diversities. No nation has uniformity of race.[5]

Herzl did not conceive of the Jewish nation as derived from theoretical criteria. Concepts, like race, were not to his liking. Only from an empirical situation he

---

[4] Ibid., 49.
[5] Theodor Herzl: Inyanei Ha-Yehudim (the Jewish Cause) Diaries 1895–1904. Jerusalem: Mossad Bialik and the Central Zionist Archives 1997, vol. 1, 258.

personally experienced would a pragmatic reflection emerge, leading him to set his sights on the objective of the Jewish State.

It is not only curiosity about Herzl's biography that impels us to retrace his path to the idea of the nation and to search for the foundational experience that drove him to conceive of the necessity of this national project. The specific circumstances that led him to Zionism explain how a certain type of nation emerges in his thinking, however imprecise it is in his formulations. For obvious reasons of chronology, the Dreyfus Affair was long considered as the main trigger. Dreyfus was sentenced and publicly degraded on January 5, 1895, and, as the legend was conveyed by Herzl himself, immediately afterwards he began to map out a rough draft of a Jewish state. Some historians consider Karl Lueger's election as mayor of Vienna to be the most decisive turning point, while ascribing a lesser role of catalyst to the Dreyfus Affair.

It seems preferable to see the two events as contributing to the emergence of his new approach, rather than to think in terms of »either … or«. In both cases, dramatic and negative experiences were clearly decisive factors behind these developments. In both cases, the nation was not a profound aspiration that had been long been contemplated but rather a sudden reaction. It was not haphazard but a necessity. It was not an object of desire that one may caress but a radical remedy. Neither was it a whim but, rather, a last resort.

It was not, as for other Zionists, a spiritual aspiration coming from afar and triggered by some cultural romanticism.[6] Nor was it a suitable device for overcoming the decadence and degeneration of this *fin-de-siècle*. What was the driving force behind the Jewish national idea, Herzl asked? His answer was not the longing for Zion, the romantic dream of gathering the exiles in order to rebuild the former home, but simply, frankly, directly, and without ornamental rhetoric: »the distress of the Jews.«[7] Herzl did not hesitate to repeat the elementary and crude message: »Only pressure attaches us to our ancient roots again.«[8] Herzl was neither a mystic, nor a poet invoking Jewish perpetuity. He was no prophet of the rebirth of Judaism, even if he was in fact fully aware that for a number of Jews such as himself Zionism would have the effect – not the function – of activating a dormant Jewish conscience.

Herzl identified in the enemy the essential factor for maintaining the idea of a Jewish nation. More so than any supposed positive particularism, it was the pervasive hostility that burst out in Vienna and in Paris that led him to resort to the idea of the Jewish nation.[9] In this sense it was neither the Bible nor the Hebrew language, neither the Promised Land nor the permanence of a Semitic race or the Jewish faith that would serve as the basis of the nation. Rather, it

---

[6]   Anita Shapira: Herzl, Ahad Ha-am, and Berdichevsky: Comments on Their Nationalist Concepts. In: Jewish History 4 (1990), no. 2, 60.
[7]   Herzl, The Jewish State (note 3), 28.
[8]   Ibid., 49.
[9]   Claude Klein: Essai sur le sionisme: de l'Etat des Juifs à l'Etat d'Israël. In: Theodor Herzl: L'Etat des Juifs. Paris: La Découverte 2003, 117.

was the danger that threatened the Jews and which, in order to parry it, necessitated their gathering beyond the reach of their persecutors. In so reasoning, Herzl was merely retracing his own path towards the nation, one initiated not by a sentiment of a racial bond or positive identity, but by the rejection Jews were subjected to as a result of antisemitism and by the search for a solution to assure their survival. His nationalism was not the secularization of the divine promise, even if it makes use of this tradition. And even if in Herzl's eyes there existed the notion of election for the Jewish people, it was entirely in a negative sense: it proceeded not from its religious origin, but from the exceptional destiny other nations have reserved for it throughout history. Here, Herzl saw cause for praising the persistence of a people's will to survive in spite of the vicissitudes and trials of persecution.

In summary, his conception of the nation is rational. To be sustained, it does not need to be founded on any theories of race or blood lineage. Neither does it require invoking the sacred character of the land of Israel or the continuity of a two-thousand year history. In this approach, one can already make out the elements that would arouse the ire of Ahad Ha-am;[10] for Herzl the Jewish nation is neither the point of departure nor an end in itself. It is not also an ancient and immemorial, rooted, organic, popular, ancestrally based and cultural community, but results from the solution conceived by Herzl to resolve the Jewish question. This solution is the Jewish State.

Herzl did not seek to link the idea of the nation to a Jewish past with which he was, for the most part, unacquainted, while in the present, it still remained but a potentiality of which he was the curator. For all intents and purposes, the nation only existed on paper before becoming embodied in the Zionist Congress, the first Jewish Parliament in contemporary history. This epic enterprise of which he took charge was the prehistory of a nation whose emergence would be definitively celebrated with the establishment of a sovereign state.

Referring to »a theory of rationality«[11] and invoking »terms of reason,«[12] Herzl conceded that the nation is a rational project that arises from an existential necessity. Herzl conceived of the Jewish nation as the result of propositions that spring from each other. The stages of his reasoning may be ordered as follows:

1) The fate of the Jews remains condemned to a condition of precariousness. Jews have been oppressed, they still are, but above all, they will remain oppressed.

2) The only institutional framework capable of assuring their protection is a Jewish State in which they will no longer be tolerated guests as a minority but masters of their own fate as a majority.

---

[10] See Ahad Ha-am: Kol Kitvei (Collected Writings). Jerusalem, Tel-Aviv: Dvir 1961, 318.

[11] Herzl, The Jewish State (note 3), 92.

[12] Ibid., 41.

3) Therefore, for a Jewish state to see the light of day and to enjoy a legitimacy of fundamental principles, Jews are compelled to constitute themselves into a nation.

This is not to say that the task will be easy or assured success. If, however, it was imperative for him to work at this immense task, it was because Herzl foresaw an imminent catastrophe which justified, indeed demanded, the creation of a Jewish State; therefore, the reorganization of the Jewish collective into a nation was a necessity. Other Jews, for similar reasons, would opt for revolution in their host countries as the sole means of assuring the survival of the Jewish people. For Herzl, recourse to the nation addressed an urgent need connected to the spread of antisemitism. He formulated prophetic warnings that European Jews should have read and believed:

> I shall now put the Jewish Question in its most succinct form: Do we already have to »get out«, and if so, where to? [...] Can we hope for better days, possess our souls in patience, and wait devoutly for the princes and people of this earth to be more mercifully disposed towards us? I say that we cannot expect the current to shift.[13]

However, rather than seeing it for what it is, the question of modern antisemitism has too often been reduced to a facile and summary vision of its permanence, a conviction Herzl reiterated when he wrote that yesterday as today, »every single one of the nations in whose midst Jews live are shamefacedly or brazenly anti-Semitic.«[14] However, the new antisemitism that Herzl denounced was not so much another variety in a continual series of unhappy episodes in the long history of hatred of the Jews throughout the ages; it was particularly revealing of a serious dysfunction in the modern state.

For Jews such as himself, recourse to the nation also addressed the desire for citizenship and a normalcy which the nation-state promised but was unable to deliver and guarantee. Hatred of the Jews, whether emanating from on high, initiated by the state, or from the political realm and party politics, or even emanating from lower levels and finding expression in the ordinary prejudice of the masses, had an obvious and undeniable impact on Herzl. Antisemitism not only destabilized his confidence and reinforced his insecurity. Above all, it undermined the idea of ethnic neutrality with which Herzl previously credited the modern state. In other words, while a nation whose hard core is ethnic may be well structured upon complementary civic foundations that allow the entry of foreign elements that progressively acclimate, its civic structure remains inherently fragile. It may function, but it may also collapse.

The universality of the Enlightenment movement produced an open and inclusive nation. Progressively however, throughout the 19th century, the nation increasingly withdrew inwardly. Thus, in spite of the fact that primordial bonds are restrained by an intentional blurring in the nation-state between

---

[13] Ibid., 44.
[14] Ibid.

citizenship and nationality, these bonds constantly threaten to undermine the logic and emancipating spirit upon which the nation-state is founded. At the cost of betraying its generous principles, the nation can be brought to exclude those it initially included. In other words, antisemitism shattered the myth of the civic nation-state.

As Herzl believed, even in a liberal state, »The majority can decide who the strangers are.«[15] In other words, ethno-cultural factors play a role even in civic nations that are supposed apparently to overcome them by principle. Therefore, in response to this catastrophic eventuality and the increasing urgency of the »Jewish question,« a Jewish State was imperative. For while the state does not always reliably provide for the welfare of its minorities, it is, however, an efficient protector of the rights and interests of the solid ethnic core that constitutes the nation's majority.

Therefore, to speak of the state is to speak of the nation. Thus, Herzl's ambition was expressed in terms of Jews gathering to form the elementary, constituent nucleus of the nation of a future Jewish State. The coupling of the term »nation-state« is indissoluble; there must be a nation for a state; and a state for a nation. Of course, land was needed. It was a necessary condition, the Vatican excepted. There is no sovereignty without a substantial piece of land. But as Herzl pointed out, there was no doubt that between the people as the subjective basis of the State and the land as the objective one, »of these two, the subjective basis is the more important.«[16]

It is only because Herzl wished for a Jewish State that he wished for a nation, without which no state could be legitimate. Without a subsequent claim to statehood, a nation made no sense. Only through the state could the nation, at last reassembled and sovereign, obtain the guaranteed protection it required. For Herzl, the nation was a *prêt-à-porter*, inspired by the prevailing spirit of the times, coming at the right moment to resolve the »Jewish question.« By constituting a Jewish nation, the Jews would definitively eliminate the contradiction that prevails in the diasporic condition between cultural and civic identity, replacing it with a homogeneous, national identity embodied in the nation-state conceived towards this end.

The need for a state, and thus for a nation, required the implementation of a primordial solidarity which Herzl and his cohorts had themselves earlier repressed. By embracing this model, the Jewish condition would at last be »normalized.« The »nationalization« of Israel would humanize Jews who are too often depicted as devils or saints, to the extent that by their adherence to the national model, Jews acknowledge that men have identical needs. If there is a universal norm (at that time conceived as a European norm) that is good for all human groups, it is fitting that the Jews should also claim it for themselves. Herzl subscribed to a logic of similitude in relation to other nations, pitting

---

[15] Ibid., 34.
[16] Ibid., 92.

him squarely against those cultural Zionists who would opt for a logic of difference or uniqueness.

II   The Jewish Nation: is it the same (old) one or is it new?

How should we view Herzl's conception of the Jewish nation in relation to other theories of nationhood? Gellner's thesis – that nations do not in fact create nationalism, rather nationalist movements define and create nations – lends itself well to Herzl's case. After all, for him the idea of the state created the nation. To be sure, the nation is not suddenly born *ex nihilo*. The Jewish group precedes the existence of the Jewish State. Ethnic solidarity is the ground on which the political process of nation-formation may be set in motion.[17] But, without a state, a people is not yet a nation, but a only a people. A people is a historical phenomenon; the nation is a modern one. As Herzl wrote: »we are a modern nation and wish to become the most modern.«[18] In this sense, and in this sense alone, the state creates the nation which can only exist if it appropriates, through the State, the political resources that will guarantee its existence. He was aware of the metamorphosis: »Our minds must first be turned into a *tabula rasa* purged of many old, outworn, confused, short-sighted notions.«[19] To transform the Jewish people into a Jewish nation, one has »to replace an old building with a new one.«[20] Herzl solemnly declared while paraphrasing the passage from the the Jewish prayer, the *Shema*: »Wir sein ein Volk. Ein Volk«. (»We are a people, *one* people«.)[21] He also wrote: »Whether we desire it or not, we are and shall remain a historical group with unmistakable characteristics.«[22] But, he was forced to recognize that it was difficult to be too prolix on just what are those »unmistakable characteristics.« When he attempted to elaborate, he evidently fell back on the Jewish religion to which he twice referred in the same terms: »We recognize our historical affinity only by the faith of our fathers.«[23] And, in another place: »The faith of our fathers is the only thing by which we still recognize that we belong together.«[24] Herzl was honest enough in both instances to admit the residual character of this common link by using the adverb »only.« For him Judaism was a link to the past, not a strong and active connection to the present. In other words, the faith of the fathers was no longer, so to speak, the faith of the sons. He asserted in

---

[17] Erika Harris: Nationalism and Democratisation. Burlington: Ashgate Publishing Company 2002, 52.
[18] Herzl, The Jewish State (note 3), 99.
[19] Ibid., 39.
[20] Ibid., 40.
[21] Ibid., 33.
[22] Ibid., 49.
[23] Ibid., 81.
[24] Ibid., 100.

the first paragraph of *The Jewish State* that he was not »inventing anything,« that his idea was an »age-old one,« and that »the material components of the edifice [he was] sketching [were] in existence.«[25] But, this denial was highly questionable in as much as Herzl seemed to pay lip-service to the Jewish past, because it was really the modernity of the project that stimulated him. Herzl was no »perennialist« in the manner of Ahad Ha-am who believed in the permanence of a »national-self.« Even if long dormant, it could, according to his understanding, be reawakened by its contact with the land of Israel and the Hebrew language. In many respects, Herzl seems close to the viewpoint of Anthony Smith, who is convinced that modern nationalist movements activate an old ethno-cultural fund which they could not invent but which they reconstruct and adapt to their needs. Accordingly, Herzl refers to the Maccabees at the end of his *Jewish State*.[26] It is clear that he sought to attract the masses by mobilizing a powerful national myth conveying will, determination, independence, and liberty. But Herzl could not relinquish totally the very claim of common origin. As Shmuel Almog has noted in this context:

> Not every ethnic or cultural group was deemed worthy of becoming a nation. [...] National movements that sought the status of nations needed a lineage similar to that of the historical nations.[27]

By not insisting upon the sources, it can be said that Herzl was perhaps the least nationalist among national leaders of 19th century Europe. He did not hesitate to admit the contingent dimension of Jewish nationalism: »Our enemies have made us one without our volition, as has always happened in history.« That he thought that Jews »might be able to merge with the peoples surrounding [them] everywhere without leaving a trace if [they] were only left in peace for two generations«[28] shows him to be a very »soft« kind of nationalist. He believed that »If the distinctive nationality of the Jews will not and need not perish«, it was »because external foes hold it together.«[29] For him, this motive did not alter in any way the legitimacy of Jewish nationalism; it provided it with a more justified basis, precisely because it was a not a romantic device of bored amateurs. Herzl did not need to profess the perennial sanctity of nations throughout the ages. For him, nations were not a metaphysical device but essentially a product of history. Instead of being the chosen, the elected people, Jews would have with Zionism the opportunity to become an elective nation. Perhaps the difference between »elected« and »elective« appears to be negligible, but for Herzl it was very significant.

---

[25] Ibid., 27.

[26] Anthony D. Smith: The Ethnic Origins of Nations. Oxford: Basil Blackwell 1986.

[27] Shmuel Almog: Was Herzl a Jewish Nationalist? In: Theodor Herzl: Visionary of the Jewish State. Ed. by Gideon Shimoni and Robert Wistrich. Jerusalem: Magnes Press 1999, 167.

[28] Herzl, The Jewish State (note 3), 49.

[29] Ibid., 37.

Herzl saw in nationalism a modern phenomenon aiming to establish a political community. It would be led by an elite that acts in the name of the people but without its explicit mandate. The Herzlian Jewish nation was a social
construct and a cultural creation of modernity designed for an age of revolution. Yet, curiously, there are certain themes which appear in his writings,
notwithstanding their naïve or enthusiastic aspect, which seem to prefigure the
theses of Ernest Gellner and Benedict Anderson on the impact of industrializa-
tion throughout the world on nationalism.[30] For Herzl, social conflicts were of
determinant importance. As his analysis of antisemitism taught him, if groups
were subjected to an ambient hostility and designated foreigners, they would
be pushed to create their own communities. In the following, Theodor Herzl's
words sound as if they could be written by Gellner or Anderson: »The dis-
tances of the surface of the earth have been overcome […] We build safe railroads in a mountain world which people once scaled on foot and with trepida-
tion.« Herzl added that the electric light was certainly invented to »solve the
problems of mankind by its glow. One of these problems, and not the least of
them, is the Jewish question.«[31] Herzl also wrote: »When the Jewish Company
has been formed, this news will be carried in a single day to the remotest ends
of the earth with the lightning speed of our telegraph wires.«[32] Without being
able to theorize the link between the rapid spread of modern communication
and nationalism, Herzl felt that there was at least some correlation between the
technological and the ideological phenomena. Herzl was eclectic. The answer
regarding whether the Jewish nation is new or old is, in his view, analogous to
the status of the land according to the title of his famous utopian novel. Thus,
for Herzl, in *Alt-neu-land* will live mainly an *Alt-neu-volk*.

The existence of a Jewish nation presented as such raises three questions re-
lating to the exterior and interior borders of the national community:

1) If the Jews are a nation, is this to say that all members of the Jewish people will be included in it, as part and parcel of it, assigned to it willy-nilly? In
other words, is the national ideal of a non-elective, imposed nation or of an
elective nation that offers the choice of participating or opting out?

2) If the Jews are a nation, is this to say that it is appropriate to conceive of
this nation as a cultural homogeneity. In other words, is it a homogeneous or
pluralist nation?

3) If the Jews are a nation and they constitute their own state, what is to be
the status of its residents who are not Jewish? In other words, are we dealing
with a state that is comprised of an ethnic or civic nation?

---

[30] Ernest Gellner: Nations and Nationalism. Oxford: Basil Blackwell 1983; Benedict
   Anderson: Imagined Communities: Reflections on the Origin and Spread of Nationalism. London: Verso 1991 (revised edition).
[31] Herzl, The Jewish State (note 3), 32.
[32] Ibid., 110.

III Designated or Elective Nation?

Regarding the first question: if the Jews comprise a nation, one might think that all Jews are a part of it without exception or choice. In other words, the national affiliation proposed by Herzl amounts to a national designation, the appointment of a residence. However, this is not really the case. Whereas the nation is indeed elective, it is this belonging to the people which proves to be imposed from the inside or outside. To understand this antinomy, it is important to understand the distinction and relation that Herzl suggests between »people« and »nation,« between an »historical group« and a »modern nation.« The nation is the people when it is assembled and politically endowed by a state. »Peoplehood« is a designation of the Jewish group in conditions of exile and dependence. Membership in the Jewish people is an exterior designation that eludes the individual. Jews, for the most part, belong to a common people by sole virtue of their birth and affiliation, on the one hand, and, on the other, by the fact that they are designated as such through hostile or oppressive intent by antisemites. Herzl underscored the role played by antisemites, in spite of themselves, in the perpetuation of the Jewish people. (Religious conversion is the only proactive step one can take to join the Jewish people.) As opposed to membership in the people, membership in the nation is voluntary: Jews are the natural candidates for membership in the Jewish nation. It is for them that the national framework is constituted though they are free to accept or reject it, to actualize its potential or to dismiss its legitimacy. In other words, although the Jewish nation addresses itself exclusively to Jews, it is not exempt from the conditional expression of an explicit individual will. As Herzl wrote: »The Jews who want a state of their own will have one.«[33] In this sense, as primordial as the Jewish nation may have been at the outset, since it is founded on a group identified beforehand as Jewish and that is propagated from generation to generation through biological lineage, it also presents an elective character that must not be underestimated. Of course, not everyone can be a part of it, but why would non-Jews want to join the Jewish nation? For Herzl, membership within the Jewish people, to which Jews have been assigned as a result of antisemitism, becomes optional in the framework of the nation. Thus, only those who make the choice to voluntarily gather on a common territory participate in the destiny of a Jewish state. The common destiny in the lands of exile must, in effect, be transcended by the affirmation of a will to join the reassembled people. Whereas it may be a political nation, defined by the possession of a territory, the existence of a state, and the promulgation of a constitution, the nation as seen by Herzl does not emulate the abstraction of a republican nation. The Jewish nation is founded on a primordial homogeneity of religious origin, but it transcends it without abolishing it.

---

[33] Ibid.

Herzl was concerned about the process of passage from people to nation during the period before the State was established. Accordingly, he conceived of *The Society of Jews,* which was defined as the state in the process of being formed. From the time of the existence of this *Society,* even before the Jewish nation is officially proclaimed, all Jews joining the movement will have expressed their desire to be part of the future nation that will be born with the proclamation of the Jewish State. This nation, which Herzl urges the Jews to found, is all the more elective in that this choice will in due time require their relocation to a land where the Jews will enjoy sovereignty. Thus, emigration illustrates, above all, the voluntary aspect of this demand Jews make upon themselves.

The Jewish nation, as Herzl conceived of it, rests on the principle defined by the titular chair of Hebrew at the College de France, the French philosopher Ernest Renan, in his celebrated text on the national question, *Qu'est-ce qu'une nation? (What is a Nation?).* »The nation,« Renan explained, »is a spiritual principle, defined not so much by its more or less faithful antecedents - geography, race, language, religion, mores, than by the expression of a will to share a common political destiny.« This is what Renan meant by the expression: »the nation, an everyday plebiscite.«[34]

Moreover, Herzl retained from Renan's text only the idea of the elective nature of this principle, whereas in his essay Renan underscored the essential role of memory in the formation of a nation. He added perceptively that this factor applies more to the memory of defeats than that of victories, citing the Jewish people as an example. Renan's thesis applies well to Herzl's Zionism. On one hand, there is the conjunction of these two elements – the memory of violent acts experienced and the everyday plebiscite constituting a nation. On the other hand, the primacy of this principal over the first is quite apparent. Herzl recognized that, paradoxically, a negative destiny, rooted in tribulations and oppression, greatly contributes towards the maintenance of an objective and subjective feeling of belonging. Indeed these negative experiences serve to recall to consciousness the origins of the humiliated person. As Herzl expressed it, this was in many respects the major obstacle preventing the Jews from integrating and disappearing among the nations. It was finally the trigger that would motivate the will to assemble the people into a nation. But if oppression was, in Herzl's eyes, a necessary condition for bringing about the transition to the nation, it is, as such, an insufficient one. Those subjected to this condition must be disposed to change as the requirement for the emergence of a national will and in order to transform a negative into a positive experience.

The consent of those Jews concerned and affected by the undertaking of politically organizing a community into a nation does not, however, imply the unanimity of all. In this regard, this nation is even more elective in that all Jews are far from likely to consent unanimously to the project. As already

---

[34] Ernest Renan: Qu'est-ce qu'une nation? Paris: Calmann-Lévy 1882.

explained, joining the nation is an optional, discretionary decision. Possible objections are of a diverse nature, as are the degrees of potential opposition. These range from honest and overt hostility to mere indifference. In any case, Herzl remained faithful to his spirit of tolerance: »Let anyone who does not want to go along, stay behind.«[35] Herzl was enough of a nationalist not to profess assimilation as such, but he was liberal enough to admit that »there is nothing discreditable about that.«[36]

Little surprised by the initial indifference and hostility to his conception, Herzl sensed that as the project would eventually be realized, he would obtain the consent of the people as a whole – *a posteriori*. This is the reason Herzl was careful to exclude, for obvious reasons, the idea of a preliminary collective consultation by referendum. A majority of the Jews would have rallied, presumably, against his national project. To justify this temporary infringement on the principle of a virtual democratic consultation, he defined the role of the Zionist movement as that of a tutor or caretaker tending to a person in danger (the Jewish people) and incapable of acting for himself. To give this role a juridical basis and legitimacy, Herzl borrowed from Roman law (it was his domain of specialization at Law School) the concept of *negotiorum gestio*. The *Society of Jews*, as he called the Zionist movement in *The Jewish State*, was the moral body to be the *Gestor*. Being the *avant-garde* of the Jewish people, the *Society of Jews* was conferred by Herzl with the status of »state-creating agency.«[37] This device would be temporary in Herzl's view, and it obviated the prospect of winning »the free consent of a majority of Jews.« Herzl added:

> It can be done against the will of some individuals, or even despite the opposition of groups of Jews who today are most powerful, but never, absolutely never, can a state act against all the Jews.[38]

Despite his reservations about democracy, reinforced during his work as the political correspondent of the *Neue Freie Presse* in parliamentary Third Republic France, he was nevertheless sensitive to the democratic legitimacy principle: »The idea depends only on the number of its adherents.«[39] His conviction proceeded from a realist point of view, since he believed,

> If only some individual pursued this idea, it would be a rather foolish thing; but if many Jews agree to work on it simultaneously, it is entirely reasonable, and carrying it out will present no major obstacles.

But the *raison d'être* of the project was essentially normative.

---

[35] Herzl, The Jewish State (note 3), 51.
[36] Ibid., 34.
[37] Ibid., 51.
[38] Ibid., 108.
[39] Ibid., 29.

This diversity of viewpoints in regard to Zionism signifies a refutation of the accusation of a »dual allegiance,« allegedly entertained or held by Zionists at the same time that they added, or even substituted, a new attachment for the state they would create in place of their allegiance to the state of which they were subjects. Logically, this accusation would not affect those Jews who did not declare themselves Zionists. If there can be a »Jewish people« in the diaspora (in the religious or cultural sense or by designating its specific origins), it can only raise itself to the rank of nation in the heart of a future Jewish State. Thus, Herzl admitted that it would not be possible to be a member of two nations simultaneously (and of two states). Herzl did not foresee the possibility of bi-nationality. Summoned to choose between the Jewish people and the Jewish nation, those preferring the first alternative will have thus proven, by staying in the diaspora, their sincere and definitive attachment to their respective homeland.[40] Herzl affirmed that not only would Zionism not harm them, it would render them, by their abstention from or their rejection of it, more patriotic in their country.

Did Herzl subscribe to the postulate that Jews are foreigners everywhere they reside? His expression of such a view was only as an acknowledgement of failure. Jews in the diaspora should not be considered foreign necessarily, but if they are, it is not because they cannot be assimilated but because their assimilation is rejected. They are foreigners not by any religious definition, according to which every Jew living outside of Eretz Israel is in a forced exile; nor are they deemed foreign because of any objective perception of an irreducible difference between Jews and non-Jews. Rather they are foreigners because in reducing their singularity to a religious particularity, in the eyes of gentiles, they remain, still and always, fundamentally »other.« As Herzl noted, this pejorative designation remained the privilege of the majority. The acquisition by Jews of linguistic, cultural, or professional competence within countries in which they reside would do nothing to change this basic situation. In times of crisis, they would always be reminded of their alleged foreignness, their »otherness.«

The elective character of the nation engenders certain contradictions. The voluntary and fundamentally personal step of joining the nation is contradicted in Herzl's *Der Judenstaat* by the excessively pre-planned character of the unfolding of the migratory operations, replete with a profusion of stages and details. In truth, in his mind, the urgency of the situation necessitates the alteration of this elective and voluntarist vision. Herzl ruled out a process whereby emigration would occur at a snail's pace, according to individual desires and aspirations. And yet, Herzl, who lost sight of his initial approach

---

[40] Herzl did not fail to mention a third option which fully commanded his respect. This is the path taken by the sympathizers who, without joining the Zionist movement today and the Jewish State tomorrow, nevertheless manifest a clear interest and goodwill towards the project.

somewhat, subsequently regained it by recalling the primary evidence in favor of the conception of the elective nature of the Jewish nation. Zionism was not merely a mass humanitarian salvage operation. Herzl wrote: »Do we not always envisage their emigration as a voluntary one?«[41] If we compare Herzl's idea of the nation with what subsequently came to pass, we must conclude that its elective character is passed on when the nation becomes autochthonous. Only the new immigrants may continue to conceive of their transformation or passage to the nation in such terms. Finally, it would have been a more equitable interpretation and application of Herzl's endeavor had Israeli law considered Israel as the State of the Jewish nation, not of the Jewish people.

IV Homogeneous Nation or Pluralistic Nation?

Herzl was sufficiently revolutionary in the project of creating a state for the Jews and in casting the Jews in a national identity which allowed him to admit some attachment to traditions and customs. Unlike Edmond Burke, he did not ponder the idea of a nation that would have to invent and create everything from scratch. Herzl intuited that there was no place for revolution in certain domains where it was proper to be modest, moderate, and prudent. He was too sensitive to the importance of sociology to imagine the Jewish people as a *tabula rasa*. He had already dismissed this idea by deeming that the Jews must endow themselves with the institutions of a parliament and political parties. As long as the economy was set up in keeping with his desires as a social reformer, this fact was enough for him to exclude the need for carrying out a cultural revolution or to impose a single language on the nation. We can see in his view of things modernist elements as well as the reproduction of certain social elements directly traced from the template of a European society. Although Herzl believed that the Jewish State would be geographically distant from Europe, he nevertheless remained attached to Europe, because therein resided his own culture. He would create or recreate Europe without the Europeans, since they have not proven themselves worthy or capable of living up to their own ideals. Because of the violence of the departure, which was more or less dictated by the nations and their states that excluded the Jews from their native societies and lands, Herzl felt that the individual Jew would need the protection and comeraderie of his fellow Jews in order to succeed as smoothly as possible in the process of transplantation. Therefore, Herzl developed a »community *aliyah*« (immigration) model. As for the Zionist movement, there would not be any imposed departure. Rather the task of planning it makes clear that »all groupings will be voluntary.«[42]

---

[41] Herzl, The Jewish State (note 3), 84.
[42] Ibid., 81.

Herzl did not preoccupy himself with the internal unity of the new nation. He did not concern himself with the cultural homogenization of the Jews. The cornerstone of the edifice of the nation was to be located in its will to maintain in unity a state whose creation is justified by the memory and the present, as well as by the continual potential of hostility encountered by the Jews in the diaspora. But, as opposed to Europe, integration into the citizenry was not conditioned upon the disappearance of cultural identities. The equality of legal and political conditions would not require the unanimity of mores and cultures. The Jewish state would have no religious requirements. No demands were to made of immigrants to break with their former homelands. While they may have left those homelands for political reasons, they would remain faithful and emotionally attached to their cultures. The revolution would have to appear as an evolution. First, the idea would receive the consent of the emigrants. Herzl understood that in order for Jews to leave Europe for the Jewish State, he had to offer guarantees: »We shall not give up our cherished customs, we shall find them again.«[43] Herzl did not ignore the task of nation-building, but he was ready to make the process an extended one. The change of place was drastic and radical enough to let the other social, cultural, linguistic and even political processes take place slowly, inspired by an incremental and reformist spirit. According to Herzl, more aggressive ways of dealing with these changes would be counterproductive. As he pointed out: »These little habits are like a thousand fine threads; each of them is thin and fragile, but together they make up an unbreakable cable.«[44] He understood that because of the necessity of leaving Europe, at least, Jews will recreate Europe in their new state. Divorce from European peoples and countries would not require divorce from their culture. In this sense, Zionism was not only a modern solution to the Jewish question, as Herzl subtitled his book, but also a practical device to solve the crisis of European cosmopolitanism.[45] He multiplied the precautions, and re-lied himself on experiment. Cultural transfer was already a reality:

> There are English hotels in Egypt and in the mountain peaks of Switzerland, Vien-nese cafés in South Africa, French theaters in Russia, German opera houses in America, and the best Bavarian beer in Paris.[46]

And all these pictures will unite together with the arrival in the Jewish State of the Jewish communities from the diaspora. The cosmopolitan *Altneuland* was already programmed in *The Jewish State.*

This was especially true regarding the question of language. Herzl did not intend to impose a *lingua franca* from above: »Everyone will retain his own

---

[43] Ibid., 39.
[44] Ibid., 90.
[45] Michael Stanislawsky: Zionism and the *fin-de-siècle*: Cosmopolitanism and Nation-alism from Nordau to Jabotinsky. Berkeley: University of California Press 2001, 14.
[46] Herzl, The Jewish State (note 3), 90.

language, the beloved homeland of his thoughts.«[47] Either a common language would emerge, or a linguistic federalism will prevail, as in Switzerland. The same was true, at least initially, regarding judiciary legislation. Herzl proposed a model of transition. During the first stage, every immigrant Jew would be judged according to the laws of the country which he has left. Legal uniformity only come afterwards.

V   An Ethnic or Civic Nation?

National and political Jewish affirmation excluded in Herzl's mind any chauvinist deviation. Every Jew in the world was naturally entitled to be a candidate to become a citizen of the future Jewish State, but the native residents deserved equal citizenship.[48] There is no ethnical division between national majority and minority. It is generally admitted that only in *Altneuland* did Herzl pay some attention to the Arab question by inventing the figure of Rashid Bey. Since Herzl had serious doubts, when he wrote *The Jewish State,* whether or not the Jewish State could come into existence in Palestine, it was evident that the Arab question need not have been raised in this text. But that fact does not mean that Herzl ignored the probability that the Jewish state would come into existence in an empty territory. He had to suppose that it would be established in a place where a native population was currently living. That is the reason why *The Jewish State,* which posited the foundations of the Jewish nation, laid down some principles connected to the presence of an autochthonous population. What was the model of nation Herzl was striving for? Was it civic or ethnic? The question whether Herzl's model of the nation was civic or ethnic is not marginal. Herzl did not ignore the native fear of mass immigration. It was for Herzl the key to claiming political independence. »Infiltration without sovereignty« increased pressure on the native population – which feels itself threatened – to bar the further influx of Jews.[49] Only sovereignty would give Jews the means to allow waves of immigration to arrive in the land without interference or disruptions. Put in other terms, only in a Jewish State might a Law of Return be implemented. The threat for the natives will not be less, but their pressure will be no longer effective. Reducing the opposition of the local population and solving the contradiction were for Herzl questions of interest in the realm of ethics. Consequently, he felt the imperative to provide a theoretical counterpart: to the authorities, he promised financial advantages and foreign investment; to the neighboring countries, benefits. And, last but not least, for the natives, in order to relieve their anxiety, he of-

---

[47] Ibid., 100.
[48] Rachel Elboim-Dror: Herzl as a Proto-Post-Zionist? In: Theodor Herzl: Visionary of the Jewish State (note 27), 167.
[49] Herzl, The Jewish State (note 3), 51.

fered »honorable protection and equality before the law,« to »men of other creeds and other nationalities come to live among us.«[50] This last device will take the form of a modern and advanced legislation that Herzl conceived as »a model code«.[51]

Herzl had no intention of placing the Arabs out of the modern enterprise led by Zionism. They were, in fact, invited by him to benefit from the modern advances, technology, and the dynamism introduced into the Middle East by the Jews, who were defined by Herzl as the »missionaries of progress.« The Arab hero of *Altneuland*, Reshid Bey, reveals a deep gratitude to the Jews for the economic opportunities and expansion that they brought to the country and from which he profited himself. He is a full member of the New Society and he participated in the work of its Executive Committee. Of course, his speech, which is recorded in the text, resembles Herzl's voice. It is the same one that created this native figure according to the paternalist and optimist tone that prevails in the genre of utopian literature.[52] But Herzl did not refrain from objecting to the hegemonic discourse of the fictional character Steineck regarding Jews being the first to bring science to Palestine. Besides, Kingscourt, who plays the role of the non-Jew sympathetic to the Zionist cause, asks Rashid Bey if his destiny, even if satisfactory to some extent, is not a lonely one, constituting an exception to the rule of collective exploitation and spoliation. Herzl did not satisfy himself with this type of query. He wanted to show that it was not enough for the Arab minority to reach the material level and guarantee social and political rights for the native population. Herzl refrained from imposing the occidental model on submissive Arabs, and he distanced himself from cultural imperialism. He depicted a situation of political and economical equality that they deserved: »We don't interfere in their creeds and their habits. We gave them a great amount of welfare.« Herzl did not present a perfect society in the novel; the debate between Littwak and Rabbi Geyer on the integration of foreigners showed well enough that the New Society is by no means a place of social perfection. This oriental society is threatened by populist demagogy, particularism, and xenophobia that may disturb the harmonious atmosphere. Therefore, the last words of the New Society's president are important to remember: »The foreigner has to be welcomed among us.« Herzl demonstrated explicitly in his *Altneuland* his personal inclination for cosmopolitism and religious tolerance. He advocated in the novel for an open society. A real sign of Jewish normalization, as expressed in terms of the novel, would be when cultural Europe will be at home in Zion, as Jews of the New Society will feel at home in Europe. The society in *Altneuland* is like the ark of Noah, or even a good tower of Babel. It is rich because it possesses all

---

[50] Ibid., 100.
[51] Ibid., 101.
[52] Rachel Elboim-Dror: Ha-Mahar shel ha-Etmol (Yesterday's Tomorrow). Jerusalem: Yad Ben-Zvi 1993.

the cultural and religious families of the earth. »We [Jews] are xenophiles,« Herzl said. He did not see any contradiction between cosmopolitism and nationalism. In the novel, the protagonist concludes: »Here in the New Society, everyone may live and be happy as he wants.« The themes of reciprocity and fraternity give some credibility to the idea of pacific coexistence grounded in mutual interest.

Herzl suggested a common citizenship, but he allowed for the maintenance of the cultural features of the different parts that constitute the body politic. He opted for the principle of separation between church and state, even if the latter is called the synagogue or the rabbinate. He intended to separate the political realm, as a sphere of interests and common values where citizens work together to achieve the public interest, from the cultural sphere, where citizens distinguish themselves by tongue, culture, habits. Herzl posed a double level of national unity: a political one where equality prevails between citizens united by the civic, juridical, territorial identity overcoming all ethnic and cultural differences, and a cultural one, by which they maintain their differences. All citizens living in the New Society will be united by the ideals of welfare and development, and they will work towards achieving a perfect society; all citizens will be faithful to their religious and cultural backgrounds. Regarding political rights, the nation is an extensive one, constituted by the citizens in the state, regardless of their ethnic attachments. The unity factor is founded on the legitimacy of the regime and the citizens' attachment to the society. The Jews would be the dominant ethnic population, but it would not have political consequences for other ethnic groups' political and cultural rights, because of the dedication to cosmopolitanism. This ideal is to succeed precisely in the area where European society failed.

The realization of the Jewish nation, as conceived by Herzl, would not preclude or prevent Jews in the diaspora from considering themselves outside of the nation. The existence of the Jewish nation does not entail a break of cultural affinities, which have been developed by Jews over centuries; the Jewish nation does not exclude the full political participation of non-Jewish populations and peoples in the new state or society as citizens and as members of the executive arm of government. National unity was subject to the free choice of the individual; political unity was subject to inclusive and integrative citizenship; cultural harmony was based on pluralist and multicultural practices. Herzl, indeed, had a right to tell *Atlneuland* readers: »If you will it, it is no legend.«

Jacques Kornberg

Theodor Herzl: Zionism as Personal Liberation*

I

There have always been quarrels about Herzl's Zionist agenda. In the last decade, the main dispute has been over his conception of the Jewish State: over how *Jewish* Herzl's Jewish State was, or how European, or how Gentile. This quarrel is really about a larger issue, for behind it are urgent controversies about the Jewish character of the state of Israel. In these controversies, different sides make competing claims about Zionism's origins and pedigree. Does it lie in liberalism, cosmopolitanism, in some mix of them along with Jewish traditions, or in nativism and religious messianism? In making their claims advocates look back to Herzl, the founder of political Zionism, for legitimacy and authority.

I will briefly review these debates, but I will also raise the question as to whether we can ever pin Herzl down on these issues. I will also move to what I think is most important about Herzl, how he changed history, which has more to do with his work as a Jewish diplomat and less to do with his theories about the Jewish State. My view of Herzl is by no means new, but I want to reiterate it and add my own perspective to it.

In the recent literature on Herzl and Zionist values, Daniel Boyarin occupies a special place, having been the most categorical in attacking Herzl's Zionism for being »unJewish,« advocating alien values, overturning age-old Jewish orientations. In his view, Herzl, as a member of a despised minority, had internalized the majority European stereotype of the Jew as a weakling, with a botched body: poorly proportioned, short, swaybacked, flat-footed. Herzl's project, according to Boyarin, was to transform Jews »into the ideal ›Aryan‹ male.« The pride of traditional Judaism, the cerebral, gentle, nurturing scholar was now viewed as unmanly, feminine. Aggressive and domineering ideals of masculinity shadowed Zionism from the very beginning.[1]

* This essay first saw the light of day as a lecture at an international conference held in Jerusalem in June 2004: Marking the Centenary of Theodor Herzl's Death: Herzl Then and Now. I wish to thank the organizers of the conference for their invitation: Professors Jacob Golomb and Robert Wistrich of the Hebrew University of Jerusalem. My thanks to Mona Kornberg for her rigorous and perceptive editorial advice at every step of the way, from lecture to final essay.

[1] Daniel Boyarin: Unheroic Conduct: The Rise of Heterosexuality and the Invention of the Jewish Man. Berkeley: University of California Press 1997, 277.

Michael Gluzman has made a similar argument. Here again, Herzl is seen to have internalized the majority European culture's stereotype of the Jewish male as »a genetically flawed and degenerated creature.« Jewish males were believed to be especially subject to »mental illness and sexual pathologies,« to hysteria, and homosexuality, in short, to being feminine. In response, Herzl's Zionism stood for a longing for masculinity. Accordingly, in Herzl's novel *Altneuland,* life in the New Society transforms the protagonist Friedrich Loewenberg from an effeminate Jew to a sturdy »oak,« who experiences heterosexual desire for the first time in 20 years. For Gluzman, Herzl's claim that Zionism promoted female equality was a fraud, for the ideal of masculinity required that femininity be its polar opposite. Women thus remained in the private sphere, helpmates to their men. The reader may remember the story of the Viennese Jew Otto Weininger, who committed suicide because he equated Jewishness with being effeminate. Herzl solved the same dilemma through Zionism, which celebrated a masculine image of national strength. Gluzman cites the well-known line from Herzl's diary: »I need to educate the youth and turn them into military men.« While Boyarin views Herzlean Zionism as promoting hardness, aggression and domination, understood as healthy masculinity, Gluzman sees Herzlean Zionism as promoting highly restrictive and one-dimensional ideals of masculinity and femininity.[2]

Gender politics has wide political implications, nowhere more evident than in the policies of states, whether fascist, communist, or liberal-democratic. Anita Shapira touches on this implication when insisting that Herzl's priority was a liberal state, valuing human rights and eliminating human want. Of course, a state had to have an army, but Herzl certainly did not dwell on this. He mentioned military education, but his thoughts on these matters were sketchy. As a matter of fact, no overriding cult of masculinity dominated Herzlean Zionism. He imagined a Jewish state created by international agreement, with the help of European states glad to be rid of their »Jewish problem.« Herzl's primary concern was with »Jewish honor and respect,« which meant placing Jewish-Gentile relations on a new footing of equality and mutual regard. For this to happen, both the Jewish state and European states would have to be liberal, tolerant societies. As for the existing Arab population of Palestine, Herzl, willfully unrealistic, did not imagine them resisting the Jewish presence. There was no need, therefore, to defeat them militarily. The cultivation of military virtues was not inherent in Herzlean Zionism, but was a

---

[2]   Michael Gluzman: The Zionist Body: Nationalism and Sexuality in Herzl's Altneu-land. »Genetically flawed« and »mental illness« on page 4 are quotations from Shmuel Almog. The Herzl quote is on page 11. See also page 15. Pages cited are from a prepublication copy Professor Gluzman generously shared with me. The piece will be published In: Feminist Readers, Jewish Texts. Ed. Rachel Biale and Susannah Heschel. Berkeley: The University of California Press, forthcoming.

later development, the result of spirited and armed Arab opposition to Zionist endeavors in the land.[3]

Yoram Hazony takes up the meaning of »Jewishness« for Herzl from another angle. Current issues shadow his thinking as well, in this case Hazony's opposition to the post-Zionist view that Israel should become a state of all its citizens, and grant no privileged legal status to those of Jewish nationality or to Judaism. At stake for him is the Jewish character of the Jewish state, and he finds pedigree for his ideas in Herzl's Zionism. He argues that Herzl revolted against the German-Jewish ideology of emancipation, with its view that the loss of the ancient Jewish state and the scattering of the Jewish people was a precondition for their divine mission. In this German-Jewish view, the Davidic kingdom was a brief moment in Jewish history and not the defining moment. It was the *loss* of statehood and power that turned Jews into the carriers of purely spiritual values, and it was their dispersion that turned Jews into the carriers of prophetic universalism to all the nations. Against this idea, Herzl reawakened glorious memories of Jewish nationhood. What is more, he viewed acculturated European Jews as divided beings with conflicted identities, racked by the need to mimic Gentiles. In a Jewish state, Jews would gain »inner wholeness.« Traditional Judaism would become the established state religion, while the state would draw its national symbols from the ancient era of Jewish kingdoms.[4]

Hazony is not disturbed by the fact that Herzl's utopian novel *Altneuland* envisages cultural pluralism in the »New Society,« for he dismisses the novel as a sheer propaganda ploy. Herzl was trying to assure Christians that Jewish rule would not threaten the Christian presence in the Holy Land. Hazony, however, does not exaggerate Herzl's Jewishness and acknowledges what he calls Herzl's »limited appreciation of the need to strengthen the Jewish national culture and consciousness.« He concludes, as others have, that Herzl's great contribution to Zionism lay elsewhere: in his creation of a Jewish National Assembly, a kind of parliament in exile, as the repository of Jewish sovereignty. And along with that, in his innovative diplomacy, the practice of »Realpolitik,« seeking access to the power centers of Europe, making the Jewish nation a player on the world stage.[5]

Numerous authors have insisted on Herzl's Jewishness, but their view of it is usually far different from Hazony's. Steven Beller sees Herzl as a »Jewish thinker,« but is careful to place this in the historical context of turn-of-the-century Vienna. For Beller, Herzl drew from the ideology of emancipation, which was a creation of the *Haskalah*. The version of this ideology Herzl

---

[3] Anita Shapira: Land and Power: The Zionist Resort to Force, 1881–1948. Oxford: Oxford University Press 1992, 11, 12, 15.

[4] Yoram Hazony: The Jewish State: The Struggle for Israel's Soul. New York: Basic Books 2000, 87–92, 114, 138–151. »Inner wholeness,« is a quote from Herzl.

[5] Ibid., 120, 127–131.

adopted came from Abraham Geiger, the great founder of Reform Judaism. For Geiger, the »divine spirit« animating Judaism centered upon the teachings of the prophets and their vision of social morality and universal peace. These teachings were rooted in ethical monotheism, which was the message Jews were to carry to the rest of humanity. Thus, for Geiger, Judaism was compatible with the best in modern values; the world needed Judaism. Similarly, for Herzl the Jewish nation was to be a »paragon of modernity.« Herzl did not seek the »normalization« of the Jews; instead, he saw Palestine as a *tabula rasa*, a virgin country, where Jews would create a model society from scratch, unburdened by Europe's heritage of feudalism and serfdom. The »Jewish mission« was to show the world how to create a society exemplifying »tolerance, freedom and humanity.« That was what Jewishness meant to Herzl.[6]

Another recent interpretation of the »Jewishness« of Herzl's Zionism, seeking to anchor it squarely in the nineteenth-century historical context, follows a similar line. Michael Stanislawski sees Herzl as a good European, a cosmopolitan who embraced universalist values that transcended national, ethnic, and religious differences. In keeping with the spirit of the eighteenth-century Enlightenment, Herzl believed that what humanity had in common was far more fundamental than their merely skin-deep national, ethnic, or religious differences. At the same time, and in seeming contradiction, Herzlean Zionism stood for Jewish self-pride, Jewish solidarity, and the preservation of Jewish ethnicity as an ultimate value. In a Jewish state, Jews would be able to define themselves, unrestrained by assimilationist mimicry. They would develop what Herzl called »our own character, not a Marrano-like, borrowed, untruthful character, but our own.« The state would shelter a national culture drawn from Jewish history; it would commemorate Jewish heroes. But this would be a new Jewish culture, what Stanislawski calls

> a subversion of traditional Jewish categories and conceptions in the name of a new form of Jewishness totally defined by the values and aesthetic of the European fin de siècle.

To be Jewish was to read the Jewish prophets as affirming universalistic and cosmopolitan values. To be Jewish, in keeping with other values of the fin de siècle, was to affirm a new virile ideal of masculinity. Thus, Stanislawski seeks to resolve the paradox of Herzl's Jewish nationalism and his universalism. For Herzl, universalism was both a European and Jewish value.[7]

---

6   Steven Beller: Herzl. London: Peter Halban 1991, xiii, 58, 103; Geiger's ideology of emancipation In: Michael Meyer: Response to Modernity: A History of the Reform Movement in Judaism. Oxford: Oxford University Press 1988, 95–99.

7   Michael Stanislawski: Zionism and the Fin de Siècle: Cosmopolitanism and Nationalism from Nordau to Jabotinsky. Berkeley: University of California Press 2001, 96; the Herzl quote is inserted by me, from: Jacques Kornberg: Theodor Herzl: From Assimilation to Zionism. Bloomington: Indiana University Press 1993, 177; Stanislawski is not critical of Herzl's synthesis, but cannot forebear quoting Cynthia Ozick's sarcastic comment: »universalism is the ultimate Jewish parochialism.« See, 12.

What can we decide after considering these differing interpretations of Herzl's vision of the Jewish state? My own conclusion is that there is some truth in all these accounts, for his conception of the Jewish State was not settled and consistent, and was even conflicted. What will the Jewish State be like, according to Herzl? Judaism will bind Jews together and be the state religion officiated by traditional rabbis, but, at the same time, Judaism will emphasize cosmopolitan and universalistic values. The state will be pacifistic, but the state will also promote a virile ideal of masculinity emphasizing bravery and courage in battle. Only in a Jewish state will Austro-German Jews finally be recognized as Germans, a recognition they could not achieve in Europe. But, also only in the Jewish state will Jews be free to develop their own true character, not a Marrano-like character distorted by assimilationist mimicry. Herzl insisted in *The Jewish State:* »The distinctive nationality of the Jews cannot, will not, and need not perish.« At the same time he was against sheltering and promoting a Jewish language. But how can one preserve a nationality without maintaining a national language? The same uncertainty appears in Herzl's utopian novel *Altneuland*: where he extols Russian Jews for whom »a Jewish nation still exists [...] [as a] living tradition, a love of the past.« He later describes »the spell of the Sabbath« descending over Jerusalem, and then imagines the New Society as indifferent to »race or creed,« equally open to Muslims and Christians. The question of the character of the Jewish State always remained an unsettled and conflicted one for Herzl. Those who seek consistency and a system will only find shifting winds. This is not unusual; most of us are conflicted on some issues. Benjamin Harshav has commented wisely:

> sensibilities and attitudes [...] are often fuzzy and ambivalent and not as systematic and coherent as ideologies would like to be. Individuals, even highly articulate ones, are often undecided on various matters, inconsistent, compromising between opposite ideas, changing their position with time.[8]

---

8   Raphael Patai (Ed.): On the leading role of rabbis. In: The Complete Diaries of Theodor Herzl. Trans. Harry Zohn. 5 Vols. New York: Herzl Press and Thomas Yoseloff 1960, I: 34, 104; see also Theodor Herzl: The Jewish State. Trans. Harry Zohn. New York: Herzl Press 1970, 81; Herzl: On cosmopolitan and universalist values. In: The Jewish State, 100; Patai (Ed.), On virile masculinity. In: The Complete Diaries of Theodor Herzl, I: 38, 55–58; Herzl, On a peace loving Jewish state. In: The Jewish State, 101; Patai (Ed.), The Complete Diaries of Theodor Herzl, I: 213; Patai (Ed.), On finally being recognized as Germans. In: The Complete Diaries of Theodor Herzl, I: 246–247. For similar statements see I: 171 and II: 694–695; »The distinctive nationality...« In: The Jewish State, 37; Herzl, On Herzl's opposition to a Jewish language. In: The Jewish State, 99–100; Theodore Herzl: Old-New Land. Trans. Lotta Levinsohn. Introduction by Jacques Kornberg. New York: Markus Wiener Publishing and Herzl Press 1987, 45, 152, 248, 259; Harshav quoted in Stanislawski, Zionism and the Fin de Siècle: Cosmopolitanism and Nationalism from Nordau to Jabotinsky (note 7), xx.

II

Herzl's great contribution to Jewish history lay far less in his conception of the Jewish State than it did elsewhere. Most historians would agree with Gideon Shimoni: »In the final analysis it was less in theorizing than in the creation of the instruments for the attainment of Zionism's objectives that Herzl made his most important contribution.« He changed history: there may well have been no State of Israel without Herzl, just as there may well have been no Bolshevik revolution without Lenin's iron will and decisiveness. Herzl made history by bringing East and West European Jews together into one political body, unifying them politically, creating a disciplined political movement, forging a Jewish National Assembly, a parliamentary body as an incipient state in exile, which sought and gained international recognition and legitimacy as a representative of the Jewish people. It was as activist rather than as theoretician that Herzl shaped history. The question to pose, then, is how did his ideas shape his creation of the instruments for the attainment of Zionism's objectives?[9]

Herzl's priority as Zionist leader was international diplomacy first, diplomacy second, and diplomacy third. David Vital put it well: Herzl wished to make the Jewish nation »a recognized and constituent element of the world of high politics.« He sought sources of Jewish power to carry out his goals, for he was transforming the Jewish-Gentile relationship. Jews were not to make humanitarian or moral appeals; diplomacy was based on *Realpolitik*, on a *quid pro quo* between state entities. But what had Jews to offer? Herzl played on exaggerated stereotypes of Jewish power by convoking an international congress of Jews in the clear light of day, with maximum publicity, conjuring up the image of a tightly unified international Jewish political movement. Pursuing *Realpolitik*, he offered financial aid to the Ottoman government in return for a charter; he also conveyed the message that Zionism would divert numerous and menacing Jewish revolutionaries from Europe; in *The Jewish State*, he depicted a Jewish state in Palestine as »the wall of defense against Asia,« a Europeanist outpost serving pan-European interests. As touched by fantasy as these ideas were, Herzl was proposing that Jews devise sources of power for their own political ends. All was to be done openly, candidly, and boldly.

Herzl faced serious opposition from Jews over convening an international political congress whose ultimate goal was the establishment a Jewish state. Many Jews feared they would be charged with lack of patriotism and were very concerned about what the antisemites would make of it. Herzl's style, in Vital's words was: »grand and ambitious«; Jews, a weak and vulnerable people, were to become legitimate and respected players on the international scene.[10]

---

[9]   Gideon Shimoni: The Zionist Ideology. Hanover, New Hampshire: University Press of New England 1995, 96.

[10]   David Vital: Zionism: the Formative Years. Oxford: Clarendon Press 1982, 61; see also 47, »Diplomacy was the whole of his policy«; Herzl, The Jewish State (note 8), 52; Herzl, On Zionism and Jewish Revolutionaries. In: The Jewish State (note 8),

Zionism prior to Herzl, or the *Hibbat Zion* movement, had followed a different course. Under the repressive conditions of Tsarist Russia, it could not openly proclaim political aims. Its goals were modest and long-term; its resources were scant. *Hibbbat Zion* aimed for agricultural colonies in Palestine, to be led by an elite of nationally-minded pioneers. Herzl considered this surreptitious national infiltration into Palestine demeaning, for Jews were counting on Ottoman sufferance rather than pressing for their right to a state. He insisted that Zionism's immediate goal was a Jewish state, while *Hibbat Zion* worried that such proclamations would lead the Ottoman authorities to tighten controls over Jewish settlements.[11]

We know that Herzl's frenetic diplomatic activity in the capitals of Europe failed. In August 1902, he publicly acknowledged that the years of diplomatic efforts at the Ottoman court had come to nothing. On reflection, how could anyone think it would be otherwise? In the nineteenth century, the Ottoman Empire had watched its ethnic minorities turn to nationalism and its European possessions shrink. Why would it invite yet another nationalistically-minded minority into its empire? Why would the Ottoman government put Jews within reach of Jerusalem? Surely, the *Sultan* was the sober-minded realist, and *Herzl* the fantasist. Why did Herzl favor this bold, extravagant diplomatic approach to Jewish nationhood, which contained more than a touch of fantasy?[12]

III

For Herzl, it was not only the goal, a state, that would liberate Jews, but the means of arriving at that goal would liberate Jews as well. Herzl's international diplomacy would get Jews used to thinking of themselves in new ways, in ways that would transform them. To understand what was behind this idea, we have to go back to Herzl's origins as an acculturated Austro-German Jew, and the way his Zionism emerged out of his Jewish ambivalence.

I have described Herzl in my book as an ambivalent Jew, not a self-hating Jew, but an ambivalent Jew, balancing on a tight-rope between Jewish self-contempt and Jewish pride and solidarity. As I describe this self-contempt: Herzl saw Jews as »inferior, cowardly, unmanly, preoccupied with money, bereft of idealism.« But he also praised their steadfastness when facing persecution, and identified with their history of victimization. He shared European stereotypes of the »despised physiognomy« of the Jews, believing the Jewish

---

44–45, 48 and Kornberg, Theodor Herzl: From Assimilation to Zionism (note 7), 180–183; David Vital: The Origins of Zionism. Oxford: Clarendon Press 1975, 334–36.

[11] Vital, Zionism: the Formative Years (note 10), 55–56 and Jacques Kornberg: »Ahad Ha-am and Herzl.« In: At the Crossroads: Essays on Ahad Ha-am. Ed. Jacques Kornberg. Albany: State University of New York Press 1983, 121.

[12] Kornberg, »Ahad Ha-am and Herzl« (note 11), 118.

character was etched in their physiognomy. Describing Jews, what Herzl attended to, first of all, was the ugly Jewish physique. Berlin business friends of
his father were »ugly little Jews and Jewesses.« Going to synagogue in Paris in
1894, for the first time in his three years there, he looked around and saw
»bold misshapen noses; furtive and cunning eyes.« Deviousness and avarice
were stamped on their faces. Even later, in his Zionist novel *Old-New Land,*
Herzl described a Viennese Jew, Leopold Weinberger, as having, »a decided
squint and very damp palms.« Nervous stealthiness was written all over his
eyes and hands. Reading an antisemitic tract by Eugen Dühring in 1882, Herzl
was compelled to agree with him in part: »The crookedness of Jewish morality
and the lack of ethical seriousness in many (Dühring says in all) Jewish actions
is exposed.« Yet in a *feuilleton* a few years later, Herzl condemned Christian
ethical teachings as cloaking »a thirst for plunder« of Mediaeval Jews, and
extolled the »heroic loyalty« of these Jews to their God. In the twistings and
turnings of ambivalence, Jews could be cowardly and avaricious, and heroic
and steadfast.[13]

For Herzl, history explained the Jewish character. In a diary entry of his
youth, he called Jews, »an aristocratic race brought down by history.« Jews
were not innately cowardly and avaricious; circumstances had made them so.
Vulnerable and restricted to commercial occupations, their only security had
been money, and acquisition the only outlet for their power drive. Sharp commercial dealing was the only way they could retaliate against their persecutors.
As a vulnerable minority, they had learned survival tactics, developing a keen
sense for when to be surreptitious and when to be submissive. Ghetto isolation
and their restriction to commercial occupations had made them what they
were. Herzl concluded: »The ghetto-walls of intolerance had restricted them
[Jews] both in mind and body.«[14]

For a long time, Herzl believed these faults and vices would be cured by
emancipation and assimilation within Europe. Once free of restrictions and
isolation, free to enter the gamut of occupations, to receive a modern education, to enter state service, to serve in the army, the Jewish character would
improve. Assimilation too, would do its work. In the early 1880s Herzl recommended intermarriage as a way of improving what he called the Jewish
»Folk-profile« (ethnic profile). However, intermarriage between Jews and
Christians was prohibited by law; to become married one of the partners would
have to convert, or register as *konfessionslos* (without religious affiliation).
Intermarriage in nineteenth-century Central Europe meant Jews assimilating
into German-Christian society. Herzl himself followed a less extreme path to
assimilation, joining a German nationalist dueling fraternity while a student at
the University of Vienna. The fraternity, *Albia,* accepted Jews, but the terms of

---

[13] Kornberg, Theodor Herzl: From Assimilation to Zionism (note 7), 2, 21, 24, 72, 84,
      142; Herzl, Old-New Land (note 8), 10.
[14] Kornberg, Theodor Herzl: From Assimilation to Zionism (note 7), 21–23, 126.

that acceptance were that they shed the »Jewish spirit« and any fidelity to Jewry, and make German history their history, and ancient German heroes and epics their own.[15]

Negative views of Jewishness affected how Herzl viewed himself. A letter he wrote in 1902 tells of a duel Herzl had cancelled seventeen years earlier (1885) with an apology because he was worried sick about his father, severely ill at the time. He admitted that for years, after canceling the duel, he was plagued by uncertainty as to whether Jewish emotionalism and anxiety had overcome him, labeled at the time as a feminine-like hysteria. He tortured himself over the thought that his father's illness had provided him with an alibi for his lack of manly Germanic hardness. What he would not consider was that his act showed exemplary filial devotion. Affected by the domineering gaze of the majority culture, Herzl turned Jewish virtues into Jewish deficiencies.[16]

For most of his life, Herzl's Jewish ambivalence remained in uneasy though tolerable balance, resulting in no more than swings of mood and feeling between what I have called,

> rage at Gentiles, wounded Jewish pride, heightened Jewish self-disdain leading him to blame Jews for antisemitism, calls for Jewish self-assertion, and renewed wishes for Jewish assimilation, for a ›Jewish submergence into the nation.‹

Herzl could favor a self-effacing Jewish assimilation to Germandom, and a little while later react with fury to an editor's suggestion that he adopt a non-Jewish sounding pen name.[17]

IV

Herzl remained in this state through the 1880s and part of the 1890s, but this ambivalence became less and less tolerable with growing antisemitism in Vienna in the 1890s. He then changed his mind about antisemitism, no longer seeing it as a surviving remnant of medievalism which would give way to growing enlightenment and eventually disappear. He now judged it a far greater threat, a dynamic modern political movement made up of a coalition of anti-liberal forces that had achieved weight through the widening of suffrage. Jews now lived in a new and dangerous age of mass political parties. The prospects for assimilation had died out.[18]

The new anti-Jewish climate in Vienna in the 1890s, not the Dreyfus case in France, changed Herzl. From the 1850s to the 1880s, Jews had seen steady progress in their rights and standing in the Austro-Hungarian Empire. By the

---

[15] Ibid., 24–25, 48–51.
[16] Ibid., 69–71.
[17] Ibid., 81, 116–117.
[18] Ibid., 99–102.

time the constitution of 1867 was promulgated, legal restrictions on choice of occupations and residence, and on buying land, had been lifted. Jews enjoyed the rights of citizenship. By the 1870s, thirteen Jewish deputies sat in the *Reichsrat*. A substantial Jewish middle class had emerged, whose sons were entering the professions. But the 1890s saw an utter reversal of these trends, marked by the rise of the antisemitic Christian Social party, a wide-ranging coalition of the respectable middle classes. Progress in opening the state service and the academy to Jews was blocked.

Most important for Herzl, in the new antisemitic climate, Jews were being ostracized from Liberal and German Nationalist political and social associations as well, exactly the objects of Jewish assimilationist yearnings. For decades, Jews had been allies in Liberal and Austro-German Nationalist associations; now they were being turned away, becoming pariahs, outcasts once again. By the 1890s, the Liberal Party had moved to de facto segregation, with separate Jewish and Gentile party branches; the *Deutscher Schulverein* (German School Association), which had once subsidized German-Jewish denominational schools, now allowed local branches to exclude Jews; the *Deutscher Klub,* a radical nationalist parliamentary caucus, removed the Jewish editor of its party newspaper, the highly assimilated champion of Germandom (*Deutschtum*) Heinrich Friedjung; and very importantly, university student fraternities formally rejected duel challenges from Jews on the grounds that Jews lacked »a sense of honor and principle.« Dueling presupposed social equals; one did not stoop to duel with outcasts.[19]

In this way, Jews were betrayed by their former allies, the German Liberals and German nationalists, as soon as the Jewish alliance began to cost them politically. Their acknowledgment that in the present climate Jews were dispensable, an embarrassment, superfluous weight that needed to be thrown overboard, affected Herzl at least as much as the rise of antisemitic political parties with their violent anti-Jewish demagogy. Betrayal by former allies made him, and Jews like him, pariahs to their reference group, that is, to those who counted for them, those whose acceptance and respect they had sought and cherished. It was no wonder Herzl equated ostracism with self-contempt. Well after he had become a Zionist leader, he would insist: »Golus, Ghetto. Words in different languages for the same thing. Being despised, and finally despising yourself.«[20]

Ghettoized once again, Jews would remain what they were, in Herzl's words, a people »debased through oppression, emasculated, distracted by money, tamed in numerous corrals.« Emancipation and assimilation had been a failure; the modern state would not grant equality to former pariahs. But now Herzl saw an alternative: antisemitism, the cause of their distress, had opened a

---

[19] Ibid., for my view of the impact of the Dreyfus Case, see Chapter 8; for the rise of the Jewish bourgeoisie in the 1870s, 27–28; For the 1890s, Chapter 4; »a sense of honor,« 106.
[20] Herzl, Old-New Land (note 8), 252.

new road for Jews. Ostracized, dehumanized, fair game for physical assault, Jews had been thrown back upon themselves; now their transformation had to come from themselves, not from European assimilation. Jews had to rid themselves of their faults, and find honor and self-respect by themselves. This would become the aim of Zionism.[21]

Herzl then altered his view of assimilation: not only would it not »improve« the Jews, but it rendered them powerless in the face of antisemitism. This new view first appeared in Herzl's play of 1894, *The New Ghetto,* which is about the human toll of assimilation on Jews: their lack of settled self-esteem, their idealization of Gentiles, their need to measure their worth »in spoonfuls of gentile acceptance.« Jews as a minority had been shaped by the domineering gaze of the Gentile majority and internalized its Jewish stereotypes. Jews saw their Jewishness as carrying the taint of materialism and cowardice. Seeing Jewish traits as vices while idealizing Gentile traits, Jews could not drain the cup of self-contempt; all they did was by definition suspect, so that they were battered by self-doubt and self-recrimination. In this condition, they could not meet antisemitism with a strong and dignified response, and would only plunge further down into the depths of victimhood, powerlessness, and self-hatred.[22]

Having seen Jews in the mirror of European society for so long, Herzl now realized how much they were intimidated and shaped by its judgments. Herzl's Zionism was to be a frontal assault on Jewish self-contempt. This accounts for his maximalism, projecting a Jewish state as the immediate goal, and his deliberate lack of prudence and caution, the brash and uncompromising way he announced his intentions. Herzl drew from images of his German nationalist student days and from the epic achievement of German unification: they were models of manliness, boldness, the politics of the fait accompli. In his diary he idealized the Prussian manner, »the forthright grand old style, open and aboveboard!« which took others aback: »the world would then have to come to terms with it.« This was the style Jews were to adopt, for the Jewish cure had to be equal to the Jewish disease. As he put it: »Nor are we doing violence to anyone except to ourselves, our habits, our evil inclinations, and our faults.« Zionist ends and means had to be both exalted and exhilarating, a cure for Jewish anxious apprehension and self-deprecation.

Ahad Ha-am caught the measure of Herzl's Zionism as an antidote to the West European Jews' »consciousness of inferiority.« As he so shrewdly put it: »The higher and more distant the ideal, the greater its power of exaltation.«[23]

Thus Herzl aimed at a sovereign state with a still negligible *Yishuv,* before the existence of a national infrastructure, before modern nationalism had touched – let alone mobilized – large numbers of Jews, before the creation of a

---

[21] Herzl quoted in Kornberg, Theodor Herzl: From Assimilation to Zionism (note 7), 126; see also, 129.

[22] Ibid., 139. For my analysis of The New Ghetto, Chapter 6.

[23] Ibid., »the forthright,« 171; »Nor are we doing violence,« 169; Ahad Ha-am quoted, 172.

sustaining Hebrew national culture, before the land held a sizable Jewish population rooted in the soil. Critics pointed to the flaws in Herzl's agenda: a Jewish state simply handed to Jews by a colonial power, on a silver platter as it were, not arising organically out of a Jewish presence in the land, lacking a Hebrew national culture, would have been without political and moral legitimacy, a frail reed, as easily uprooted as granted.[24]

Herzl's diplomatic campaign in the capitals of Europe was part of his effort to transform Jewry. Many have noted that Herzl had no desire to pursue a range of nationalist strategies in tandem, but pressed for only one: gaining diplomatic recognition for a Jewish state. Though he was to make adept concessions to Zionists with other agendas in order to hold the movement together, he himself wished to exclude other nationalist strategies, such as creating a foothold in the homeland, fostering a national language and cultural revival, military preparations, demanding national rights wherever a portion of the nation resided.[25]

For Herzl these other strategies lacked boldness and the quality of »thinking big,« and, even worse, they would not draw the Great Powers into the Zionist enterprise. This was essential, for there was a pan-European interest in a Jewish state; Jewish statehood was to be a joint Jewish-Gentile enterprise. In one way, Herzl's strategy was shrewd and realistic: nationalist movements often seek the support and protection of a client-sponsor relationship with an existing state. What Herzl started, culminated in the Balfour Declaration, which came out of an extravagant British belief in Jewish power, a factor that Herzl played on in his own diplomacy. This strategic victory gave Zionists the opportunity to create an impressive base and infrastructure in mandatory Palestine. In another way though, David Vital has best captured the coexistence in Herzl of both »well-founded judgment and wild surmise,« For just as Herzl believed that Jewishness was a stigma that could only be overcome by Zionism, he also believed that a Jewish state would bind Jews and Gentiles together in a new relationship of mutual equality and esteem.[26]

Discussing Jewish emigration from Europe to the Jewish State, Herzl commented in his diary: »We shall depart as respected friends.« So intent was he on this that in *The Jewish State,* he conceived of an »amicable expropriation.« The Jewish Company, arranging for the sale and lease of Jewish assets in Europe, would have a European staff made up of Gentiles, including »respectable anti-Semites« to make sure that Jewish economic cunning not work to the Gentile disadvantage. An extravagant belief in the size of Jewish wealth led Herzl to imagine that not only would the transfer of Jewish wealth in Europe favor Gentiles, but would enhance general prosperity, and even temper social discontent. Herzl's idea of an »amicable expropriation« presupposed, as well,

---

[24] Ibid., 172.
[25] Shimoni, The Zionist Ideology (note 9), 97–99.
[26] Kornberg, Theodor Herzl: From Assimilation to Zionism (note 7), 170, 178–180; Vital, The Origins of Zionism (note 10), 233.

that European states would consider it in their interest to allow a mass immigration of Jews to a Jewish state, that Christian rulers would accept a Jewish state in the Holy Land, and that the Ottoman authorities would be willing to create a beachhead for another nationalist movement within their tottering empire.[27]

How do we account for Herzl's fantasy? Why his exclusive concern with Gentile political recognition? Herzl's deepest obsession was with Jewish self-respect and Jewish honor. Just as he saw Jewish self-contempt as due to the majority's contempt for a minority, so he saw Jewish honor and dignity as tied to Gentile esteem. Honor was a social category, a matter of self-respect, but also of the confirmation of that respect by others. There were two parts to the equation: Jews first had to cease being supplicants and make their declaration of independence from Gentiles; they would then gain Gentile esteem.[28]

Jewish commentators early on were struck by Herzl's obsession with Gentile esteem. Adolf Böhm saw in it »a touch of ghetto-like feelings.« Robert Stricker observed that »Herzlean Zionism was, in the first instance, an appeal not to the Jewish world, but to the Gentiles.« Ahad Ha-am made the most cutting commentary of all by comparing Herzl's aim to an old lady abandoned by her lover:

> There is an old lady who, despairing utterly of regaining her lover by entreaties, submission and humility, suddenly decks herself out in splendor and begins to treat him with hatred and contempt. Her object is still to influence him. She wants him to at least respect her in his heart of hearts, if he can no longer love her.

For Ahad Ha-am, Herzlean Zionists were not much different than assimilated Jews: the latter sought »love« from Gentiles, while Herzl sought »respect.«[29]

Ahad Ha-am may have hit the nail on the head. For Herzl, pressing for statehood as an urgent, immediate goal, was a way of curing Jews of self-contempt and minority timidity, and a way of gaining honor in the eyes of Gentiles. But Herzl's obsession with Jewish honor and self-respect made history. When he arrived on the scene, *Hibbat Zion* was at a low ebb. Cautiously muting its nationalist aims for fear of repercussions from the Tsarist and Ottoman authorities, the movement was unable to capture the Jewish imagination. Unable to amass resources, its colonies in Palestine were subject to Rothschild largesse and Rothschild control. As one *Hibbat Zion* adherent described the change wrought by Herzl: »The new, unprecedented manner, the candid proud language was a striking contrast to our hitherto inconspicuous conspiratorial method of operation.« Herzl's maximalist proclamations and sense of urgency »captured the imagination of Jews, raised Zionism's standing in the Jewish world, and implanted Zionism in the European political arena.«[30]

---

27 Patai (Ed.), The Complete Diaries of Theodor Herzl (note 8), I: 183; Herzl, The Jewish State (note 8), 68–69; On the impact of the transfer of Jewish wealth, Kornberg, Theodor Herzl: From Assimilation to Zionism (note 7), 180.
28 Kornberg, Theodor Herzl: From Assimilation to Zionism (note 7), 185.
29 The quotes are in: ibid., 184–187.
30 Z. Bychowski quoted in ibid., 173; Kornberg quoted, 173.

Benno Wagner

Leaders 1904. Masaryk – Herzl – Kafka

In the summer of 1904 Theodor Herzl died of a pre-existing heart condition after a severe quarrel over the geographical destination of Jewish mass emigration,[1] an emigration that, according to his plans, would finally lead to the foundation of a modern Jewish state. In the same summer of 1904, Franz Kafka, then a law student at Charles University in Prague, bought and obviously read very closely the new Czech edition of a book that the Czech national leader and later President of the Czechoslovakian Republic, Thomas Garrigue Masaryk, had first published in 1881, in German: *Der Selbstmord als sociale Massenerscheinung der modernen Civilisation.*[2] Here, Masaryk offered both a diagnosis and a therapy for what he called in the rhetoric of his day the »sickness of our century.«[3] The decay of morals and increase of semi-education in an ever more complex modern world could only be healed by a new religion, combining the most suitable elements of Protestantism and Catholicism. Until the invention of such a remedy, Masaryk warned, one would have to deal with the statistical symptoms of the disease: mass emigration and suicide. The latter was comprised of »those anomalous kinds of death brought about by an unintentional interference of the subject with his life process, whether by positive, active self-participation or a negative, passive attitude towards the dangers of life. In this sense, for example, the one who commits suicide is one who meets a premature death through an immoral or imprudent life [...].«[4] In this very summer of 1904, when the fate of one national leader in the Hapsburg »Völkerkerker« seemed to fulfill with disquieting precision the prognosis of another such leader, Franz Kafka began to realize *his* fate, a fate that would again lead to premature death: He started writing.

---

[1] For a resumé of the so-called »Uganda conflict« see: Adolf Böhm: Die zionistische Bewegung: Tel Aviv: Hozaah Ivrith 1935, vol. 1, 254ff.

[2] Suicide as a Social Mass Phenomenon of Modern Civilization. The American edition has been published under the title: Thomas G. Masaryk: Suicide and the Meaning of Civilization. Chicago and London: University of Chicago Press 1970. Following references are taken from this latter edition.

[3] Ibid., preface.

[4] Ibid., 7.

I

No other modern author has been haunted more intensely by factors signified by the key terms of my introductory remarks – the modern masses, their misery, and the question of leadership – than Franz Kafka, the professional »Schrift-Führer« of Bohemian social insurance. In his uncompleted first novel, the *Description of a Struggle* of 1904/05, two obviously morally disoriented males are taking a walk on a Prague winter night, discussing their meaningless lives characterized by fears of physical insecurity and Chaplinesque manouevres of assimilation.

While the ego narrator tries in vain to escape from the hopeless situation into some Nietzschean superman phantasies, his company finally admits that his life strategy, namely sexual adventurism and an eventual marriage, is also bound to fail: »Nothing is certain, no one can tell the direction or the duration for sure. If I go into a tavern with the intention of getting drunk, I know I'll be drunk that evening. But in this case!«[5] And when he considers the options of becoming a criminal or »going off to a distant land,« the narrator, obviously a reader of Masaryk, tells him smilingly: »I'm afraid no misdeed, no unfaithfulness or departure to some distant land will be of any avail. You'll have to kill yourself.«[6]

From the very beginning the need for and impossibility of leadership were lingering at the margins of Kafka's writing. In February 1917, when the new emerging global power was preparing to cut through the Gordian knot of social, cultural, and political »questions« which in 1904 had still been hopelessly entangled, Kafka envisaged leadership not only as an impossibility, but even as a danger and a threat inherent in modern culture: »Nowadays,« he wrote in his short story *The New Advocate*,

> there is no Alexander the Great. There are plenty of men who know how to murder people [...] but no one, no one at all, can blaze a trail to India. Even in his day the gates of India were beyond reach, yet the King's sword pointed the way to them. Today the gates have receded to remoter and loftier places; no one points the way, many carry swords, but only to brandish them, and the eye that tries to follow them is confused.[7]

These few lines of early 1917 display the intricate structure of the modern concept, or rather problem, of political leadership. In its actual, pragmatic sense, leadership has been made impossible by the complexity and normative polycentrism of modern society. If you still want to rely on leadership, you

---

[5]   Franz Kafka: Description of a Struggle. In: Franz Kafka: The Complete Short Stories. Ed. by Nahum M. Glatzer. London: Vintage 1999, 49.

[6]   Ibid., 49.

[7]   Franz Kafka: The New Advocate. In: Kafka, The Complete Short Stories (note 5), 415.

have to change your maps, so to speak. Or rather, and first of all, you have to survey the unmarked territory of a new set of collective orientations. To ignore the remoteness of this territory, to claim unquestioned leadership on the grounds of some arbitrarily selected norms or ideas, will only unleash pure violence and inevitably lead to murder. At the same time, leadership remains a problem to be tackled; it is obviously more than merely a romantic desire. Kafka makes this point very clear in December 1917, when the Hapsburg Empire is in fact already doomed: »They were given the choice of becoming kings or the kings' messengers,« his famous parable runs:

> As is the way with children, they all wanted to be messengers. That is why there are only messengers, they charge through the world and, since there are no kings, call out their now meaningless messages to one another. Gladly would they put an end to their miserable life, but they dare not do so because of their oath of allegiance.[8]

In the following »revolutionary winter« of 1918/19, Germany was flooded with messengers and murderers. This was the period between the establishment of the Weimar Republic and the assassination of Walter Rathenau; 376 political murders had been counted. Max Weber gave his famous lecture on *Politics as a Vocation* at this time. Here Weber expressed his contempt for the »sterile excitation« of the sword brandishing new class of political dilettantes, trying to occupy the vacant center of political power.[9] At the same time, he seemed to affirm Kafka's diagnosis of the leadership dilemma, when he described the only choice for modern political organization: either »leadership democracy« with a party machine blindly following a charismatic leader, or »leaderless democracy,« namely, the rule of professional politicians without a calling, without the inner charismatic qualities that make a leader. Usually, this means what the party insurgents in the situation usually designate as the rule of the clique.[10] And it was on the razor's edge between these two evils that Weber outlined his political ethos for the new generation of politically interested students who were his audience.

In this paper I attempt to analyze the concept of leadership in Herzl, Masaryk, and Kafka. However, my goal is not to arrive at a final ethical judgement, based on the easily available wisdom of the retrospective observer. Rather, I would like to explore the discursive potential of a notion deeply entangled in the catastrophe of the 20th century, as it existed in the last two decades *before* the great catastrophe, and at its very edge.

Nonetheless Weber and Kafka, icons of the sociology and mythology of leadership, mark the boundaries and the specific tension of my investigation – or rather, of my project description. What should be noted here is that the pe-

---

[8] Ibid.
[9] Max Weber: Politics as a Vocation. In: Essays in Sociology. Ed. by H. H. Gerth and C. Wright Mills. New York: Oxford University Press 1946, 115.
[10] Ibid., 113.

riod in question provides an interesting case for the study of political leadership. The phenomenon of the typical modern mass leader, he himself a man from the crowd, was only to become predominant in the decades after World War I. Whoever wanted to claim top level political leadership in Central Europe before the Great War had to compete with, or more precisely, to confront and to challenge the system of traditional leadership, that is, the monarchic principle. In the same period we witness in the field of philosophy what Arnold Gehlen has called the loss of a »grand key attitude,«[11] a cognitive gesture claiming to penetrate all aspects of life. But despite, or rather because of the ever increasing complexity of modern societies, this attitude of a comprehensive world view has survived in many individuals as an empty model. And it seems that between the philosophical death of the »grand key attitude« in the middle of the 19th century and the end of »the age of discussion« proclaimed by Carl Schmitt immediately after World War I,[12] it is the successful transfer of the former from philosophy to politics – that is exactly the gesture of »pointing the way to India« – that constitutes the strongest challenge to traditional leadership. Thus, political ideology was linked to philosophical knowledge in a way different from the period between the World Wars, different from the post war period, and different again from our present time.

To begin, I would like to identify four general elements of a typical case of modern political leadership: 1) a social or ethnic group that could be defined by a vital *problem* (a so-called »question,« as the German language expresses it: »Arbeiterfrage«, »Frauenfrage«, »tschechische Frage«, »Judenfrage«; 2) an individual with a *biography* that proves belonging to the group »in question«; 3) a significant *experience* or event (»Erlebnis«) that enables a new view of that problem and a vision of its solution; 4) the ability subsequently to develop an *interpretation* of that group, an interpretation in the double sense of understanding or knowing the group and of defining and guiding it. Today, electronic media have closely integrated these two aspects of political interpretation in one informational circuit: as public opinion research and propaganda. A century ago, the merging of men and media in politics had just begun while philosophy and literature were still considered as resources for the programmatic as well as the experimental aspect of politics. Under these two aspects – leadership as an (inevitable?) political risk and leadership as a media phenomenon – I shall now look at Masaryk, Herzl, and Kafka as different, though closely related discursive economies of leadership.

---

[11] Arnold Gehlen: Über kulturelle Kristallisation. In: Studien zur Soziologie und Anthropologie. Neuwied, Berlin: Luchterhand 1961, 315.

[12] Cf. Carl Schmitt: The Crisis of Parliamentary Democracy. Trans. by Ellen Kennedy. Cambridge: The MIT Press 1988, preface.

II

Masaryk offers a most instructive comparative case vis-à-vis Theodor Herzl. The biography of Tomas Garrigue Masaryk presents the classical example of a social upstart, a *homo novus*. He was born in 1850, in the aftermath of the 1848 revolution, as the son of a Slovakian coachman and a German household servant. When he was eleven his mother, a deeply religious and socially ambitious woman, sent him to German »Realschule« (junior high school) to become a teacher. A Catholic priest advised him to go to high school in Brno where he developed into a mediocre pupil and an eager scholar of Greek philosophy and world literature, from Shakespeare via Schiller and Goethe to Wells and Zola. He went to Vienna in 1872 to study classical philology and philosophy and he wrote his doctoral thesis on the *Essence of the Soul in Plato*, in 1876. Meanwhile, three times Emperor Franz Joseph had made and revoked his promise to grant the Czechs national rights equivalent to those of the Hungarians. Nevertheless, Masaryk's first gesture of leadership was aimed at society rather than at the nation.

By merging the discourses of social statistics, medicine, and religion in his study on suicide, he combined the absolutely modern stance of the sociologist with the pre-modern gesture of the doctor-priest. According to Masaryk, modern semi-education and its physiological symptom, nervousness, had their common cause in the rapidly spreading network of modern media and of accelerating traffic. In the suicide book, we find such creative applications of national statistics as the correlation between the national consumption of paper per head and the inclination to suicide.[13] Dr. Masaryk's remedy was a humanistic education that forms the basis for a modern religion, a *re-ligio* of information to a deeper knowledge. In a later essay he offered this prescription for journalism, the »modern form of brainwork [Geistesarbeit]«:

> We think in a telegraphic and stenographic mode, that is we are asking for compact, precise, and diverse information. The journalist must therefore be laconic as long as he can rely on the deep and comprehensive basic education of his reader. But most of all the journalist must himself have this education; otherwise he is just a ›journalier‹, he is literally a day laborer, even less, an hour man, a minute apparatus.[14]

When Masaryk split with the Young Czech party in 1893, it was exactly because, in his view, their political program was no more than an association of political slogans and nationalistic archaisms, an early chaotic form of the very »media-politics« our civilisation has driven to electronic and professional perfection.

Masaryk was looking for a different path. In 1893 he founded *Naše Doba* (*Our Times*), a review for »science, arts, and social life,« and in 1897 he was

---

[13] Cf. Masaryk, Suicide and the Meaning of Civilization (note 2), 68ff.

[14] Jean d'Armes: Masaryk. Proletariersohn – Professor – Präsident. Berlin: C. A. Schwetschke & Sohn 1924, 15.

appointed to the chair of ethics at the university in Prague. At the time the Hapsburg minister of education remarked that Masaryk might function as a »calming element« in face of increasing national tensions. It was only in 1899 that he began his transformation into a political leader, involuntarily, but also irrevocably. In the fall of that year a Jewish day laborer, Leopold Hilsner, was facing criminal charges for allegedly having killed Agnes Hruza, a young tailor apprentice in the southern Bohemian village of Polna. For a few months, the Czech and the German nationalist papers stood united in proclaiming a case of ritual murder and spreading antisemitic hysteria throughout the country. Though during the entire trial ritual murder was never mentioned as an explicit motive, evidence against Hilsner was collected along the lines of the medieval blood libel narrative. When Hilsner was found guilty and sentenced to death, Masaryk took a stand and publicly called for a revision of the judgement. »In my following analysis of the Polna trial«, he wrote,

> I will try to make up for the shame of our national journalism that by its slanderous and hate-mongering coverage of the Hilsner affair has created a Bohemian and Austrian Dreyfusiade for us. [...] so much lack of judgement and consideration, so much inhumanity on the verge of cruelty [...] such a phenomenon can only be explained by the nervous overexcitement and the abnormal situation of our Bohemian and Austrian life in general.[15]

In a word, nationalism was not the answer to the national question for Masaryk. The national question was rather to be translated into a social question, which in turn was not to be understood in a materialistic way, but as the cultural and ethical question of »giving the spirit predominance over matter, of illuminating the hearts and minds of the people.«[16] In 1900, while suffering severe attacks from almost every quarter of Czech society for »siding with the Jews« and thereby »siding with the Germans,« Masaryk founded his own political party, the Czech People's Party, also known as the Realist Party. The party's platform, the humanity program of 1902, was based on an apparently non-selective approach towards the national question. »Humanity,« it should be noted, was not simply an obsolete ideal associated with Goethe. For a small nation in a modern world on its way to a cosmopolitan society, the peaceful co-existence of different nations on the same territory was, according to Masaryk, to be seen as the only possible way of a thinking nation. »Humanity,« as a crucial passage of the program ran, »is our highest goal, but there is no humanity outside of the nations who form humanity, after all.«[17]

---

[15] Thomas G. Masaryk: Die Nothwendigkeit der Revision des Polnaer Processe. Offprint from the weekly paper *Die Zeit*, Vienna 1899, 1.

[16] Masaryk, Česká Otázka (The Czech Question), quoted in Roland J. Hoffmann: T. G. Masaryk und die tschechische Frage. Nationale Ideologie und politische Tätigkeit bis zum Scheitern des deutsch-tschechischen Ausgleichsversuchs vom Februar 1909. Munich: Oldenbourg 1988, vol. 1, 150f.

[17] Ibid., 49.

This formula is of crucial importance for our topic. It exposes precisely how the modern »*Jewish* question« was essentially a result of the way in which the modern *national* questions were being posed and answered. If Masaryk in his neo-archaic idiom of the doctor-politician was complaining about the »abnormal« situation of the Czech people in the Hapsburg monarchy he was in fact offering a set of disquieting choices to the Jews: they could either completely assimilate in their host nations and hence disappear as a distinct ethnic and cultural group; or they might claim to be considered as a nation, but then, compared to the »abnormal« nations in the »Völkerkerker,« they would be a *completely* »abnormal« one, without a territory, a national language, a state, a political leadership and so on. Or, if they, like a collective Bartleby, »preferred rather not to« either assimilate or nationalize, they would inevitably be excluded from humanity.

III

When Masaryk's book on suicide was first published in Vienna, Theodor Herzl, ten years his junior, was still a law student at the university. A member of the German students' fraternity Albia, which was gradually turning from nationalist to racist in those days, he had to witness the suicide of a Jewish fellow member unable to bear the mere threat of being expelled from the »Männerbund« sooner or later. Though Herzl was aware enough of the new order of racial nationalism to leave the corporation by his own decision, he too did not receive his calling for leadership so soon. And maybe it was more than pure coincidence that he first had to prove to be a good journalist in the strict sense of Masaryk's definition. His first feuilletons for the *Wiener Allgemeine Zeitung* and the *Neue Freie Presse* were soon widely recognized for their elegant style and their deep emotion. So it may be true for Herzl as for Masaryk that they did not turn into leaders overnight. But in any case, it was another antisemitic trial that triggered his emergence as a leader: the infamous Dreyfus affair, beginning in 1894, that was already being used as an historical analogy for the Hilsner affair.

I can only indicate here that in fact Herzl and Masaryk make a most instructive case for the comparative study of political leadership. While Masaryk was anxious to calm down the overheating nationalism in Bohemia, Herzl's secular feat quite to the contrary consisted in the discovery of a hidden energy among his people, a literal »Korach« that resulted from their very exclusion from the family of nations.[18] According to Herzl, the creation of a Jewish state is in the first place a matter not of mechanics, but of energetic engineering. In his foreword to *The Jewish State* he compares the situation of the oppressed Jews to a

---

[18] Cf. Josef Fraenkl: Theodor Herzl. A Biography. London: Ararat 1946, 37; and Böhm, Die zionistische Bewegung (note 1), 152f.

boiling tea kettle: »Now I believe that this power, if rightly employed, is powerful enough to propel a large engine and to dispatch passengers and goods, the engine having whatever form men may choose to give it.«[19]

While – at least until 1909 – Masaryk's ideal leader is a doctor or a priest,[20] Herzl's key figure is that of an engineer of »human energy.«[21] In his conversation with the Baron Hirsch, he called »a unified political organization« a precondition for the solution of the Jewish question.[22] Hence the completely different role of imagination and poetry in the two concepts of leadership. Masaryk conceives of poetry as a passive or receptive medium of »leaderly« interpretation: »Poetry enhances our imagination, and we need it in politics to see the future and the others' soul. Imagination enables the politician to understand the people and the nations.«[23] For Herzl, on the contrary, imagination, or »the idea,« is the formative agent of politics; »leaderly« interpretation is therefore an active, transformative communicative force. In his 1902 novel *Old-New Land* the protagonist David Littwak, while watching a theater play about the false messiah Shabbetai Zevi, explains the success of false leaders: »it was not that the people believed what these charlatans told them, but the other way round – they told them what they wanted to believe.«[24] Nevertheless, even true leaders cannot succeed without the poetic power of invention: »Only the phantastic is able to move the masses,« Herzl writes to Hirsch after their conversation – to move them not only in a figurative but also in a literal sense.[25]

Of course, all these differences between Herzl and Masaryk may be traced to one obvious fact. Herzl's state was a *creatio ex nihilo*. As opposed to the Czechs (and any other emerging nation), the Jews had no political organization, no territory, no common language. Herzl's diary may help to understand the extremely dynamic character of his political imagination: »Great things need no solid foundation. […] The earth floats in mid-air. Similarly, I may be able to found the Jewish State without any firm support. – The secret is movement.«[26] Obviously, Herzl regarded as a panacea what Masaryk had identified as the cause of the modern disease – the acceleration of bodies and information through vehicles and media. *The Jewish State*, and even more so his 1902 novel *Old-New Land*,

---

[19] Theodor Herzl: The Jewish State. New York: Scopus Publishing Company 1943, 14.
[20] Or even Christ who »redeemed mankind« exactly because he refrained from any kind of political agitation (cf. Masaryk, Suicide and the Meaning of Civilization [note 2], 222).
[21] A glance at Anson Rabinbach's significant study, The Human Motor. Energy, Fatigue, and the Origins of Modernity. Berkeley: University of California Press 1992, reveals to what extent Herzl had in fact relied on the discursive energies of the energetic discourse of his day as the territory of his political manoeuvres.
[22] Cf. Theodor Herzl: Tagebücher 1895–1904. Erster Band. Berlin: Jüdischer Verlag 1922, 23.
[23] Quote in d'Armes, Masaryk. Proletariersohn – Professor – Präsident (note 14), 49.
[24] Theodor Herzl: Old-New Land. Haifa: Haifa Publishing Company 1960, 83.
[25] Herzl, Tagebücher 1895–1904. Erster Band (note 22), 33.
[26] Ibid., 398f.

are transmodern speed trips. For the Jews, to close this list of differences, emigration was not a symptom of a civilisation's disease, but a way to a healthier life.

But despite all these differences, it is crucial to see that Herzl's imagined evolution of technology and social organization and Masaryk's imagined evolution of the human soul can be considered as two different ways of repressing one and the same vital problem, in fact the original sin of national discourse: the question of the inevitable selectivity of national ideas, and of the idea of the nation itself. The protagonist of Herzl's novel, David Littwak, is fighting fiercely for a non-restrictive immigration policy for the Old-New Land. In the novel, the quantitative aspect of population as well as the qualitative one, the existence of an autochthonous Arab population, is solved by the mere dynamics of technical and social development. Also, for all the details of description, the northern and southern boundaries of the country that is not a state remain unclear. In fact, as Friedrich Loewenberg, another main character, puts it: »This New Society could very well exist anywhere, in any country of the world.«[27] So whereas Masaryk's concept of humanity, his idea of an inward revolution of the human imagination and soul, is an attempt to gently dissolve the Gordian knot of ethno- and geopolitics (the improbability of a one-to-one correspondence of territory and ethnic group), Herzl tries to simply leave it behind by means of his proliferating technological and biopolitical phantasy. It has been said that Herzl's blunder about the importance of territory for leadership had actually contributed to his premature death in 1904. This is owing to his tentative suggestion at the Sixth Zionist Congress to consider Uganda as a provisional solution for the suffering Jews in Eastern Europe and the crisis it created. Still, Masaryk lived through World War I. The Great War reminded him of the fact that national leaders have to deal not only with peoples, but with territories. The opening remark in his famous inaugural lecture on *The Problem of Small Nations in the European Crisis*, delivered at King's College in October 1915, builds a bridge to the final section of my paper: »it would help us greatly if I could show you a good map of the European nations; but no such map exists. [...] you will find political maps, maps of railroads, etc., but no ethnographical ones.«[28]

IV

In the writings of Franz Kafka the correlation between leadership and poetry is inverted. Leadership is a function of poetry; it serves writing as a model of organization: »Great, tall commander-in-chief, leader of multitudes,« Kafka

---

[27] Herzl, Old-New Land (note 24), 215.
[28] Thomas G. Masaryk: The Problem of Small Nations in the European Crisis. Inaugural Lecture at the University of London, King's College. London: Council for the Study of International Relations 1917, 11.

addresses himself in his diary in the winter of 1922 in Spindelmühle, Giant
Mountains, immediately after having unleashed his dogs to write the most
breathtaking, disquieting, and precise novel of the 20th century, *The Castle*,
»lead the despairing through the mountain passes no one else can find beneath
the snow. And who is it that gives you your strength? He who gives you your
clear vision.«[29] Kafka, too, had received his calling as a leader in the famous
»Laurenziberg vision« of his student days,[30] where he figures himself a »leader
of writing,« a *Schrift-Führer*. For him, the *Schriftführer* (German for »secre-
tary«, »clerk«) not only in the Bohemian Workmen's Accident Insurance Institute, but also in a unique poetic project one might call »culture insurance,« the
function of the leader is merely a cognitive one. It consists of the discovery
and surveying of territories (and of the risks and chances inherent in them) that
are invisible to others, to supply maps that do not exist.

In the spring of 1917, when the timeless Hapsburg Monarchy is drawing nigh
to its end and the birth or rebirth of its nations appears as a shining promise to
many, Kafka puts the modern drama of leadership on stage in a seemingly fantastic but in fact stenographic and telegraphic China. In his narrative fragment
entitled *The Great Wall of China*, the highly cultivated Chinese, threatened by
uncivilized nomads from the North, rely on the great wall as a safeguard against
attacks. However, the reflections of the narrator, he himself a »subordinate supervisor«[31] of the building project, soon make it clear that the Great Wall is
fragmentary, in fact it consists of more gaps than wall. Thus, his reflections
wander to the question of leadership, namely the intentions or purposes that the
high command connected to the system of piecemeal construction. It should be
noted here that *The Great Wall of China*, as all of Kafka's narratives, must be
read as a stenographic protocol for a complex series of different problems: from
poetic production via the birth of culture out of the clash of Apollonian and Dionysian powers, Austrian accident insurance, and the threat of antisemitism to the
question of the political fate of Europe during and after the Great War. But it is
the problem of leadership that connects it closely to the writings of Masaryk and
Herzl, and of cultural Zionism, typical of Prague. The figure of the first-person
narrator inscribes Kafka's autobiography into Masaryk and Herzl. He is one of
those semi-educated professionals who precisely fit into Masaryk's cultural
criticism, insofar as he is only capable of fragmentary and erratic reflections. His
self-introduction, on the other hand, copies the opening scene of *Old-New Land*,
to the extent that the narrator himself is a complex stenograph of Kafka, the
accident insurer, and Kafka, the writer, and of Herzl's Friedrich Loewenberg:

---

[29] Franz Kafka: Diaries 1914–1923. Entry of February 10, 1922. Ed. by Max Brod.
New York: Schocken 1965, 220.
[30] Cf. Franz Kafka: Tagebücher. Bd 3: 1914–1923 (Gesammelte Werke in zwölf Bänden. Nach der Kritischen Ausgabe hg. Von Hans-Gerd Koch. Bd 11). Frankfurt am
Main 1994, 179.
[31] Franz Kafka: The Great Wall of China. In: Kafka, The Complete Short Stories (note
5), 237.

I was lucky [...] for many who before my time had achieved the highest degree of culture available to them could find nothing year after year to do with their knowledge, and drifted uselessly about [...] and sank by the thousands into hopelessness.[32]

His seemingly bizarre description of the relation between the Chinese people and its leaders is in fact a precise protocol – and a grandiose parody – of the leadership discourse of nation building. In an attempt to put an end to his ponderings on the system of piecemeal construction, the narrator confesses:

We [...] did not really know ourselves until we had carefully scrutinized the decrees of the high command, when we have discovered that without the high command neither our book learning nor our human understanding would have sufficed for the humble tasks which we performed in the great whole. In the office of the command – where it was and who sat there no one [...] knew – in that office one may be certain that all human thoughts and desires revolved in a circle, and all human aims and fulfillments in a countercircle. And through the window the reflected splendors of divine worlds fell on the hands of the leaders as they traced their plans.[33]

At first sight, this is the point of view of a »subordinate supervisor« for safety measures towards the irrational rule of government supervision (»Staatsaufsicht«) in all fields of bureaucracy in the Hapsburg Empire. And, according to its own neo-mythical self-description, this Empire served as Europe's bulwark against the barbarous Slavs. But here one spots a possibly fatal inheritance of the new nations emerging from the ruins of the Monarchy. They obviously cannot get rid of that blind spot of human knowledge that was so deeply inscribed in the absolutist model of divine legitimation. Thus, in his foreword to the *Czech Question*, Masaryk produces a stunningly »Chinese confession«:

I believe [...] that the history of the peoples is not accidental, but that it is the fulfilment of a determined plan of providence. Therefore, it is the task of historians and philosophers, it is the task of every people to understand this plan and to know its place in it. [...] But I also believe that even the most penetrating spirit would not be able to reveal these plans of providence.[34]

One may note, at the same time, how closely Kafka's Chinese subordinate supervisor describes the position that Herzl assigns to *his* readers. Herzl, too, imagines his state as a bulwark of culture, namely as »a portion of a rampart of Europe against Asia, an outpost of civilization as opposed to barbarism.«[35] His outline of the Jewish State also follows the principle of piecemeal construction – »short aphoristic chapters will therefore best answer the purpose«[36] – as not

---

[32] Ibid., 236f. In the course of Herzl's novel (which Kafka read at the time of his entry into the Workmen's Insurance), Loewenberg makes his Masaryko-Herzlian way from the potential suicide via the bad emigrant (to an isolated island) to a good immigrant: into Palestine.

[33] Ibid., 239f.

[34] Quote in Hoffmann, T.G. Masaryk und die tschechische Frage (note 16), 138.

[35] Herzl, The Jewish State (note 19), 45.

[36] Ibid., 30.

to tax the intellectual capacities of his readers. In a résumé article on the first Zionist Congress in Basel, he assigns the job of legitimizing the leaders of the Zionist movement against any suspicion of profit-making to the scrutiny of the philosophers and poets: »They must be able to read the inner meaning of our words and to vouch for our opinions.«[37] But just as in Kafka's China, for all the scrutiny and for all the worship to the organization of labor and planned development, the last purposes of the high command – the New Society of the Jewish State and Old-New Land – inevitably remain beyond the grasp of the masses. Still, Herzl legitimizes his high command, the Society of Jews, which represents »a mixture of human and superhuman.«[38] In the case of the Jewish State, this mixture emerges from the role of the Zionist movement for which Herzl finds a precedent in the ancient Roman legal institution of »negotiorum gestio«: »When the property of an oppressed person is in danger, any man may step forward to save it. This man is the *gestor*, the director of affairs not strictly his own. He has received no warrant – that is, no human warrant; higher obligations authorize him to act.«[39] Here is, at last, the only remaining »key attitude« of political leadership in the 20th century: the gesture of exceptionalism as the modern form of political theology.

But Kafka's literary stenographs are much more than simple descriptions or parodies. In fact, his a-territorial lands and trans-ethnic populations serve as a laboratory for a controlled series of experimental variations of the major cultural risks in his turbulent days. Masaryk's ideal of brotherhood through common labor on the project of human civilization, an ideal that Herzl's David Littwak will carry to civilization's outpost at Neudorf, Palestine – reverberates in Kafka's China as a dream:

> Every fellow countryman was a brother for whom one was building a wall of protection, and who would return lifelong thanks for it with all he had and did. [...] Shoulder to shoulder, a ring of brothers, a current of blood no longer confined within the narrow circulation of one body, but sweetly rolling and yet ever returning throughout the endless leagues of China.[40]

In 1920, Kafka adds a codicil to this building scenario, a short story entitled *The City Coat of Arms*. As a consequence of conflicting ideas on how to build the new Tower of Babel, another architectural project of Chinese unity, the people's powers were paralyzed so that eventually

> they troubled less about the tower than the construction of a city for the workmen. Every nationality wanted the finest quarter for itself, and this gave rise to disputes, which developed into bloody conflicts. These conflicts never came to an end [...] but by that time everybody was too deeply involved to leave the city. All the legends

---

[37] Herzl, The Basel Congress, Contemporary Review 1897; dt. 22.
[38] Herzl, The Jewish State (note 19), 90.
[39] Ibid.
[40] Kafka, The Great Wall of China (note 31), 238.

and songs that came to birth in that city are filled with longing for a prophesied day when the city would be destroyed by five successive blows from a gigantic fist.[41]

1914 – 1915 – 1916 – 1917 – 1918: the end of Old Europe, the beginning of the catastrophe of the nations.

But there are also more hopeful variations of the leadership scenario available. Kafka's Chinese supervisor tires of his metaphysical reflexions on the invisible high command who »absorbed in gigantic anxieties, know of us, know our petty pursuits, see us sitting in our humble huts.«[42] At that point, he suggests a surprising change of perspective. To understand the nature of the Empire, he suggests, one must not turn to the teachers of political law and history, whose few precepts are hidden under a fog of confusion created by the mere process of teaching them. Instead, »the common people should be asked to answer« »this question of the empire,« »since after all they are the empire's final support.«[43] Here, the process of interpretation we have been discussing so far is inverted: the masses are now the subject, and the leaders the object of understanding. It must be emphasized that what follows is *not* an anticipation of centralized and standardized public opinion research (of which Kafka was one of the first experts, since he was professionally in charge of the distribution of safety questionnaires for Bohemian factories).[44] In fact, in this sense, Kafka's China is the very contrary of Old-New Land: space and time still rule over politics, communication is organized via slow, contingent, and even hopeless human transmission – such as messengers or traveling inspectors. These are the direct opposite of the motorized and ubiqitous traveling offices in Old-New Land: »If once, only once in a man's lifetime, an imperial official on his tour of the provinces should arrive by chance at our village, make certain announcements in the name of the governments [...] – then a smile flits over every face.«[45] And why? Because though every village is loyal to the Emperor – invisible, in far away Peking and over the clouds – this loyalty refers to a different Emperor in each of them: »Long-dead emperors are set on the throne in our villages, and one that only lives on in song recently had a proclamation of his read out by the priest before the altar.«[46] But it is exactly that double weakness of the empire: the government's failure to develop the institution of the empire with sufficient precision, and the »feebleness of faith and imaginative power on the side of the people« that the Chinese supervisor considers as »one of the greatest unifying influences among our people; indeed [...] the very ground on which we live.«[47]

---

41 Franz Kafka: The City Coat of Arms. In: Kafka, The Complete Short Stories (note 5), 433f.

42 Ibid., 241.

43 Kafka, The Great Wall of China (note 31), 242.

44 Cf. Franz Kafka: Amtliche Schriften. Ed. by Klaus Hermsdorf and Benno Wagner. Frankfurt: S. Fischer 2004, 123ff. and 819ff.

45 Kafka, The Great Wall of China (note 31), 245; Cf. Herzl, Old-New Land (note 24), 163.

46 Kafka, The Great Wall of China (note 31), 245.

47 Ibid., 247.

V

Today, of course, we know too much to return to such a non-selective and heterogeneous federalism of imperial imaginations. But maybe there is, finally, a helpful hint in one of Kafka's funniest stories about the fatality of leadership. It was Masaryk who assigned to his people the habitus of a malingering accident-insured workman towards the insurance doctor: »So strong is the inclination of the Czechs toward inertia,« he once wrote, »that we believe in false martyrdom; everbody is walking about showing their little wounds and expecting admiration.«[48] Herzl conceived of the Jewish diaspora as a wound in the body of his people, and he saw himself as the one who had the proper prescription to heal it. Kafka's famous country doctor is called to the bed of an ill patient in a remote village one stormy winter night. But alas, he has no horse. His perplexity is overcome by a truly Herzlian experience. From the uninhabited pig-sty of his house suddenly emerges, with unheard of energy, the steam of two enormous horses. »Energy, doctor. Energy is everything,« shouts not the country doctor's groom, but old Kingscourt in *Old-New Land*.[49] The trip to the patient is a pastiche of the comfortable travel conditions in Old-New Land's workmen's trains. Having arrived in no time at the peasant hut, the doctor lives through Masaryk's experience during the Hilsner affair. First, he sees no sign of injury on his patient's body. But then, after an archaic ritual with some maddening allusions to the protocols of the Hilsner trial, he finally agrees to see a gaping wound fitting exactly the alleged ritual wound of Hilsner's alleged victim.[50] And in the very moment he entrusts his medical art to this popular imagination, he finds out that this case is beyond repair. But after the boy has deceased, all the marvellous energy of his horses is gone. »Slowly, like old men, we crawled through the snowy wastes. [...] Never shall I reach home at this rate; my flourishing practice is done for; [...] in my house the disgusting groom is raging; Rosa [the doctor's housemaid; B. W.] is his victim.«[51] When Kafka wrote this little protocol of misguided, or »misled« leadership, Masaryk had left his country for the national cause, leaving his house, daughter, and mentally suffering wife to the henchmen of the Hapsburg police. But beside these allusions to a dark spot in an otherwise brilliant biography, we can extract from the story three prescriptions for taking home.

The first and most famous is the line (from *A Country Doctor*): »A false alarm on the night bell once answered – it cannot be made good, not ever.«[52] –

---

[48] Quote in d'Armes, Masaryk. Proletariersohn – Professor – Präsident (note 14), 14.
[49] Herzl, Old-New Land (note 24), 23.
[50] For a detailed analysis see Benno Wagner: »Das ist ein schlechter Wundarzt«. Die Hilsner-Affäre und die Politik des Tabus bei Thomas G. Masaryk und Franz Kafka. In: Juliette Guilbaud/Nicolas Le Moigne/Thomas Lüttenberg (eds.): Normes culturelles et construction de la déviance. Geneva 2005, 173–192.
[51] Franz Kafka: A Country Doctor. In: Kafka, The Complete Short Stories (note 5), 225.
[52] Ibid.

It serves to remind political leaders, and all of us, of the dangers of alarmist discourse.

The second: »To write prescriptions is easy, but to come to an understanding with the people is hard.«[53] This quotation is another reminder of the close connection of leadership to techniques and skills of communication, and it has been of undisputable importance for nation building – or nation fixing – up to this day.

But, in this context, perhaps it is the housemaid's wisdom which will be most suitable. She exclaims, at the expected sight of the powerful horses: »You never know what you're going to find in your own house.«[54] This statement offers, at last, a chance to reconcile the discourses of Herzl, Masaryk, and Kafka. Today, as politics is clearly and dramatically running out of solutions in view of nation building, we might, at the risk of losing valuable time to follow false alarms, have a look around in our cultural households. Maybe, instead of hidden or forgotten energies, we may discover a source of hidden or forgotten fantasies: literature as a resource for a new »Chinese« federalism of world views.

---

[53] Ibid., 223.
[54] Ibid., 220.

Michael Berkowitz

Re-Imagining Herzl and other Zionist Sex Symbols

In no small measure, Zionism attained viability as a political movement due to distinct qualities of its founder, Theodor Herzl. Despite Herzl's dearth of typical prerequisites for legitimacy with respect to Jewish and non-Jewish constituencies of the *fin-de-siècle*, as well as westernized Jewry's general distaste for overtly separatist Jewish agendas, his leadership proved to be compelling to a significant portion of Jewry. There are, of course, numerous reasons why Herzl was the man of the moment, why he succeeded where others – particularly his forerunners in *Hibbat Zion*, such as Leo Pinsker – had failed.[1] It was crucial that Herzl, as well as a smattering in his cohort, looked the part. It furthermore is highly significant that Herzl and political Zionism assiduously undertook to utilize and spread his image as perhaps the most essential element of the fledgling movement. Even the most perspicacious of Jewish scholars have underestimated the infiltration of Herzl's countenance in Jewish national consciousness. Yosef Hayim Yerushalmi's handsome volume on illustrated *Haggadot*, for instance, neglects to mention that the officer pictured as leading the seder in a 1956 *Haggadah* of the Israeli Defense Forces is obviously the incarnation of Herzl.[2] In a less sonorous vein, Israeli cartoonist Shmulik Katz portrayed a tour group visiting »The Herzl Museum near Herzl's Tomb on Mt. Herzl« in the early 1970s, where the tourguide and tourists – including an Israeli soldier, and local and foreign visitors – all look exactly like Theodor Herzl.[3] Even in Herzl's own time his unmistakable form was featured in pro- and anti-Zionist broadsides in the Jewish press, and lampooned in the first Zionist humor magazine, *Schlemiel*.[4]

For the purpose of clarification and orientation, I wish to emphasize that I mainly am concerned with Zionism in the West – that is, how the movement functioned in Jewish life and consciousness outside of Eastern Europe and Palestine before the rise of Hitler. Hence, this chapter pertains more to the

---

1 The most authoritative account and interpretation of Herzl's life is Steven Beller: Herzl. London: Peter Halban 2004.

2 Illustration by Jacob Zimberknopf, Plate 188. In: Yosef Hayim Yerushalmi (Ed.): Haggadah and History. Philadelphia: Jewish Publication Society 1975.

3 Shemuel Katz: Jerusalem: Holy Business as Usual. Ramat Hasharon: Yanat 1978 (no pagination).

4 Cesar Augosto Merchan Hamann: Life and Works of Sammy Gronemann (Diss.). University of London 2002, 36–9.

Diaspora – as opposed to the *Yishuv*, the Jewish settlement in Palestine, and later, the State of Israel. Second, on a personal as well as historiographic note, I wish to acknowledge my inestimable indebtedness to my late teacher, George L. Mosse (1918–1999). Especially in the final decade of his extraordinary life, Mosse stressed the importance of things visual in the modern age. He was fond of asserting that by the nineteenth century, »people don't read – they see.« Of course, this was a self-conscious, provocative exaggeration. He knew full well that people read, see, and form impressions from an infinite variety of sources, conditioned by all sorts of predispositions. Mosse believed, however, that historians had long been reluctant to use visual material, in comparison to their preference for evidence such as official records, pronouncements, and memoirs of supposedly great men. He furthermore made a concerted effort to incorporate popular culture, which to a great degree overlapped with the visual domain, into cultural history. All of this, as opposed to traditional »intellectual history« and the »history of ideas« was dedicated to uncovering and analyzing patterns of perception that cut across various social, political, economic, and religious distinctions.[5]

These concerns of George Mosse inspire the following attempt to investigate and interpret what Jews »saw« in the late nineteenth and early twentieth centuries. I am interested in images that played a role in the formation of Jewish ethnic and political consciousness, how these images came into being, and how they functioned – particularly in the Western lands where Jews were assumed to be engulfed by the stream of assimilationism.[6]

As a final point of departure, I will repeat the canard enshrined as popular wisdom – that Jews generally have an aversion to the »graven image« that goes beyond the prohibition on portraying human forms for religious purposes.[7] This convention has been eroded, for centuries, in Jewish culture. In the last few years scholars including Marc Epstein, Steven Fine, Richard Cohen, Mark Gelber, David Shneer, and Yael Zerubavel have showed a fine sensitivity to the visual and material in Jewish life.[8] Nevertheless, most sophis-

---

[5] See Stanley G. Payne/David J. Sorkin/John S. Tortorice (Eds.): What History Tells: George L. Mosse and the Culture of Modern Europe. Madison: University of Wisconsin Press 2004; George L. Mosse: Nazism: A Historical and Comparative Analysis of National Socialism (An interview with Michael A. Ledeen). New Brunswick: Transaction 1978.

[6] Paula E. Hyman: Was There a ›Jewish Politics‹ in Western and Central Europe? In: The Quest for Utopia: Jewish Political Ideas and Institutions Through the Ages. Ed. by Zvi Gitelman. London, Armonk/New York: M. E. Sharpe 1992, 105–118.

[7] See Kalman P. Bland: The Artless Jew: Medieval and Modern Affirmations and Denials of the Visual. Princeton: Princeton University Press 2000; for a more traditional view see Lionel Kochan: Beyond the Graven Image: A Jewish View. Houndmills, Basingstoke, Hampshire: Macmillan 1997.

[8] Steven Fine: Art and Judaism in the Greco-Roman World: Toward a New Jewish Archaeology. New York: Cambridge University Press 2005; Marc Michael Epstein: Dreams of Subversion in Medieval Jewish Art and Literature. University

ticated discussions involving Jews and images serve the understanding of antisemitism, such as the splendid studies of Sander Gilman on the milieu of Franz Kafka and Marc Weiner's exploration of visual symbols associated with Richard Wagner.[9] By no means do I mean to discount these important efforts. But the motive here is different. I aspire to look over the shoulder of previous generations of Jews, to see how they imagined themselves and their leaders. It seems that the standard evocations of *shtetl* and ghetto life, and antisemitic renderings of Jews of all walks of life did not have great resonance among the Jews themselves.[10] I have come to the conclusion that numerous politicized groups of Jews from the late nineteenth century onward deployed symbols and images, and attempted to muster their forces with pictures of their heroes. Zionism, however, was the Jewish movement *par excellence* that sought to influence its constituents with portrayals of its leadership and its movement in action. In his voluminous diaries, Zionism's founder, Theodor Herzl, made clear his intention to mobilize the Jews in the same manner that other nations came to be galvanized – with banners, ribbons, and flags – and by positively exploiting his people's collective fantasies.[11] The movement took this up in earnest, as one of its most striking acts was to present on the Jewish and world stage a new Jewish type – a new Jewish man and even new Jewish woman. The movement's media featured the »New Jews« who were nurturing, and themselves being nurtured, by the revived Promised Land.[12] Relatedly, Zionism's concern with documenting and illustrating the productiveness of the Jews in Palestine was similar to other groups' efforts to show that Jewry under their auspices were eminently productive, as opposed to having a parasitic

---

Park/Pennsylvania: Penn State University Press 1997; Mark H. Gelber: Melancholy Pride: Nation, Race, and Gender in the German Literature of Cultural Zionism. Tübingen: Max Niemeyer 2000; David Shneer: Yiddish and the Creation of Soviet Jewish Culture, 1918–1930. New York, Cambridge: Cambridge University Press 2004; Richard I. Cohen: Jewish Icons: Art and Society in Modern Europe. Berkeley, Los Angeles, London: University of California Press 1998; Yael Zerubavel: Recovered Roots: Collective Memory and the Making of Israeli National Tradition. Chicago: University of Chicago Press 1995.

[9] Sander L. Gilman: Franz Kafka, the Jewish Patient. New York, London: Routledge 1995; Marc A. Weiner: Richard Wagner and the Anti-Semitic Imagination. Lincoln and London: University of Nebraska Press 1995.

[10] See Michael Berkowitz: Viewing the Jewish Masses: Easing (?) and Interpreting Entry to the New World. In: Zutot 2001: Perspectives on Jewish Culture 1. Ed. by Shlomo Berger, Michael Brocke and Irene Zwiep. Amsterdam: Kluwer 2002, 151–6.

[11] Carl Schorske: Fin-de-Siècle Vienna: Politics and Culture. New York: Vintage 1981, 146–174; Robert Wistrich: The Jews of Vienna in the Age of Franz Josef. Oxford: Littman 1990, 421–493; Amos Elon: Herzl. New York: Holt, Rinehart and Winston 1975; Ernst Pawel: The Labyrinth of Exile: A Life of Theodor Herzl. New York: Farrar, Straus and Giroux 1989.

[12] New Year's greeting postcard from the Jewish National Fund, A2 6/7/1/1, Central Zionist Archives, Jerusalem (hereafter cited as CZA).

relationship with the general economic order. This discourse originated in the debates about Jewish emancipation in the eighteenth century. It is not surprising, then, that the United Hebrew Trades in the United States, the various territorialist movements, and the Alliance Israelite Universelle in France, enshrined productivization as a main hallmark.

An important caveat, however, must be addressed, especially with regard to the study of Daniel Boyarin, *Unheroic Conduct: The Rise of Heterosexuality and the Invention of the Jewish Man*, as it pertains to Zionist images and ideology.[13] I want to stress that Zionism was not visually monolithic. There were a number of visual discourses and strategies that operated in early Zionism, many of which were apparently contradictory. To a certain extent »gentile« ideas and looks were espoused, while it was nevertheless possible for one to be recognizably »Jewish« and beautiful. Furthermore, one of the consistent, prominent motifs was idealized and reverential representations of traditional Jews by artists such as Hermann Struck and Joseph Budko.[14]

Herzl himself had recognized the growing power of his own legend, as well as the charismatic attraction of his chief lieutenant in Zionism, Max Nordau, and his successor as President of the Zionist Organization, David Wolfssohn.[15] To the extent that Herzl and his cohort partially succeeded at »conquering« the Jewish communities,[16] this was achieved in no small measure by lionizing his movement's leaders, the most significant of whom was Herzl himself. Their message also was conveyed through the evolving spectacle of Zionism's chief institution, its Congress, in which its leaders were embedded.[17] The Congress was an unprecedented pseudo-parliamentary body in the Jewish world; the attempt to secure a Jewish homeland in Palestine was, of course, the focus of the movement's politics.

To be sure, Zionism was a minority movement within a minority, and an embattled one at that. Compared with other alternatives for immigration, Palestine was not the people's choice, despite the fact that it obviously became an important locus of Jewish settlement, particularly in the years between the wars, and during and after the Holocaust. What most concerns us here, how-

---

[13] Daniel Boyarin: Unheroic Conduct: The Rise of Heterosexuality and the Invention of the Jewish Man. Berkeley: University of California Press 1997, 278–312.

[14] See Michael Berkowitz: Between Orthodoxy and Modernism: Hermann Struck's Influence on the Countenance and Soul of Zionism. In: A Land Flowing With Milk and Honey: Visions of Israel from Biblical to Modern Times. Ed. by Leonard J. Greenspoon and Ronald A. Simkins. Omaha: Creighton University Press 2001, 261–284.

[15] Marvin Lowenthal (Ed.): Theodor Herzl, entry for 15 July 1896; entry for 3 September 1897. In: The Diaries of Theodor Herzl. Gloucester/Massachusetts: Peter Smith 1978, 182–3, 224–5.

[16] Theodor Herzl: Opening Address at the Second Zionist Congress (Delivered in Basel on August 28, 1898). In: Theodor Herzl: Zionist Writings: Essays and Addresses. Trans. by Harry Zohn. New York: Herzl Press 1975, vol. 2, 16–7.

[17] Postcard, 3. Zionisten-Congress in Basel, 1899, Emil Buri photographer, CZA.

ever, is how Zionism became a factor of Jewish identity outside of Eastern Europe and Palestine. In dwelling on these Zionist-disseminated images I do not wish to suggest that a majority of western Jews called themselves Zionists. It seems, however, that Zionism had a disproportionately large impact on the self-image of modern Jews, affecting even those who were only mildly interested in, or indifferent to its aims. One did not have to be a Zionist to have been regularly exposed to Zionist media, and throughout the west Zionist politics came to be more and more intermingled with formerly anti-Zionist bodies ranging from trade unions to rabbinical seminaries.[18] Hence, Zionism's share in comprising the self-image of western Jews loomed larger than its limited, if not paltry, membership rolls.

Simply put, Theodor Herzl is the most significant Jewish icon of modern times.[19] It is little wonder that Herzl's countenance, more than any other, came to epitomize Jewish political aspirations during the *fin-de-siècle*. Even for non-Zionists, it was possible to exalt him, as did Sigmund Freud, as a champion of »the human rights« of the Jews.[20] The exhilaration generated by Herzl's physical presence during his brief tenure at the head of Zionism, and reproductions of his photographed, drawn, painted, and sculpted torso – which were ubiquitous beginning in 1897 – provided a figure above all others in the Jews' national self-imagination. Herzl embodied simultaneously a cultured Viennese, a dignified European statesman, and the ideal new man that Zionism aspired to create. That he also was seen as a messianic incarnation is beginning to be explored by historians;[21] in Herzl's own time, this was part of the case waged against him by the Orthodox establishment.

During the six Zionist Congresses over which he presided, and the mass meetings he addressed in London, Vienna, Basel, Vilna, and elsewhere, thousands of Zionists gazed upon Herzl's face. Others came to know him not only through his speeches and writings, and reportage of his Zionist activity, but by scores of pictures that circulated throughout the Jewish world. Although it is too simple to say that Herzl's image was the preeminent bond of Jewish solidarity, the power of his countenance, in the service of Zionist nationalization, was remarkable. Herzl's picture helped Jews imagine themselves as members of a vaguely defined, yet emerging Jewish nation – no matter where they lived. Gershom Scholem, who would later discover and analyze the ways that Shab-

---

[18] See Michael Brown: The Israeli-American Connection: Its Roots in the Yishuv, 1914–1945. Detroit: Wayne State University Press 1997, 212–3, 186–8, 92–3.

[19] For a survey of Herzl images from a more high-brow perspective see Cohen, Jewish Icons (note 8), 241–244.

[20] Quoted in Pawel, The Labyrinth of Exile (note 11), 456; Pawel, in this translation, mistook the name »Neuda« for Nordau.

[21] Robert S. Wistrich: Theodor Herzl: The Making of a Political Messiah. In: The Shaping of Israeli Identity: Myth, Memory, and Trauma. Ed. by Robert Wistrich and David Ohana. London, Portland/Oregon: Frank Cass 1995, 1–37.

betai Zevi's image inculcated and spread the myth of his false messiahship,[22] felt his attraction to Zionism intensified when presented with a portrait of Herzl as a Christmas present.[23]

The most popular image of Herzl was the etching by Hermann Struck of the early 1900s.[24] This picture was copied, sometimes accurately, sometimes grossly, in scores of settings. It appeared in several editions of the *Jüdischer Almanach*,[25] served as the model for scores of portraits woven into rugs and wall hangings, was used to adorn the official Congress postcards of 1909 in Hamburg, and that of 1913, which was held in Herzl's city, Vienna.[26] Numerous photographs of Zionist groups conspicuously include a reproduction of the Struck etching.[27] There is no evidence that Herzl, Struck, or the Zionist Organization tried to control the promulgation and hawking of likenesses of the work. In addition to postcards and pictures per se, David Tartakover has shown how Herzl's image, often a crude version of the Struck etching, decorated hundreds of consumer goods, such as teapots, drinking glasses, pocket watches, cigarette packages, and tobacco pouches.[28] The sentimental attachment to the Struck Herzl-etching might also have been enhanced due to the respect accorded the artist Hermann Struck, a German-Jew who was a founder of the Orthodox arm of the Zionist movement, Mizrachi. Struck was known, as well, for sympathetically depicting East European Jews, the *Ostjuden*.[29] The affection for Struck, the man, seems to have abetted appreciation for Struck, the artist.[30]

---

[22] Gershom Scholem: Sabbatai Sevi: The Mystical Messiah, 1626–1676. Trans. by R. J. Zwi Werblowsky. Princeton: Princeton University Press 1975.

[23] David Biale: Gershom Scholem: Kabbalah and Counter-History. London, Cambridge/Massachusetts: Harvard University Press 1979, 53.

[24] Theodor Herzl »personality« file, CZA; frontispiece, Jacob de Haas: Theodor Herzl: A Biographical Study. Chicago, New York: Leonard 1927, vol. 2.; there is no mention in the text of the portrait.

[25] Hermann Struck: Reproduction of Etching of Theodor Herzl. In: Juedsicher Almanach. Ed. by Berthold Feiwel. Berlin: Juedischer Verlag 1904, vol. 2, 107.

[26] Postcard, XI. Zionisten Kongress in Wien, 2–9 September 1913, XI. Zionist Congress file, CZA.

[27] Teachers of the Jerusalem Hebrew Gymnasium, 2286, photo collection, CZA.

[28] David Tartokover (Ed.): Herzl in Profile: Herzl's Image in the Applied Arts. Tel Aviv: Tel Aviv Museum 1978–79, 28, 30, 19, 27.

[29] See Arnold Zweig: Das Ostjuedische Antlitz. Wiesbaden: Fourier 1988; originally published in 1920, with 25 pictures by Hermann Struck; the most recent edition is Arnold Zweig: The Face of East European Jewry. Ed. and trans. by Noah Isenberg. Berkeley: University of California Press 2004, with 52 Drawings by Hermann Struck. See also David Brenner: Marketing Identities: The Invention of Jewish Ethnicity in ›Ost und West‹. Detroit: Wayne State University Press 1998; Noah Isenberg: Between Redemption and Doom: The Strains of German-Jewish Modernism. Lincoln: University of Nebraska Press 1999.

[30] Arnold Fortlage/Karl Schwarz: Das Graphische Werk von Hermann Struck. Berlin: Paul Cassirer (no date), 1–3; Heinrich Hirschberg: Der Humor bei Struck. Berlin:

The next most popular, and likewise frequently appropriated picture of Herzl was a view of him, photographed by E. M. Lilien, overlooking the Rhine Bridge in Basel during the First Zionist Congress. Similar to Struck, Lilien was well-known in Zionist circles, and considered to be a great »national« artist. Mark Gelber has recently illuminated Lilien in his superb study of German cultural Zionism.[31] Lilien primarily was identified, however, with a pen-and-ink drawing, an agricultural scene showing the regenerating Zion, which was used for the Fifth Zionist Congress postcard and Zionist fundraising appeals.[32] Lilien's earlier photographic effort identified Herzl with Basel, the European locale most associated with the movement and its Congress. For the next century, this picture would serve as a synecdoche for Zionism, encompassing the vast ideological and historical sweep of the movement. Herzl's glance in the picture suggested that although he was above the Rhine, he was contemplating the Jewish future in a faraway place. Herzl himself was pleased with this picture. It easily melded with the epigraph of his utopian novel, *Altneuland* (Old-new Land), »If you will it, it is not a dream.« The famous Rhine-bridge image, however, might be used to illustrate what may be termed the instability of supposedly realistic images, in that after Herzl's death, this picture was imposed on a view of Jerusalem and other settings, which were used for Jewish National Fund stamps and other publicity.

There are many re-settings of a side-view photograph of Herzl, with arms folded; after 1904 the portrait or postcard version sometimes had a black border, to denote mourning.[33] Although this particular pose is distinctive, other frontal portraits of Herzl are reminiscent of photographs of Jewish sages, and even Jewish family-member portraits, often featuring the departed's thick beard.[34] Despite the fact that Herzl's beard was neatly trimmed, there was something believed to be Jewish and even messianic about it. Two of Herzl's closest associates in the movement, Max Nordau and David Wolffsohn, also boasted full complements of facial hair. Somehow the majestic and the rabbinical could be construed in the bushy beards; of Wolffsohn it was said that he looked the part of a leader: calm and manly.[35]

Verlag des Herausgebers 1919; Adolph Donath: Hermann Struck. Berlin: Juedische Buecherei 1920.

[31] Israel Zangwill: introduction to a portfolio of heliogravures by Ephraim Moses Lilien: The Holy Land. Berlin and Vienna: Benjamin Harz 1922, no pagination.

[32] KKL printed materials file, CZA; see Berkowitz: Zionist Culture and West European Jewry before the First World War. Cambridge: Cambridge University Press 1993, 127–9.

[33] Herzl »personality« file, CZA; one of these spelled his name, uncharacteristically, as »Theodore Hertzl«.

[34] See Cohen, Jewish Icons (note 8), 266, n. 25; Elliot Horowitz: Visages du judaism. De la barbe en monde juif et de l'elaboration de ses significanctions. In: Annales Histoire, Science Sociales 49 (1994), 1080–86.

[35] Jewish Chronicle, 12 September 1913, 18, 26; Jewish Chronicle, 18 August 1911, 22.

So as not to mistake the traditionally Jewish aspect of these images, sometimes picture-postcards of the bearded ones were accompanied by quotations. One of David Wolffsohn quotes a Congress address of his intoning, in Hebrew: »One God, one people, one land, one language«.[36] In truth, Wolffsohn began the speech in Hebrew, but he delivered most of it in the Congress vernacular, German. Likewise, a popular postcard and portrait image of Nordau was embellished with the following statement, attributed to Nordau: »We carry our Judaism like a jewel.«[37] Interestingly, the quotation is in Yiddish, and it is not certain if Nordau actually knew more than a smattering of Yiddish. Furthermore, Nordau was famous for having broken with traditional Judaism and scorning all forms of organized religion as part and parcel of civilization's »conventional lies.« Herzl, especially after his death, was pictured amidst traditional, distressed-looking Jews, most of whom seem unaware that he is with them.[38] Picturing Herzl in the bosom of more traditional Jews was not necessarily wishful thinking or cynical manipulation. A popular wall-hanging of immigrant Jews in Britain and Ireland between the wars featured a micrograph of Theodor Herzl, with his portrait composed of a Yiddish translation of *Der Judenstaat.*[39]

Herzl and Nordau also were pictured with other Jewish and world leaders, which speaks volumes about the aspirations, if not pretensions of the movement. A privately produced greeting card, apparently made for members of an early Zionist society, situated Herzl and Nordau – as well as Moses Gaster, Bernard Lazare, and Max Mandelstamm – alongside Christopher Columbus and George Washington.[40] Herzl was, indeed, accustomed to being introduced as the new Moses or Columbus, which he dismissed as exaggerations, yet he made no effort to dispel such rhetoric.[41] In a less ostentatious manner, this trend was continued, as Chaim Weizmann was similarly depicted on the same page with United States President Warren Harding, British Prime Ministers David Lloyd George and Ramsay MacDonald, Lord Balfour, and General Allenby during the Mandatory years.[42] The Zionists therefore legitimated themselves through their association with non-Jewish world leaders and luminaries – and Arab leaders. Later on, the appropriation of Eleanor Roosevelt correctly reflected the perception that she was passionately devoted to US and world Jewry.[43] There is little doubt, however, that the Zionists were infinitely

---

[36] Postcard, Wolffsohn »personality« file, CZA.
[37] Postcard, Nordau »personality« file, CZA.
[38] Postcard, Herzl »personality« file, CZA.
[39] Personal collection of the author; also on exhibit at the Jewish Museum, Dublin.
[40] Greeting card, Herzl »personality« file, CZA.
[41] Marvin Lowenthal (Ed.): diary entry for 13 July 1896. In: The Diaries of Theodor Herzl (note 15), 180.
[42] Palaestina-Bilder-Korrespondenz (May 1929), 3; Palaestina-Bilder-Korrespondenz (October 1928), 30.
[43] Franklin Roosevelt (pictured) in Kinder-Tsurnl (April 1943), 15.

more titillated when Marilyn Monroe went on the stump for the movement in the next decade.

But sex appeal did not always function in the most obvious manner. Jewish icons also were seen as embodying sex appeal; the most notable case are the numerous testimonies, by men, to Herzl's manly beauty. But in the decade of the 1920s, Zionism's unrivalled sex symbol became Albert Einstein – whose role in Zionism is often understated. His was the figure treasured, above all, as Diaspora Zionism's greatest claim to fame, and played an immeasurable role in the Jewish self-imagination.[44] Zionists the world over heartily agreed that Professor Einstein was their most spectacular attraction. Strangely, he has not been given his due in most Zionist historiography. Einstein's importance in boosting Jewish pride and confidence in the general direction of Zionism, and Jewish self-assertion in general, defies comparison. Few Zionists would have disputed that Einstein was

> the personification of every great quality a man can have: goodness of heart, honesty, and boundless love for all living creatures. It would have been almost impossible to discover a character defect in him. But perhaps his most amazing quality was his absolute simplicity. He was what he was in a perfectly natural way, without any effort.[45]

Despite the fact that his theories were incomprehensible except to a very narrow elite, it was generally known that he »introduced a new scientific conception of space and time and of their relation to the physical world.« It was likewise known, particularly among Jews, that »the foremost Jewish genius of our age is a modest, unassuming, kindly gentleman, almost childlike in his simplicity, with a keen sense of humor.«[46] Although there is an unkempt quality to many pictures of Einstein, he also was regarded as physically attractive, with a pleasing countenance.

Einstein's portrait became a universal symbol of scientific genius with a human face, and Zionists were ecstatic to be able to appropriate him as one of their own.[47] They showed his picture and talked about him on every possible occasion.[48] Everyone wanted to soak up his wisdom, meet him, shake his hand,

---

[44] Albert Einstein, cover, Palaestina-Bilder-Korrespondenz (March 1929). On the reception of Einstein from a cultural perspective, see Alan J. Friedman/Carol C. Donley: Einstein as Myth and Muse. Cambridge: Cambridge University Press 1989; Gerald Holton/Yehuda Elkana (Eds.): Albert Einstein: Historical and Cultural Perspectives. Princeton: Princeton University Press 1982, 281–343.

[45] Nahum Goldmann: Mein Leben als deutscher Jude. Munich: Langen Mueller 1980, 177–78.

[46] Herman Bernstein: Celebrities of Our Time. London: Hutchinson 1924, 243.

[47] Portrait of Einstein dedicated to Arthur Ruppin (1923), CZA; Stephen S. Wise to Julian Mack, December 17, 1930, MSS. Col. #19, 25/15, American Jewish Archives, Cincinnati.

[48] Portrait of Einstein by Max Liebermann on cover of Menorah [Paris Zionist organ], 1 April 1928.

and be photographed with him.[49] His presence at public Zionist functions resulted in huge crowds that could barely control their adulation.[50] Whatever he had to say was taken as a solemn pronouncement to be pondered, regardless of its novelty.[51] Zionists also liked to believe that when Einstein spoke, the rest of the world listened intently.[52] Whenever he took to the road his movements were tracked by Zionist organs with the fervor of gossip sheets looking for any scrap of information about a Hollywood celebrity;[53] his pilgrimages to Palestine were regarded as sacred events.[54]

Stories about Einstein, some of them apocryphal, became part of Zionist and Jewish lore. The best known (true) story is from the State of Israel: in 1952, upon the death of Chaim Weizmann, Einstein was offered the Presidency of the State of Israel, albeit a largely ceremonial position – despite the fact that he did not live, and had never lived, in the country.[55] His brief response to the extraordinary request was perfectly in character:

> I am deeply moved by the offer from our State of Israel, and at once saddened and ashamed that I cannot accept it. All my life I have dealt with objective matters, hence I lack both the natural aptitude and the experience to deal properly with people and to exercise official functions. For these reasons alone I should be unsuited to fulfill the duties of that high office, even if advancing age was not making increasing inroads on my strength. I am the more distressed over these circumstances because my relationship to the Jewish people has become my strongest human bond, ever since I became fully aware of our precarious situation in the world.[56]

Similar to the perception of Brandeis, Einstein, too, was seen as having a rather weak connection to Jewish culture and politics before his turn to Zionism.[57] Like Gershom Scholem, his encounter with East European Jews was

---

49 Inscribed photograph of Stephen S. Wise and Albert Einstein, to Brandeis (L. D.): »From two humble fellow Zionists,« CZA.

50 Juedsiche Rundschau, 24 June 1921, 359; »Der Aufbau Palaestinas als Aufgabe der Judenheit: Eine juedische Massenkundgebung« in Berlin. In: Juedische Rundschau, 6 July 1921, 371.

51 »Professor Einstein ueber sein Eindruecke in Palaestina.« In: Juedische Rundschau, 24 April 1923, 195–6; »Eine Botschaft Einsteins. Die Antwort auf das Weissbuch muss verdoppelte Arbeit sein.« In: Juedsiche Rundschau, 5 December 1930, 644.

52 See »Das Echo des Einstein-Briefes.« In: Juedische Rundschau, 22 October 1929, 555, on the impact of Einstein's letter to the *Manchester Guardian* of 12 October 1929.

53 »Prof. Einstein faehrt nach Palaestina.« In: Juedische Rundschau, 6 October 1922, 521; »Einstein in Singapore.« In: Juedische Rundschau, 5 January 1923, 5; »Einstein in Wien.« In: Juedische Rundschau, 26 September 1924, 551; »Einstein in New York.« In: Juedsiche Rundschau, 19 December 1930, 672.

54 »Einstein in Palaestina.« In: Juedische Rundschau, 16 Febraury 1923, 75.

55 Yitzhak Navon: On Einstein and the Presidency of Israel. In: Holton/Elkana (Eds.), Albert Einstein: Historical and Cultural Perspectives (note 44), 293–96.

56 Quoted in Jeremy Bernstein: Einstein. New York: Viking 1973, 214.

57 Goldmann, Mein Leben als deutscher Jude (note 45), 178.

pivotal in his attraction to Judaism and Zionism. Despite his sincere intolerance for chauvinism, Einstein was explicit about the necessity of a national movement for world Jewry, and Zionism in particular. Einstein clearly articulated the notion that to be a Jew, and to be a Zionist, required an unconditional love for the entirety of the Jewish people, and especially the Jews' »poor (East European) Jewish brethren,« the *Ostjuden*.[58] »Let us just leave anti-Semitism to the non-Jews,« he wrote, »and keep our hearts warm for our kith and kin.«[59] Not since Herzl's early addresses and writings had a Zionist leader's call for Jewish unity been received as a sign of integrity, generosity, and compassion, as opposed to a tactical ploy. Also like Louis Brandeis, Herzl, and Nordau, Einstein embodied the notion of »returning to the fold.«[60] Again echoing the thought of Herzl, Einstein stated: »I regard the growth of Jewish self-assertion as being in the interests of non-Jews as well as of Jews. That was the main motive of my joining the Zionist ranks.«[61]

Yet Einstein went further than any other Zionist leader in defining and condoning the existence of Zionism in the diaspora, which made him uniquely suited for heroic stature in the western Jewish communities, especially the United States. His was the most lucid argument articulated in support of diaspora-nationalism, without intoning the pious Zionist hope that all Jewry would eventually settle in Palestine. »For me,« Einstein wrote,

> Zionism is not merely a question of colonization. The Jewish nation is a living thing, and the sentiment of Jewish nationalism must be developed both in Palestine and everywhere else. To deny the Jews' nationality in the Diaspora is, indeed, deplorable. If one adopts the point of view confining Jewish ethnic nationalism to Palestine, then to all intents and purposes one denies the existence of a Jewish people. In that case we should have the courage to carry through assimilation as quickly and as completely as possible.[62]

Although he freely admitted his disdain for »undignified assimilationist cravings and strivings,« Einstein nevertheless repeated Herzl's and Brandeis's claim that Zionism and other nationalities need not be mutually exclusive.[63]

Einstein was, therefore, a Zionist and national Jew whose appeal to the Jewish world at large was perhaps greater than any other in the twentieth century. The way Einstein was received suggests a blurring of conventional categories

---

58 See Steven Aschheim: Brothers and Strangers: East European Jews in German and German-Jewish Consciousness. Madison: University of Wisconsin Press 1982, and Jack Wertheimer: Unwelcome Strangers: East European Jews in Imperial Germany. New York, Oxford: Oxford University Press 1987.

59 Albert Einstein: Assimilation and Nationalism (1) (1920). In: About Zionism. Ed. and trans. by Leon Simon. London: Soncino 1930, 23–4.

60 Abraham Pais: Subtle is the Lord: The Science and Life of Albert Einstein. New York: Oxford University Press 1982, 317, 315.

61 Einstein, Assimilation and Nationalism (note 59), 27–8.

62 Ibid., 28.

63 Ibid., 37.

of esteem for integrity, super-intelligence, dignity, depth of spirit, and even beauty. The magnetism of his image shows little sign of abating, although some seventy years after his pronouncements for Zionism his role in Jewish politics, and Zionism in particular, command little notice.

The comprehensive transformation of the Jewish people, according to Zionist ideology, could only take place in Palestine. Nevertheless, the movement's heads, in the years between the wars, cultivated the legends of Jewish and Zionist heroes, as well as the generic New Jew said to be coming into existence in the Yishuv. Herzl's implicit and explicit message was that all Jews, regardless of settling in Palestine, would be fundamentally, positively changed through even their expressed sympathy with Zionist aims. In the eyes of later cartoonists they would, quite literally, become »Herzls.« Overall, a multiplicity of visual discourses, or pictorial polemics, assisted in launching and sustaining the Zionist movement. The most important underlying notion, I think, is that of Zionism as a transformative process – of a land and a people. As our age is increasingly dominated by images and image thinking, it is hoped that a more critical interrogation of image creation and reception – including the concept of »sex appeal« – in the Jewish and Zionist worlds, will enter more and more into general, constructive discussion.

Eitan Bar-Yosef

A Villa in the Jungle: Herzl, Zionist Culture, and the Great African Adventure

In *Soumchi*, a children's book published in 1978, Amos Oz returns to his early days in Mandatory Jerusalem, to that magical summer of first love, and to his fantasy of traveling from the Holy City to Africa. Time and again, the eleven-year old boy, nicknamed Soumchi, imagines how he would set off on his new bicycle, »via Bethlehem, Hebron and Beersheva, via the Negev and Sinai deserts, towards the heart of Africa and the source of the river Zambezi, there to brave alone a mob of bloodthirsty savages.«[1] Later, after exchanging the bike for a toy train, Soumchi's daydream becomes even more elaborate; like the great entrepreneur Cecil Rhodes – straddling over Africa in the famous *Punch* cartoon (1892), one foot planted in the Cape, the other in Cairo[2] – Soumchi now envisions a train track cutting across a miniaturized African landscape that seems to extend from his own backyard:

> I would dig a winding river, I thought, and fill it with water and make the railway cross it on a bridge. I'd raise hills and scoop out valleys, run a tunnel beneath the hanging roots of the fig tree and from there my new railway would erupt into the wilderness itself, into the barren Sahara and beyond, up to the source of the river Zambezi in the land of Obangi-Shari, through deserts and impenetrable forests where no white man had ever set foot.

And elsewhere he adds, »where no white man had ever set foot, and to which my heart goes out.«[3]

To be sure, Soumchi never makes it to Obangi-Shari. Instead, he reaches another place to which his heart goes out – the room of his beloved classmate Esthie. A girl's room, Oz writes, »feels like a foreign country, utterly other and strange, its inhabitants not like us in any way«.[4] Freud had famously declared that the woman's psyche is the Dark Continent; and as the colorful elephants

---

1   Amos Oz: Soumchi (1978). Trans. by Amos Oz and Penelope Farmer. New York: Harvest 1993 [¹1980], 14.
2   As Peter Merrington has recently shown, while Rhodes's Cape-to-Cairo dream reflected an extraordinary imperial vision, it also revealed an almost infantile desire to literalize the /c/-sound alliteration. See Peter Merrington: A Staggered Orientalism. South Africa and the Cape-to-Cairo Imaginary. In: Poetics Today 22 (2001), 323–364, here 329.
3   Oz, Soumchi (note 1), 23–24, 36.
4   Ibid., 60.

on Esthie's pajamas suggest, her room is an appropriate (though perhaps temporary) substitute for the jungles in which Soumchi has yet to set his white foot.

Soumchi may dream of a wild and exotic Africa, but in other texts by Oz,
Africa is often associated with horror, madness, even death. Jacqueline Rose,
who has traced these sporadic references, has written that South Africa appears
in Oz's novels »as the unlived life of Israel: mundanely, almost contingently,
as the place where the Israeli might have chosen to go; more troublingly, as the
sign wherever it appears – hysteria, fanaticism, apocalypse – of the barely
imaginable, barely acknowledgeable, political unconscious of the nation.«[5]
Rose makes no mention of *Soumchi*, but there seems to be an uncanny affinity
between the guilty anxieties that permeate Oz's adult texts and Soumchi's
colorful, uninhibited, African fantasy; that is, between the colonial desire and
the post-colonial guilt. Africa, for Oz, is a »foreign country, utterly other and
strange,« but also conspicuously familiar; a magnificent daydream, but also a
nightmare; a sin, but also a punishment.

Amos Oz is not the only Israeli Jew to daydream about Africa. Ehud Barak's assertion that Israel is a »modern and prosperous villa in the middle of
the jungle« – »No hope for those who cannot defend themselves,« he warned,
»and no mercy for the weak« – demonstrates that even today, images of Africa
are still central to Zionism's self-fashioning.[6] Ironically, Barak's »villa in the
jungle« parable came just three months after the assassination of Prime Minister Rabin, an event which seemed to call into question Israel's smug image as
the last outpost of civilization in the Middle East: as her husband was preparing for the large peace rally in Tel-Aviv, 4 November 1995, Lea Rabin won-
dered why the security officials begged him to put on a bulletproof vest.
»What, are we in Africa?« she asked: »What sort of idea is this?«[7]

Africa, then, remains a space in which personal and national fantasies can
be acted out, made explicit: it is precisely the broadness and complexity of
»Africa« that makes the metaphor so ubiquitous in Zionist cultural history –
and so flexible. Thus, while the analogy between Israel and Apartheid South
Africa has become increasingly prevalent in recent years among Israel's critics, it is often forgotten that in the 1950s Israel made zealous attempts to distance itself from the Apartheid regime by offering assistance to – and identifying with – the emerging Black nations in Africa. As Golda Meir has written in
her autobiography, although it is certainly true that Israel was hoping to improve its diplomatic status, »The main reason for our African ›adventure‹ was
that we had something we wanted to pass on to nations that were even younger
and less experienced than ourselves. [...] We went into Africa to teach, and

---

[5]   Jacqueline Rose: States of Fantasy. Oxford: Clarendon 1996, 45.
[6]   Address by Foreign Minister Ehud Barak to the Annual Plenary Session of the
      National Jewish Community Relations Advisory Council, 11 February 1996,
      http://mfa.gov.il/mfa/go.asp?MFAH016g0.
[7]   Ha'aretz, 5 November 1995 [Hebrew].

what we taught was learned.«[8] Yet, it is indicative of Israel's ambiguous position, historically and ideologically, that Daniel Malan, the leader of the South African Nationalist Party who became Prime Minister in 1948, was the first foreign head of state to visit the young Israel; and that thirty years earlier, Jan Smuts, the legendary South African statesman, became the hero of the young Jewish *Yishuv* in Palestine thanks to his contribution to the issue of the Balfour Declaration.[9] »We are not Rhodesians,« Menachem Begin proclaimed in the Knesset in November 1970;[10] but it was Begin himself, as Prime Minister, who would initiate the massive building of Jewish settlements in the West Bank. By the end of the 1990s, the combination of militarized colonial outposts, road blockades, and highways for Jews would only bring Israel closer than ever before to Cecil Rhodes's African visions.

Considering the numerous references to Africa in Zionist culture and history, it is perhaps not surprising that the first Zionist fantasy of the Dark Continent surfaced shortly after the formal creation of the Zionist movement. I refer, of course, to the Uganda Proposal of 1903, when Theodor Herzl was offered by the British Government a chance to establish a Jewish colony in British East Africa, in the Guash Ngishu plateau not far from Nairobi. The Uganda affair is very often presented either as an embarrassment for Herzl or as a marginal episode in Zionist history. Isaiah Friedman, for example, has insisted that Herzl never intended to implement the plan: »For him, it was merely a ploy to obtain British recognition of the Zionist movement, recognition of Jews as a people, and to gradually bring Britain to the conclusion that only in Palestine would the Jewish problem be solved.«[11]

Even if Friedman is correct in his assessment of Herzl's tactics, what his analysis fails to consider is the significant role played by Africa in Herzl's work – Africa as a place, an idea, an imaginary. As this essay will demonstrate, to trace these recurring images of what Golda Meir had called the »African ›adventure‹« – as well as other imperial-type escapades, like the desert-island fantasy – is to highlight desires and anxieties that are emblematic of Herzl's Zionist project and its legacy: racial fantasies, colonial visions, but also, on a more fundamental level, that unadulterated sense of pleasure described so skillfully in Amos Oz's *Soumchi*. My objective is not to offer a

---

8 Golda Meir: My Life. New York: Dell 1975, 306–307.
9 Benjamin Joseph: Besieged Bedfellows. Israel and the Land of Apartheid. Westport: Greenwood Press 1988, 10, 7. On Smuts's contribution to the creation of Apartheid see, for example, Benjamin Pogrund: War of Words. Memoir of a South African Journalist. New York: Seven Stories Press 2000, 32.
10 Divrei HaKnesset [Knesset Proceedings]. Vol. 59 (2 November 1970 – 10 February 1971), 181.
11 Isaiah Friedman: Herzl and the Uganda Controversry. In: Theodor Herzl and the Origins of Zionism. Ed. by Ritchie Robertson and Edward Timms. Edinburgh: Edinburgh University Press 1997, 39–53, here 40.

systematic analysis of the colonial dimensions of Herzl's Zionist ideology;[12] rather, I illustrate how various imperial plots, tropes, and insignias, typical of the *fin-de-siècle*, have shaped Herzl's imagination – and through it, twentieth-century Zionist culture.

I   A Man's Book

An array of travel narratives, ethnographical studies, and cartographical accounts published throughout the nineteenth century constructed the image of Africa in popular European culture. Like Marlow, the narrator of Joseph Conrad's *Heart of Darkness* (1902), numerous European boys must have gazed at the huge maps of Africa and said to themselves, »When I grow up I will go there.« By the time they had become men, the scramble for Africa, underway since the 1880s, was already reshaping the image of the continent: »It had ceased to be a blank space of delightful mystery – a white patch for a boy to dream gloriously over,« says Marlow: »It had become a place of darkness.«[13] Nevertheless, a range of popular novels – imperial romances like Henry Rider Haggard's *King Solomon's Mines* (1885), dedicated »to all the big and little boys who read it«[14] – presented this »darkness« as an ideal site for adventure, the stuff that imperial dreams are made of.[15] No wonder, then, that one of the most disturbing nightmares recorded by Freud in *The Interpretation of Dreams* was triggered by Rider Haggard's *She* (1886).

It seems that for Herzl, too, this kind of »boys' literature« – »an adventurous journey to an undiscovered country,« Freud wrote, »a place almost untrodden by the foot of man«[16] – fed into the making of a dream: the Zionist dream. In June 1895, when Herzl told his friend, the author Alphonse Daudet, that he wished to write a book »for and about the Jews,« Daudet asked: »A novel?« He was thinking about something along the lines of *Uncle Tom's Cabin*. »No«, replied Herzl, »preferably a man's book!«[17]

---

[12] On this question see, among many others, Derek J. Penslar: Zionism, Colonialism and Postcolonialism. In: Journal of Israeli History 20 (2001), 84–98; Avi Bareli: Forgetting Europe. Perspectives on the Debate about Zionism and Colonialism. In: Journal of Israeli History 20 (2001), 99–120.

[13] Joseph Conrad: Heart of Darkness (1902). Ed. by Robert Hampson. Harmondsworth: Penguin 1995, 21–22.

[14] H. Rider Haggard: King Solomon's Mines (1885). Ed. by Dennis Butts. Oxford: Oxford University Press 1989 (The World's Classics), 1.

[15] Cf. Joseph Bristow: Empire Boys. Adventures in a Man's World. London: Routledge 1991; Patrick Brantlinger: Rule of Darkness. British Literature and Imperialism, 1830–1914. Ithaca: Cornell University Press 1988, 227–253.

[16] Sigmund Freud: The Interpretation of Dreams (1900). Trans. by A. A. Brill. New York: Modern Library 1950, 318.

[17] The Complete Diaries of Theodore Herzl. Ed. by Raphael Patai. Trans. by Harry Zohn. 5 vols. New York: Herzl Press 1960, i.12.

What, we might ask, is »a man's book«? One answer to this question can be found in the first page of the remarkable diary Herzl began writing in June 1895, as he was formulating his first Zionist ideas: »For some time past I have been occupied with a work of infinite grandeur. At the moment I do not know whether I shall carry it through. It looks like a mighty dream. But for days and weeks it has possessed me beyond the limits of consciousness [...]. Title: The Promised Land!« Herzl then goes on to make a fascinating analogy: »Stanley interested the world with his little travel book *How I Found Livingstone*. And when he made his way across the Dark Continent, the world was enthralled – the entire civilized world. Yet how petty are such exploits when compared to mine. Today I must still say: compared to my dream.« And a few days later, envisioning the first Jewish pioneers who would arrive at the new Jewish State, he adds, »For the future legend, have a distinctive cap designed, *à la* Stanley.«[18]

Henry Morton Stanley, author of *Through the Dark Continent* (1878) and *In Darkest Africa* (1890), was a journalist like Herzl, but it is nevertheless striking that the first analogy that springs to Herzl's mind is one between finding a solution to the Jewish question and finding Livingstone at the heart of Africa.[19] This reference, it is important to note, was not marginal or eccentric. In 1895, for example, weighing his Zionist scheme against Baron Hirsch's projects, Herzl claimed that »This exodus is to the earlier one as the present-day scientific exploration of the Witwatersrand gold fields is to the adventurous exploration of Bret Harte's Californians.«[20] Indeed, throughout his career, Herzl seemed to have been fascinated by colonial-style expeditions sent out to survey foreign and exotic terrains. We see this in his diary in the close attention he paid to the work of the Zionist commission sent to explore El-Arish in 1903, and in his insistence, later that year, to send a scientific expedition to survey East Africa. There was even a peculiar exchange of letters in the Anglo-Jewish press about the question of a pilgrimage to Palestine organized by the Maccabeans club (and its leaders, Israel Zangwill and Herbert Bentwich), which was scheduled for spring 1897. In a letter read at a public Zionist rally in East London in January 1897, Herzl described the Maccabeans' voyage as a national scientific expedition. Bentwich, in response, complained in a letter to the *Jewish World* that »those who are taking part in the Pilgrimage [...] have no such far-reaching scheme on foot as Dr. Herzl's fervid imagination would attribute to them [...]. The Pilgrimage is what its name denotes, and not an ›Expedition‹ nor an ›Investigation Commission,‹ as Dr. Herzl suggests.«[21]

We can only speculate what brought Herzl's »fervid imagination« to evoke Stanley's journey to find Livingstone in the first page of his diary. It may have

---

[18] Ibid., i.3, 4, 91.
[19] On the relationship between Livingstone and Stanley, geography and empire, see Felix Driver: Geography Militant. Cultures of Exploration and Empire. Oxford: Blackwell 2001, esp. 68–89, 117–145.
[20] Herzl, Diaries (note 17), i.43.
[21] Ibid., ii.513.

been the image of an old problem, finally solved. Or maybe it was the frantic sense of excitement that Herzl was experiencing in summer 1895, similar to the thrill one might feel during an exotic journey in the jungle. But it is equally significant that the Zionist scheme was associated, in Herzl's mind, with a manly, masculine, mission to Africa, an expedition into the Dark Continent which would make the white body appear even whiter. Much has been written about Herzl's tendency to internalize the antisemitic image of the Jew as feminine, physically inferior, sexually deviant, even – as Sander Gilman has shown – the Jew as black.[22] Indeed, Herzl's Zionism was also an attempt to transform the defective Jewish body of the Diaspora: as Daniel Boyarin has argued, it was precisely by transforming them into colonists that Herzl hoped to convert the physically-inferior Jews into virile white men.[23] Read against this racial and sexual fantasy, it is no wonder that the Zionist manifesto must also be a »man's book«.

It is difficult to assess whether *The Jewish State*, the book that Herzl eventually wrote after his conversation with Daudet, was indeed the »man's book« he had in mind.[24] *Altneuland*, on the other hand, clearly displays some of the themes and images that one associates with Stanley's escapades: the book is indebted not only to the utopian literature prevalent in the *fin-de-siécle*[25] – works like Edward Bellamy's *Looking Backward* (1888), William Morris's *News from Nowhere* (1890) or H. G. Wells's *When the Sleeper Wakes* (1899) – but also to the imperial romances and juvenile adventure stories written by authors like Stevenson, Haggard, Henty, or Verne. The book describes two visits to Palestine – the first in 1902, the latter in 1923. What is often overlooked is the fact that the twenty years in between are spent by the two friends, Kingscourt and Loewenberg, on a desert island in the South Seas. This is how Kingscourt – a tall German nobleman, broad-shouldered and manly – describes his isle:

---

[22] Sander Gilman: Jewish Self-Hatred. Anti-Semitism and the Hidden Language of the Jews. Baltimore: Johns Hopkins University Press 1986, 6–12; id.: The Jew's Body. London: Routledge 1991, 171–200.

[23] Daniel Boyarin: The Colonial Drag. Zionism, Gender, and Mimicry. In: The Pre-Occupation of Postcolonial Studies. Ed. by Fawzia Afzal-Khan and Kalpana Seshadri-Crooks. Durham: Duke University Press 2000, 234–265.

[24] Elsewhere in the diary (11 June 1895) Herzl returned once more to the meeting with Daudet: »He reminded me of Uncle Tom's Cabin. I told him then and there that I desired a more manly form of announcement. At that time I was still thinking of the Enquête [treatise] to be entitled The Situation of the Jews. Today, the more I think about it the more it seems to me that it would really be beneath my dignity to make my plan palatable to the masses through love affairs and little jests, as Bellamy did in his utopian novel«. Here, the »man's book« is constructed more explicitly as the opposite of the (melodramatic, chatty, and hence feminine) novel. See Herzl, Diaries (note 17), i.75.

[25] See Rachel Elboim-Dror: Yesterday's Tomorrow. Vol. I, The Zionist Utopia. Jerusalem: Yad Izhak Ben-Zvi 1993 [Hebrew].

Life on the yacht is freedom, but no real solitude. You must have a crew about you, you have to put into a harbor occasionally for coal. [...] But I know an island in the South Seas where one is really alone. It is a rocky little nest in Cook's Archipelago. I bought it, and had men come over from Raratonga to build me a comfortable home. It is so well hidden by the cliffs that it cannot be spied on any side from the sea. Besides, ships rarely come that way. My island still looks uninhabited....I live there with two servants, a dumb Negro whom I had in America, and a Tahitan whom I pulled out of the water at Avarua harbor when he tried to drown himself over an unhappy love affair. Now I have come to Europe for a last visit to buy whatever I shall need for the rest of my life over there – books, apparatus for physics, and weapons.[26]

Reading this, one is naturally reminded of that great ancestor of the late nineteenth-century imperial romance, a novel which presents a seminal myth of the colonial adventure: *Robinson Crusoe*. Many of the elements that make up Defoe's »man's book« are present in this passage: the fantasy of being all alone, master-of-all-I-survey; the comfortable abode, hidden in such a way that the island still appears uninhabited; a world with no women; and, last but not least, the presence of a faithful native whom the white man had saved from death. In fact, the native here has been split into two – a mute African and a Tahitan, who seems more articulate, or at least has more of a history.

This was not the first time that Herzl evoked Robinson Crusoe in the context of his political vision. In July 1898, in an interview he gave to the *Young Israel* journal (a juvenile paper published in London), Herzl observed that »At the present time our movement has to cut its way through the brushwood« – not unlike Stanley in the jungle, of course. Describing the Colonial bank he was struggling to establish, Herzl continues: »all the instruments that we require we must make for ourselves, like Robinson Crusoe on his island – your readers will appreciate that allusion. In time to come, the development of Zionism will read like a wonderful romance.«[27]

What is interesting about *Altneuland* is that whereas the Jew is certainly not Friday, nor is he Robinson Crusoe. Friedrich Loewenberg, the young, melancholic, effeminate Jew who joins Kingscourt in the desert island, is situated in the middle of this racial spectrum, between the white manly European and the helpless, toiling natives. As Michael Gluzman has shown, the twenty years spent on the island have transformed Friedrich's body:[28] »What a green, hollow-chested Jewboy you were when I took you away«, says Kingscourt: »Now you are like an oak.«[29] Gluzman's analysis demonstrates the affinity between masculinity and the Zionist project: life on the island may have strengthened

---

[26] Theodor Herzl: Altneuland (1902). Trans. by Lotta Levenson. New York: Bloch 1941, 31.

[27] Young Israel, July 1898, 106.

[28] Michael Gluzman: Longing for Heterosexuality. Zionism and Sexuality in Altneuland. In: Theory and Criticism 11 (1997), 145–162 [Hebrew].

[29] Herzl, Altneuland (note 26), 54.

his body, but it is only in Palestine that Friedrich can forgo his homoerotic relationship with Kingscourt and attain a truly heterosexual identity. It is telling, however, that Loewenberg's transformation is mirrored, in the novel, in the change undergone by David Littwak, the poor, meager Oestjuden boy who becomes, in Palestine, a »tall, vigorous man [...] whose sunburnt face was framed in a short black beard.«[30] What Friedrich achieves in his South Seas hideout, Littwak is able to achieve in the Holy Land. The »development of Zionism will read like a wonderful romance« because Palestine – just like Robinson Crusoe's desert island, or the Stanley-type African expedition – is where the Jew can finally become a man (and, we should perhaps add, a *white* man, whose fair face is sunburnt).

It is worthwhile noting that the desert-island fantasy – a typical colonial variation on the »African adventure« theme – continued to shape Zionist culture long after Herzl's death: in these daydreams, Palestine becomes an uninhabited, detached piece of land, floating independently of any geographical affiliation, a space which the Zionist recluse can develop, civilize, and rule. A typical example is Zvi Lieberman's *Oded Hanoded* (»Oded the Wanderer«), a children's book published in 1932 (and filmed the following year, the first Israeli children's movie).[31] Oded, a young Sabra from a new Zionist settlement embarks with his school friends on a long journey »to the great and wild mountains in the East«. But when he strays away from the others (to record his impressions of the landscape in peace), the thoughtful Oded suddenly finds himself all alone in the wilderness. Surveying the area, building a comfortable abode in a cave, working diligently and reading the Bible, this miniature Crusoe wonders whether he is doomed to »grow savagely and become a savage« like »those savages in Africa«: »What a horrible thought!« But, needless to say, Oded's mission is to bring civilization, not to go native: stunned, after a week, to discover a sign of human habitation (not a footprint but a distant fire), Oded reaches an Arab village, where the »filthy« inhabitants stare at him with amazement, »never having seen a man wearing European clothes«. Teaching the thankful savages to read and to write (in Arabic!), Oded eventually selects a local Friday, and together they return to the Zionist outpost.

A more subtle desert-island fantasy figures in the opening sentence of one of the most influential Israeli novels, Moshe Shamir's *With His Own Hands* (1951):

> Elik was born of the sea.
> That's the way father used to tell it when we would be sitting down to supper on the veranda of our little house on summer evenings. All around lay empty sandy lots,

---

[30] Ibid., 60.
[31] Tzvi Liebeman: Oded Hanoded. Tel-Aviv 1959 [¹1932] (no publisher, no page-numbers). My translation. On the film see Ella Shohat: Israeli Cinema. East/West and the Politics of Representation. Austin: University of Texas 1989, 27–38.

and on the walls and ceiling the little lizards would be scurrying away from the light
[...].
Father used to say: »We found you in a barrel that the sea washed ashore.«[32]

The ambiguous meaning of Elik's sea-birth has generated much debate among critics: does it embody the Zionist desire for a fresh start, free from the diasporic Jewish past, from the burden of history and culture? Or is it, on the contrary, suggesting an intimate return to the Mediterranean culture that forged the Judaic civilization in the first place? What is illuminating for our present discussion, however, is the remarkable image of being washed ashore, to the empty sand dunes – not unlike the survivor of a shipwreck who must begin a new life. Interestingly, this mythical birth merges in the opening paragraphs of the novel with another Zionist fantasy, more typical of the 1940s and 1950s: »»We turned you up inside a cauliflower, a big one.‹ I also remember the version: ›Actually we found you among the Bedouins in the desert,‹ which smarted worst of all.«[33] Here, Crusoe-Elik is re-imagined as a native: first as a product of the indigenous soil, then as a local Friday, one of those savages Oded had set out to educate.

In recent years, the desert-island fantasy has attained a more subversive expression: the growing rift within Israeli society has meant that, since the 1980s, the seacoast city of Tel Aviv (the name was famously borrowed from the title of Sokolow's translation of *Altneuland*) has increasingly become a cultural, social, and political island, drifting away from the rest of Israel. To disassociate itself from the rest of the Holy Land, Alona Nitzan-Shiftan has written, is »to split the national body itself – to detach the dream from its authentication, the ›neuland‹ from its ›altland‹, the utopia from the settlement«. Artists-architects Ganit Mayslits Kassif and Ehud Kassif have taken this fantasy *ad absurdum* by constructing »Neuland«. Exhibited at the ninth Venice Biennale for Architecture (2004), the work offers a duplicated mirror image of Tel Aviv, an island which is placed in the sea, opposite the real city as a provocative (or inspiring) alternative. »Released from the internal conflicted landscape of utopia and oppression, Neuland suggests an ironic, speculative, and utterly impossible escape,« writes Nitzan-Shiftan: »In Neuland, the state that was envisioned by Herzl [...] could finally find its appropriate setting – on land which is the result of cartographic manipulation, the genetic/graphic cloning of a vision without the nastiness of its implementation.«[34] It is indicative of Herzl's imaginative vigor that this island fantasy is already present in *Altneu-*

---

[32] Moshe Shamir: With His Own Hands (1951). Trans. by Joseph Shachter. Jerusalem: Israel Universities Press 1970, 1.

[33] Ibid.

[34] Alona Nitzan-Shiftan: Tel Aviv Lands. In: Back to the Sea. Catalogue of the Israeli Pavilion, the Ninth International Architecture Exhibition, Venice. Ed. by Sigal Bar-Nir and Yael Moria Klein. Tel Aviv 2004.

land, sandwiched in between the Alt and the Neu: the post-Zionist subversion is merely prefigured in the authoritative Zionist text.

II   The White Jew's Burden

The geographical dimensions of the colonial adventure are inseparable from its racial implications. If the island episode in *Altneuland* evokes the desire of transforming the Jewish body, it is later in the novel that this racial fantasy is played out much more explicitly: one of the chapters describes a visit to the laboratory of the celebrated bacteriologist Professor Steineck who, having cured Palestine of its malaria, now prepares to do the same for Africa. »That country can be opened up to civilization only after malaria has been subdued,« explains the visionary scientist: »Only then will enormous areas become available for the surplus populations of Europe. And only then will the proletarian masses find a healthy outlet.« The visitors, somewhat baffled, ask whether the aim is »to cart off the whites to the black continent«:

> Not only the whites!« replied Steineck gravely. »The blacks as well. There is still one problem of racial misfortune unsolved. The depths of that problem, in all their horror, only a Jew can fathom. I mean the Negro problem. Don't laugh, Mr. Kingscourt. Think of the hair-raising horrors of the slave trade. Human beings, because their skins are black,[35] are stolen, carried off, and sold. Their descendents grow up in alien surroundings despised and hated because their skin is differently pigmented. I am not ashamed to say, though I be thought ridiculous, now that I have lived to see the restoration of the Jews, I should like to pave the way for the restoration of the Negroes.[36]

Herzl stresses the affinity between Jewish and African histories – centuries of persecution and subjugation – but he is also careful to position the Jews and the blacks on opposite sides of the racial spectrum (which is undoubtedly why Golda Meir quoted this episode from *Altneuland* in her autobiography[37]). The Jew is cast here as the civilized colonist whose sacred duty is to bring civilization, first to the desolate plains of Palestine, then to the darkness of Africa. Activists in the Pan-African movement that began to crystallize in the 1890s have often acknowledged their debt to Zionist ideology.[38] It is telling, for example, that the first Pan-African Congress convened in London in July 1900,

---

[35] Note that the original reads, »Menschen, wenn auch schwarze Menschen [...]«: human beings, *although* their skin is black.

[36] Herzl, Altneuland (note 26), 170.

[37] Meir, My Life (note 8), 308–309.

[38] Cf. Robert G. Weisbord and Richard Kazarian, Jr.: Israel in the Black American Perspective. Westport: Greenwood 1985, esp. 7–28; Benyamin Neuberger: W. E. B. Du Bois on Black Nationalism and Zionism. In: Jewish Journal of Sociology 28 (1986), 139–144.

just three weeks before the third Zionist Congress was held in the same city.[39] Seen from Herzl's perspective, however, this Jewish-African bond always preserves the desire of maintaining a strict binary opposition between the two races.

On the one hand, Steineck's vision clearly evokes Rudyard Kipling's well-know poem *The White Man's Burden* (1899). Written during the Philippine-American War, the poem has come to represent the imperial frame of mind:

> Take up the White Man's burden –
> Send forth the best ye breed –
> Go, bind your sons to exile
> To serve your captives' need;
> To wait, in heavy harness,
> On fluttered folk and wild –
> Your new-caught sullen peoples,
> Half devil and half child.[40]

At the same time, it is typical of the ambivalent status of the Jew – part Crusoe, part Friday – that the nature of his burden is more complex than Kipling allows. In a speech delivered (in English) in London, June 1899, Herzl presented the Zionist scheme as an imperial venture that would benefit Britain: »We shall carry culture to the East, and Europe in turn will profit from this work of ours. We will create new trade routes, and none will be more interested in this than Great Britain with its Asiatic possessions. The shortest route to India lies through Palestine.« Herzl's conclusion, however, struck a less celebratory note:

> I do not believe that our people have borne their yoke so long under such sad circumstances merely to bring a new method of trade back to their home. The sufferings of our much-tried people must have another meaning – a yearning after justice, after humanitarianism must be in us and we must satisfy it. One is perhaps not in the most elegant company, when one strives for a goal in the company of »beggars and starvelings,« but I do not speak from the pulpit of a synagogue, and so I may be permitted to say that we Zionists do not shrink from joining beggars and starvelings when the end is righteousness. (Cheers.) Perchance by this means we will discover the possibilities of social improvement, and by realizing this ideal, thus aid other much-burdened nations. Then shall we be true Israelites.[41]

While Herzl's attitude towards his brethren is captured in that twice repeated phrase, »beggars and starvelings«, what is remarkable here is his usage of »burden«: this is no longer the colonial burden of bringing salvation to the Fridays of the world, but rather the more obvious, less ostentatious, burden of being an oppressed and suffering people. The real wretched of the earth – and not the white man – are those who carry a burden that must be relieved by the Jews.

---

[39] Jonathan Schneer: London 1900. The Imperial Metropolis. New Haven: Yale University 2001, 220–225.

[40] Rudyard Kipling: The Complete Verse. London: Kyle Cathie 1990, 261.

[41] The Messenger of Zion, July 1899, 14.

It is ironic that Ahad Ha-am, in his acidic critique of *Altneuland*, refuses to acknowledge this humanistic aspect of Herzl's work:

> Here the bacteriologist Steineck grieves for the fate of the blacks and devotes his power to remove the obstacles hindering them from returning to their land, and all in the name of Zionism. From this we can draw to ourselves a »black movement,« headed by the leader of the Zionists, who writes »Altneuland« to depict for us [...] the realization of the »black« ideal after twenty years – and therefore we ask: how would the black Altneuland differ, then, from the Zionist one?
> And I think I would not be exaggerating I if say that few and slight are the changes that the author would have been compelled to make in his book in order to make it »black.«[42]

By suggesting that *Altneuland* could well be presenting the Black, not Jewish, regeneration, Ahad Ha-am was merely subverting and ridiculing Herzl's blueprint: as we have seen, it is precisely to render the Jews *less* black that Herzl turned his vision to Africa. At the same time, so keen is Ahad Ha-am to condemn Herzl's »ape-like mimicry« of the West,[43] that he fails to appreciate the truly altruistic basis of Herzl's black Zionism. As a result, whereas Herzl exhibits a much more ambiguous moral and racial stand towards the Africans (and, we should perhaps add, towards his East European brethren), it is Ahad Ha-am who emerges from this feud as the (European, imperialistic, racist) bigot.

Herzl's ambivalence towards the Africans can also be traced in his representation of Oriental natives. On the one hand, during a visit to Egypt in March 1903, Herzl vowed that Zionism would also secure the future of those poor peasants. Describing a drive to the pyramids, he writes, »The misery of the *fellahin* by the road in indescribable. I resolve to think of the *fellahin* too, once I have the power.«[44] And yet, when he envisions the Jewish State, Herzl has no difficulty imagining how natives would clear the snakes and fight malaria for the Jewish colonists: »If we move into a region where there are wild animals to which the Jews are not accustomed – big snakes, etc.,« he wrote in June 1895, »I shall use the natives, prior to giving them employment in the transit countries, for the extermination of these animals. High premiums for snake skins, etc., as well as their spawn.«[45] Similarly, during his visit to Palestine in 1898, Herzl explained that to drain the swamps, »Such Arabs as are immune to the fever might be used for the work.«[46] Admiring Professor Steineck's vision of curing malaria, we should not forget who, in fact, would be doing the dirty work.

---

[42] Ahad Ha-am: Altneuland. In: Kol Kitvei Ahad Ha-am [»Complete Writings of Ahad Ha-am«]. Tel-Aviv: Dvir 1965 [¹1956], 319. My translation. Also see Shulamit Laskov: The Altneuland Dispute. In: Hatzionut 15 (1990), 35–53 [Hebrew].

[43] Ibid., 320. Also see Steven J. Zipperstein: Elusive Prophet. Ahad Ha'am and the Origins of Zionism. Berkeley: University of California Press 1993, 195–199.

[44] Herzl, Diaries (note 17), iv.1454.

[45] Ibid., i.98.

[46] Ibid., ii.741.

My point is that all these different allusions to African adventures or colonial romances hinge on an ambivalent image of the Jew: white, but not quite, as Homi K. Bhabha has written in a somewhat different context.[47] A remarkable demonstration of this ambiguous position can be found in a dream Herzl had in January 1904, just a few months before his death. »Dreamt of the German Kaiser last night,« he wrote in his diary: »He and I were alone on a bark at sea.«[48] Just like the yacht that carries Kingscourt and Loewenberg to the South Sea, Herzl's dream evokes, yet again, the image of a manly German and the sickly, self-hating Jew who will one day become a man, perhaps, once he reaches his Robinson-Crusoe island. But in the meanwhile, he is still floating somewhere in the ocean, very far from his final destination.

III   A miniature England in reverse

Until now we have examined some of the African day-dreams and imperial adventures that can be traced in Herzl's writing up to 1903. The Uganda proposal, made to Herzl several months after the publication of *Altneuland*, offered a unique chance to realize, politically, some of these racial and colonial desires: after all, defined against the indigenous East-African savages, the Jews' paleness would shine afar. Even the British settlers in East Africa, who fiercely resisted Chamberlain's vision of an African Zion, even they had to admit that the Jews were »possibly the lowest class of white men«.[49] Not quite, but still white.

Paradoxically, the proposal emerged just as the Royal Commission on Alien immigration, set up in April 1902 – Herzl himself was invited to give evidence in July – submitted its Report, in which it recommended to limit, considerably, the Jewish immigration into Britain.[50] Chamberlain acknowledged openly that the British made the African offer because they were keen to divert the flood of East-European Jews who were migrating to London's East End: »the best solution of this question«, Chamberlain explained in a speech in 1904, »was to find some country in this vast world of ours where these poor exiles can dwell in safety without interfering with the subsistence of others«.[51] The Jews, in other words, were too black to be admitted to the metropolitan centre, but white enough to colonize the empire for His Majesty's government.

---

[47] Homi K. Bhabha: The Location of Culture. London: Routledge 1994, 89. My argument is indebted to Boyarin, Colonial Drag (note 23).

[48] Herzl, Diaries (note 17), v.1606.

[49] Quoted in Robert Weisbord: African Zion. The Attempt to Establish a Jewish Colony in the East Africa Protectorate 1903–1905. Philadelphia: The Jewish Publication Society of America 1968, 84.

[50] Cf. Bernard Gainer: The Alien Invasion. The Origins of the Alien Act of 1905. London: Heinemann 1973; Colin Holmes: Anti-Semitism in British Society, 1876–1939. London: Edward Arnold 1979.

[51] Quoted in Weisbord, African Zion (note 49), 122.

This racial indeterminacy is echoed in Herzl's defense of the Uganda Plan, when he explained that the Jewish colony would function as a »miniature England in reverse.«[52] Herzl meant that whereas the British metropolitan center established colonies overseas, the Jewish colonies overseas would eventually establish a metropolitan centre in Palestine itself. Still, just like other witnesses to the Royal Commission on Alien Immigration, who were complaining that Jews were both the epitome of difference _and_ so alarmingly alike, Herzl's phrase – a »miniature England in reverse« – preserves the imperfect colonial mimicry that stood at the heart of Herzl's Zionist project, and which was exposed so explicitly in the Uganda affair and in his decision to align himself with the British Empire.

Mimicry is a key term in Herzl's thought. As Jay Geller has noted, before arriving at Zionism, Herzl offered a number of answers to the Jewish question; in addition to mass conversion, he also proposed a Darwinian mimicry: Antisemitism »represents the education of a group [namely, the Jews] by the masses, and will perhaps lead to its being absorbed. Education is accomplished only through hard knocks. Darwinian mimicry will set in. The Jews will adapt themselves.«[53] And although Herzl soon dropped this version of ultra-radical assimilation, mimicry continued to inform his work (as Ahad Ha-am was quick to note when he ridiculed Herzl's »ape-like mimicry« in _Altneuland_).

To see this mimicry in action, we can turn to the Israeli painter Nahum Gutman, who joined the British Army in 1917, enlisted in the special Jewish Battalion. In his memoirs, Gutman recalled how the awkward attempts made by the Jewish Tommies to adopt the manners and mannerisms of British soldiers merely infuriated their British commander. »Is this an army or isn't it?«, he hollered at them. »Please go down to the brothels in Jaffa. Do some sport, write letters home and that's it. Be soldiers, for heaven's sake, like all his Majesty's soldiers.«[54] Mimicry, writes Homi Bhabha, »is at once resemblance and menace«;[55] the Zionist attempt to imitate the British soldier merely produces miniature British soldiers in reverse. Indeed, as Gutman himself testified, »most of the Jewish soldiers were very short. A special application had to be made to obtain little pith helmets that would fit their skulls.«[56] The Stanley-

---

[52] Quoted in Amos Elon: Herzl. New-York: Holt, Rinehart and Winston 1975, 375.

[53] Herzl, Diaries (note 17), i.10. On Herzl and mimicry see Jay Geller: Of Mice and Mensa. Anti-Semitism and the Jewish Genius. In: Centennial Review 28 (1994), 361–385; Boyarin, Colonial Drag (note 23).

[54] Nahum Gutman/Ehud Ben-Ezer: Ben Holot U-Khol Shamaim [»Between the Sands and the Blue Sky«]. Tel-Aviv: Yavneh 1980, 171–172. My translation. On Gutman's own African adventures see Eitan Bar-Yosef: Painter or Hunter. Nahum Gutman, Lobengulu King of Zulu and the South-African Book. In: Theory and Criticism 20 (2002), 113–136 [Hebrew].

[55] Bhabha, Location of Culture (note 47), 86.

[56] Gutman/Ben-Ezer, Holot (note 54), 172–173.

type caps that Herzl was planning for his pioneers attain, in Gutman's narrative, an almost Lilliputian essence.

This mimicry, which is parodic, flawed, demonstrates the limited extent to which Zionism could take on, or adapt, colonial features. To claim, like Edward Said, that »one Semite went the way of Orientalism, the other, the Arab, was forced to go the way of the Oriental,«[57] would be to ignore the hybridity of »the Jew« and the ambivalence that characterizes the Jew's interaction with the British Empire on the one hand, and the dark continent on the other.[58] By transforming them into colonists, Herzl may have hoped to convert the effeminate Jews into white virile men: but this process, by definition, was doomed to fail. Even in Africa, there was always someone whiter.

Herzl's phrase, »a miniature England in reverse,« then, encapsulates the hybridized racial position of the (miniature, reversed) Jew, but it also reflects an explicit, straightforward identification with the British colonial project. In the speech he delivered in London in June 1899, Herzl asked,

> What can I, a poor barbarian from the Continent, say about [industry and progress] to the inhabitants of England? [...] You are far ahead of us in all technical industries, just as the great politicians of your country were the first to see the necessity for extending your Colonial possessions. This is the reason why the flag of Greater Britain waves over every sea, and, to my mind, this is why the Zionist idea, which is a colonising plan, should be easily and quickly grasped in England.[59]

Herzl was fascinated by that great metropolitan capital, the heart of the British Empire. In March 1901, following Professor Kellner's proposal that he should move to London, Herzl wrote in his diary: »The suggestion continued working in me all night. I could already see everything in London: my house in Regent's park, my parents' apartment nearby, the Congress Office, the office of the two editions of the *Welt*, my communication with the East End in weekly articles in the Yiddish edition (letters to the East End: ›My Dear East End.... Your friend Th. H.‹), my visits of inspection to the Colonial Trust which will flourish because of my presence – a whole full life.«[60] Herzl was well known for the swiftness with which he could visualize »a whole full life.« But there are enough hints suggesting that England, in particular, held a special charm for him.[61]

---

[57] Edward W. Said: Orientalism. Western Conceptions of the Orient. Harmondsworth: Penguin 1995 [¹1978], 307.

[58] On the ambivalence of the »Jew« see Bryan Cheyette: Constructions of the »The Jew« in English Literature and Society. Racial Representations, 1875–1945. Cambridge: Cambridge University Press 1993; Ivan Davison Kalmer/Derek J. Penslar: Orientalism and the Jews. An Introduction. In: Orientalism and the Jews. Ed. by Ivan Davison Kalmer and Derek J. Penslar. Waltham: Brandeis University Press 2005, xiii–xl.

[59] The Messenger of Zion, July 1899, 14.

[60] Herzl, Diaries (note 17), iii.1069–70.

[61] Cf. Steven Beller: Herzl's Anglophilia. In: Robertson/Timms (Ed.), Theodor Herzl (note 11), 54–61.

The afternoon spent with the poet laureate Alfred Austin and his wife in April 1898 offered, as Amos Elon has noted, some of the most pleasurable hours Herzl was to spend in the last few years of his life.[62] And this pleasure is related, in Herzl's diary, to the quintessential Englishness of it all: »A quiet park, a delicious garden, silence all around the venerable manor. [...] What charming jingoists these two are, proud of their beautiful England, which they call the first, foremost, finest power in the world. *Mon avis!* [...] These are the people, this is the milieu that I need for my well-being. *Comme je les comprends, les Juifs assimilés de l'Angleterre!* If I lived in England, I might be a *jingo.*«[63] On the one hand, the Austins embody all those values that Herzl admired: aristocracy, order, beauty. At the same time, one wonders whether Herzl's sympathy was not rooted in the fact that the British poet, too, was a miniaturized England. »With all my liking for the *laureate*,« Herzl writes, »a few comic touches did not escape my notice. He is a *guerrier en chambre*, a conqueror of colonies in his quiet flower garden. Mrs. Austin is taller by three heads than he is; he likes to put his hand on her shoulder, just as he patted mine reaching up from below.«[64]

Some of Herzl's opponents were hardly amused by his over-identification with the British Empire. Ahad Ha-am complained that the only aspect of the educational system in the new Jewish state described in *Altneuland* is the fact that the children's bodies are made physically fit by encouraging »competitive games – cricket, football, rowing – like the English«.[65] But Ahad Ha-am, of all people, should have recognized at least some of the benefits of an English education: for Ahad Ha-am was residing in Hampstead at the time, enjoying the imperial metropolis and working as a head-clerk at the Wissotzky Tea Company – that most archetypal of colonial commodities. Years later, after moving to the Hebrew Utopia that was Tel Aviv, Herzl's old adversary would find himself yearning for London, »simply for London. For its streets and stores more numerous than its inhabitants, for the dark ›City‹ where I spent many years without either light or air, for the suffocating fog....«[66]

IV   Heart of Darkness

The most disturbing manifestation of Herzl's infatuation with British imperialism can be found in his ardent determination to meet Cecil Rhodes.[67] On January 11, 1902 he writes,

---

[62] Elon, Herzl (note 52), 320.
[63] Herzl, Diaries (note 17), iii.937–938.
[64] Ibid., iii.939.
[65] Herzl, Altneuland (note 26), 80; Ahad Ha'am, Altneuland (note 42), 317.
[66] Letter to Dubnow, March 1913, quoted in Zipperstein, Elusive Prophet (note 43), 321.
[67] On Herzl and Rhodes see Mark Levene: Herzl, The Scramble, and a Meeting that Never happened. Revisiting the Notion of an African Zion. In: The »Jew« in Late-

In fact, all things considered, you are the only man who can help me now. Of course, I am not concealing from myself the fact that you are not likely to do so. The probability is perhaps one in a million, if this can be expressed in figures at all.

But it is a big – some say, too big – thing. To me it does not seem too big for Cecil Rhodes. This sounds like flattery; however, it does not reside in the words, but in the offer. [...]

You are being invited to help make history. That cannot frighten you, nor will you laugh at it. It is not in your accustomed line; it doesn't involve Africa, but a piece of Asia Minor, not Englishmen, but Jews.

But had this been on your path, you would have done it yourself by now.

How, then, do I happen to turn to you, since this is an out-of-the-way matter for you? How indeed? Because it is something colonial, and because it presupposes understanding of a development which will take twenty or thirty years. There are visionaries who look past greater spaces of time, but they lack a practical sense. Then again there are practical people, like the trust magnates in America, but they lack political imagination. But you, Mr. Rhodes, are a visionary politician or a practical visionary. You have already demonstrated this. And what I want you to do is not to give me or lend me a few guineas, but to put the stamp of your authority on the Zionist plan and to make the following declaration to a few people who swear by you: I, Rhodes, have examined this plan and found it correct and practicable. It is a plan full of culture, excellent for the group of people for whom it is directly designed, not detrimental to the general progress of mankind, and quite good for England, for Greater Britain. [...]

What is the plan? To settle Palestine with the homecoming Jewish people.[68]

I have quoted from the letter in some length because it suggests how Herzl is able to move from admiration to mimicry, even to the point of mimicking the voice of Rhodes himself, of taking up his persona: »I, Rhodes, have examined.« (It is telling that when Chamberlain was discussing the El-Arish plan with Herzl, he made him promise not to perform another Jameson Raid from Sinai to Palestine – as if Herzl was in fact impersonating Rhodes.[69]) For critics of Zionism, Herzl's letter to Rhodes could be said to anticipate the unholy alliance between Israel and South Africa that was gradually forming up in the 1970s. These critics would probably point to Herzl's desperate attempts to obtain other territories in Africa. In May 1903 he described how he »started out from Chamberlain's Uganda suggestion – and hit upon Mozambique«.[70] Two months later Herzl decided it was time to meet King Leopold to secure a Charter in Congo. In a letter to Franz Philipson he wrote, »The Congo State has land enough which we can use for our settlement. We can take over part of the responsibilities, that is, pay an annual tax [...] to the Congo State, in return for which we naturally lay claim to *self-government* and a not too oppressive

---

Victorian and Edwardian Culture. Between the East End and East Africa. Ed. by Eitan Bar-Yosef and Nadia Valman. London: Palgrave, forthcoming.

[68] Herzl, Diaries (note 17), iii.1193–1194.

[69] Ibid., iii.1369.

[70] Ibid., iv.1487.

vassalage to the Congo State.«[71] What started as a romantic gesture to Stanley's journey – an exciting African romance, a sort of »Dr. Herzl, I presume« – now attains a more sinister aspect, a Zionist version of Conrad's *Heart of Darkness*.

The letter to Rhodes was never sent, and one can only speculate what Rhodes would have been able to do for the Zionist cause. What would have happened, had an African Zion been established? Could we imagine »the horror« of it all? This specter of an alternative Zionist history and its disturbing affinity with history as we know it brings us back, full circle, to Soumchi's Rhodes-like projects and to Amos Oz's novels, in which Africa occasionally flickers as the unlived life of Israel, »as the sign of the barely imaginable, barely acknowledgeable, political unconscious of the nation«.[72]

But it is equally significant that while Herzl dreamt about being Rhodes, his unique position as carrying both burdens – the white and the black – also allowed him to see what Rhodes and the British could not. In March 1903, attending a lecture on irrigation in Cairo, Herzl turned from the boring lecture to gaze at the

> striking number of intelligent-looking young Egyptians who packed the hall.
> They are the coming masters. It is a wonder that the English don't see this. They think they are going to deal with the *fellahin* for ever.
> Today their 18,000 troops suffice for the big country. But how much longer?
> [...] This [English] boldness makes them magnificent *merchant adventurers*; but it also always makes them lose their colonies later.
> What the English are doing is splendid. They are cleaning up the Orient, letting light and air into the filthy corners, breaking old tyrannies, and destroying abuses. But along with freedom and progress they are also teaching the *fellahin* how to revolt.
> I believe that the English example in the colonies will either destroy England's colonial empire – or lay the foundation for England's world dominion.
> One of the most interesting alternatives of our time.
> It makes one feel like coming back in fifty years to see how it has turned out.[73]

Celebrated for his vision of the Jewish State, Herzl here offers a sober, almost chilling analysis of decolonization, of the long and violent process in which the European colonial powers would gradually lose their grip over other lands and peoples. But this should come as no surprise: Herzl would have been the first to recognize that journeys that begin with the gusto of an African expedition can sometimes end with a melancholic dream about a German Robinson Crusoe and his Jewish Friday, floating together in a small boat somewhere in the middle of the ocean, very far from the promised island of their dreams.

---

[71] Ibid., iv.1512.
[72] Rose, States of Fantasy (note 5), 45.
[73] Herzl, Diaries (note 17), iv.1449.

Daniel Hoffmann

»Dieses schlicht verschwiegene Bekenntnis«.
Gustav G. Cohen, ein unbekannter Freund Theodor Herzls

Nach seiner Rückkehr nach Wien beschließt Theodor Herzl am 3. September 1897 eine ausführliche Tagebucheintragung über den Verlauf des Basler Kongresses und die unterschiedlichen Emotionen zwischen Euphorie und Gelassenheit bei seinen Teilnehmern mit einer Erinnerung privater Art.

> Und die beste Erinnerung aus diesen Congresstagen sind mir ein paar Plauderviertelstündchen Nachts auf dem Balkon des Hôtel trois rois, mit dem alten feinen Banquier Gustav G. Cohen, dem ich nach dem kleinen französischen Wein den er bei Tische trank, ›Beaujolais fleuri‹ zubenannt hatte.[1]

Herzl hat diesen angenehmen Eindruck nicht vergessen. In seinem ersten Brief an Cohen nach dem Kongress verwendet er den Kosenamen sogar in der Anrede und schreibt dazu:

> Mit meinem Sinn dafür, in den gegenwärtigen Vorkommnissen dasjenige herauszufinden, das mir die liebste Erinnerung sein wird, habe ich Sie in Basel so gern zum Plaudern aufgesucht. Und wirklich ist vom Trubel dieser Tage, die jedenfalls der Geschichte der Juden angehören, das bischen Schwätzen auf dem Rheinbalcon mir die freundlichste Erinnerung.[2]

Herzls später immer wieder brieflich geäußerter Wunsch nach einer Fortsetzung dieser abendlichen Begegnungen und die weitgehende Ausblendung politischer Tagesfragen der zionistischen Bewegung lassen den Eindruck entstehen, dass er in Cohen weniger den aktiven Mitstreiter als den Freund schätzte, der für ungetrübte Augenblicke des Lebens unentbehrlich war.

Der Beginn ihrer Bekanntschaft steht hingegen unter einem ganz anderen Stern, und doch birgt er schon den Keim für Herzls spätere eher private Wertschätzung des Zionisten Cohen.

---

[1] Theodor Herzl: Briefe und Tagebücher. Bd 2. Zionistisches Tagebuch 1895–1899. Bearbeitet von Johannes Wachten und Chaya Harel. Berlin, Frankfurt am Main 1983, 543.

[2] Herzl: Brief an Cohen vom 18.9.1897. In: Theodor Herzl. Briefe und Tagebücher. Hg. von Alex Bein u. a. Bd 4. Briefe. Anfang Mai 1895 – Anfang Dezember 1898. Bearbeitet von Barbara Schäfer. Berlin, Frankfurt am Main 1990, 346f. Siehe auch den Brief vom 27.7.1900. Bd 5. Briefe. Anfang Dezember 1898 – Mitte August 1900. Bearbeitet von Barbara Schäfer. Frankfurt am Main 1991, 508, in dem sich Herzl auch für den Londoner Kongress »unsere guten Plauderstündchen« erhofft.

Unter dem Titel *Aus den Anfängen der Herzl'schen Tätigkeit. Drei Briefe von Theodor Herzl* hat Cohen im August 1904 in *Ost und West*, der Illustrierten Monatsschrift für Modernes Judentum, eine Erinnerung an diesen Beginn veröffentlicht. Aus der Vielzahl der Briefe, die er von Herzl besaß, hat er drei ausgewählt und sie mit einem Kommentar versehen. Der begleitende Text vergegenwärtigt nicht nur Cohens Freundschaft mit Herzl, sondern er bietet auch einen autobiographischen Rückblick Cohens auf seine »zionistischen« Anfänge, die in die frühen 80er Jahre des 19. Jahrhunderts zurückreichen.

Cohen schildert, wie er in »freudigster Erregung« Herzls Judenstaat, auf den er durch eine Zeitungsbesprechung aufmerksam geworden war, gelesen hat und durch Vermittlung des Wiener Kaufmanns Martin Hinrichsen seine eigenen zionistischen Darlegungen, die er in einer Broschüre mit dem Titel *Die Judenfrage und die Zukunft* privat hatte drucken lassen, ohne Namensnennung Herzl zukommen ließ.[3] Herzls Antwortbrief an Hinrichsen vom 8. April 1896, der in *Ost und West* im Faksimile abgedruckt ist, enthält die einzige ausführliche Auseinandersetzung mit Cohens zionistischen Gedanken. Herzl schreibt:

> Ich erkannte gleich nach den ersten Worten die geistige Structur dieses Mannes, und was ich dann weiter las, kam mir nur selbstverständlich vor, so wie ihm in meiner Schrift Alles selbstverständlich vorgekommen sein muss. Wenn es für mich noch einzelner Beweise für die tiefe nationale Zusammengehörigkeit der Juden bedürfte, so wäre dieses schlicht verschwiegene Bekenntniss meines unbekannten Verwandten ein vollgiltiger. [...] Ich werde mich freuen, wenn er sich mir nennt, aber ich dringe durchaus nicht darauf. Mir genügt es, ihm auf diese Weise die Hand zu drücken, und wenn er glauben wird, dass er für die Sache unserer Nation etwas leisten kann, wird er sich schon melden. Ich kenne meine Juden, ich weiss was in uns steckt, was in uns stecken musste, wenn wir die schwersten Prüfungen überstanden, die je ein Volk der Geschichte durchmachte.[4]

Die Prüfung, die Cohen den Weg zum Zionismus finden ließ, war eine Familientragödie.

1881, zwei Jahre nachdem Cohen in seine Heimatstadt Hamburg zurückgekehrt war, starb sein einziger Sohn an Meningitis. Cohen zog sich für einige Wochen auf die Insel Sylt zurück, um mit dem Schmerz über den Verlust des Sohnes zurechtzukommen. Dort las er den 1876 erschienenen Roman *Daniel Deronda* der englischen Schriftstellerin George Eliot.

> Es war einige Zeit nachdem ich George Eliots ›Daniel Deronda‹ gelesen, dass eines Tages – es war Anfangs der 80er Jahre – der Gedanke plötzlich in mir auftauchte, die Verfasserin sei im Recht, das einzige Heilmittel für die Judenkrankheit liege in der Wiederherstellung eines jüdischen Staates in Palästina, hier sei das Ideal, welches unser Volk bewegen könnte, sich aufzuraffen. [...] Als ich später meine Ge-

---

3   Gustav G. Cohen: Aus den Anfängen der Herzl'schen Tätigkeit. Drei Briefe von Theodor Herzl. In: Ost und West. Illustrierte Monatsschrift für Modernes Judentum, IV 8–9, August 1904, 593–600, 595.

4   Herzl: Brief an Martin Hinrichsen vom 8.4.1896. In: Theodor Herzl. Briefe und Tagebücher. Hg. von Alex Bein u. a. Bd 4. Briefe (Anm. 2), 88f.

danken niederschrieb, dachte ich nicht an eine Veröffentlichung, von der ich nur den Vorwurf der Lächerlichkeit erwartete, sondern das Interesse, welche sie bei meinen späten Nachkommen erwecken könnten, wenn das Geahnte, Erhoffte vielleicht wirklich eingetreten. Die wenigen Bekannten, denen ich das Manuskript zeigte, waren entweder gleichgültig oder entschieden gegnerisch. Der Funke wollte nicht zünden.[5]

Dass er diesen Funken nur schwer hätte zünden können, lag an Cohens stillem, zurückhaltendem Naturell, das auch an diesen rückblickenden Worten leicht abzulesen ist. Denn er hatte, so bekennt er hier aus dem Abstand von beinahe einem Vierteljahrhundert, zwar die Hoffnung, dass das Ideal eines jüdischen Staates eines Tages Wirklichkeit werden würde, für seine Verwirklichung hatte er sich aber nicht aktiv einsetzen wollen. Er scheute es sogar, seine Gedanken zum Zionismus namentlich zu zeichnen und beließ es mit ihrer Publikation als Privatdruck, der nur einen ausgewählten und damit begrenzten Kreis ansprechen konnte. Herzls Wort vom verschwiegenen Bekenntnis charakterisiert Cohens Haltung deshalb in doppelter Hinsicht.

In seinem Beruf ist Cohen hingegen ein sehr erfolgreicher Mensch gewesen. Als Sohn eines Kaufmanns wurde er am 17. Februar 1830 in Hamburg geboren. Seinen Wunsch zu studieren, musste er nach einem schweren geschäftlichen Rückschlag des Vaters aufgeben. So ergriff er ebenfalls den Beruf des Kaufmanns und begab sich 18jährig nach Südafrika, wo ein Onkel von ihm lebte. Zwanzig Jahre lang blieb er dort und gelangte zu großem Wohlstand. »Er wurde englischer Bürger und übersiedelte 1869 nach Manchester«.[6] 1879 kehrte er als Privatier nach Hamburg zurück, wo er bis zu seinem Tod am 10. Dezember 1906 lebte.

Cohen ist ein typischer Vertreter des assimilierten deutschen Judentums. »Er erhielt Gymnasialbildung, wuchs in einer feingebildeten, vom Aufklärungsgeist erfüllten Familie auf, ohne mit jüdischer Art und Sitte bekannt zu werden. [...] So war er bis zur Unkenntlichkeit assimiliert«.[7] An dieser Welt deutschen Geistes hielt er jedoch nicht fest. Als er nach Südafrika geht, entwickelt er eine hohe kulturelle Anpassungsfähigkeit an die englische Welt, so dass er schließlich zum Präsidenten der Handelskammer gewählt wird. Seine Wende zum Zionismus zeigt eine ebenso tiefe Entschlossenheit, sich in den Dienst der neuentdeckten Idee zu stellen. Sein anfänglich rein theoretisches Interesse, das in der Niederschrift des ersten Teils der Broschüre *Die Judenfrage und die Zukunft* seinen Ausdruck findet, wandelt sich Anfang der 90er Jahre zu einem praktisch ausgerichteten Zionismus.

Diesen Wandel dokumentiert eindrucksvoll der Aufbau der Schrift *Die Judenfrage und die Zukunft*. Sie gehört zu den zahlreichen Texten, die zu Beginn der 1880er Jahre den zionistischen Gedanken propagieren, jedoch oftmals ohne Kenntnis der Mitstreiter. So lassen sich weniger gegenseitige Abhän-

---

5 Cohen, Aus den Anfängen (Anm. 3), 594f.
6 Siehe Nachruf in der *Jüdischen Rundschau* vom 21.12.1906, 754–755.
7 Siehe Nachruf in *Die Welt* vom 21.12.1906, 13–14.

gigkeiten oder Beeinflussungen als gemeinsame Gedankenstrukturen fest-
stellen, die sich zum historischen Gesamtphänomen des Zionismus zusam-
menschließen.

In ihrem ersten Teil ist sie eine Art von Programmschrift, die sich mit der
Judenfrage unter dem Gesichtspunkt der gesellschaftlichen und politischen
Situation der Juden in Deutschland befasst. Sie stellt das Ideal einer Selbstän-
digkeit der Juden als Nation heraus und plädiert für einen ersten Versuch, die
Juden wieder an ihre Staatlichkeit heranzuführen, der auf Zypern stattfinden
soll. Cohen entwickelt für sein Zypern-Projekt jedoch keine konkreten Vorstellungen. Es dient ihm vor allem dazu, die Idee einer neuen staatlichen Existenz
durch ein nicht aussichtslos oder illusionär erscheinendes Projekt wieder ins
Blickfeld der europäischen Juden zu rücken.

> Man wird fragen: Gesetzt, eine solche Ansiedelung [auf Zypern – D. H.] würde ge-
> deihen – was dann? Wie soll Palästina in den Besitz des Judenthums übergehen,[8]
> wie würde sich die ansässige Bevölkerung, wie das orthodoxe Judenthum der Welt
> verhalten, das in der neuen Pflanzung möglicherweise eine Rotte Abtrünniger erbli-
> cken würde, die mit aller Macht zu bekämpfen wäre? – Wie das, in andern Ländern
> ansässige moderne Judenthum, das nicht geneigt sein würde, die Genüsse europäi-
> scher Grossstädte mit der primitiven Lebensweise im neuen Staat zu vertauschen?
> Es ist unmöglich, diese Fragen jetzt schon zu beantworten. Es kann nur wiederholt
> werden, dass es sich hier nicht um ein fertiges Projekt, sondern vorerst nur darum
> handelt, die Idee der nationalen Wiederherstellung zu pflegen, und dem Judenthum
> ein neues Interesse, ein Ideal zu geben.[9]

Die vorsichtige Zurückhaltung, mit der Cohen hier argumentiert, offenbart
auch der Schlussabsatz dieses ersten Teils. Er hat ihm nicht die Form einer
flammenden Rede gegeben, sondern er begnügt sich mit einem indirekten
Aufruf an das jüdische Volk, den er in die Form des Optativs kleidet. »Man
sollte es aufrütteln mit einem: ›Ermanne Dich, erhebe Dich‹«.[10] Den Abschluss
bildet ein Zitat aus Eliots *Daniel Deronda*.

> Ich kann nicht besser schliesen, als mit Geo Eliot's Worten: Revive the organic cen-
> tre: Let the unity of Israel, which has made the growth and form of its religion, be an
> outward reality. – Looking towards a land and a polity, our dispersed people in all
> the ends of the earth may share the dignity of a national life, which has a voice

---

8 Dass es schon seit den 1860er Jahren jüdische Siedlungsprojekte in Palästina gab,
   die jedoch in starker finanzieller Abhängigkeit von der Diaspora standen (unterstützt
   z. B. von Edmond de Rothschild oder Chibat Zion), ist Cohen wohl nicht bekannt
   gewesen. Siehe dazu: Jehuda Reinharz: Old and New Yishuv. The Jewish Community in Palestine at the Turn of the Twentieth Century. In: Jewish Studies Quarterly,
   Nr 1, 1993/94, 54–71.
9 Gustav Gabriel Cohen: Das Ideal des eigenen Staates. Zwei Schriften aus den Anfängen des Zionismus. Hg., eingeleitet u. kommentiert von Daniel Hoffmann, mit
   einem Beitrag von Hanne Lenz. IBA – Media & Book, Berlin 2003, 67.
10 Ebd., 72.

among the peoples of the East and the West, which will plant the wisdom and skill of our race so, that it may be, as of old, a medium of transmission and understanding.[11]

Mit diesem Zitat kehrt Cohen zu der Inspirationsquelle seiner zionistischen Gedanken zurück. Es bildet den Extrakt seiner eigenen, noch spekulativen Überlegungen und zeigt, wie stark sie in ihrem Kern von literarischen Fiktionen geprägt sind.

Der zweite Teil der Schrift, der den Titel *Spätere Notizen* trägt und auf den Zeitraum von August bis Dezember 1891 datiert ist, gibt hingegen eigene Erfahrungen Cohens wieder. Er ist ein aufrüttelnder Bericht, der unmittelbar mit dem Elend der 1890 aus Moskau vertriebenen jüdischen Flüchtlinge konfrontiert und keinen Raum mehr für abwägende Reflexionen über grundlegende Fragen zur Lösung der Judenfrage lässt. Um den verfolgten Juden zu helfen, wurden in Deutschland Rettungskomitees gegründet, so auch in Hamburg das »Hilfskomitee für die russischen Juden«, deren Mitglied Cohen war. In seinen Schilderungen findet er zu neuen Bewertungen und auch zum Eingeständnis von Irrtümern. So revidiert er seine negative Meinung über die orthodoxen Juden aus dem ersten Teil und hebt bewundernd ihre Hilfsbereitschaft hervor.

> Ich habe vorhin gesagt, dass ich Irrthümliches in meinen früheren Anschauungen entdeckt und mich dessen gefreut habe. – Es betrifft das orthodoxe Judenthum, das ich bisher hier nur oberflächlich kennen gelernt und dessen Kraft und Befähigung ich unterschätzt hatte, auch bei dem russischen ist dies der Fall. Es ist im Elend, aber wer es mit einigermaassen wohlwollenden Augen betrachtet, entdeckt unter diesem Elend auch gute Züge.[12]

Er erkennt, dass die Notwendigkeit eines radikalen Neuanfangs der verfolgten Juden in einem eigenen Staat nun unabdinglich geworden ist. Vor allem aber entdeckt er das Zusammengehörigkeitsgefühl, das Juden aus unterschiedlichen Ländern miteinander verbindet.

> Und ich habe noch etwas bei dieser Gelegenheit entdeckt. Dass das Racen-Gefühl unter Juden doch stärker ist, als ich früher angenommen. – In meiner vorhergehenden Schrift hatte ich doch nur einen engen Kreis im Auge, als ich von der herrschenden Gleichgültigkeit, ja Abneigung sprach. – Man hatte mich schon früher darauf aufmerksam gemacht, dass ich nicht nur nach hiesigen Verhältnissen urtheilen dürfe. – – – Als die Januar-Berichte über die jüdische Auswanderung eintrafen, als der Aufruf zur Hülfe erging, da zeigte es sich, dass das alte Stammes-Gefühl nicht erloschen war, dass es lebte, und auflodere, wie man es kaum geahnt hatte.[13]

Herzl hat in seinem Brief an den Wiener Kaufmann Hinrichsen diese *Späteren Notizen* hervorgehoben, weil sie auf einer unmittelbaren Begegnung mit der Not der Juden beruhen und damit aus dem Bereich rein spekulativen oder ideellen Bedenkens der Judenfrage ein für alle Mal herausführen. »Besonders

---

[11] Siehe in der deutschen Übertragung von Jörg Drewitz, Zürich 1994, 675f.
[12] Cohen, Das Ideal des eigenen Staates (Anm. 9), 77.
[13] Ebd., 79.

dankbar war ich dem Verfasser des Manuscripts für die Schilderung der Comité-Tätigkeit in der Zeit der russischen Judenaustreibung. Diese Schilderung hat einen bleibenden literarischen Werth«.[14]

Zum Abschluss dieses zweiten Teils gestattet sich Cohen jedoch eine idealistische Emphase, indem er an eine gleichnisartige Darstellung des Assimilationsprozesses der Juden im Exil die Hoffnung auf einen biblischen Exodus anknüpft.

> Das Judenthum ist mit einer Pflanze des Ostens verglichen worden, deren Saat die Winde dahintragen und über die ganz Erde verstreuen. Wo sie fällt, da keimt sie, gleichviel wie unzuträglich auch die Beschaffenheit des Bodens und Climas. Unter günstigen Verhältnissen gelangt sie zu solcher Entwickelung, dass sie der einheimischen Flora einen grossen Theil ihres Terrains abgewinnt. – – Das Gleichniss ist zutreffend, könnte indess weiter ausgesponnen werden. Der Eigenthümer des Bodens will die fremdartige Pflanze nicht. Die Frucht, welche sie trägt, mag eine heilsame sein, aber ihm schmeckt sie wie eine bittere Medicin. – Und die üppig wuchernde Pflanze entzieht seiner Meinung nach zu viel Nahrung, beeinträchtigt das Gedeihen der heimischen und ihm zusagenden. Er sucht sie daher in der Entwickelung zu hemmen, wo er kann, und unter dem Mangel von Pflege, auf dürftiges Erdreich beschränkt, den stärksten Winden ausgesetzt, verkümmert sie häufig und es bildet sich ein wildes Gestrüpp, verletzend für das Auge des Beschauers und jammervoll gegen den Blumenschmuck wohlgepflegter Beete abstechend. – – Wo sie doch zu hoher Entwickelung gelangt, da strebt man, ihr durch Pfropfen mit einheimischen Reisern nach und nach den ursprünglichen Character zu nehmen. – Jetzt schmeckt die Frucht auch dem verwöhntesten Gaumen des Landes, aber dass sie desselben Stammes wie jenes Gestrüpp, welchem nahe zu kommen man sich scheut, davon ist die Kenntniss verloren gegangen.
>
> Das Land, in welchem sie einst zu hoher Blüthe gelangte, liegt zum Theil verödet. – – – Ist es ganz undenkbar, dass man es dennoch – gestützt auf neue Erfahrung und auf die Kenntniss der schädlichen Einflüsse, welche weiteres Gedeihen auf heimischem Boden hemmten – wieder mit einer Pflanzung auf demselben in grösserem Styl versucht? – Wer wird einst, ein neuer Moses, die Stimme aus dem feurigen Busch hören?[15]

Im Juni 1896 ergänzt Cohen seine Broschüre mit einem Nachwort und gibt sie erneut in Druck. Er verweist in ihm auf neue Lektüreeindrücke, auf Israel Zangwills *The Children of the Ghetto*, aber vor allem auf Herzls *Judenstaat*. Dass er inzwischen in brieflichen Kontakt mit Herzl getreten ist und dieser zu den Lesern seiner zionistischen Darlegungen gehört, verschweigt er jedoch. Seine Beurteilung von Herzls Ideen unterstreicht hingegen noch einmal die unterschiedlichen Wirkungsmöglichkeiten, die in ihrer beider Persönlichkeit angelegt sind: das zurückhaltende, auf begrenzte Aktionen beschränkte Naturell Cohens und den revolutionären Impuls in Herzls Auftreten.

---

[14] Herzl, Brief an Martin Hinrichsen (Anm. 4), 89.
[15] Cohen, Das Ideal des eigenen Staates (Anm. 9), 87f.

Einige Jahre später fand ich mit freudiger Ueberraschung manches, meinen Gedanken Verwandte einem der Charactere in Mr. Zangwill's wunderbarem Buch ›the children of the Ghetto‹ in den Mund gelegt; (einige der Stellen, die mir dabei besonders aus der Seele geschrieben waren, füge ich hier bei) und in einer vor kurzem in Wien erschienenen Brochure ›Der Judenstaat‹ von Herrn Dr. Theodor Herzl, erhält das, was mir in unbestimmten Umrissen vorgeschwebt, greifbare Form und frisch pulsirendes Leben. Ich bin, so sehr ich den Muth und die Hingebung des Verfassers bewundere, noch der Ansicht, dass er betreffs des vorhandenen Materials und des jetzigen Zeitpunktes zu sanguin ist und seiner Zeit vorauseilt, aber das letztere mag nothwendig sein. Zu so vielen grossen Bewegungen wurde der erste Anstoss in einer Periode gegeben, die ihnen kein Verständniss entgegenbrachte. Dass ich meinerseits in meinem Urtheil über das heutige Judenthum zu sehr durch Wahrnehmungen, die auf einen engern Kreis beschränkt blieben, beeinflusst wurde, habe ich bereits in Vorstehendem bereitwilligst zugestanden.[16]

Interessant sind die beiden Mottos, die Cohen seiner Broschüre vorangestellt hat. »Was waren wir? Was sind wir? Was sollten wir sein?« —— »Dass er nicht/ Soll irre werden, wenn des Staubes Weisheit/ Begeisterung, die Himmels Tochter lästert.«/ Schiller, Don Carlos.[17] Die drei Fragen vermitteln den Wunsch nach einer grundlegenden historischen Standortbestimmung, mit der Vergangenheit, Gegenwart und Zukunft des Judentums geklärt werden sollen. Das anschließende Zitat aus Schillers *Don Carlos* stellt diese nüchtern-knappen Fragen jedoch in ein ganz anderes Licht. Ihre Bedeutung enthüllen diese Verse aber erst, wenn man ihren Kontext berücksichtigt. Im 21. Auftritt des 4. Aktes treffen die Königin und der Marquis von Posa zusammen. Sein gewagtes Spiel sieht der Marquis für sich verloren. Der Königin übermittelt er seine letzte Botschaft an den Prinzen.

Er mache –/ O sagen Sie es ihm! das Traumbild eines neuen Staates wahr,/ Das kühne Traumbild eines neuen Staates,/ Der Freundschaft göttliche Geburt. Er lege/ Die erste Hand an diesen rohen Stein./ Ob er vollende oder unterliege –/ Ihm einerlei. Er lege Hand an. Wenn/ Jahrhunderte dahin geflohen, wird/ Die Vorsicht einen Fürstensohn, wie er,/ Auf einem Thron, wie seiner, wiederholen,/ Und ihren neuen Liebling mit derselben Begeisterung entzünden. Sagen Sie/ Ihm, daß er für die Träume seiner Jugend/ Soll Achtung tragen, wenn er Mann sein wird,/ Nicht öffnen soll dem tödenden Insekte/ Gerühmter besserer Vernunft das Herz/ Der zarten Götterblume – daß er nicht/ Soll irre werden, wenn des Staubes Weisheit/ Begeisterung, die Himmelstochter, lästert.

Auch in dieser Rede werden die drei Dimensionen der Zeit vergegenwärtigt und zwar im Blick auf die Verwirklichung eines Traumbildes. Im Vordergrund steht aber das unbedingte Festhalten an der Vision, über alle möglichen Enttäuschungen hinweg. Die Begeisterung, der idealistische Enthusiasmus ist für Posa entscheidend. Sie soll stets lebendig bleiben. Der bereits über 50 Jahre alte Cohen hat diesen Enthusiasmus für die zionistische Idee in geradezu ju-

---

[16] Ebd., 88f.
[17] Aus Friedrich Schiller: Don Carlos. 4. Akt, 21. Auftritt, Verse 4278–4296.

gendlicher Weise entwickelt und bis an sein Lebensende bewahrt. Im Nachruf der *Jüdischen Rundschau* steht zweimal der Hinweis auf Cohens jugendliche Begeisterung für den Zionismus. Auch wenn er sich selbst für die praktische Umsetzung des Ideals nicht in dem Maße engagiert hat wie Herzl, so hat er doch die Frage »Was sollten wir sein« Anfang der 80er Jahre für sich in einem unmissverständlichen und nicht mehr revidierten Sinne beantwortet.

In Cohens *Die Judenfrage und die Zukunft* finden wir die vier grundlegenden Überzeugungen der zionistischen Bewegung wieder, die Gideon Shimoni in seinem Buch *The Zionist Ideology* als gemeinsamen Nenner der unterschiedlichen zionistischen Strömungen, die sich vom Beginn der 1880er Jahre bemerkbar machen, zusammengestellt hat. Da sind 1.) Die Definition der Juden als einer Gemeinschaft, 2.) Die Diagnose der augenblicklichen problematischen Situation dieser Gemeinschaft, 3.) Das Eintreten für eine Lösung dieser Situation und 4.) Vorschläge, welche Mittel oder Wege zur Erreichung dieser Lösung verwendet werden sollen.[18]

Cohen schildert im ersten Kapitel die gesellschaftlichen Erscheinungsformen des Antisemitismus des späten 19. Jahrhunderts, die soziale und berufliche Ausgrenzung und den Vorwurf der Zersetzung einer geschlossenen kulturellen Welt der Deutschen. Sehr klar sieht er die Möglichkeit, dass sich diese Zustände in Notzeiten zu Exzessen ausweiten können.

> In Zeiten der Ruhe trägt solche Saat keine andern Früchte als die der erwähnten Gehässigkeiten. – Wie aber, wenn einmal eine Periode grosser Erregung, der Misserfolge, des Elends über das Land kommt? Dann liegt die Gefahr nahe, dass die besonnen und edel Denkenden überstimmt werden und der langverhaltene Hass sich mit Heftigkeit Bahn bricht.[19]

Cohen hat seine Diagnose der gefährdeten Situation des europäischen Judentums und seine Gedanken für eine Lösung jedoch aus einer spezifischen Perspektive heraus entwickelt, nämlich als englischer Staatsbürger, der die alte und ihm fremd gewordene Heimat in ihrer antisemitischen Einstellung mit dem Blick des Fremden betrachtet. In diesem Punkte findet sich eine überraschende Ähnlichkeit mit Moses Hess' Schrift *Rom und Jerusalem*. Zu Beginn des vierten Briefes konstatiert Hess: »Hätte ich nicht in Frankreich gelebt, es wäre mir schwerlich in den Sinn gekommen, mich für die Wiederherstellung unsrer Nationalität zu interessieren«.[20] Erst der Blick vom Ausland her auf die Verhältnisse in dem Land, aus dem er stammte, hat ihn zur Diagnose der prekären Situation der deutschen Juden geführt.

Eine solche vermittelte Perspektive, die vom Fremden her das fremdgewordene Eigene anders zu beurteilen vermag, hat auch Cohen aufgrund seiner in

---

18 Gideon Shimoni: The Zionist Ideology. Hanover, London 1997, 52.
19 Cohen, Das Ideal des eigenen Staates (Anm. 9), 46.
20 Moses Hess: Rom und Jerusalem. Die letzte Nationalitätsfrage. In: ders.: Ausgewählte Schriften. Ausgewählt und eingeleitet von Horst Lademacher. Köln 1962, 221–320, hier 234. Hess lebte ab 1853 in Paris, wo er auch gestorben ist.

England verbrachten Jahre eingenommen. Und wie Hess sich von Frankreich Unterstützung versprach bei der »Gründung von Kolonien«[21] in Palästina, so hat auch Cohen seine Hoffnung auf Englands Hilfe gesetzt. Für ihn ist England keineswegs das Musterbeispiel eines Landes, in dem seine jüdischen Bürger eine unangefochtene gesellschaftliche Präsenz errungen haben, die er sich zum Vorbild für Deutschland nähme. Vielmehr verspricht er sich, ebenso wie Hess von Frankreich, von England die nötige Sensibilität und das Verständnis dafür, dass die Judenfrage nicht in den Ländern der Diaspora zu lösen ist, sondern nur in Palästina.

Es giebt eben nur einen Ausweg: nationale Wiederherstellung, und wenn es hoffnungslos erscheint, das Judenthum des Festlandes, wie es heute besteht, für die Idee zu begeistern, bei den englischen Juden fände sich jene Pietät, jene Anhänglichkeit an ihren Stamm, jenes Selbstbewusstsein, welches zu einem Schimmer von Hoffnung berechtigt. Leider nur zu einem Schimmer! Aber wenn je eine gemeinsame Action des Judenthums in jener Richtung stattfinden kann, ich glaube, von England würde sie ausgehen, oder doch unter den Juden Englands ihre kräftigste Stütze finden. Wer England nicht kennt, glaubt, es sei ein Land der Nüchternheit. Und doch sind gerade ihm grosse Ideen entsprungen, und in ihm hat sich die Begeisterung, die Festigkeit, die Ausdauer zur Ueberwindung aller Schwierigkeiten gefunden. Von diesem Geist haben auch seine jüdischen Söhne etwas angenommen. – Unter ihnen, wenn irgendwo, könnten sich einst die Männer finden, welche bereit sind, Hand anzulegen, und auf diesem Boden wären sie der Sympathie und wahrscheinlich auch der Mitwirkung ihrer christlichen Mitbürger sicher.
Der Anstoss käme vielleicht in einer Zeit, in welcher die Judenfrage zu einer brennenden geworden. – Der aufs äusserste getriebene Antisemitismus würde statt der Krankheit, als welche man ihn betrachtet, gerade ein Heilmittel für das Judenthum. In den anscheinend dem Verfall preisgegebenen Körper dürfte gerade er vielleicht neue Lebenskraft giessen. Auf mich hat die Bewegung schon lange den Eindruck gemacht, als könne gerade durch sie, das Judenthum neu erstarken, sich erheben und veredeln.[22]

Cohen teilt zudem Hess' Kritik an den Emanzipationsbestrebungen des Reformjudentums, für das das jüdische Volk durchaus seine »Mission« in der Diaspora zu erfüllen hat.[23] Denn dass die modernen Juden ihr nationales Gefühl, und sei es auch noch so rudimentär, besser aufgeben sollten, weil die politischen Bedingungen für seine Verwirklichung fehlten, erkennt Hess als einen Trugschluss. Die Juden gehörten vielmehr »zu den totgeglaubten Völkern, welche im Bewusstsein ihrer geschichtlichen Aufgabe ihre Nationalitätsrechte geltend machen dürfen.«[24] Hess konstatiert, dass »die Auferstehung der

---

[21] Ebd., 277.
[22] Cohen, Das Ideal des eigenen Staates (Anm. 9), 62.
[23] Siehe ebd., 58, Anm. 11. Bei Hess, Rom und Jerusalem (Anm. 20), 241 und 262 über die jüdischen Rationalisten: »Nach ihnen wäre die *Zerstreuung* der Juden der *Beruf* des Judentums«.
[24] Hess, Rom und Jerusalem (Anm. 20), 223.

Toten [...] nichts Befremdendes mehr zu einer Zeit [hat], in welcher Griechenland und Rom wieder erwachen, Polen von neuem aufatmet«.[25] Für Cohen
bedeutet die erfolgreiche nationale Befreiung der Völker Europas – »Griechenland, Italien, die Balkan-Völker«[26] – ebenfalls eine wichtige Motivation, es
ihnen gleichzutun und sich nicht von der Selbstaufgabe durch Assimilierung
fesseln zu lassen. Weder die Ratschläge aus dem eigenen noch aus fremdem
Haus zur Emanzipation will er als vernünftige Lösung gelten lassen. »Nur wir
allein, sollen uns nach einer Existenz von mehr als 3000 Jahren, und noch voll
von Lebenskraft, todt erklären!«[27]

Dass die Vorstellung von Israel als einer Nation wie jede andere, als ein
Volk unter Völkern in gleichberechtigter Stellung, von dem traditionell religiösen Verständnis der Einheit des jüdischen Volkes abweicht, die nicht territorialen Ursprungs ist, sondern sich vom Bundesschluss und von der Thora her
legitimiert sieht, spielt für Cohen, der kein religiöser Mensch gewesen ist,
keine entscheidende Rolle. Die Idee der nationalen Wiederherstellung ist für
ihn keine religiöse Forderung, sondern ein sittliches Ideal der Selbstbewusstwerdung eines gedemütigten Volkes, das den Ansprüchen aus seiner Geschichte erneut gerecht werden soll.

> Und wir haben fast eine grössere Berechtigung, ich möchte sagen, Pflicht, an unse
> rem Dasein festzuhalten, als die andern, denn wir haben so viel gut zu machen. [...]
> Wir sind beschmutzt, und wir müssen wieder rein dastehen, der Name ›Jude‹ muss
> wieder zu Ehren kommen.[28]

Im Unterschied zu Cohens wesentlich moralischem Verständnis der Aufgabe
der nationalen Wiederherstellung, ist sich Hess ihrer religiösen Dimension
durchaus bewusst gewesen.

Cohen bleibt in seiner Skizzierung des Lebens der Juden in Osteuropa im
ersten Teil seiner Schrift allzu vage,[29] wenn er den Gedanken der nationalen
Wiederherstellung bei ihnen eine »sehr untergeordnete Rolle« spielen sieht
und hinzufügt: »Es überlässt alles dem lieben Gott«.[30] Cohen spricht ihnen
also eine passive Haltung zu. Dass er die ›Chibat Zion‹-Bewegung im Osten,
die sich Anfang der 80er Jahre im Zuge der Pogrome gebildet hat und die mit
Pinskers 1882 erschienenen Broschüre *Autoemancipation* im Westen bekannt
geworden ist, in seiner Schilderung nicht erwähnt, mag dafür sprechen, dass
dieser Teil von Cohens Darlegungen tatsächlich auf das Jahr 1881 zurückgeht.
Hess, dessen Schrift Cohen kaum gekannt haben dürfte, hatte hingegen schon
sehr klar erkannt, dass die Wurzeln des Nationalgefühls bei den Juden Osteuropas tiefer reichen und historisch weniger versehrt wurden als bei den assimi

---

[25] Ebd.
[26] Cohen, Das Ideal des eigenen Staates (Anm. 9), 49.
[27] Ebd.
[28] Ebd.
[29] Ebd., 52.
[30] Ebd., 53.

lationsbereiten Juden im Westen. Den Grund dafür sieht er gerade in der religiösen Sphäre, nämlich im täglichen Gebet.

> In jenen Ländern, welche den Okzident vom Orient scheiden, in Rußland, Polen, Preußen, Österreich und der Türkei, leben Millionen unserer Stammesgenossen, die Tag und Nacht die inbrünstigsten Gebete für die Wiederherstellung des jüdischen Reiches zum Gott der Väter emporsteigen lassen. Sie haben den lebendigen Kern des Judentums, ich meine die jüdische Nationalität, treuer bewahrt als unsre okzidentalen Brüder, die alles im Glauben unserer Väter neu beleben möchten, nur nicht die Hoffnung, die diesen Glauben geschaffen.[31]

Cohen schränkte jedoch die Tragweite seiner Bemerkungen über das Ostjudentum ein, weil er sie nicht aus eigenem Erleben beglaubigen konnte. Das änderte sich in dem Augenblick, als die Flucht vor den Pogromen die russischen Juden auch nach Hamburg brachte. An ihrer Not erkennt Cohen, dass das politische Schicksal des jüdischen Volkes keine halbherzigen Aktionen mehr duldet.

> Ich [bin] in meiner Meinung bestärkt worden, dass alles was jetzt geschieht, nur Paliativ-Mittel sind, und dass die jetzigen Versuche zu Ansiedlung in anderen Weltheilen, so segensreich sie sich auch für die Einzelnen erweisen mögen, die Stellung des Judenthums in der Welt nicht dauernd verbessern können. – Im Gentheil, ich fürchte noch mehr als früher, dass sie die Krankheit in Lande tragen werden, die bislang von ihr verschont geblieben.[32]

Er verteidigt deshalb sein Zypern-Projekt gegen Kritik und plädiert für einen neuen Versuch.

Im Nachruf der *Welt* vom 21. Dezember 1906 wird Cohens Position in der zionistischen Bewegung mit der der großen Vertreter des Zionismus seiner Zeit verglichen.

> So viel ist gewiß, daß Cohen wie Herzl im letzten Grunde als künstlerisch veranlagte Kulturmenschen von der Schönheit der Idee und der subjektiv erfaßten psychischen Judennot ausgingen. Das Moment des wirtschaftlichen Judenelends überwiegt bei Heß und Pinsker. Den anfangs reinen Judenstaatlern Pinsker und Herzl stehen Heß und Cohen gegenüber, die vom ersten Augenblick an in der Erlangung Palästinas die selbstverständliche Voraussetzung für die Lösung der Judenfrage erblickten. […] Cohens Entwicklung ging vom spekulativen Zionsideal zum vollwertigen Nationalismus. Er begann als kluger Menschenfreund und endete als Jude.[33]

---

[31] Hess, Rom und Jerusalem (Anm. 20), 244.
[32] Cohen, Das Ideal des eigenen Staates (Anm. 9), 81.
[33] Nachruf in *Die Welt* vom 21.12.1906, 14.

Jacob Golomb

Transfiguration of the Self in Herzl's Life and in his Fiction

»*Eretz Israel* is not California,« wrote a Zionist writer in a Socialist Party organ in 1920. »We do not celebrate its land because it contains golden nuggets but because on its ground we hope to mend *the flaws of our souls.*«[1] Herzl aspired to »mend these flaws,« namely to overcome, by Zionism, his problematical syndrome of typical *Grenzjude*. Namely, Herzl attempted to change his existential profile as a German-speaking »marginal Jew« by means of a radical transfiguration of his own self. But before or during performing this formidable task, he delineated and analyzed such transfigurations in his literary fiction, notably in a collection of short stories: *Philosophische Erzählungen*[2] (Philosophical Tales). Thus, Herzl's literary fiction assisted him in the transfiguration of his self by functioning as an experimental laboratory for his existential transformation.

To substantiate this thesis I shall deal with this syndrome of marginality, then analyze several short stories, and finally deal with Herzl's ambivalent attitude toward technological progress. This ambivalency has its roots in his existential objectives. By stressing this ambivalency, which comes to the fore in his short stories, I also wish to correct the view, claimed for example, by David Ben-Gurion, that Herzl »had unlimited faith in science and technology.«[3] This view requires serious qualification, because Herzl's ambivalence toward technology derives from his pragmatic understanding that technology may indeed improve the material well-being of the whole state, but is irrelevant to existential self-transfigurations of individuals like himself and his generation of marginal Jews.[4]

---

1 Azar Rabinovitz: Hirhurim (Meditations). In: Ha-Adamah (The Earth). Tel Aviv: Nissan 1920 (my emphasis).
2 Theodor Herzl: Philosophische Erzählungen. Berlin 1919.
3 See David Ben-Gurion's preface to Theodor Herzl: A Portrait for This Age. Ed. by Ludwig Lewisohn. Cleveland 1955, 14.
4 This section draws heavily from my other publications on this fascinating syndrome of »Jewish marginality«. See Jacob Golomb: Nietzsche and the Marginal Jews. In: Nietzsche & Jewish Culture. Ed. by Jacob Golomb. London, New York: Routledge 1997, 158–192; id.: Nietzsche und die jüdische Kultur. Wien: WUV-Universitäts-Verlag 1998, 165–184; id.: Nietzsche und die ›Grenzjuden‹. In: Jüdischer Nietzscheanismus. Hg. von Werner Stegmaier und Daniel Krochmalnik. Berlin, New York: Walter de Gruyter 1997, 228–246. See also my: Jewish Self-hatred between

I   Herzl as *Grenzjude*

Herzl as a young individual was a very sensitive and highly impressionable Jew in the midst of acute personal crises that involved existential agonies concerning his personal and professional identity. Hence he deeply suffered from what is now labeled as »the syndrome of marginality.«

In this category of *Grenzjuden* (marginal Jews) or stepchildren,[5] one may include, in addition to Herzl,[6] prominent Western European Jewish intellectuals, such as Arthur Schnitzler, Jakob Wassermann, Stefan Zweig, Franz Kafka, Franz Werfel, Kurt Tucholsky, Walter Benjamin, Karl Kraus, Ernst Toller, Gustav Mahler, Sigmund Freud, Max Nordau,[7] and many others. They were *Grenzjuden* in that they had lost their religion and tradition, but had not been fully absorbed into secular German or Austrian society. For some, hatred of their ancestral roots led to self-destruction and breakdown (as in the notable case of Otto Weininger's suicide).[8] These doubly marginal individuals tragically lacked an identity: they rejected any affinity with the Jewish community, but were nonetheless unwelcome among their non-Jewish contemporaries.

According to Gershom Scholem: »Because they no longer had any other inner ties to the Jewish tradition, let alone to the Jewish people,« these marginal Jews »constitute one of the most shocking phenomena of this whole process of alienation.«[9] Yet, despite their desperate attempts to be accepted as Austrians and Germans, most recognized the traumatic truth that, as Arthur Schnitzler put it, »for a Jew, especially in public life, it was impossible to disregard the fact that he was a Jew.«[10]

Central European Jews proposed a wide spectrum of solutions to their unbearable state of uprootedness, from full assimilation, including even conversion to Christianity (Gustav Mahler), to identification with some definite ideological or political cause such as Socialism (Kurt Tucholsky, Ernst Toller) or Zionism (Herzl, Nordau, Buber).

    Universality and Particularity: Nietzsche, Freud and the Case of Theodor Lessing. In: Leo Baeck Year Book 50, 2005.

5   Solomon Liptzin: Germany's Stepchildren. Philadelphia 1944.

6   See Jacob Golomb: Thus Spoke Herzl: Nietzsche's Presence in Herzl's Life and Work. In: Leo Baeck Year Book 34, 1999, 97– 124.

7   See chapter 2 in Jacob Golomb: Nietzsche and Zion. Ithaca: Cornell University Press 2004, 46–64.

8   See Part IV of: Nietzsche and the Austrian Mind. Ed. by Jacob Golomb. Wien: Wiener Vorlesungen und Studien 2004, 191–254.

9   Gershom Scholem: Jews and Germans. In: Commentary. November 1966, 35. The Hebrew version of this article, based on his lecture before the World Jewish Congress held in Brussels on August 1966, appeared in the Israeli daily Ha-aretz on 14.9.1966.

10 Arthur Schnitzler: My Youth in Vienna. Trans. by Catherine Hutter. New York 1970, 6.

Most ideologues of Zionism were primarily focused on establishing a Jewish state and securing a safe shelter for the Jewish people. Many of Zionism's founding fathers were also preoccupied with the creation of socialist institutions in *Eretz Israel*. However, Herzl's socio-political thought, unlike that of his Eastern European followers, who were profoundly influenced by socialist and Marxist movements, was primarily based on the liberal British paradigm and was open to the needs of individuals to express their personal identities. Thus, I concur with Jacob Talmon's perceptive observation: »Herzl's Jewish nationalism« derives from liberal and individualistic categories of thought.«[11] Here, far from claiming, like Ian Buruma, that Herzl was an exponent of European »Anglomania,«[12] I wish to show that Herzl was the first among the Zionist thinkers who believed that Jewish nationhood is a very effective means to attain individual identity and personal authenticity.

Clearly, during his pre-Zionist period, (during which most of his »*Philosophical Stories*« were written), Herzl epitomized the class of the German-speaking *Grenzjuden*. He understood that despite his untiring attempts to be accepted by Austrians as Austrian, he could not disregard the fact that he was a Jew. Hence he wrote bitterly that all the political experience he had gained while working as a correspondent for the *Neue Freie Presse* in France had been for nothing: »It will only benefit those who have the opportunity to enter political life. But for myself? A Jew in Austria!«[13]

Zionism, as envisioned by Herzl, would foster the emergence of a new and unique (that is, authentic) image of the Jew in a society without God and political dogmas. This example of anti-dogmatic, Nietzschean free-thinking has been sometimes narrowly regarded by some historians as shrewd pragmatism. But examining the father of political Zionism through this existentialist prism reveals him as the pioneer of an exciting historical experiment of fostering personal authenticity by creating it for the whole nation.[14] This perspective

---

[11] Jacob L. Talmon: Types of Jewish Self-Awareness: Herzl's ›Jewish State‹ after Seventy Years (1896–1966). In: id.: Israel among the Nations. London 1970, 88–127. See also Ernst Ludwig Ehrlich: Liberalismus und Zionismus. In: Theodor Herzl Symposion. Wien 1996, 35–43.

[12] Ian Buruma: Voltaire's Coconuts: or Anglomania in Europe. London: Weidenfeld & Nicolson 1999.

[13] Herzl's letter to Hugo Wittmann, dated March 30, 1893. Theodor Herzl: Briefe und Tagebücher. Ed. by Alex Bain et. al. Berlin 1983, vol. 1.

[14] Cf. Robert Weltsch's claim that »Zionism is a personal task imposed upon every individual [...] the whole life of the young Jew undergoes a transformation.« Robert Weltsch: Theodor Herzl and We. In: The Young Jew. Series 2. 1929, 23, 24. Recently, these rather neglected ramifications of the Zionist revolution have attracted new attention. For example, Eyal Chowers rightly asserts that »Zionism meant more than political independence in Palestine. It promised both material and spiritual transformation«. Eyal Chowers: Time in Zionism: The Life and Afterlife of a Temporal Revolution. In: Political Theory. 5, October 1998, vol. 26, 652–685. On the

shows that *Der Judenstaat* was not written solely as a reaction to the failures of emancipation and assimilation, but also as an attempt to provide a constructive solution to the syndrome of marginality that at the individual level was the most hideous symptom of this failure.

Herzl believed that the free, creative, and authentic Jew would be more likely to evolve in Zion on virgin ground unstained by what his friend Max Nordau called European »degenerate culture.«[15] In his eyes, the Zionist solution was more authentic than the continuation of assimilation, dissimulation, and the prolongation of the dangerous game of being a »free spirit« in Europe.[16] And this was an historic point in time, when European national and antisemitic oppression had inflicted upon the Jews the crisis of identity that had brought many, including Herzl himself, to the desperate search for authenticity.

If we adopt Nietzsche's formula for authenticity, then Herzl »becomes what he is« by overcoming what he is not:[17] neither an Orthodox Jew, nor a Christian, nor, finally, a marginal Jew. He overcame these potential identities until he became what he wanted to be: a free, secular Zionist and an authentic Jew, who proudly belonged to his people.

The German-speaking marginal Jews were obliged to suppress some of their most vital elements. By doing so, they were prevented from attaining personal harmony and from spontaneously expressing their genuine nature, as Herzl, the herald of Jewish authenticity, claims: »The very act of going this way will change us into different people. We regain once more our inner unity that we have lost and together with it we also gain some character, namely our own, not the false and adopted character of the marranos.«[18]

By the time he left Paris in 1895, Herzl had abandoned his dream of becoming a famous playwright (like his celebrated friend Arthur Schnitzler) and had ceased to live in the existential conditions of the »New Ghetto,« which were unbearable for him. With *Der Judenstaat*, Herzl committed himself to a Jewish-Zionist identity. Nevertheless, the posture of ironic disguise and narrative distance is already quite conspicuous in the *Philosophische Erzählungen* where one of the main philosophical-existentialist leitmotifs is the search on the part of the heroes and heroines for personal authenticity and their desperate attempts to foster for themselves genuine self-transfigurations.

---

   ideal of personal authenticity see Jacob Golomb: In Search of Authenticity from Kierkegaard to Camus. London, New York, Routledge 1995.

[15] See chapter 2 on Nordau in Golomb, Nietzsche and Zion (note 7), 46–64.

[16] See: Jacob Golomb: Stefan Zweig. The Jewish Tragedy of a Nietzschean ›Free Spirit‹. In: Nietzsche and the Austrian Mind (note 8), 92–126.

[17] On the Nietzschean aesthetic model of authentic selves see Jacob Golomb: Nietzsche on Authenticity. In: Philosophy Today 34 (1990), 243–258, and id., In Search of Authenticity from Kierkegaard to Camus (note 14), chapter 4.

[18] Speech before the Israeli Union. In: Pollack (Ed.): Ko Amar Herzl (Thus Spoke Herzl). Tel Aviv 1940, 30 (Hebrew). All quotations from this useable collection are mine.

The title, »Philosophical Tales,« was the title Herzl insisted on giving to his collection of short stories. This fact reveals his aspiration to be considered a thinker, not just a capable journalist; hence some remarks about his attitude to philosophy are called for.

II   Herzl and Philosophy

Herzl's enduring interest in philosophy is already attested to by the fact that his private library in Vienna contained mainly philosophical works and not, as one might expect, books of law. Actually, Herzl, the lawyer, never practiced much. Most of the books from Herzl's private library in Vienna are now located in Jerusalem, in the Central Zionist Archives and in the Herzl Museum. Thus, one may inspect them. Besides most of Nietzsche's books in expensive editions,[19] one can find there a French edition of Francis Bacon; a four-volume edition of Herder; Kant's *Kritik der reinen Vernunft*; five volumes by Lessing; volumes by Rousseau; and a twelve-volume edition of Schopenhauer. A significant part of this library is made up of books that present British political philosophy, a fact that accords with Herzl's liberal socio-political thought.

Besides this evidence of Herzl's special attraction to philosophy, we have other weighty proof for the fact that he aspired to be more than just a serious dabbler in philosophy. For example, in his *Jugendtagebuch*, 1882–1887, he refers to Plato, Aristotle, Kant, Feuerbach, Schopenhauer, Fichte, Hegel, Schelling, and Brentano.[20] In a diary entry of March 21, 1897, he notes that he has sent *Der Judenstaat* to Herbert Spencer with a short letter in which he called Spencer a »great spirit.« Admittedly, Herzl, was not satisfied to approach only businessmen and politicians regarding Zionism. He was very eager to enlist the support of the leading philosophers of his time for the Zionist project, thereby giving the impression that his Zionist agenda had an important philosophical aspect.

Moreover, in his diary he was critical of Rousseau, and he quoted from works by Kant, More, and Voltaire that can be still found in his private library. Furthermore, after Herzl had moved with his family from Budapest to Vienna in 1878 and began studying at the law faculty of the University of Vienna, he attended Brentano's lectures on practical philosophy. This shows that from the beginning of his academic studies Herzl was attracted to philosophy to such an

---

[19] Herzl's private library contains the following editions of Nietzsche's works: Jenseits von Gut und Böse. Leipzig 1886; Zur Genealogie der Moral. Leipzig 1887; Morgenröte. Leipzig 1887; Also sprach Zarathustra. Leipzig 1886; Die fröhliche Wissenschaft. Leipzig 1887; Die Geburt der Tragödie. Leipzig 1886; Der Fall Wagner. Leipzig 1888; Menschliches, Allzumenschliches. Leipzig 1886; Unzeitgemässe Betrachtungen. Leipzig 1886; Götzen-Dämmerung. Leipzig 1889.

[20] Herzl, Briefe und Tagebücher (note 13), vol. 1, 585–648.

extent that he even took extracurricular courses and studied philosophy with the very famous Austrian philosopher, Franz Brentano.

Sigmund Freud also attended Brentano's lectures while studying medicine at the university as a contemporary of Herzl. It may well be that these two great Jewish figures met – they were virtually neighbors – without, however, becoming friends. One may imagine the possible comic scenario where Herzl, lying on the psychoanalytical sofa of his friend in Bergasse 19 says: »Dear Dr. Freud, I had a dream of a Jewish State […].« Surely Herzl would become cured of some of his neurotic symptoms, but whether he could be cured of his dream of a Jewish State seems doubtful!

III   The Search for Authenticity in the *Philosophische Erzählungen*

The Zionist revolution would enable »new Jews« to decide whether to go to Zion or stay in Europe. However, for such a mental transfiguration, Herzl needed the kind of psychology that Nietzsche called the »bitter psychology« which unmasks weaknesses that must be overcome.[21] Herzl frequently conducted psychological examinations along these lines: »I found out that the great are petty, as petty as myself.« However, Herzl's »petty self« aspired to attain the greatness of a Bismarck, an »active psychologist who read individual souls as well as of the soul of the crowd.«[22] Such a reading of the human soul is manifested in the *Philosophische Erzählungen*. These stories were written not long before as well as after Herzl's transfiguration into the new figure of a Zionist Jew – indeed, the very act of writing them assisted him in this painful process. The main existential motifs of these stories are: the search for an authentic existence beyond dissimulation and deceit; the transfiguration of one's character from its low level of passive, feeble existence to active, proud, vital patterns; and insights into the nature of human beings and their »human, all too human« elements (to use the title of Nietzsche's work that was found in Herzl's private library).

What is more, the stories are impressionistic and unstructured, with a flow of spontaneous associations that evidence more concern with aphoristic brilliance than with systematic consistency. All these literary characteristics corroborate Raoul Auernheimer's observation that Herzl owed a large debt to Nietzsche's style and literary genius.[23]

More important, however, the content of these stories also bears a distinctive Nietzschean-existentialist imprint. One of Herzl's stories, *Der Ge-*

---

[21] See Nietzsche and Depth Psychology. Ed. by Jacob Golomb, Weaver Santaniello and Ronald Lehrer. New York: University of the State of New York 1999.
[22] Pollack (Ed.), Ko Amar Herzl (note 18), 108, 89.
[23] Raoul Auerhheimer: Uncle Dori: Memories of a Cousin and a Literary Colleague. In: Theodor Herzl: A Memorial. Ed. by Meyer W. Weisgal. New York 1929, 35.

dankenleser (»The Mind Reader«) written in 1887[24] before the beginning of his Zionist period, depicts the search for authenticity and the rejection of falsehood, in a kind of Nietzschean thought-experiment. It deals with a man who »sees falseness everywhere,« who observes the shifts in behavior patterns from »*echt*« (genuine) to »*unecht*.« Herzl's hero claims that »it is a disaster to know how to read our thoughts.« However, fully authentic life is not possible in European society, as Nietzsche had also claimed. Thus, Nietzsche situated his hero of optimal authenticity, Zarathustra, in a cave, far removed from human society. In contrast to Nietzsche's hero, the hero of Herzl's story has »social inclinations« and is married (though, like Herzl, not happily). Herzl, who at that time was also preoccupied in finding a political solution to the problem of Jewish authenticity, could not entertain Nietzsche's idea of the splendid isolation of the authentic *Übermensch*. Hence he did not wish to sever authenticity so radically from the social sphere.

Nonetheless, it is clear that during his intensive search for a political solution to the Jewish Question, Herzl was also deeply preoccupied with the issue of authenticity that had bothered him as a *Grenzjude*. He deals with this existentially crucial problem by a conscious use of Nietzschean formulae. For example, the key formula of Nietzschean authenticity – »How does one become what one is?« – is phrased by Herzl in *Der Gedankenleser*[25] in a similar manner : »This is the question of experiences that make me what I am.« Herzl also adopts a psychologizing attitude when he encounters, with the hero of his story, »all the ugliness and filth that stirs and lives in the soul.« These Nietzschean motifs reappear in two other philosophical stories: *Die Garderobe* and *Pygmalion*, but this time another Nietzschean leitmotif is added: the belief in our ability to transfigure ourselves so that we become what we are. A fateful change takes place in the heroine behind the mask of make-up in the theater in *Die Garderobe* and she becomes »completely different from what she was.« In *Pygmalion* it appears that Herzl, like most existential thinkers, does not believe in a rigid and permanent human essence. Instead, he adopts the dynamic-evolutionary view of the free creation of personality. The impresario, who is the chief character of the story and who probably represents Herzl himself, undergoes a significant transformation from playwright to political director on the stage of the reborn nation. In other stories, estrangement is prevalent, and their wandering heroes manifest syndromes of marginality and fluctuate from one definition of identity to another. Herzl himself, from the dubious status of an assimilatory *Grenzjude*, underwent »a fateful shift« and »a full transfiguration of the spirit« to become a proud statesman with a definite vision and identity.

---

24 Theodor Herzl: Der Gedankenleser. In: Wiener Allgemeine Zeitung, May 25, 1887.
25 Surprisingly, this philosophically significant story was not included in *Philosophische Erzählungen*. It appeared first in the *Wiener Allgemeine Zeitung* and then in: Theodor Herzl: Neues von der Venus. Plaudereien und Geschichten. Leipzig 1987.

Such an aesthetic staging of identity is arranged by Herzl under the ironic disguise of the figure of the impresario, the narrator and hero of the 1888 story, *Der Aufruhr von Amalfi*. Herzl's theatrical experience is applied in this story to arouse the dormant Jewish masses for a significant move from the new and old ghettos. »The real impresario is capable of staging street-shows« and political theater, in which Herzl excelled. Thus, the impresario of this story, who adopts a condescending, paternalistic, and aristocratic tone toward the »mob,« arranges an ecstatic mass orgy in which the »mob« wants to tear the impresario apart as a result of »the crazy and wild drives that erupted.«[26] Herzl deals in this story with the lowest motivating force: unrestrained greed. He uncovers regions of the ›psyche‹ and he directs their energy into political activity. His writings are a kind of a psychological laboratory, whose findings he applies in life itself: »The marketplace in Amalfi is the world with its ugly life of rioting.«[27]

Herzl also expresses the inner pathos of his protagonists, their reflections, and introspection in their attempts to comprehend their »roots« and their existential experiences. In *Die schöne Rosalinde* Herzl presents the extreme experience of a character who sees his own skeleton and draws existential conclusions from this encounter with finality and death. Another Nietzschean motif appears here: overcoming sickness to attain psychological insights: »The sickbed made more than one into a philosopher.«[28] The same truly Nietzschean spirit is also expressed in a reference to the »birth-pangs of a self-knowledge« by a character who wishes to return from his inauthentic »escape« from himself.[29] In this context Herzl mentions the search by the »modern man« for »a remedy« and meaning, and reflects about »philosophy« and »true poetry« and about the disabling effects of reflection.

The »small letters« of the »human, all too human« soul, namely our most secret drives, appear as a motto in *Eine Gute Tat*. The epigraph reads: »You have done a good deed, be careful to conceal its reasons.«[30] This aphorism and the theme of the story show a deep suspicion of our conscious motives for our actions. The motif finds its expression in the aphorism that so excited Freud, who (like Herzl) was deeply influenced by Nietzschean psychology: »›I have done that,‹ says my memory. ›I cannot have done that,‹ says my pride, and remains inexorable. Eventually – memory yields.«[31]

Herzl could also have employed this aphorism for another short story, *Sarah Holzmann*, in which he states that »the motives for our actions are sometimes quite odd and most of the time very gloomy.« These actions are rooted mainly in the unconscious, as he indicates by quoting the term *unbewusst* from a poem by Friedrich Rückert.

---

[26] Herzl, Philosophische Erzählungen (note 2), 91ff.
[27] Ibid., 93.
[28] Ibid., 179.
[29] Ibid.
[30] Ibid., 221
[31] Friedrich Nietzsche: Jenseits von Gut und Böse. Leipzig 1886, section 68.

This last motif recurs in several stories, conspicuously in *Die Raupe*, in which the hero Fritz reads a chapter from Hyppolyte Taine's *De l'intelligence* on the »metamorphosis of the caterpillar into a butterfly.«[32] *Das Wirtshaus zum Anilin*, written the same year as *Der Judenstaat*, expresses the belief that a new image of mankind can be created and shaped by sublimating despair. This story focuses on the sublimation of »the most offensive material,«[33] in that Herzl employs chemical terms that lie at the root of the concept of *Sublimierung*. He proclaims the existential significance of death for self-overcoming on the way to greatness, since »one cannot reach philosophical height if one has not squarely faced death.«[34]

Herzl deals in most of these stories with the »attractive power of the abyss« and returns in *Die Heilung vom Spleen* to the fundamental idea of his play *Solon in Lydien*, namely that »we human beings, cannot live without distress.« The Nietzschean and Freudian motifs of sublimating our more basic drives to create aesthetic and cultural values and the »metaphysical comfort« of art, (the leitmotif of Nietzsche's *Birth of Tragedy*), reappear in the story *Sarah Holzmann*. It presents »a little Jewess« who sings and plays music produced by the sublimation of her sufferings since »our best achievements were reached out of our torments.« The conclusion of this story is presented directly by the narrator, who confesses: »Art has always been a great comforter in my life, because it is capable of turning pain into flowers that give joy to other people, especially to those who are troubled and oppressed.«[35]

This remark is clearly autobiographical. Herzl, with his own troubled personal life, sublimates his marginality through creative writing and overcomes it through political activity. The main aim of this activity is to provide the right conditions for the creation of a new image of a Jew who sublimates his sufferings as the marginal »slave« to become a »master.«

Although Herzl cites Schopenhauer in his story *Die Güter des Lebens,* written in 1898, and calls him »the great pessimist,« he emphatically rejects Schopenhauer's metaphysical pessimism. This is a story about a literary-philosophical experiment – the prearranged meeting of four friends twenty years after they have graduated, each of whom has followed his own path to find meaning and value in life. Three of them depict their disappointments with materialism and the social value of wealth, the shallow and illusory value of honor, and the emptiness of the values of family and subsistence. Only the fourth friend, Wilhelm, asked at the start of his existential journey about »that which fulfills a man.«[36] Hence, only he succeeds in gaining the »internal results of the success« in »this philosophical wager,« in which appearances and

---

[32] Herzl, Philosophische Erzählungen (note 2), 214.
[33] Ibid., 263.
[34] Ibid., 264.
[35] Ibid., 55.
[36] Ibid., 121.

external layers are illusions and there are no guarantees for attaining a truthful life or a meaningful answer to the existential question of »why« and »what for.« Wilhelm, like Herzl himself, »when he finished his studies at the university, tried for a while to be a writer.« He went »on trips to England and France« to learn »about modern movements of social welfare.«[37] This was undoubtedly Herzl's hint at the nature and the objectives of his Zionist project.

Also important is the fact that in sharp contrast to Schopenhauer's view of ›blind Will‹ and its manifestations as pure evil, Herzl emphasizes the sober optimism that values the very act of willing and of hope as ends in themselves, since belief in the future »is the only thing in which one is never disappointed – because the future is never here.« Thus, Herzl adopts the attitude expressed in most of Nietzsche's writing: that the way is the goal. A similar idea is presented by Herzl in the story since only Wilhelm, who sought an existential goal that cannot be fully reached, namely personal authenticity, attained his goal. This existential insight is expressed politically by Herzl's famous claim: »Zionism is the Jewish people on the road.« Herzl, who according to the popular simplistic perception was a »romantic dreamer« or »a naïve prophet,« appears here as a cautious, realistic optimist.

It is likely that Zionism, which engrossed Herzl during the writing of these stories, and which sealed his troubled journey to shape his own authentic identity, is what prevented him from becoming seriously engaged with psychological philosophy. As a genuine »impresario« or composer of his own life, Herzl managed to transfigure it, and in doing so to attain his own authentic identity. It may well be that Herzl was even more optimistic than Nietzsche. Perhaps Nietzsche's optimism was too weak and restrained for Herzl. We should not forget that Herzl sought to advance the Jewish people and their culture to reach the sublime achievements represented in *Die Güter des Lebens*, in which he expresses his enthusiasm for »our great cultural achievements. For we live in a time that reminds one of the glorious age of the Renaissance and the Reformation.«[38]

But, on the more personal level it becomes clear that Herzl aspired to overcome the inauthentic existential marginality, which was characteristic of him and other acculturated European Jews, by means of Zionism. His attempts are vividly portrayed in his *Philosophical Stories* which could also be called: »In Search of Herzl's Personal Authenticity.«

IV   Herzl on Technology

Herzl's preoccupation with authenticity accounts, in my view, for his ambivalence regarding technological and cultural »progress.« These cannot be of any help in his attempts to foster a transfiguration of the self. In fact, the common

---

[37] Ibid., 129.
[38] Ibid., 128.

belief that Herzl believed unreservedly in progress and in the »heaven« that science and technology would bring to humankind and to Zion is far from exact. In *The Dirigible Airship*, one of his »technological« stories and also a fable about Zionism, Herzl tempers his enthusiasm for this revolutionary invention. He asserts that people are not worthy of flying: »The way they now are crawling is still good for them.«[39] There is therefore a good chance that they will misuse this invention for evil deeds and thereby »bring new forms of misery.« He repeats his warning regarding technological progress elsewhere: »The scientific revolutionaries prepare salvation from known distresses, thereby immediately instigating new miseries.«[40] It appears that Herzl's faith in technological progress stemmed solely from pragmatic Zionist needs and that he harbored no illusions about it. Such an attitude is incompatible with the optimistic outlook of someone who fully believed in Enlightenment, progress, education, human reason, and the moral improvement of humankind resulting from the advancement of science. Still, it seems that despite these reservations about our »human, all too human« nature and about the increasing gap between ever-improving technological knowledge and deteriorating morality, an element of optimism does appear, since these technological inventions will bring »an improvement in the welfare and mores« of humankind. Thus, Herzl's optimism is tempered by »human, all too human« nature, which could turn technological and scientific progress into a moral nightmare.

Moreover, Herzl's revolutionary Zionism was nourished by the collapse of religious and secular linear historical narratives that believed in teleological or rational progress. Historical time and consciousness became open to any kind of »monumental« adventure or intervention without any clear course, and without commitments to earlier eschatological stories of coming salvation and deliverance. Herzl had arrived on the European scene in an age when belief in God was declining, and when the prevalent ethos derived from the Enlightenment's metanarrative of progress was in an accelerated process of what after Nietzsche was called a »*décadence*.« Herzl's Zionist ideology celebrated the Jewish people's capacity to begin something completely new where nothing had existed before but the relics of the »destroyed Old Temple.« These historic »infinite horizons« and opportunities became open to fresh cultural and social projects that Nietzsche was enticing people »to experiment with.« Herzl, with his determination, imagination, and personal courage, was exactly the right man at the right time to follow this Nietzschean call to overcome the »old« time. In so doing he would begin a radically new history that would sweep away the maladies of the new and old ghettos and overcome the syndromes of marginality and tradition.

Still, Herzl believed in the positive consequences of the notion of cyclicity and recovery of the ancient language, land, and values, which necessitated a

---

[39] Ibid., 38.
[40] Pollack (Ed.), Ko Amar Herzl (note 18), 88.

move backward to the point of origin where authenticity and harmony had resided. These positive dimensions made Zionism into a viable ideology and successful mass movement without which the present state of Israel would have been inconceivable. Despite the inherent tension between negative and historically open dimensions and positive, past-related values and legacies, both were required by Herzl in his Zionist program. However, for the practical implementation of his vision he also needed to employ pragmatic tools such as technology and scientific advancement.

It seems that Herzl accepted technological advancement as a lesser evil out of the sober and affirmative realization that this development »cannot be restrained and halted,« as he wrote in »Der sterbende Fiaker,« in *Neue Freie Presse* in April 1898. Furthermore, Herzl, as a genuine liberal pragmatist, argued in favor of the use of technology for the well-being and freedom of the individual. This notion is vividly expressed in his story *Radfahren*, which appeared in the *Neue Freie Presse* in November 1896. But Herzl is well aware of technological flaws and of the price to be paid for them, hence his cautious and sometimes ironic attitude. This irony reaches a pinnacle in his story *Das Automobil*, written in 1899: »The machine has, as it were, the capacity to be improved, which cannot be said with the same certainty about living creatures.« Here, Herzl ironically terms the crisis of modernity, *pace* Hobbes: »Bellum omnium contra omnibus.« Given all this, one can certainly understand that Herzl's psychology softened his pragmatic »technological« inclinations. »How quick becomes our driving [...] how slow is our wisdom,« he declares in a brilliant aphorism[41] characteristic of the period of his life when he began his transfiguration from »caterpillar« to authentic »butterfly,« from marginality to Zionism.

Conclusion

Marginal Jews considered Jewish orthodoxy, in the words of one of their eloquent spokesmen, Franz Werfel, to be the »holiest fossilization.«[42] Herzl's image of the »new Jew« demanded that the Jews overcome their rabbinical consciousness, around which they had structured their Jewish »antiquarian« identity in the diaspora. Herzl stipulated that they adopt instead a »monumental« approach centered around the grandeur of their glorious days in ancient Israel. Thus Herzl, who returns »home,« insisted upon returning to the historical and authentic sources of the Jewish people: »Zionism is a return to Israel before the return to *Eretz Israel*,« and »though we had to become a new people, we will not deny our ancient race«.[43]

---

[41] Theodor Herzl: Das Automobil. In: Neue Freie Presse, August 6, 1899.
[42] Franz Werfel: Between Heaven and Earth. Trans. by Maxim Newmark. London 1947. Foreword (1944), VIII.
[43] Pollack (Ed.), Ko Amar Herzl (note 18), 13, 76.

Herzl, indeed believed in the slow but more reliable process of education, cultivation, and development of habits of thought and living, that is, in the creation of a »second nature.« This quite monumental task required a »monumental« historical consciousness, which would assist the Jewish people, in general, and marginal Jews, in particular, in withstanding the torments of transfiguration and help them to attain their glorious future. Thus, Herzl nurtured a »monumental« mission and distinguished between »mundane history« and »glorious history«: »All these petty, unknown, noisy, and insignificant men, who devise plots, overturn governments, and do not sense where they are directed [...] act in history [...] without any objective and choice.«[44] In a sharp contrast, Herzl stresses his own »monumental« vocation: »I feel within myself a great power which is ever-increasing toward the splendid mission.« He looks to the past of the Jewish people through the selective prism of »monumental« consciousness and asserts that »owing to all our troubles we became decadent and the opposite of what we have once been: a nation gifted with tremendous talent.« He refers to heroic ages and seeks to revive Jewish greatness: »I believe that on this earth will grow a generation of wonderful Jews. The Maccabees once more will come into being.« As the leader of a national revival of a glorious past, Herzl sees himself and his companions from the monumental historical perspective: »I will fight courageously. But all these who are accompanying me will become great historical figures.«[45] He reflects on the fate of an eminent leader vis-à-vis the pettiness of the masses: »I know that the highest objective of democracy is to get rid of singular individuals for the sake of the common good [...]. Great men of spirit [...] are estranged from their people just as well as the people are strangers to them [...].«[46]

Herzl does not shun greatness, because »it is he who seeks greatness that is in my eyes a great man, not the one who has attained it.« He draws the strength for his determination and his aspirations for greatness from the splendid past of his people. Zionism is a political-practical materialization and revival of this »monumental« past: »I am not presenting to you a new ideal; on the contrary it is a very old one. This is the idea that dwells in each of us, it is as ancient as our people, who never have forgotten it.« Therefore, »we need Maccabees who know how to work: to work with their spirits and their hands.«[47]

In his speeches and writings, Herzl emphasized the »normal« work that »new Jews« would undertake in their old-new state. To arrive at this conception, of course, he had to align himself with the Jewish masses in the diaspora. Despite his »aristocratic« aversion to them, Herzl was well aware that his Zionist revolution needed the Jewish masses. Thus, he sought to entice his

---

[44] Ibid., 83–84.
[45] Ibid., 72, 106.
[46] Ibid., 87, 92.
[47] Ibid., 92, 31, 7. Herzl identified with another »monumental« leader of ancient Israel, Moses, about whom he planned to write »a biblical drama« (ibid., 109).

people, using symbolic rituals to enable them to uncover in themselves personal and national powers that had remained dormant in the diaspora. The masses needed slogans. Thus, this charismatic man supplied the Jewish masses with slogans and phrases in an attempt to entice them to transform themselves, as he transformed his own self. However, he confined his personal journey towards an authentic life to a heroic attempt of overcoming the syndrome of marginality within his subjective experience. This process took place in the deepest mental recesses of Herzl's soul, since »we ourselves want to advance to a new morality,« and »one who wants to attain to greatness has first of all to conquer his own self.«[48]

---

[48] Ibid., 90, 97.

Klaus Hödl

Theodor Herzl and the Crisis of Jewish Self-Understanding

In 1882 *Kadimah*, the first Jewish nationalist student organization in Western Europe, was founded in Vienna. It was to become one of Theodor Herzl's earliest and strongest supporters.[1] Its early members, such as Reuben Bierer, Moritz Schnirer, Perez Smolenskin, et al., were almost all exclusively of East European origin.[2] They banded together primarily to react to the prevailing indifference of the city's highly integrated Jewry to Judaism.[3]

Little more than a decade later the Viennese Jewish museum opened its doors to visitors interested in Jewish culture and history. It was established by the »Gesellschaft für Sammlung und Conservirung von Kunst- und historischen Denkmälern des Judentums« (hereafter referred to as »museum society«), the members of which consisted of some highly acculturated Jews.[4] At that time Vienna could boast having the first Jewish museum in the world.[5] Kadimah and the Jewish museum were not the only institutions that made the Habsburg capital a trailblazer for new developments. Vienna, by electing Karl Lueger its mayor, also gained the questionable reputation of being the first capital in Europe to be governed by an antisemitic party.[6] Furthermore, at least until Theodor Herzl's death in 1904, the Austrian capital could declare itself the center of political Zionism.

All four instances bespeak a cultural milieu that characterized Vienna and distinguished it from other cities. To be sure, the Jewish museum and political Zionism did not retain their hue of being exclusively Viennese. It did not take long for Zionist headquarters to move to Berlin, and Jewish museums, or at least the exhibition of Judaica and the presentation of Jewish historical narratives in a museum setting, could also be found in Germany soon after the es-

---

[1] Robert S. Wistrich: The Jews of Vienna in the Age of Franz Joseph. Oxford: Littman 1990, 349.
[2] The only exception was the Viennese-born Nathan Birnbaum.
[3] Nathan Birnbaum: Gegen die Selbstverständlichkeit. In: Festschrift zur Feier des 100. Semesters der akademischen Verbindung *Kadimah*. Ed. by Ludwig Rosenhek. Mödling 1933, 30.
[4] Oesterreichische Wochenschrift 43 (1897), 861.
[5] Klaus Hödl: Jüdische Identität und Museum. Das Wiener jüdische Museum im 19. Jahrhundert. In: transversal 1:3 (2002), 47.
[6] Steven Beller: Theodor Herzl. Wien: Eichbauer Verlag 1996, 46.

tablishment of the museum in Vienna.[7] Neither was antisemitism a phenomenon restricted to the Habsburg capital. Nevertheless, specific Viennese conditions cannot be totally disregarded in explaining why it was first in this city that a Jewish museum and a Jewish nationalist student organization were established, why a declared antisemite was elected mayor, and why Herzl set out to organize (political) Zionism.

Delineating the impact of the Viennese cultural setting on Herzl will be one of the two purposes of this essay. The other aim is to explore Herzl's ties to Judaism, especially to the organized Jewish community.

In the 1880s and early 1890s, Herzl pursued assimilation.[8] In various statements he disparaged Jews, distanced himself from them, and expressed his desire to become a full-fledged citizen of the larger society.[9] Yet, all his assimilationist endeavours notwithstanding, Herzl's views of Jews and Judaism were in line with perceptions of other liberal Jews, locating him in a particular Jewish discourse rather than on the brink of cutting all bonds with the Jewish milieu. Sometimes, Herzl's conceptions even adhered to a specific Jewish intellectual tradition. He was thus firmly rooted in a community of like-minded Jews, consisting mostly of assimilationists. Like Herzl, they strove to become accepted members of the society at large, no longer stigmatized by their Jewishness. In not yet being fully acknowledged by Gentiles, but already estranged from traditional Judaism, they occupied a site that might be designated as the Third Space,[10] situated in the border area between traditional Jewish and non-Jewish cultural spheres. However, since these Jews were largely acting alone without the Gentiles, their performance was overwhelmingly a Jewish undertaking. Thus, Herzl as an assimilationist did not really step beyond a Jewish sphere.

Stressing this perspective of Herzl means that his later development into a Zionist was not a journey from utmost alienation from the Jewish world to Jewish nationalism, but rather a reorientation of a certain kind of Jewishness. He did not articulate his assimilationist orientation as an outsider to the Jewish world, and Zionism was not »the ultimate version of that practice dubbed co-

---

7   See Katharina Rauschenberger: Jüdische Tradition im Kaiserreich und in der Weimarer Republik. Zur Geschichte des jüdischen Museumswesens in Deutschland. Hannover: Verlag Hahnsche Buchhandlung 2002 (Forschungen zur Geschichte der Juden, Abteilung A: Abhandlungen; 16); Jens Hoppe: Jüdische Geschichte und Kultur in Museen. Zur nichtjüdischen Museologie des Jüdischen in Deutschland. Münster: Waxmann 2002, 31–34.

8   Michael Brenner: Warum München nicht zur Hauptstadt des Zionismus wurde – Jüdische Religion und Politik um die Jahrhundertwende. In: Zionistische Utopie – israelische Realität. Religion und Nation in Israel. Ed. by Michael Brenner and Yfaat Weiss. München: C. H. Beck 1999, 41.

9   Bernard Avishai: The Tragedy of Zionism. Revolution and Democracy in the Land of Israel. New York: Farrar Straus & Giroux 1985, 36.

10   Jonathan Rutherford: The Third Space. Interview with Homi Bhabha. In: Identity. Community, Culture, Difference. Ed. by Jonathan Rutherford. London: Lawrence and Wishart 1990, 211.

lonial mimicry,« as Daniel Boyarin wrongfully claims.[11] Rather, Herzl must be understood within a larger Jewish context.

The second part of this paper pursues a different approach. Its purpose is to show that Herzl's conversion to Zionism was very much embedded in the Viennese cultural context, which also led to the founding of Kadimah, to the establishment of the Jewish museum, as well as to the election of Lueger. It goes without saying that the city's specific cultural make-up influenced not only various segments of the Jewish community, but had a major impact on non-Jewish groups as well. Since Jews and Gentiles constituted the cultural setting, its impact came to bear on both groups. It is not surprising that many similarities between Jews and non-Jews existed. As Schorske has shown, there were concrete resemblances between Herzl and non-Jewish politicians, even with those who pursued an antisemitic policy, such as Georg Ritter von Schönerer and Karl Lueger.[12] These similarities, however, were not related to the content of their respective policies, but only to their performance.

By emphasising the impact of an intellectual Jewish milieu as well as the Viennese cultural setting on Herzl's activities, I hope to add new perspectives to an understanding of his achievements.

Theodor Herzl in the Viennese Jewish Setting

Theodor Herzl changed his attitude about the relationship between Jews and non-Jews several times before he arrived at his conception of Zionism. All these stages were characterized by his striving to nullify extant antisemitic stereotypes and to attain Gentile acknowledgement of the Jews as equals. Although he remained steadfast to these aims, the means he deemed to be efficacious for achieving them altered. As Jacques Kornberg has delineated, they included assimilationist approaches such as conversion, intermarriage, or the mastery of duelling, followed by the realization of socialist teachings, and, lastly, the founding of a Jewish state.[13] These plans were not viewed as optional solutions to the »Jewish question,« but they were proposed over time in succession. Their elaboration was heavily influenced by the cultural configuration of Vienna in the late nineteenth century.

In the early stage of his preoccupation with the »Jewish question,« Herzl proposed assimilation as the most appropriate means for its solution.[14] He thought that the absorption of the Jews by the Gentile population would trans-

---

[11] Daniel Boyarin: Unheroic Conduct. The Rise of Heterosexuality and the Invention of the Jewish Man. Berkeley: University of California Press 1997, 305.

[12] Carl E. Schorske: Fin-De-Siècle Vienna. Politics and Culture. New York: Cambridge University Press [6]1981, 133.

[13] See Jacques Kornberg: Theodor Herzl. Bloomington: Indiana University Press 1993.

[14] Schorske, Fin-De-Siècle Vienna (note 12), 146.

form the Jews, thereby erasing all differences between them and non-Jews and finally bringing about a relationship between the two that was based on mutual respect. He did not doubt the existence of »Jewish peculiarities,« which in itself may already be regarded as an outcome of his assimilationist stance. There was thus a »tautological logic« on which Herzl's whole undertaking was predicated: He expressed opinions about Jewish deficiencies that he had adopted from the Gentile population, because of his dominant assimilationist orientation. He favored Jewish assimilation because he thought the Jews were stricken by these shortcomings. Herzl considered the Jewish body to be peculiar body and the Jewish mental physiognomy[15] to be debased and effeminate.[16] All these abnormal characteristics were to be »normalized« through adaptation to the larger society.

Although Herzl adopted contemporary anti-Jewish stereotypes, he still differed from antisemites in that he adduced different reasons for Jewish peculiarities. For him it was not their biological constitution that caused their assumed physical and psychological deformation. Rather, historical circumstances under which Jews had to eke out their existence were largely responsible for this situation. A revealing case in point for Herzl's attitude is represented by his reading of Eugen Dühring's *The Jewish Problem as a Problem of Racial Character and Its Danger to the Existence of Peoples, Morals and Culture*, one of the earliest racial antisemitic books in German. The author described Jews as having a crooked morality and a lack of ethical seriousness – ideas with which Herzl readily agreed.[17] In contrast to Dühring, however, he did not consider race as the decisive factor for the Jews' »faulty character.« Instead, he traced it back to the particular living conditions in their past, especially to their oppression by Gentiles.[18]

Herzl's partial concurrence with Dühring and other antisemites in their view of Jews indicates the large extent to which he shared a mode of thinking that was predominant towards the end of the nineteenth century. However, in bringing forth an explanation of the alleged Jewish mental and physical properties that differed from the reasons voiced by most non-Jews, Herzl's line of argument was very much embedded in a Jewish discourse. This view was largely maintained by assimilationist Jews, although religiously-minded Jews, such as the Viennese Rabbi Adolf Jellinek,[19] shared it as well. According to the latter, there was no doubt that Jews were effeminate and that anyone who wanted to understand the Jewish character had to study the female psyche.[20]

---

[15] Theodor Herzl: Briefe und Tagebücher (8.2.1882). Jugendtagebuch 1882–1887. Berlin: Propyläen 1983, vol. 1, 609.
[16] Herzl, Briefe und Tagebücher (Brief an Moriz Benedikt, 27.12.1892), 506.
[17] Herzl, Briefe und Tagebücher (9.2.1882) (note 15), 612.
[18] Ibid.
[19] Wistrich, The Jews of Vienna in the Age of Franz Joseph (note 1), 114–121.
[20] Adolf Jellinek: Der jüdische Stamm. Wien ²1886, 31.

Herzl's notion of the effeminate Jew, though, was not only in accordance with perceptions held by Jellinek, but was voiced by many other Jews as well. It found its most elaborate expression in the book *Geschlecht und Charakter* by Otto Weininger.[21] The conception of Jewish differences, especially of the effeminate Jew, was thus in wide circulation around the turn of the twentieth century.[22] It was articulated not only by antisemites, but also by many – and not only assimilationist – Jews.

Against this background, it is fair to state that an understanding of Herzl's views of the Jews requires a closer examination of Viennese Jewry, or at least of a particular segment of the city's Jews. Even though Herzl, as an assimilationist, seemed to be willing to leave the Jewish world behind, he was very much entrenched in a milieu of like-minded Jews. Thus, the Viennese cultural setting was a major influence on Herzl's design for a Jewish state, as I will demonstrate, and the Jewish intellectual milieu exerted a decisive impact on Herzl's assimilationist stance.

Theodor Herzl's Participation in the Jewish Discourse

In the nineteenth century, especially in its closing decades, purportedly scientific studies on differences between Jews and non-Jews abounded.[23] With secularization – religion's loss of influence not only on people's lives but also as an explanatory factor for phenomena in the realm of nature – and the emergence of physical anthropology and biology as leading scientific disciplines,[24] the distinction between Jews and Gentiles was being determined anew. Difference was no longer seen as having a religious origin, but came to be located in the body. Jews were held to differ from Gentiles in their specific susceptibili-

---

[21] Cf. Otto Weininger: Geschlecht und Charakter. Eine prinzpielle Untersuchung. München: Matthes & Seitz 1980; Nachdruck von 1. Auflage, Wien: Braumüller 1903, 403–440. Im Weiteren: Jews and Gender. Responses to Otto Weininger. Ed. by Nancy A. Harrowitz and Barbara Hyams. Philadelphia: Temple University Press 1995; Jacques LeRider: Der Fall Otto Weininger. Wurzeln des Antifeminismus und Antisemitismus. Wien: Löcker Verlag 1985.

[22] Klaus Hödl: Die Pathologisierung des jüdischen Körpers. Antisemitismus, Geschlecht und Medizin im Fin de Siècle. Wien: Picus 1997, 164–232.

[23] See Ludwig Stieda: Ein Beitrag zur Anthropologie der Juden. In: Archiv für Anthropologie 14 (1882), 61–71; Bernhard Blechmann: Ein Beitrag zur Anthropologie der Juden (gedr. Med. Diss.). Dorpat 1882; Constantin Ikow: Neue Beiträge zur Anthropologie der Juden. In: Archiv für Anthropologie 15 (1884), 369–389.

[24] Cf. George W. Stocking, Jr.: Victorian Anthropology. New York: Free Press 1987; George W. Stocking, Jr.: Race, Culture, and Evolution. Essays in the History of Anthropology. Chicago: The University of Chicago Press ²1982; Peter J. Bowler: The Mendelian Revolution. The Emergence of Hereditarian Concepts in Modern Science and Society. Baltimore: John Hopkins University Press 1989.

ties to disease,[25] their peculiar bodily measurements[26] and their mental physiognomy.[27] These alleged Jewish characteristics were deemed to be scientifically proven, the outcome of numerous »objective« studies.

The introduction of the concept of race[28] provided a new dimension for the whole undertaking of dealing with the »Jewish question« in a scientific way, in that Jews were no longer held to have the possibility of shedding their assumed peculiarities by altering their living conditions, which had been the belief not only of Jews, but also of many liberally-oriented Gentiles since the Enlightenment.[29] Consequently, it widened the gap between perceptions of Jews and non-Jews. Whereas the latter increasingly tended to back racial theories, Jewish scientists continued tracing the cause of specific »Jewish characteristics« to particular historical and environmental circumstances.[30]

The fact that Jewish scientists did not normally question the concept of »Jewish difference« altogether should not be a great surprise. Due to their education and professional training, they were hardly in a position to doubt the data provided by numerous studies in medicine or anthropology. Both Jewish and non-Jewish scientists constituted a scientific community whose members worked with the same paradigms.[31] Anyone who repudiated them would have been ousted from this community, barred from professional advancement and, to a large extent, also from access to publishing. Being a maverick in the field of science can sometimes be a decisive prod to reach new insights, as Sigmund Freud himself attested.[32] Yet, in most cases, it is tantamount to being neglected by colleagues and, ultimately, to professional failure. This must have been a

---

[25] Cf. Hödl, Die Pathologisierung des jüdischen Körpers (note 22); Klaus Hödl: Gesunde Juden – kranke Schwarze. Körperbilder im medizinischen Diskurs. Innsbruck: Studien Verlag 2002; John M. Efron: Medicine and the German Jews. A History. New Haven: Yale University Press 2001; Heinrich Singer: Allgemeine und spezielle Krankheitslehre der Juden. Leipzig: Benno Konegen 1904.

[26] Cf. Sander L. Gilman: The Jew's Body. New York: Routledge 1991; Mitchell B. Hart: Social Science and the Politics of Modern Jewish Identity. Stanford: Stanford University Press 2000.

[27] See Max Sichel: Über die Geistesstörungen bei den Juden. In: Neurologisches Centralblatt 8 (1908), 351–367; Alexander Pilcz: Geistesstörungen bei den Juden. In: Wiener klinische Rundschau 47 (1901), 888–890.

[28] Cf. Ashley Montagu: Man's Most Dangerous Myth. The Fallacy of Race. Walnut Creek: AltaMira Press 1997.

[29] Cf. Johann Ludwig Ewald: Projüdische Schriften aus den Jahren 1817–1821. Heidelberg: Manutius Verlag 2000 (Exempla Philosemitica; 2); Christian Wilhelm Dohm: Über die bürgerliche Verbesserung der Juden. Berlin 1781.

[30] See John M. Efron: Defenders of the Race. Jewish Doctors and Race Science in Fin-De-Siècle Europe. New Haven: Yale University Press 1994, 58–90.

[31] Ludwik Fleck: Entstehung und Entwicklung einer wisenschaftlichen Tatsache. Einführung in die Lehre vom Denkstil und Denkkollektiv. Frankfurt/M.: [2]1993.

[32] Dennis B. Klein: Jewish Origins of the Psychoanalytic Movement. Chicago: University of Chicago Press [2]1985, 86.

central reason for the Jewish failure to question the data on »Jewish difference.« However, although they accepted the data as facts, they very often found sufficient latitude in interpreting them without necessarily resorting to race theories.

Herzl's concept of abnormal Jewish peculiarities was in congruence with the views of many Jewish scientists. Accordingly, he considered Jews to be especially susceptible to certain diseases and to have peculiar bodily characteristics.[33] His perception resulted from his participation in the intellectual and cultural life of his social environment. As a journalist he could not distance himself from contemporary strands of thinking. Yet his views did differ from those of his intellectual surroundings to a certain and decisive extent in that he did not agree on the reason for the Jews' unique characteristics. Had he accepted the notions of Jewish characteristics circulating in the larger society at face value, he would have had to consider himself as a fundamental »other,« essentially different from the Gentile population and unable ever to close the alleged, racially determined gap between him and the non-Jewish part of society. This, however, was not in accordance with his assimilationist stance. In consequence, he provided an explanation for »Jewish physical and psychological deficiencies« that considered them to be the outcome of social circumstances. In this way he could contrive ways and means for Jews to alter their characteristics and become fully integrated into society.

The second characteristic that defines Herzl as being firmly rooted in a community along with many other assimilationist Jews concerns his view of the past. His assertion that historical living conditions must be held accountable for the Jews' purported physical and psychological shortcomings can be placed in an intellectual tradition, the beginning of which dates back to the activities of a small group of reform-minded Jews sometimes called the Science of Judaism, in the early nineteenth century.[34] Their central achievement was the introduction of historical consciousness into modern Judaism.[35] Up to this time, Diaspora Jewry had hardly developed historical thinking. By and large, they conceived their history as a period that lay between their ancient past, when they were still in possession of a homeland of their own, and the future advent of the Messiah.[36] The Diaspora itself was basically seen as a static time, when nothing fundamentally changed and history was not characterized by progress, but by its circular course.[37]

---

[33] Alex Bein: Theodor Herzl. Wien: [2]1974, 192.

[34] Michael A. Meyer: Jewish Religious Reform and Wissenschaft des Judentums. The Positions of Zunz, Geiger and Frankel. In: Leo Baeck Institute Year Book 16 (1971), 21.

[35] This view has also been challenged lately. Cf. Shmuel Feiner: Haskalah and History. The Emergence of a Modern Jewish Historical Consciousness. Oxford 2002.

[36] There were also exceptions to this mode of thinking, however rare they were, especially in the sixteenth century. Cf. Yosef Hayim Yerushalmi: Zachor: Erinnere Dich! Jüdische Geschichte und jüdisches Gedächtnis. Berlin: Wagenbach 1996, 68.

[37] Amos Funkenstein: Perceptions of Jewish History. Berkeley: University of California Press 1993, 120.

The Science of Judaism set out to interpret history rationally, i.e., without any reference to a metaphysical agency and by introducing the concept of development.[38] At the same time, its representatives divided the past into a magnificent era of Sephardic Jewry that lasted until their expulsion from Spain in 1492 and an ignoble Ashkenazic past, characterized, as Leopold Zunz (1794–1886) described it, by »vulgar rabbinism« and »its sophistic method of studying the Talmud.«[39] Abraham Geiger (1810–1874), another founder of the Science of Judaism, claimed that Ashkenazic Jews lived in a »dark Age, incapable of thinking thoughts other than those dictated by the very rabbinic authorities who had kept them in a stranglehold for centuries.«[40] According to these views it was not only the oppression by Gentiles that caused the Jews' alleged deficiencies, but also the Jews' imperviousness to contemporary intellectual life, their clannishness, and self-isolation.

It was in the intellectual tradition of the Science of Judaism that Herzl expressed part of his Jewish identity. Whereas he took much pride in his – purported – Sephardic origin, claiming that his great-grandfather was a Spanish Jew,[41] he repudiated Ashkenazic Judaism. He held the Talmud and the role of the rabbis as outmoded.[42] Herzl expressed criticism concerning pre-emancipatory Ashkenazic Judaism, as well as regarding its present-day traditional variety that he located in Eastern Europe. He disparaged Eastern Jews by calling them, for instance, »semi-Asiatic.«[43]

Herzl lashed out against Eastern Jews because he blamed their tenets of Judaism for not being in accordance with the thinking and values that were considered normative by the Gentile part of society. It was traditional Jewish life that provided the major reason for the Jews' abortive attempts to become fully integrated. However, in his endeavour to make Jews abandon all their characteristics that seemed to prevent full integration, he waged his battle in a Jewish intellectual environment, in line with other assimilationist Jews. Whereas many Gentiles tended to consider all Jews as diseased and degenerate and therefore not fit for full integration, Herzl and his Jewish allies saw only the Eastern Jews as corresponding to this category.

A third characteristic that put Herzl firmly in the fold of other assimilationist Jews was his specific kind of attachment to Judaism. Even though his ties to

---

[38] Michael A. Meyer: Judaism within Modernity. Essays on Jewish History and Religion. Detroit: Wayne State University Press 2001, 128.

[39] Ismar Schorsch: From Text to Context. The Turn to History in Modern Judaism. Hanover/NH: Brandeis University Press 1994, 213.

[40] Talya Fishman: Forging Jewish Memory: Besamim Rosh and the Invention of Pre-Emancipation Jewish Culture. In: Jewish History and Jewish Memory. Essays in Honor of Yosef Hayim Yerushalmi. Ed. by Elisheva Carlebach, John M. Efron and David N. Myers. Hanover: Brandeis University Press 1998, 72.

[41] Kornberg, Theodor Herzl (note 13), 76.

[42] Ibid., 23.

[43] Ibid., 80.

the Jewish religion were very loose, he maintained an allegiance to it. The same holds true for other liberal-minded Jews of his time. Many of them were estranged from the religious world and slack in performing their religious duties. However, like Herzl, they continued to cling to Judaism. This was primarily a result of their memories. Their own religious experiences belonged to the past and could only be recollected. Owing to them, in fact, they were part of the family life of their childhood, which exerted a formative impact on their Jewish identity. Hence, it was primarily their remembrance of their parental families that constituted their adherence to Judaism.[44]

Herzl's ties to Judaism can be taken as exemplary for the purposeful replacement of religious practices in the present with family memories as the predominant form of expressing Jewishness. His »tie to Jewry,« writes Jacques Kornberg, »had nothing to do with Jewish knowledge or belief; it was maintained through a filial bond.«[45] Herzl remembered fondly or in a positive spirit his attendance of synagogue services with his father, and through his recollections he maintained an allegiance to the Jewish world.

Memory thus represented the central tie to Judaism for Herzl and other assimilationist Jews in the late nineteenth century. This finds its paradigmatic expression in the Viennese Jewish museum. The central part of its exhibition was the *Gute Stube*, a room conveying the atmosphere of a Sabbath celebration. It was designed to evoke a time when Jews still observed this day in a religious way. The museum's aim can be seen to have been achieved, according to the view of the Russian-Jewish anthropologist S. Weissenberg, who visited it in the early twentieth century. He described his impressions of the museum in an article that he published shortly afterwards. He pointed out that in looking at the *Gute Stube*, the visitor is overwhelmed by wistful feelings for the long-lost, good old days; the visitor finds himself transported back to his childhood, and instinctively looks around, searching for his grandparents to wish them »a good Shabbes.«[46] For Weissenberg, Sabbath celebration belonged to the past and was intimately connected with memories of his grandparents.

Performing religious duties had been largely abandoned by many Viennese Jews by the end of the nineteenth century. It solely existed in their memories, thereby being bound up with recollections of family life with their parents. Remembering that lost world constituted the only attachment to Judaism. This, however, was so common among Jews that it generated a widespread feeling of nostalgia for the past, leading to expressions of cultural memory.[47] In this

---

[44] Miriam Gebhardt: Das Familiengedächtnis. Erinnerung im deutsch-jüdischen. Bürgertum: 1890 bis 1932. Stuttgart 1999 (Studien zur Geschichte des Alltags; 16).

[45] Kornberg, Theodor Herzl (note 13), 84.

[46] Samuel Weissenberg: Jüdische Museen und Jüdisches in Museen. Reiseeindrücke. In: Mitteilungen der Gesellschaft für jüdische Volkskunde 23:3 (1907), 87.

[47] Regarding the notion of »cultural memory« cf. Jan Assmann: Das kulturelle Gedächtnis. Schrift, Erinnerung und politische Identität in frühen Hochkulturen. München: C. H. Beck ²1999.

way, Jewish identity was strengthened again. Herzl's position may thus be called assimilationist, but it hardly signified his looming abandonment of his Jewish ties. It was rather the expression of a state typical of many liberal-minded Jews in his time, which even led to a solidification of Jewish consciousness.

To summarise the material regarding Herzl's assimilationist stance, it is fair to say that he was acting within a Jewish milieu. In his alienation from Judaism and even repudiation of it, he did not distinguish himself much from many of his fellow Jews, who, like Herzl, also sought integration into society and acknowledgement by the Gentiles. Herzl's endeavours were thus in line with the strivings of many other Jews; he participated in a collective Jewish undertaking. Herzl never left the Jewish fold, however radical his solutions to the »Jewish question« may have appeared.

Herzl's allegiance to Jewry and Judaism was strengthened in the 1890s when he developed from an assimilationist to a Zionist. The Viennese cultural setting was of central importance to his conversion. In this article, two major components of this cultural configuration will be emphasized. Neither of these elements was specifically Viennese. Nevertheless, in their particular hue and correlation to each other they generated a peculiar climate that had a decisive impact on Herzl.

Fin-de-Siècle Vienna

Vienna underwent dramatic changes in the second half of the nineteenth century. Among the most conspicuous developments was a staggering increase in its population, caused by migration from the various provinces under the Habsburg crown. Within the range of its present day geographic boundaries, Vienna encompassed only 401,000 residents in 1830, whereas by 1910 it was home to some two million people.[48] The city's Jewish population increased at an even greater pace. In 1830 around 1,000 Jews lived in Vienna, and by 1910 they numbered 175,000.[49] The growth in population exerted an indelible impact on the city, especially on its political and cultural configuration. Among the many effects on the city, two aspects will be emphasized which characterized Vienna probably more than any other European city and thus influenced the setting in which Herzl founded the Zionist movement.

---

[48] Michael John/Albert Lichtblau: Schmelztiegel Wien. Einst und Jetzt. Zur Geschichte und Gegenwart von Zuwanderung und Minderheiten. Wien: Böhlau 1990, 12.

[49] Marsha L. Rozenblit: Die Juden Wiens 1867–1914. Assimilation und Identität. Wien 1989, 24.

The Shift from the »Written« to the »Spoken« Word

The first aspect heavily influenced and shaped by the many migrants arriving in the Austrian capital is related to its cultural profile. The newcomers settled mostly in the suburbs of the city, on its periphery, at a distance from the center, where not only the emperor reigned, but where all the important political and administrative institutions were located, and where wealth resided and imperial glamour was at home.[50] Vienna's topography came thus to be structured according to the status, that is, the occupation, wealth, education, etc. of its residents.

In accordance with these parameters was a cultural divide. The suburbs were largely characterized by a confluence of the various cultural heritages immigrants had brought with them from their home provinces. They constituted an oral culture, that is, one based on the spoken word. People adhering to this culture tended to express themselves through »performances«;[51] their self-perception lay with the performative element.[52] This is not to say that the newcomers were all illiterate. Rather, in this particular case, »performance« refers to a cultural realm characterized by popular culture, festivities, ceremonies, rituals, customs, and traditions.[53] It can be contrasted with the elite culture that was strongly influenced or characterized largely by the written word. The geographical space associated with this written culture's predominance was Vienna's first district and its adjacent neighbourhoods, where the major educational institutions, libraries, and theatres could be found. It may therefore also be called the realm of textual culture.

This topography, dividing Vienna into two culturally distinguishable zones, was connected to the distribution of power, the centre of which was largely congruent with the realm of the written word. The apparent confluence of textual culture and power, as opposed to the lack of power characteristic of oral culture, was mirrored in a political demonstration which took place in September 1911, against the economic policy responsible for rising food prices. The demonstrators gathered in Vienna's periphery, moved towards the center of the city, and destroyed schools, libraries, laboratories, etc. in their path.[54] The representative demonstrators from the world of the spoken word thus vented their anger and lamented their powerlessness vis à vis current

---

[50] Wolfgang Maderthaner/Lutz Musner: Die Anarchie der Vorstadt. Das andere Wien um 1900. Frankfurt/M.: Campus 1999.

[51] The notion of performance has various meanings. Cf. Mieke Bal: Kulturanalyse. Frankfurt/M.: Suhrkamp 2002, 263–294; Uwe Wirth (Ed.): Performanz. Zwischen Sprachphilosophie und Kulturwissenschaften. Frankfurt/M.: Suhrkamp 2002.

[52] Erika Fischer-Lichte: Theater als Modell für eine performative Kultur. – Zum *performative turn* in der europäischen Kultur des 20. Jahrhunderts. Saarbrücken 2000 (Universitätsreden; 46), 4.

[53] Maderthaner/Musner, Die Anarchie der Vorstadt (note 50), 38–47.

[54] Ibid., 22–33.

economic policies by attacking those institutions that symbolized the culture of the written word and which legitimized the current power structure.

Vienna's peculiar cultural divide was also reflected in its party politics. The inner city seemed to be the stronghold of the Liberals, whereas the periphery tended to provide the constituency for the parties relying on the masses. It was fertile ground for those ideologies that addressed the plight of the poor and offered alternatives to their miserable material existence. Thus, the periphery was the home base of Socialism and the anti-capitalist teachings of the Christian-Socialists. Karl Lueger, who headed the latter group, defeated the Liberals for the first time in the 1895 municipal elections. It was not only a victory against political competitors, but also a major success for the power of the spoken word and for political antisemitism.

Antisemitism as a Political Factor

Beside the various political and cultural consequences of Lueger's victory for society at large, it had particular repercussions for Jews. Many of them, a far greater proportion than non-Jews, belonged to the Liberals, be it due to ideological conviction or because they, at the least hesitatingly, fought antisemitism. Consequently, the Liberals' defeat left many Jews not only without an influential ideological home, but also without a political party that was in a position to counter antisemitic activities. The Social Democrats, who also attracted Jewish politicians and voters and who fought, at least to a certain extent, antisemitism, had very little political power at the time and therefore did not yet represent an adequate alternative for many Jews.[55]

The Liberal's electoral loss was concurrent with a cultural shift in Viennese policy, namely from the written word to the spoken word in the sense I have elaborated above. Among other things, this meant that Jews not only lost an ally in their fight against antisemitism, but that its political and cultural preconditions changed as well. In the heyday of political liberalism, and thus of the realm of the written word, specific wishes of particular social entities were usually brought to the attention of politicians by way of personal intervention by the groups' representatives. This procedure was most successful the more the respective interlocutors could argue that the whole society would benefit from the realization of their interests. Consistently, the fight against antisemitism was led by the representatives of the board of the Jewish community, and they sought to persuade politicians that suppressing anti-Jewish activities would be beneficial for the entire monarchy.[56] The Jewish community

---

[55] Wistrich, The Jews of Vienna in the Age of Franz Joseph (note 1), 228.
[56] Walter R. Weitzmann: Die Politik der jüdischen Gemeinde Wiens zwischen 1890 und 1914. In: Eine zerstörte Kultur. Jüdisches Leben und Antisemitismus im Wien

thus kept largely quiet in public; while it seemed to be rather passive, it eagerly worked for its own interests »behind the scenes.«

This closed-door policy became increasingly threatened by the culture of the spoken word by the end of the nineteenth century. Politics in the realm of the spoken word was politics for the masses. Making politicians aware of specific political interests was no longer solely a matter of personal intervention, but could be achieved by pressure from the populace. Lueger himself was swept into office by the masses. He benefited from an electoral reform in 1882 that granted the right to vote to people who paid five florins or more in taxes,[57] significantly increasing the number of eligible voters. Among these new voters were the lower middle classes and artisans, who opposed liberal policies and advocated protective measures against economic competition.[58] Lueger capitalized on this fact by supporting their claims.[59] Another factor contributing to his political success was antisemitism. He employed it as a means to unite his nationally diverse constituency, in that it gave them an enemy they could all agree on.[60] Their anti-liberal and anti-capitalist grudge could thus find a vent and be projected onto a concrete foe.

Lueger also won people over to his party by making use of the performative element. In contrast to attracting voters mainly through political programs and goals, mass politics strongly appealed to people's emotions. Political campaigns were turned into shows and events. Lueger grasped the new performative trend faster than any of his competitors and became an expert in political performance. His party »staged rallies, parades, and demonstrations throughout the city, with bands playing their new campaign song, ›The Lueger March.‹«[61] The shift in culture from text to performance, which could be called the »performative turn,«[62] thus produced a new form of politics, contributing to the political ascent of Lueger and thereby to the growing importance of antisemitism as a political factor.

The culture of the spoken word, relying on the performative element and on support from the masses, was rabble-rousing, demagogic, and employed antisemitism. In contrast, efforts to combat antisemitism belonged mostly to the

---

seit dem 19. Jahrhundert. Ed. by Gerhard Botz, Ivar Oxaal and Michael Pollak. Buchloe 1990, 199f.

[57] Peter Pulzer: The Rise of Political Anti-Semitism in Germany and Austria. Cambridge/MA: Harvard University Press ²1988, 168.

[58] John W. Boyer: Political Radicalism in Late Imperial Vienna. Origins of the Christian Social Movement 1848–1897. Chicago: University of Chicago Press 1981, 184–246.

[59] George E. Berkley: Vienna and Its Jews. The Tragedy of Success 1880s–1980s. Cambridge/MA: Abt Books 1988, 97.

[60] Wistrich, The Jews of Vienna in the Age of Franz Joseph (note 1), 229.

[61] Berkley, Vienna and Its Jews (note 59), 99.

[62] Erika Fischer-Lichte: Ästhetische Erfahrung. Das Semiotische und das Performative. Tübingen 2001, 13.

culture of the written word. The rise of the spoken word was thus congruent to the demise of exactly that culture that was averse – even though more superficially than profoundly – to Judaeophobia and thus provided methods to counteract it. At a time when antisemitism was as fierce as never before and reached a new climax,[63] the familiar protections against antisemitic excesses became obsolete. This can be demonstrated by the record of the »Verein zur Abwehr des Antisemitismus,« established in 1891 by a few non-Jewish liberals, such as Arthur Gundaccar Freiherr von Suttner, the husband of the Novel Prize winner Bertha von Suttner, the famous physician Hermann Nothnagel, Friedrich Freiherr von Leitenberger, and others.[64] Their goal was to ward off the antisemitic onslaught. However noble their aims, the Verein disbanded after only a few years of existence due to a lack of resonance. The cause for its failure might partially be seen in its reluctance to employ oral and populist methods of communication, i.e. to focus on the performative element. Only once, in 1892, did the Verein organize a demonstration and send its supporters onto the streets. This was when the Verein exerted its greatest influence.[65] However, the Verein usually pursued its goals by intervening with politicians, even though this approach no longer seemed to be very efficacious.

The 1890s, the decade in which Theodor Herzl became a Zionist, was thus characterized firstly by a new political culture in which the performative element played an increasingly important role and secondly, although closely related to the first, a growth in antisemitism, probably best reflected in Lueger's election as mayor. They were two conspicuous, intimately related characteristics of Vienna's culture at the end of the nineteenth century. They questioned any feeling of Jewish belonging and shattered many people's identities. All social strata and groups were touched by these developments, but due to Judaeophobia, Jews were probably affected more than others.

Both antisemitism and the rise in the performative component in culture were not unique to Vienna. In the Habsburg capital, however, they were more salient than anywhere else; they played a greater role and gave the city a distinctive character. This was especially the case with the »performative turn,« i.e. the shift from the written to the spoken word. Although it could be observed all over Europe,[66] one of its central expressions, the theatrical element in public life, was probably nowhere else as prevalent as in the Austrian capital. This feature may be traced, possibly, to its Baroque heritage.[67]

---

[63] Peter Pulzer: Jews and the German State. The Political History of a Minority, 1848–1933. O.O.: Wayne State University Press ³2003, 105.

[64] Cf. Jacques Kornberg: Vienna in the 1880s. The Austrian Opposition to Anti-Semitism. The Verein zur Abwehr des Antisemitismus. In: Leo Baeck Institute Yearbook XLI (1996), 161–163.

[65] Ibid., 170.

[66] Fischer-Lichte, Theater als Modell für eine performative Kultur (note 52), 7.

[67] Allan Janik: Vienna 1900 Revisited. In: Rethinking Vienna 1900. Ed. by Steven Beller. New York: Berghahn Books 2001 (Austrian Studies; 3), 35.

In the following section, I delineate aspects of Herzl's Zionist stance as a response to the two aspects of Vienna's cultural configuration mentioned above. His Zionism will be contrasted to the stated policy of the Viennese Jewish Museum. The goal of this comparison is to outline Herzl more clearly as a figure acting in a particular Viennese context.

The Response to Antisemitism

The upsurge of antisemitism Viennese Jews had to face in the 1880s and 1890s differed from former waves of hostility. It was no longer tied to narrow or specific aims, such as barring the Jews from economic competition, but was also employed to marginalize or even socially exclude them. Jews responded to these challenges in various ways. One reaction consisted in the pursuing of assimilation even more doggedly than before. The rise in intermarriage may be taken as indicative of this trend.[68] Another response points towards a strengthening of Jewish consciousness, reflected by intensified social relations among Jews themselves, as the growing number of Jewish societies indicated,[69] and by a greater interest in their own cultural heritage, especially in their history and literature.[70]

This development, usually summarized under the term »Jewish Renaissance,« is frequently equated with endeavours to halt further social integration.[71] However, this was not always the case. Some segements of Jewry also initiated new efforts to achieve the goal of becoming an acknowledged part of the larger society, all anti-Jewish hostility notwithstanding. Such a course was mainly taken by Jews who had been very acculturated and to a large extent had already shed their Jewish heritage, when antisemitism awakened them to their being Jewish.[72] Consequently, they were impelled to deal with their Jewish-

---

[68] Rozenblit, Die Juden Wiens 1867–1914 (note 49), 134.

[69] Michael Pollak: Kulturelle Innovation und soziale Identität im Wien des Fin de siècle. In: Botz/Oxaal/Pollak, Eine zerstörte Kultur (note 56), 89.

[70] See in general: Jacob Borut: Vereine für jüdische Geschichte und Literatur at the End of the Nineteenth Century. In: Leo Baeck Institute Yearbook 41 (1996), 93; Louis Maretzki: Geschichte des Ordens Bnei Briss in Deutschland 1882–1907. Berlin 1907, 156.

[71] Olaf Blaschke: Bürgertum und Bürgerlichkeit im Spannungsfeld des neuen Konfessionalismus von den 1830er bis zu den 1930er Jahren. In: Juden, Bürger, Deutsche. Ed. by Andreas Gotzmann, Rainer Liedtke, and Till van Rahden. Tübingen: Mohr Siebeck 2001 (Schriftenreihe wissenschaftlicher Abhandlungen des Leo Baeck Instituts; 63), 63.

[72] A case in point was the Jewish merchant and member of the Board of the IKG, Sigmund Mayer, who started to become aware of being Jewish with the growth of antisemitism. In his autobiography he writes: »Ich hatte eigentlich schon ganz vergessen, daß ich Jude war. Jetzt brachten mich die Antisemiten auf diese unangeneh-

ness and determine its content. Due to their background, they showed only little readiness either to relate it to religious Judaism or to associate it with loosening the ties to their non-Jewish social environment. Instead, they tried to identify with a version of Judaism that would allow them to adhere to their acculturated habits and even to continue to cling to integration. In order to achieve this aim, they reinterpreted the Jewish religious heritage from a present-day perspective and did thus invent new Jewish traditions.[73] Thereby, they wanted to present an image of Judaism to Gentiles, with which the latter would find favor. In this way the barriers set up against their complete integration by the new outburst of antisemitism would be overcome.

The »museum society« as well as Herzl pursued this approach. They both reacted to antisemitism by constructing new Jewish traditions, which were designed to enhance Jewish self-consciousness and to improve the negative notion of Jews harbored by Gentiles. The means, however, by which they tried to reach this goal, differed. In contrast to Herzl, the »museum society,« at least in its early years, did not encourage Jews to emigrate to Palestine. Instead, they articulated the aim of becoming fully enfranchised citizens in the Diaspora in Vienna.[74] Although they were aware that assimilation had ultimately failed, they did not relinquish their hope of becoming integrated. They merely altered the strategy to meet this end. At issue was no longer the extent to which Jews should jettison their cultural heritage, but the degree to which they could assert their distinctiveness in order to become socially respected. The Jewish museum thus made efforts to display a version of Judaism that encompassed values that Gentiles also held in high esteem. Central to these was the family.[75] In this way, as the members of the »museum society« assumed, they would induce non-Jews to revise their negative attitude towards Jews and Judaism.

As the »museum society's« General Assembly in 1900 attests, this strategy seemed to be successful. A Dr. Cornill, a Protestant theologian from the University of Breslau, had been invited to deliver a guest lecture. In his speech he touched upon the »Jewish sense of family« that in his view was »highly developed.«[76] He also admonished Jews not to neglect their family ties, because, if anything, it would be their exemplary family life that would put an end to antisemitism.[77] Cornill's lecture, especially the conclusion, was very much in accordance with the aim of the museum. Firstly, Judaism was set in a positive light, and secondly, Jews were provided with the prospect that Judaeophobia

---

me Entdeckung.« (Sigmund Mayer: Ein jüdischer Kaufmann 1831–1911. Lebenserinnerungen. Leipzig: Dunker & Humblot 1911, 289).
[73] On this point see Eric Hobsbawm/Terence Ranger (Ed.): The Invention of Tradition. Cambridge: Cambridge University Press [3]1985, 4.
[74] Hödl, Jüdische Identität und Museum (note 5), 56.
[75] Klaus Hödl: The Turning to History of Viennese Jews: Jewish Identity and the Jewish Museum. In: Journal of Modern Jewish Studies 3:1 (2004), 25–26.
[76] Oesterreichische Wochenschrift 51 (1900), 909.
[77] Ibid., 900.

might disappear. Additionally, both points were stressed not by a fellow Jew expressing only his hope of improved relations between Gentiles and Jews, but by a non-Jew, even an assertive Christian. Cornill's lecture basically seemed to render the museum's goal achievable: to counteract antisemitism by making Judaism socially respectable.

As was the case with the »museum society,« Herzl also realized the failure of his assimilationist efforts of the 1880s and early 1890s. He similarly set out to alter his strategy pursued thus far, without ever swerving from the goal to become acknowledged by Gentiles as an equal. Similar to the »museum society,« Herzl wanted to present a form of Judaism that would no longer serve as a target of scorn, but would meet with favourable resonance. Amongst other values, he also held Jewish family life as exemplary, as he emphasised in his play, »The New Ghetto.«[78] The major – and indeed decisive – difference between the Jewish museum and Herzl lay in the latter's design to establish a Jewish state. Herzl's plan was based on the assumption that Jews could only jettison their purported malicious traits caused by their Diaspora experiences in their own homeland, and thus be transformed into respectable people. The aim of a Jewish state thus did not deviate from the former goal pursued by assimilation, that is to say to become acknowledged as equals by Gentiles; only the strategy differed. As Jacques Kornberg formulated it: »The purpose of the Jewish departure from Europe and of statehood was to reconcile Jews and Gentiles, not to renounce Europe but to identify with it, not to emphasize differences between Jews and Gentiles, but to eliminate them.«[79]

To summarize the impact of antisemitism on Viennese Jews, it can be stated that it was a major impetus for Herzl's conversion to Zionism, as well as for the establishment of the Jewish museum. Both responses to the flare-up of anti-Jewish hostility in the 1890s were directed at asserting Jewishness or Jewish identity. This is not to say, however, that they pursued this aim at the cost of severing ties with Gentiles. Rather, the display of Jewish distinctiveness was to serve the goal of becoming respected by the Gentiles. Regarding the »museum society« the goal was further integration, while for Herzl the aim was for Jews to be acknowledged as equals.

The Response to the New Importance of Performance

The rise of antisemitism was closely connected to the gain in importance of the culture of the spoken word. Cultural meaning was increasingly expressed by way of performance, as was, for instance, the articulation of social adhesion and exclusion. Lueger, just to provide an elucidating example, heavily drew on

---

[78] Kornberg, Theodor Herzl (note 13), 140.
[79] Ibid., 179.

the performative element in order to encourage cohesiveness among the lower middle classes and to distinguish them from the Jews.

To the extent that Herzl and the Jewish museum responded to the outburst of antisemitism, they also reacted to the rise in relevance of performative culture. As has been mentioned above, the Jewish museum was an institution through which highly acculturated Jews sought integration into society at large. In the nineteenth century, Viennese Jews frequently expressed allegiance to the dominant culture by asserting their distinction from Eastern Jews. This cultural positioning became especially exigent when thousands of Jews from Eastern Europe, especially from Galicia, started to migrate to Vienna.[80] Although they brought with them a cultural heritage that differed from the cultural outlook of the integrationist Viennese Jews, Gentiles normally lumped all Jews together into one category of undesirables. The members of the Viennese museum society reacted to their being confounded with the Eastern Jews by drawing a clear line between the immigrants and themselves. In marking the cultural difference, they were engaging in »performance.«

This approach found its paradigmatic expression in a play on the ghetto of Prague, performed by the renowned actor at the famous Burgtheater, Adolf von Sonnenthal.[81] Besides his appearance at the theatre, Sonnenthal was Vice-President of the »museum society.« He thus represented a Jew who was widely acculturated and integrated into society at large; his ennoblement by the Emperor, to which the »von« in his name attests, bespeaks this fact. Simultaneously, he asserted his Jewish identity, as his affiliation with the Jewish museum indicates.

On the occasion of the first General Assembly of the »museum society« in 1897, Sonnenthal entertained people who were present at the event by simulating a conversation between two old »Ghetto-Jews.«[82] In order to do so he spoke Yiddish, that is, he tried to imitate it. He had to take pains in order to make his Yiddish sound authentic and thereby the whole performance took on a humorous tone.[83] Amusing the audience with imitations of ghetto types, however, was tantamount to deriding their culture. In this way, Sonnenthal (through his acting) as well as the audience (through their reactions) expressed their disapproval of Eastern European Jews and distinguished them and their religion from the religious and cultural heritage of Viennese Jews. Sonnenthal drew the line between Galician and Viennese Jews solely by means of his performance, and, as a matter of fact, through the interaction with the audience, whose interpretation of Sonnenthal's acting was likewise important for the constitution of its meaning. He did not have to explain the negative connotation of Yiddish. His parody sufficed to ridicule the language and, consequently, the whole of East European Judaism.

---

[80] Cf. Klaus Hödl: Vom Shtetl an die Lower East Side. Galizische Juden in New York. Wien 1998; Klaus Hödl: Als Bettler in die Leopoldstadt. Galizische Juden auf dem Weg nach Wien. Wien: Böhlau 1994.

[81] Berkley, Vienna and Its Jews (note 59), 4.

[82] Oesterreichische Wochenschrift 20 (1897) 413.

[83] Ibid., 413.

In this case, the museum supporters drew upon the performative element in order to articulate their familiarity with the dominant culture and thereby their worthiness to become socially accepted by it. They tried to overcome the hindrance to their integration by depicting the Eastern Jews as those who displayed those purportedly Jewish characteristics which provided antisemites a reason to marginalize Jews in general. Therefore reprehensible Jewishness became associated with the Eastern Jews. By distinguishing themselves from the immigrants, the museum supporters asserted their intention to become acknowledged as ful-fledged members of society.

Theodor Herzl drew upon »the performative« in order to enhance his Zionist cause as well, even though he had his doubts about the advantages of the culture of the spoken word. On the one hand, he stressed the importance of negotiation, rebuffed mass politics, and condemned demagoguery. In this sense he clung to the realm of the written word. »The most important aspect of his work,« writes Arthur Hertzberg, »was in diplomacy – among others he negotiated with the Sultan of Turkey, Kaiser Wilhelm, the king of Italy and Pope Pius X [...]«[84] In this way, Herzl's strategy resembled more that of the liberal Jews, who tried to accomplish their political goals by direct intervention with politicians. According to this perspective, a discernible break with the policy of diplomacy occurred only after Herzl's death under the influence of the next generation of Zionists. They tended to copy the style of the spoken word, which at that time was employed successfully by Lueger. The similarity in the mode of political acting of the Zionists and Lueger was also observed by Max Nordau. In a letter to Oskar Marmorek he referred to these young Zionists as being raised in an atmosphere influenced by the Christian-Socialists, the ideological home of Lueger. Accordingly, these young Zionists had adopted the methods of the antisemites.[85]

On the other hand, there is no denying that Herzl was adept at performance. One of the best examples of his inclination to make use of it was his plan to bring about the mass conversion of Austrian Jews to Catholicism at St. Stephen's Cathedral in Vienna, in order to win papal protection against antisemitism. In 1893, shortly before Herzl became a Zionist, he wrote in his diary: »The conversion was to take place in broad daylight, [...] with festive processions and amidst the pealing of bells. [...] And because the Jewish leaders would remain Jews, escorting the people only to the threshold of the church and themselves staying outside, the whole performance was to be elevated by a touch of great candor.«[86]

Mass conversion was to be staged as an open-air performance to impress the Gentiles and thereby to enhance the image of the Jews among them. Herzl

---

[84] Arthur Hertzberg: The Zionist Idea. A Historical Analysis and Reader. New York: Atheneum 1986, 203.

[85] Weitzmann, Die Politik der jüdischen Gemeinde Wiens zwischen 1890 und 1914 (note 56), 208.

[86] Translation by Boyarin, Unheroic Conduct (note 11), 281.

knew exactly how to appeal to people. As a playwright he had the relevant expertise, and in later years he deliberately made use of this in order to advance the Zionist cause among the Jewish masses. The First Zionist Congress in Basel (1897) paradigmatically corroborates this assertion. Here he tried to persuade Max Nordau to wear a black suit, the formal attire of the festive opening session, because it would provide the event with an aura of dignity and thus give more legitimacy to the Zionist cause.[87]

Hinting at Herzl's performative side raises the question of his similarity to Lueger.[88] Both employed the same means to find resonance for their ideas among people and convince them of the logic of their political goals. This is not to say, however, that the content of their messages could be confused or the danger of Lueger's antisemitism ignored. Their political style was similar not due to ideology but because of their contemporary context. Lueger and Herzl were pursuing their respective goals in a period when textual culture gave way to that of the spoken word and when performance gained political importance at the cost of the written word. The failure of the »Verein zur Abwehr des Antisemitismus« is a telling instance of this development. The fact that Vienna's Socialists and the Jewish museum also drew upon performance in order to transmit their messages to the larger population is one more reason to refute the assumption that comparing Herzl's and Lueger's style is tantamount to downplaying Lueger's antisemitism.

The conclusion that can be drawn from Herzl's (as well as other Jews') employment of performative elements is that with regard to their methods to pursue their political goals, they did not differ from non-Jews. This accounts for the fact that Jews as well as Gentiles were both part of Viennese culture and familiar with its symbols and codes. To understand Jewish behavior in fin-de-siècle Vienna, one must take the interactive processes between Jews and non-Jews into account. Herzl did not adopt the performative style because he wanted to adapt to Viennese culture. He employed performative components because he was part of this culture. It was not solely the Gentile Lueger who introduced the performative style into politics; neither was it the Jews alone who adopted it through acculturation. Instead, both Jews and non-Jews constituted the culture in which performance played such an important role. In actuality, it was the Jewish physician and politician Ignaz Mandl, Karl Lueger's personal friend and mentor, who introduced this style into municipal politics. In the end, Herzl was a representative of liberal Viennese Jewry who, especially due to antisemitism, underwent an identity crisis at the end of the nineteenth century. He formulated various solutions, ranging from assimilation to Zionism. Whatever he proposed, he simply acted as a Viennese Jew.

---

[87] Michael Berkowitz: Zionist Culture and West European Jewry before the First World War. Chapel Hill 1993, 26; Bein, Theodor Herzl (note 33), 339.

[88] Cf. Robert S. Wistrich: Theodor Herzl: Between Theater and Politics. In: Jewish Frontier (1982), 9–12.

Bernhard Greiner

»What Will People Say?« Herzl as Author of Comedies

For two of Theodor Herzl's written works one can doubtless adopt Hugo von Hofmannsthal's assessment of his own comedies: »the attained social.«[1] What it means exactly to »attain the social,« though, is left an open question by Hofmannsthal. He did provide a hint about its possible meaning in a note to his drama *Elektra*, completed in 1903:

> Content: Transition from pre-existence to existence: This is in every transition to every action. The action presupposes the transition from the conscious to the unconscious.[2]

The transition from pre-existence to existence is linked to a prior transition from the conscious to the unconscious. Apparently the unconscious is to be transferred into the space of existence. For Hofmannsthal it is the unconscious that – in the medium of comedy – should »attain the social.« Seven years before Hofmannsthal's drama of the transition from the world of signs to action (i.e. *Elektra*), Herzl's political tract *The Jewish State* (completed in 1896) and his utopian novel *Altneuland* (1902) gave an entirely new dimension to the notion of literature's attaining the social. In the sense of a fulfillment or realization (in Hebrew »hagshama«[3]), the written word arrives at a territory, in such a way that the provisional and placeless life of the diaspora changes course in order to enter upon history. As with the unconscious in Hofmannsthal, here something fundamentally withheld »attains the social.« National restitution is not left up to the coming of the Messiah, but is taken up directly as a theo-political heresy that parallels an aesthetic one. From the noncommittal aesthetics that characterize life in the diaspora, there is a transition to an absolute aesthetics in the sense that the space of the diaspora is breached with signs it itself provides. Aestheticization was a way for Judaism to turn the world of idolatry, that is, the surrounding non-Jewish worlds, into a neutral space, thus making acculturation possible. This neutral space is to be

---

[1] Hugo von Hofmannsthal: Reden und Aufsätze III. Ed. by Bernd Schoeller and Ingeborg Beyer-Ahlert. Frankfurt/M.: Fischer 1980, vol. 3, 611.

[2] »Gehalt: Übergang von der Prae-existenz zur Existenz: dies ist in jedem Übergang jedem Tun. Das Tun setzt den Übergang aus dem Bewußten zum Unbewußten voraus.« (Ibid. [Engl. Trans. of the quotation by Nell Zink]).

[3] In the Hebrew term the materiality, the corporeality of the process of realization is implicit.

thought through and demolished with the same principle of aestheticization. Herzl was quite aware of the heretical thrust of his writings on fulfillment. In his utopian novel, the protagonists are faced with the choice of spending an evening at a theatrical performance – a »sublime« drama on Moses – or an opera about the false messiah Shabbetai Zevi, whose destiny represents the unavoidable reversal inherent in the course of fulfillment. They decide to attend the opera.[4]

In his fulfillment writings, Herzl as author provides a positive alternative to art, as well as to the aesthetic reflection of modernity, both of which bear the stamp of negativity. In its full aesthetical significance, this move has seldom been remarked. The aesthetics of Zionism reveals itself from this angle in an entirely new light.[5] But Herzl's literary career – as a dramatist and essayist – did not reveal this perspective for a long time. As it is well known, Herzl began as a writer of comedies, with limited success. In this area, he did not »attain the social.« Before the appearance of *The Jewish State*, he had written ten comedies for the stage, the first in 1880, as well as two dramas. After 1896 there followed again two comedies as well as two more dramas.[6] Theatrical success, though not for the long term, was reserved for a comedy written with Hugo Wittman, *Wilddiebe* (*Poachers*). It premiered in 1889 at the Vienna Burgtheater and was afterwards produced by a number of German companies. His next work, *What Will People Say?* (1890), rejected by the Burgtheater, was produced in Prague and Berlin, where it failed miserably. Herzl's best dramatic work, the drama *The New Ghetto* (1894), was produced in 1895 at the Carltheater but nowhere else. This drama, unique among Herzl's pieces, deals with a resolutely Jewish theme – the question of Jewish emancipation. Presenting a roadmap to equality, it recommends full and unquestioning adoption of the contemporary gentleman's code of honor, including the practice of dueling. To be recognized as capable of rendering satisfaction becomes the ultimate proof of parity. It may be useful to refer to the works of Arthur Schnitzler, to whom Herzl maintained close contacts and who helped him in the effort to find a theater to produce *The New Ghetto*. Schnitzler's drama *Liebelei* (*Flirtations*, 1895), which the Burgtheater accepted while rejecting *The New Ghetto*, or the short story *Lieutenant Gustl* (1901), which led to Schnitzler being relieved of the rank of officer in a court martial may be cited in this context. Instead of accepting the class consciousness of the time and recommending its adoption by Jews, Schnitzler subjected it to fundamental doubts. Dramaturgically, Herzl showed himself to be closer to an author like Hermann Sudermann (for example, the 1889 drama *Ehre* [*Honor*]) than to any radical critique of society, whether from the naturalistic perspective of Gerhart Hauptmann or through Arthur Schnitzler's analysis of fin-de-siècle feeling.

---

[4] Cf. Theodor Herzl: Altneuland. In: Theodor Herzl: Gesammtelte zionistische Werke in fünf Bänden. Tel Aviv: Hozaah Ivrit 1935, vol. 5, 217f.

[5] See Philipp Theisohn: Die Urbarkeit der Zeichen. Zionismus und Literatur. Stuttgart: Metzler 2005.

[6] See the list of Herzl's early plays in the appendix.

But, it is unproductive to compare Herzl's dramas with those of contemporary authors for the sake of proving the literary inferiority of the former. It is more promising to make an internal comparison, that is, to query the relationship between Herzl's comedies and his fulfillment writings. Actually, they do achieve exactly that which the aesthetics of modernity aspires to: the attainment of the social, the transition from the world of signs to that of action, opening the space of representation for the experience of presence. In this regard, four possible relationships are conceivable. The comedies could distort the idea of fulfillment; they could prepare the way for it; they could have nothing whatsoever to do with it; or they could show a certain disposition to favor it, which, however, due to certain dramaturgic assumptions, they cannot further develop. The last possibility is naturally most productive for a discussion of Herzl's comedies. In addition, within the horizons comedy imposes, comparisons to the dramatic work of other contemporary authors are possible without disqualifying Herzl's work from the outset.

In reviewing the considerable number of comedies that Herzl wrote, one notices that all of them appeal to the same comic genre: the comedy of the put-down, of laughing at something, the comedy of incongruity. No inroads are made on the other side of comedy, which would be that of elevation, which one can laugh along with. This side of comedy includes the release of the oppressed or the repressed, the destruction of the existing order, anarchic comedy – that is, the comedy of carnival.[7] At the center of each of Herzl's comedies stands the figure of the deceived deceiver, one of the more popular objects of ridicule from time immemorial. The comedies invoke him as libertine, with the accent always on his play-acting in the realm of love, as a professional actor, or generally as one who fakes life situations. The deceived deceiver is a pretender who either stumbles over his own intrigues, opening himself to devastating ridicule, or he finds his way, through unforeseen developments in the game, back to his true self, and abandons his performance. Laughing at him then becomes constructive as it reintegrates him into the moral order. I will sketch several instances of this basic figure in Herzl's comedies, since familiarity with the comedies, almost all of which are available only in the author's vanity printings, can hardly be expected.

Compagniearbeit (*Company Work*, 1880): Two libertines want to write a drama for which they have only a title: *The Jealous Lover*. Since nothing in the way of a plot occurs to them, they try to provoke a couple they meet into jealousy by feigning being in love, intending to write the piece based on the resultant real-life events. But to save themselves from the eventual consequences, one of the libertines must pretend, in the progress of the play, that his now real

---

[7] For these two main modes of the comic see: Hans Robert Jauß: Über den Grund des Vergnügens am komischen Helden. In: Das Komische. Ed. by Wolfgang Preisendanz and Rainer Warning. München: Fink 1976, 153–164; Bernhard Greiner: Die Komödie. Eine theatralische Sendung: Grundlagen und Interpretationen. Tübingen: Francke 1992.

love is merely literary, while the other is forced to fulfill a pretended love through an unwanted marriage.

Die Causa Hirschkorn (*The Hirschkorn Case*, 1882): Two law clerks pretend to a female client that they are familiar with her case, about which they know nothing. During their now theatrical consultations with the client, the case takes a turn for the better which their ignorance keeps them from recognizing. One of them misses the reversal completely; the other becomes its beneficiary, having become emotionally close to the client in the course of the consultations.

Wilddiebe (*Poachers*, 1889): Three libertines pursue women, which is their form of »poaching.« One recognizes among their selected victims his former wife and his daughter, whom he had left many years before. Now he must deter his friends from their pursuits of them. In the process he is reconciled with his wife and opens the way for his daughter to marry freely for love instead of a marriage of convenience arranged by her mother.

Was wird man sagen? (*What will people say*, 1890): An engaged couple becomes estranged. She admires a friend of her fiancé, while he turns his attentions to a duchess who is in search of unconditional love without regard for social considerations (that is: »what people will say«). The fiancé seems to rise to the occasion, but in the end he remains caught up in the world of »what will people say?« The duchess recognizes instead in her companion, actually a servant she had been passing off as her husband for her own protection, the unconditional love she sought.

Unser Käthchen (*Our Katie*, 1899): An ex-lover returns from 20 years in Australia to visit the family of his former mistress. He is also on good terms with her husband, who knows nothing of the wife's earlier affair. (Analogously, in the novel *Altneuland* written shortly thereafter, two refugees return to Europe after 20 years; but instead of revisiting old romantic entanglements, they experience with amazement the new reality of the Jewish state.) The woman has a child from her lover that the husband regards as his own. It is the »Käthchen/Katie« of the title. The former lover wants to bestow a large fortune on his daughter, who knows nothing of her true parentage, without arousing either her suspicions or those of the nominal father. The plan goes awry; all suspect the true state of affairs, while continuing to maintain appearances. Meanwhile, the lawyer entrusted with the matter and the daughter Katie fall in love. Their true love is plainly intended to represent the opposite of the completely superficial relationships of the others. It is not clear whether the comedy itself believes this or denounces it.

The plot summaries presented here all revolve around the figure of the deceived deceiver. From this perspective, the comedies show themselves to be of simple construction and intended exclusively for entertainment. That is not a reason to dismiss them. Many pieces of the *commedia dell'arte*, for example, are laden with similar plot devices. The figures of Pantalone and the Dottore are predestined for the role of the deceived deceiver, albeit integrated into an intergenerational conflict. They embody the old in contrast to the young lovers, whose connections they try to impede. In this conflict, however, there is simultaneously a political-social aspect in effect. The people (the servant figures of the commedia dell'arte) and the first and second estates (nobility and church, which are not to be laughed at in the *commedia dell'arte*), represent two social groups that unite in opposition to the ever more powerful bourgeoisie. (Pantalone is a merchant of Venice, the Dottore a legal scholar from Bologna) and hold it up to ridicule. Herzl's comedies are devoid of such aggressive impulses. They are distinct as well from the formulations of the deceived-deceiver figure in Nestroy, who had celebrated theatrical triumphs in Vienna only a generation before Herzl with, for example, *Einen Jux will er sich machen* (*He wants to make a joke*) or *Frühere Verhältnisse* (*Prior Relations*). One of Herzl's comedies, *Prinzen aus Genieland* (*Princes from Genius-land*) was produced in 1891 in the Carltheater, which was one of the Viennese public theatres for which Nestroy wrote and performed. It was the third public theatre (»Volkstheater«) in Vienna, next to the Theater in der Josephstadt and the Theater an der Wien.

In a conspicuous way, all the characters in Herzl's comedies are play-actors, not only the respective protagonists as deceived deceivers. They pose; they act in roles ill-suited to them (for example, as man of the world, as ladies' man, or as unconditional lover) or that they have been forced by circumstances to adopt. But the characters do not see themselves as performing. When they try to convince other characters of something because their intrigues demand it, they are unaware that the Ego that here plays at comedy is already a comedian of itself as well. Thus the play-within-the-play configuration is universal in these comedies. It is an excellent precondition for successful comedy. But the pretense does not enter the realm of conscious awareness and thus cannot become productive, whether on the higher level of the relation of the piece to the audience (in contrast, for example, to Schnitzler's *Anatol*-drama, where the prologue announces: »So we enact theatre / Act in our own works / Precocious, delicate and sad / The comedy of our soul«[8]). Nor does the universal play-acting in the dramatic configuration enter the awareness of the characters in the represented world (again, one can cite a counterexample from Schnitzler, the final statement of a character in the drama *Paracelsus*: »We are always play-acting; whoever knows it is clever«[9]). Play-acting in the sense of trying to put one over on oneself and others is universal in Herzl's comedies. The comedy of ridicule that is developed out of the plot pattern of the deceived deceiver does not, however, possess in Herzl an analogous universal tendency. It is, rather, limited to relations within the represented world. The hero is compelled, or manages on his own, to abandon his staged performance. So the

---

8   »Also spielen wir Theater,/ Spielen unsre eignen Stücke,/ Frühgereift und zart und traurig,/ Die Komödie unsrer Seele [...]«. (Arthur Schnitzler: Anatol. In: Arthur Schnitzler: Das dramatische Werk. Frankfurt: Fischer 1977, vol. 1, 29).

9   »Wir spielen immer, wer es weiß, ist klug.« (Arthur Schnitzler: Paracelsus. In: Arthur Schnitzler: Das dramatische Werk. Frankfurt: Fischer 1978, vol. 2, 240).

notion of universal theatre is reduced to an opposition of being and seeming in the represented world that can be unquestioningly resolved within the world of appearances. The world of being is secure, untouched by further inquiry. The comedy of ridicule here does not examine its own norms, but rather defines them: Instead of devoting oneself to seeming, one has rather to confess to being as one is. One finds one's way back to »true« feeling in order to regain one's identity as a person of solidity who can make reference to a re-cognized moral order. The characters either attain this position, or, should they fail, they are handed over to contemptuous laughter. Thus Herzl's comedies are shown to be comedies of socialization, with a safe point of reference in ridicule, comparable with the German comedies of the Enlightenment before Lessing.

The world of being that Herzl's comedies posit, simultaneously the norm for their comedy of ridicule, is itself a fiction whose validity the comedies do not call into question. That dooms the comedies to triviality. The notion of fulfillment, that is, the hope of transcending the space of universal representation to open it up for presence, certainly implicit in the opposition of being and seeming, is redirected back into the space of representation. A transition from this space into that of presence, the action that gives a foundation to reality as Hofmannsthal makes the key question of his drama *Elektra*, cannot even come under consideration. The derisive review of all the play-actor figures engaged in fooling themselves, their fellow characters, and the audience never attacks their foundations. That, again, suggests a comparison with Schnitzler's *Anatol*. We see Anatol, how he gives himself up completely to a mood (for example, in the decadent atmosphere of a red-lighted room, at twilight, at the piano, a woman at his feet) while simultaneously knowing and enjoying his situation.[10] Or, we see him as a great magician, a hypnotist according to whose will the figures around him move and, at the same time, as one who shies away from the certainty that this power offers him (that others can speak nothing but the truth, for example, whether they are faithful to him), preferring to turn it back into a noncommittal mood.[11] This is a comic simultaneity of contrasting elements. The one position (Anatol's fantasy of an omnipotent, grandiose ego, manipulating other characters from a position of superiority) becomes ridiculous in the context of the other (his claims of immediate experience, his devotion to a stream of moods, to an experience of »life« that softens every distinctive feature). To the comic contradiction the drama adds yet another perspective, whether in the questions of Anatol's alter ego Max, or, dramaturgically, through the sequence and mirroring of individual scenes. It is the idea that these two positions or orientations of Anatol's are not at all contradictory – that the aspect of disillusionment, of self-awareness as producer-director of moods (the element of representation) is merely the reverse of absorption in such moods, an overcompensating reaction-formation to the experience of a

---

[10] Schnitzler, Anatol (note 8), scene »Episode«.
[11] Ibid., scene »Die Frage an das Schicksal«.

»centerless« ego[12] (as an experience of presence). Conversely, it is also the case that such experience is itself the jumping-off point for the delusions of grandeur in which Anatol is a self-possessed »player.« The norm for ridicule (that against which the ridiculous is measured and comes up short) is nullified just as its object. That pushes Schnitzler's figures over the edge into the abyss. However, Herzl's are either retired with a certain »Schadenfreude«, having shown themselves incapable of reform, or they attain new strength of character. Both exist in a world that is never called into question and which thus becomes, for the audience, implausible.

As play-actors who deceive themselves and others, Herzl's characters wear masks while pursuing, beneath the masks, their own egotistical interests. A comparison can be made with the figures in Sternheim's »Comedies of Heroic Bourgeois Life« (»Komödien des bürgerlichen Heldenlebens«), written between 1909 and 1916, whose protagonist bears the striking name »Theobald Maske.«[13] He pretends to those around him that he is short, plain, and of limited intelligence so that, behind the mask, he can live out his urges without regard for others. Like Herzl, Sternheim exposes the masquerade, but Sternheim's comedies affirm the reactionary's right to self-serving egotism in the mask of the bourgeois. Sternheim goes farther; he also questions the power in effect behind the mask. He shows that the »dionysian« conformist also wears the mask inside-out. He knows how to employ it as a secure footing, a structure that keeps the »inner nature«[14] he indulges from getting the upper hand. In the bipolarity of their view of life behind the mask, the comedies of Sternheim bring the ambivalence of their heroes, the unabashed social climbers of the Wilhelminian petty bourgeoisie, into the reality of literary discourse. In providing such »fulfillment« of their equally theatrical characters on the level of dramatic discourse, the comedies of Herzl miss the mark, as they let theatricality on the level of dramatic discourse founder on the strict opposition between being and seeming, character and mask. The pieces reap their comedy of ridicule from the contradiction between the structure of the imagined world, in which play-acting is universal, and the reality of literary discourse, in which the differentiation between being and seeming is constitutive. It is this contradiction that lays the foundation for the figure of the deceived deceiver. But the contradiction becomes an ideological leg-iron. That is, it encourages the construction of a false appearance of reality when it must be admitted that the generalized masquerade on display in the represented world is also valid for the real world of discourse. Such totalization of play-acting is however a central notion in Jewish self-reflection in the situation of advanced assimilation.

---

[12] In his aphorisms Schnitzler uses the term »seedless men« (»kernlose Menschen«). Cf. Arthur Schnitzler: Gesammelte Werke. Aphorismen und Betrachtungen. Ed. by Robert O. Weiss. Frankfurt/M.: Fischer 1967, 53f.

[13] Cf. Carl Sternheim's Comedy »Die Hose« (»The Pants«), written 1909.

[14] Carl Sternheim: Die Hose. In: Carl Sternheim: Gesamtwerk. Ed. by Wilhelm Emrich. Neuwied, Berlin: Luchterhand 1963, vol. 1, 96.

A contemporary of Herzl, the Jewish poet, cultural philosopher, and theater critic Theodor Lessing (1872–1933) developed this issue through an intense discussion and employed it in founding his own theory of Jewish affinity for the theater. His ideas also provide an approach to explaining the phenomenon of the high level of Jewish participation in the German theatrical avant-garde since the final decade of the 19th century, as authors, directors, actors, producers, theater critics and, no less importantly, in the audience. In his volume *Theater=Seele* (*Theater-Soul*, 1907) Lessing confirms a »disproportionately large influence of the Jewish element in the performing arts.«[15] His explanation begins – in a rather unoriginal way – with existence in the diaspora, that is, with Jewish existence as a minority whose right to exist is challenged by the surrounding majority culture. This »historical state of emergency,« – »everywhere enemies, limitations, accusations, burnings at the stake«[16] – has produced a double-masking, a »slipping into another skin«[17] on the historical-empirical level as well as on that of ideal existence. Here, Lessing's explanation begins to show originality. On the former level, the always precarious life situation has encouraged the formation of an artistic class that »behind every momentarily required mask [that is, the opportune mask in the respective concrete situation] is able to protect itself.«[18] On the level of ideal existence, however, Theodor Lessing sees this self-preservation behind masks being counteracted by a second kind of theatricality equally born of the necessity of history – that is, through a transformation into the opposite on the spiritual level: Judaism, in essence conservative, casts its lot with revolution. The originator of the dogma centered on skepticism, the »patriarchal fanatic,« becomes a relativist.[19] Behind the mask is thus another mask. As the undeniable consequence of such universality of the theatrical, however, Lessing asserts the loss of self. The ego loses itself in the play-acting of a merely aesthetic existence, since it »continually speaks in foreign words, sees with foreign eyes, and hears with foreign ears.«[20] Lessing provides different responses to this finding. First, he orients himself to the »Philosophy of Life« movement, and later (beginning in the 20s) he gravitates in the direction of Zionism. At the same time he makes the case for a genuinely Jewish theatricality concretized in the figure of Esther. Of interest to us is only his first response. Against universalized theatricality, he proposes a being that transcends the theatrical, analogous to the opposition in the contemporary »Philosophy of Life« movement which puts »spirit« or »form« on one side and boundless »life,« »nature,« and the primitive on the other. For the return to the sources, to authentic »life,« Lessing will later propagate Zionism.

---

[15] »Ein unverhältnismäßig großer Einschlag des jüdischen Elements in Bühnenkünsten« (Theodor Lessing: Theater=Seele. Studie über Bühnenästhetik und Schauspielkunst. Berlin: von Priber & Lammers 1907, 36).

[16] Ibid., 39.

[17] Ibid.

[18] Ibid., 38.

[19] Ibid.

[20] Ibid., 9.

Theodor Lessing is mentioned here because he creates an explicit connection between the universalization of the notion of theatre and the Jewish experience, and he goes on to ask after possibilities of overcoming this (in principle) theatrical being. That sharpens our perception of analogous questions in Herzl's comedies of the 1890s. There we find impulses aiming at a transtheatrical reality which is not adequately expressed in the unquestioning opposition of being and seeming on the level of dramatic discourse, pointing at this opposition as merely theatrical, an objection encountered in more pointed form in the contemporary drama of Schnitzler. If such impulses can be proven, there would be two consequences: For one, the precondition of the comedy of ridicule, the stable norm in contrast to which comic incongruities first become apparent, and in this case the differentiability of being and seeming, begins to falter. Thus, the door opens to a new type of comedy. Secondly, the search for a fundamental trans-theatrical reality displays a will to provoke the theatre itself to self-destruct – that is, to negate the medium of negation, an act that would pull the rug out from universal play-acting, while simultaneously offering the hope of sudden change to an absolutely new beginning.

On the basis of two late comedies written by Herzl, we may ask whether and to what extent they display such impulses in the direction of transcending universal theatricality. The first, written in 1890, comes from the Herzl who was still striving for a career as a playwright, after experiencing his first big success. The second was written at a time (1899) following the publication of *The Jewish State* and the first Zionist Congress, when Herzl had given the idea of fulfillment proceeding from the space of literature an entirely new content.

As already discussed, all the characters in the comedy *What Will People Say?* wear masks. They orient themselves either towards a social facade behind which they are completely empty, or they produce a facade (for example, of being a lover who has been deceived) in order to follow, behind the mask, their egotistical goals (say, to get rid of a woman one has become tired of). The ensemble of self-enacting comedians is enlivened by the aforementioned Russian duchess, who embraces the contemporary Philosophy of Life. She travels the world in search of the man who, for her love alone, will ignore all societal considerations and break every social bond. In opposition to »spirit« and »form,« and concretized in the world of »they,« stands »life« as immediate, unconditional love. Since, however, unconditional love can also be faked, the duchess comes up with a test, but it only propels her anew and ever more deeply into the world of masks. She views her companion, who as son of her estate foreman is more or less her serf, as her husband. Thus, each aspiring lover must overcome not only the social considerations of his own world, but also those he supposes to exist in hers. She seems to find such an unconditional lover, but in the end he remains a prisoner of societal considerations based on falsity. Only a single character can break out of the masquerade, namely, the duchess's companion and proto-husband. He is compelled to wear a double mask. Outwardly obliged to play the husband, without however being permitted any intimacy with the duchess, he is inwardly forced to hide his love from both her and himself. That his eventual rejection of »seeming« entails the removal of two masks (tantamount to the annulment of the masking of a masquerade) creates the impression of a fundamental transport like what the duchess is looking for. Accordingly, in the end the two play the loving couple with prospects of marriage. On this note, such comedies traditionally conclude. But it remains doubtful whether this unmasking is a leap beyond the theatrical or has merely led to a new mask.

The comedy seems to demand that a fundamental departure from all theatricality occur at this point. The desire of the protagonist to break out is not merely affirmed, but also satirized from the beginning as a mere pose by one who lays claim to melancholy, »Weltschmerz,« and a striving after »the true« and »the unconditional.« The comedy shows the »unconditional love« the duchess recognizes in her serf to be not unconditional at all; the duchess is the one who defines, distributes, and structures it. Perhaps the comedy was a failure because its aspiration to transcendence remains unclear. On one hand the comedy concedes such an aspiration to its protagonists, while on the other hand it takes it away. The play insinuates that pulling the mask off the mask has not led to the true essence of unconditional love, but rather to a new, even more impenetrable mask – that is, to self-deception. A bit of dialectic could have shown this from the start. In a world of all-encompassing mediation, love should be involuntary, a pure immediacy of feeling. That entails setting up »the true« in the midst of general untruth, whereby it inevitably becomes itself untrue.[21] Seen in this way, the comedy is remarkable for its rigorous totalization of masked being, which is simultaneously castigated as a life in falsity. (This aspect was surely not noticed by the theaters that rejected the piece.) The impulse towards the trans-theatrical becomes, on this basis, an urgent theme while remaining purely within the negative sphere.

Universal comedy-acting before oneself and others and entrance into the world of the unconditional and immediate stand in unmediated opposition to one another in *What Will People Say?* After the literary-theoretical turning point that the publication of *The Jewish State* signalizes, it is not surprising that Herzl, in writing his first comedy after this landmark publication, makes the question of mediation the motivating force of the plot. In *The Jewish State* fulfillment is already part of the work itself, no longer merely its Other, for the act of publication of the work is already the beginning of the fulfillment of that of which the text speaks.

Life behind masks is depicted in the piece *Unser Käthchen* (*Our Katie*), in classic comic style, as a love triangle: a boring husband, a frustrated wife, and her lover who is at the same time the husband's »best friend.« The lover enacts his part in this constellation while at the same time trying to transcend it. Thus, he stands for the dubious position of an immanent transcendence of the given bourgeois double morality. He has fathered a child with the unfaithful wife but

---

[21] Theodor W. Adorno gives a striking formulation of this structure in his Aphorism »Constanze« (cf. Theodor W. Adorno: Minima Moralia. Frankfurt: Suhrkamp 1979, 226–27).

this remains the secret of the couple; at the same time he becomes upset about the falsity of their relationship and has therefore removed himself to the greatest possible distance (i.e. Australia). Having become rich, he returns. He wants on the one hand to allow »his« child – Katie – a share in his wealth. On the other, he does not wish to disturb the various false relationships. He wants to establish a true father-daughter relationship in the context of the false one, but not in an immediate sense as in the earlier comedy. Rather, he proceeds pragmatically by engaging a mediator, a lawyer who will realize his aim by means of a clever transaction. The project fails, as gradually all involved are able to guess the true state of affairs, though they preserve the appearance of propriety, providing many comic opportunities – the more so as the marriage's second, »legitimate« daughter is drawn into an analogous love triangle. Meanwhile, the unsuccessful mediator and the illegitimate daughter for whom he should have performed his mediation find their way to each other in true love: The act to be performed is shifted metonymically to its supposed agents. Instead of establishing »the true« – through mediation – within »the false,« »the true« arises between the mediator and his intended beneficiary through a mediation that is denied success.

Does the comedy itself believe this escape from being is comedy? With the metonymic shifting of the task, it creates, structurally, a place for the sought after »Other.« Conversely, and simultaneously, however, it casts doubt on the act of transcendence – again metonymic – by way of the figures that achieve it. Katie owes her existence to false relationships, and sees through them the least of anyone. The lawyer, likewise, never acts on his own initiative. He merely reacts, remaining an object of the strategies of others. Thus the nascent authentic love is reclaimed as the mere obverse of love under the false, masked conditions into which it is then, logically, reintegrated. That the comedy does not believe in its imagined opening into a world beyond the theatrical, is demonstrated by its bringing, entirely unmediated, another kind of anti-world into play. Here, it is the world of the working class, in which true love, genuine marriage – beyond all ceremonial form – and, generally, true happiness are possible: »They are better people beyond a doubt! Where does that come from? From the happiness of labor!«[22] the returned ex-lover ponders. That is certainly social romanticism, labeled as such by the other characters (»You with your new sentimentality!«[23]), when compared with contemporary naturalistic depictions of the misery of the working class milieu. Perhaps we already hear the Zionist, speaking of the happiness of the pioneer, who by the labor of his hands creates a new reality in the promised land. The wealthy returnee, in any case, resolves to leave his riches to those who seek happiness in hard work.[24]

---

[22] »Es sind bessere Menschen – kein Zweifel! .. Woher es kommt? Vom Glück der Arbeit!« (Theodor Herzl: Unser Käthchen. Wien: Selbstverlag 1899, 117).
[23] Ibid.
[24] Cf.: »SIEVERS (zu Sofie). Ein Wort! .. Ich weiß jetzt, was ich mit den zweihunderttausend Mark mache. SOFIE. Nun? SIEVERS. Und mit meinem ganzen Geld' .. Ich

Thus, one can recognize in Herzl, after the shift marked by his fulfillment-writings, the beginnings of a productive literary answer to the question posed in his comedies of how the world of universal comedy can be transcended. But, Herzl went no further in the field of comedy. *What will people say?* Literary criticism has said only some few words about Herzl's comedies up to this point.[25] It has probably done him a favor, but at the same time it has missed an opportunity to assess, along with authors like Schnitzler, Hofmannsthal, Felix Salten, and Sternheim, an additional analyst of comic being, albeit one who did not »attain the social« in the field of comedy.

Appendix

Theodor Herzl: Early Plays (not published in the »Gesammelte Zionistische Werke«)

Comagniearbeit. Lustspiel in einem Act. Wien: Wallishaussersche Buchhandlung 1880.

Die causa Hirschkorn. Lustspiel in einem Act. Wien: Im Selbstverlag 1882.

Tabarin. Schauspiel in einem Act. 1884.

Muttersöhnchen. Lustspiel in vier Acten. Wien: Im Selbstverlag 1885.

Seine Hoheit. Lustspiel in drei Acten. 1885

Der Flüchtling. Lustspiel in einem Aufzug. Leipzig (Reclam Universalbibliothek Nr. 2387, Philipp Reclam jun.) 1887.

Wilddiebe. Lustspiel in vier Acten [gemeinsam mit Hugo Wittmann geschrieben, anonym gedruckt]. Berlin: Felix Bloch Erben 1889.

Was wird man sagen? Lustspiel in vier Acten. Wien: Gabor Steiner 1890.

Die Dame in Schwarz. Lustspiel in vier Acten [gemeinsam mit Hugo Wittmann geschrieben, anonym gedruckt]. 1890

Prinzen aus Genieland. Lustspiel in vier Acten. Wien: A. Entsch 1892.

Die Glosse. Lustspiel in einem Act. (1894). Dresden, Leipzig, Wien: E. Pierson 1895.

Unser Käthchen. Lustspiel in vier Acten. Wien: Selbstverlag 1899.

Gretel. Schauspiel in vier Acten. 1899

I love you. Lustspiel in einem Act. Wien: Selbstverlag 1900.

Solon in Lydien. Ein Schauspiel in drei Acten (1901). Wien, Leipzig: Wiener Verlag 1904.

Das Neue Ghetto. Schauspiel in vier Acten. Wien 1894, Verlag »Die Welt« 1897, 2. u. 3. Aufl., Wien: Selbstverlag 1903. Neue Ausgabe, Wien, Berlin: R. Löwit Verlag 1920 und in: Bd V der Gesammelten Zionistischen Werke, Tel Aviv 1934–1935.

See bibliography in:

Alex Bein: Theodor Herzl, Biographie. Frankfurt 1983 (Ullstein Materialien, Ullstein Buch; 35163), 343 (Bibliographie).

---

     verwend' es für Arme! SOFIE (zischt). Diese Herzlosigkeit sieht Ihnen ähnlich!« (Herzl, Unser Käthchen [note 22], 121).

[25] See: Alex Bein: Theodor Herzl, Biographie. Frankfurt: Ullstein 1983 (first edition: Wien: Fiba 1934, translated into Hebrew 1976); Josef Fraenkel: Theodor Herzl: Des Schöpfers erstes Wollen. Wien: Fiba 1934; Ernst Pawel: The Labyrinth of Exile: A Life of Theodor Herzl. New York: Farrah, Straus and Giroux 1989; Oskar K. Rabinowicz: Herzl the Playwright. Reprinted from: Jewish Book Annual. 1960–61, vol. 18, 100–115. New York: The Jewish Book Council of America 1961.

Vivian Liska

A Vision out of Sight.
Theodor Herzl's Late Philosophical Tales

At times, minutiae sprung from the poetic imagination can capture a shift in the needs and hopes of a nation better than sociological inquiries and political programs. One such instance is the well-known little scene drawn by the Israeli poet Yehuda Amichai, in which a man – presumably the poet – is sitting on the steps near the gate at David's Citadel and sets down two heavy baskets beside him. A group of tourists stands around their guide who points at the man: »You see the man over there with the baskets? A little to the right of his head there's an arch from the Roman period. A little to the right of his head.« »But he's moving, he's moving!« the man says to himself, and concludes: »Redemption will come only when they are told, ›Do you see that arch over there from the Roman period? It doesn't matter, but near it, a little to the left and then down a bit, there's a man who has just bought fruit and vegetables for his family.‹«[1]

Amichai's inconspicuous little scene has become part of the Israeli literary canon and has been praised as an illustration of the poet's »unflagging zest for the tangible particulars of the ordinary world.«[2] For some, however, the shift in emphasis encouraged in Amichai's lines goes well beyond the expression of an individual poetic sensibility and can be perceived as a sign of the dwindling belief in the grand ideals and the world historical force that once fuelled the Zionist endeavour. For traditional Zionists, the insistence on the primacy of a basket of vegetables over a monument bearing witness to former triumphs, of the cares and concerns of everyday life over past heroic acts, might be seen as a threat to the pride and vigour of the nation. Yet, far from questioning the Zionist cause, Amichai's miniature can be read as a confirmation of the vitality of its aims and as a vision of its ultimate fulfillment.

Two details in Amichai's text support this view. The poet's call for a change of perspective occurs after the emphatic remark that the man is »moving, he's moving!« This exclamation points to the fact that the man cannot be used as a point of reference for the historical monument, as a means to get the

---

[1] Yehuda Amichai: Tourists. Jerusalem 1967, see: http://www.english.eku.edu/Pellegrino/worldpoetry/amichai.htm+yehuda+amichai+roman+arch&hl=de&ie=UTF-8, consulted 17.03.04.

[2] Robert Alter, quoted in Joseph Lowin: Basket Case Yehuda Amichai's ›Tourists‹: http://www.google.be/search?q=cache:wOFgwmbhKSwJ:www.ivrit.org/html/literary/tourists.htm+Amichai+Robert+Alter+roman+arch&hl=en&ie=UTF-8, consulted March 17, 2004.

arch into focus because, unlike the static historical remnant, he is alive. His movements, the changing givens and circumstances of his life, necessarily alter his distance and relation to the arch. Amichai's image can be translated into a larger picture. It is precisely in a living society and for a nation on the move, one that undergoes continuous transformations, that the relevance and impact of the past is subjected to change and requires constant revisions and reassessments. Furthermore, one would be mistaken if one were to read the man's final reflection as an invitation to give up greater perspectives. Amichai's story doesn't call for a demise of visionary hopes but, on the contrary, evokes a redemption, the vision of an ideal state of being that is yet to come. Just as a Chassidic belief famously invoked by Walter Benjamin suggests that the coming of the Messiah does not involve any violent change but only a slight readjustment of the world – »dass er nicht mit Gewalt die Welt verändern wolle, sondern nur um ein Geringes sie zurechtstellen werde«[3] –, so does Amichai intimate that salvation may not require more than a minute change in the focus of a sight.

The figure of Theodor Herzl has, in many ways, become a monument, an arch of triumph in its own right. His portrait adorns the walls of official buildings and offices, he figures on stamps, coins and telephone cards, and his grave is a site of pilgrimage for tourists and Zionists nostalgic for uplifting heroic ideals. His photograph behind the seat of the head of parliament keeps referring the politicians of today to the myth of this founding figure of political Zionism. At the same time, and as befits a mythical figure, the concrete particulars of Herzl's life and work have receded into oblivion. In several passages in his writings Herzl envisioned that, as a founding father of the Jewish State to come and as a magnanimous benefactor of humanity at large, he would eventually become a legend and a revered icon of world history. He expresses this prophecy most succinctly in one of his diary entries from the 16th of June 1895, at the time when he started believing – or encouraged himself to believe – that his ambitious project could actually materialize: »Ich glaube, für mich hat das Leben aufgehört und die Weltgeschichte begonnen.« (Tagebücher, 116), (»I think for me life has ended and world history has begun.«) In Herzl's diary this line stands alone and, in the absence of comments, one is led to hear the solemn tone of this statement. But some of his more intimate diary reflections indicate that he was well aware of the dangers inherent in such self-aggrandizing mystification: »Mich vor Selbstüberschätzung, Hochmuth und Narretei hüten, wenn's gelingt. Wenn's misslingt, hilft mir die Literatur [...].« (»To guard myself from overestimating myself, from arrogance and foolishness in case it succeeds. In case it does not, literature will help me.«) As still another diary entry shows, he omits this concern very consciously from the political sketches of his project: »Aber, wenn ich, wie in

---

3 Walter Benjamin: Franz Kafka. In: Angelus Novus. Frankfurt a. M.: Suhrkamp 1988, 248–263, 263.

meinen literarischen Arbeiten Selbstkritik geübt hätte, wären die Gedanken verkrüppelt worden.« (»If I would have been as self-critical [in my political sketches] as I am in my literary works, my thoughts would have become crippled.« Tagebücher, June 11, 1895, 84) Herzl obviously believed that the ideational and rhetorical élan needed to carry out his grand visionary project would be hampered by open displays of self-doubt or hesitation. Literature, however, was another matter. The distinction he makes between his political and his literary writings points to one of the key functions Herzl assigns to his fictional prose. Far from being merely a psychological »help«, a comfort to his ego in case of failure and in the face of defeat, or a laboratory for his visionary imagination, literature is, for him, a reservoir of doubts, hesitations, and afterthoughts. This is particularly true for his late philosophical tales that can be read as self-reflections about his own ambitions of becoming a heroic player on the stage of world history and of the ideal of public or heroic life in general.

The opposition between »Leben« and »Weltgeschichte,« between »life« and »world history« Herzl so strikingly evokes in his diary entry of June 16, 1895 leaves no noteworthy traces in his political writings and is only rarely mentioned in his diary entries or in his earlier collection of seventeen stories published under the title *Philosophical Tales* in 1900. But between 1900 and 1902 he writes four additional stories collected in a section also entitled »Philosophical Tales« that makes up the final chapter of his volume of minor writings, *Feuilletons*. In these tales written half a decade after the ominous diary entry announcing his departure from »life« and his grand entrance on the scene of world history, the tension between »Leben« and »Weltgeschichte« becomes the central topic.[4] Like his novel *Old New Land*, most of the stories published in the earlier volume of 1900 can be read as literary enactments and affirmations of his political and diplomatic activities in those years. The last tales, however, obviously written under the impact of the first signs of ageing and increasing fears that his chances for practical success were disintegrating,[5] reconsider in often complex ways the primacy of a commitment to »world history« at the expense of private life. These tales can undoubtedly be read as mid-life reassessments of his own personal successes and failures, choices and errors. However, the medium he chooses for these reflections – inspired by Voltaire's *Contes Philosophiques* – and their curious mixture of allegorical tableau and realistic narrative, point beyond purely biographical or psychological concerns to insights into aspects of Herzl's thinking that have so far remained underexposed.

---

4   Theodor Herzl: Feuilletons, quoted here from the 2nd edition, 1911, Epaphroditus, 1900, Däumerle und Bäumerle oder die Zukunft, 1902, Die linke Glocke, 1901, Die Brille, 1902.

5   See Theodor Herzl: Zionistisches Tagebuch 1899–1904. Berlin 1985, 980. On May 2, 1901, a disillusioned Herzl wrote in his diary: »Today I am forty-one years old.... Almost six years ago I started this movement that made me old, tired and poor.« Theodor Herzl: Vision und Politik. Die Tagebücher Theodor Herzls. Frankfurt a. M.: Suhrkamp 1976, 189.

The tone, literary mode, and stylistic register of Herzl's four »late« philoso-phical tales are far from unified. The first, »Epaphroditus,« narrates a fictional-ized episode of a factual moment in Roman history. The second, »Däumerle und Bäumerle oder die Zukunft,« is a humorous allegorical tale with both satirical and moralizing undertones. The third, »Die linke Glocke,« stands in the tradition of the homecomer's story and the popular genre of the *Lügengeschichte*, the liar's tale, and the last, »Die Brille,« is cast as a nostalgic letter written to a former classmate. Despite their differences, these stories are linked by several common denominators: all four relate a decisive turn in the life of a middle aged or ageing man and involve the perspective of one who looks back on former triumphs and defeats, on past dreams, choices and priori-ties. The plot of all four tales hinges, to different degrees, on the narrative device of dramatic irony. The surprise caused by an unexpected and ironic turn in the story re-enacts the turn taken by the respective protagonists and releases the philosophical insight promulgated in the story. However, unlike in parables or traditional fables, these insights are not merely nuggets of truth or argu-ments dressed up as stories. Their literary value derives from the nuances and ambiguities that convey Herzl's self-questioning of issues that remained for him unresolved. As philosophical tales these stories invite the translation of specific figures and events into general insights while at the same time retain-ing the »reality effect« (Roland Barthes), the sense of contingency and com-plexity that prevents them from petrifying into mere prescriptive parables, principles, and precepts. This dual nature – both concept and narrative – inher-ent in the very notion of the philosophical tale perfectly suits the topic of these stories. They dramatize the tension, but also blur the line, between private life and public role, between heroism, might, and glory and the experience of life's compromises, contingencies, and contradictions.

Epaphroditus

The first of Herzl's philosophical tales, »Epaphroditus« imagines the last days of the mighty Roman dictator Sulla. Still at the height of his power, this shrewd and ruthless ruler unexpectedly resigns. Just as his rivals, Marius and Cinna, have given up hope of challenging his position, Sulla withdraws from his public functions, turns his back on politics, and travels southwards to the seashore, where he indulges in the common joys of life, in food, wine, women, music, dance, and spectacle. He relishes the excitement of cities and the beauty of sunsets, rejoices in the fleeting and intense experiences of the senses and – as his self-chosen nickname indicates – wholeheartedly devotes himself to the cult of the love goddess Aphrodite. He deems himself the happiest of mortals, considers himself protected from the wrath of his enemies, and mocks those who continue to strive for power and glory.

One day, on the occasion of a gladiators' fight in the circus, a beautiful woman standing behind him puts her hand on his shoulder. Sulla turns around and is instantly infatuated by her. After demonstrating her superiority and coldness by lowering her thumb and thereby deciding on the death of the wounded gladiator, the woman runs off and disappears. Before leaving the arena to pursue this seductive stranger, Sulla turns to Pompeius and reaffirms that he is the happiest of men, and wants only to discover one more thing: how to die a happy death. He also warns Pompeius of a group of former rivals who invited him for dinner. Sulla predicts that these power-thirsty men will try to involve him in their bloody plottings. Pompeius disregards Sulla's warning, and is indeed caught up in a conspiracy against Sulla. The former dictator's rivals do not believe that he has really given up his power. Convinced that Sulla's retreat into privacy is merely a strategic move to mislead his enemies, they decide to kill him. Meanwhile, Sulla has joined the beautiful woman who turns out to be Fannia, Caesar's mistress. It also becomes clear that her seduction of Sulla is a trap. The conspirators pressure Pompeius to join them and rush off to Fannia's bedroom to kill Sulla, but they come too late. The »Epaphroditus« died minutes earlier in the arms of Caesar's beautiful mistress, finding the happy end he sought. »Now,« concludes Pompeius in referring to Sulla's desire to know what a happy death is: »Now he knows.«

It is not difficult to read Herzl's story autobiographically and see in it the fantasy of a politician who, at the height of his glory but besieged by enemies escapes them by willingly relinquishing his power and retreating into privacy. Herzl may very well have identified somewhat with the historical Roman leader Sulla who is described as a handsome and charismatic self-made man with aristocratic leanings and a deft leader of his people. But there is more to Herzl's story than this.

»Epaphroditus« is based on an actual episode in Roman history, the conflict in 88–87 BC between the optimates – the aristocrats commanded by Lucius Cornelius Sulla – and the populares representing the pro-plebeians led by Marius. Herzl's story is to a large extent a faithful retelling of Plutarch's *Life of Sylla*. Not only key parts of Herzl's plot but also many details, excerpts of dialogues, character traits, and events in »Epaphrodites« are strikingly similar to Plutarch's historical narrative. Practically all the protagonists, the description of Sulla's personality, sections of the plot, his self-designation as »Epaphrodites,« as well as many details and scenes are taken straight and often literally from Plutarch's account. But whereas Plutarch's Sulla will eventually marry the lady of high birth and die only later from a gruesome illness, the end of Sulla's life in Herzl's tale no longer coincides with Plutarch's account.

The striking similarities with Plutarch's *Life of Sylla* make Herzl's changes and additions particularly significant. At the plot level these consist essentially of the failed conspiracy and Sulla's happy death. How can these deviations from Plutarch's narrative be understood? Possibly, in introducing the dramatic irony of Sulla's ultimate escape from his rivals through his death in the love bed of his enemy's mistress, Herzl does not merely let the dictator retreat into a serene privacy within which he will waste away towards an equally private death. Instead, he turns Sulla's very retreat from power into a victory over his enemies, and ultimately over the bloodshed committed in the name of power and glory, over »world history« itself.

A dialogue in an early scene literally taken over from Plutarch's account suggests an alternative to the heroic ideal. Plutarch relates that Sulla, after his unexpected resignation of power »not only declined to seek that office, but in the forum exposed his person publicly to the people, walking up and down as a private man.«[6] Similarly, in Herzl's story, Sulla, after his conversion, walks on the market place unarmed and unprotected. Valgus, an old centurion, approaches him and remarks that nothing, not even the fiercest of battles, required as much courage as this walk. But Valgus also teasingly remarks that Sulla is no longer a powerful man and reminds him that »Die Götter und insbesondere die Göttinnen lieben nur die Starken.« (»The gods, and especially the goddesses only love the strong.«) Upon this, Sulla replies with a triumphant smile: »Woher weisst du das? Vielleicht fange ich erst jetzt an, ein Starker zu sein [...]« (250). (»How do you know this? Maybe I'm only starting to be a strong one now.«) If Sulla's wisdom that true strength does not reside in weapons and armies but in the daring freedom to expose oneself unshielded and step onto the market place as a private man is transported back into Herzl's vision, its truly utopian dimension is revealed. It suggests not only the virtue but also the success of what one would call today unilateral disarmament.

It is in some ways ironic that Herzl's philosophical tale uses the foil of a historical episode and turns to »public history« to narrate a man's conversion from public to private life. A possible explanation may be that the triumph of the private over public existence is thereby not treated as mere refuge or resignation, but is introduced into the very course of »world history« as an alternative and a critique of its values dictated by power and glory. However, Herzl's tale should not be misread as a one-dimensional parable propagating the virtues of private happiness over public grandeur. The double-edged ending of the story reveals the tragic irony that Sulla's final escape – like the knowledge he gains of a happy death – occurs only in death itself. Pompeius' last words about the dead Sulla, »now he knows« (»what a happy death is like«) suggest the melancholic, almost Schopenhauerian insight that man, as long as he is alive, is inevitably enmeshed in the dealings of world history, be it as victim or as perpetrator. Although Sulla escapes through his timely death, his relinquishing of power – his unilateral disarmament – does not suffice to make his rivals believe that the battle is over. A true and ultimate escape from the games of power may not be attainable in life as it is. Possibly, and in accordance with Amichai's little scene, only a redeemed time will have obliterated those forces,

---

6   http://ancienthistory.about.com/library/bl/bl_textplutarch_sylla.htm, consulted 17.03.04.

drives, and motives that murderously »save republics« and build archs of triumph in its glory.

The Other Stories

The other three »philosophical tales« included in the *Feuilletons* center around a similar tension between »world history« – heroic ideals and glorious visions – on the one hand, and private, everyday life on the other. »Däumerle und Bäumerle,« literally »little thumb and little tree« features two contrasting friends strongly reminiscent of Don Quixote and Sancho Panza. Däumerle, the shorter of the two friends, is practical, realistic, and pragmatic, concerned with material goods, physical well-being, and the needs and necessities of the day as opposed to tall and skinny Bäumerle, a dreamer and visionary, who constantly and unremittingly looks into the future. The tale unfolds as a retrospective narrative of how the idyllic suburb where the two friends are taking a walk at the beginning of the story came into being. Herzl's tale reads like the story of a successful colonization and seems to embrace wholeheartedly the visionary's far-sightedness and endurance against all odds. However, a closer look at several details in the story blurs the seemingly clear-cut evaluation of the opposition embodied by the two contrasting figures. In the ironic treatment of the idealist and the sympathetic depiction of the pragmatist it reveals Herzl's self-mockery of the excesses of Bäumerle's – and his own earlier? – visionary pose. The story ends on a walk the two friends take amidst the newly built beautiful villas and gardens after the successful colonization of the formerly empty fields. Däumerle, the practical man, asks Bäumerle, the idealist: »Where is the future now?« Bäumerle points his finger at more empty fields in the distance just as he did at the beginning, when the friends still dwelt in narrow, foul smelling streets, and replies: »Over there!« In those closing lines of the story Bäumerle's successful project of colonization eventually puts itself into question. It is suggested that the visionary's gaze onto the distant horizon is no longer related to the miserable conditions which are no longer actual at the time of their final walk, and that his fixation on future conquests will go on, endlessly and unhappily forever, with no satisfaction, no present in sight.

Like »Däumerle and Bäumerle,« »The Left Bell« develops out of a retrospective narrative and tells the story of what at first seem to be the successful adventures of a man called Wendelin who left his hometown to seek his fortune elsewhere. One evening upon his return Wendelin overhears one of the rich and powerful members of the town's establishment confidently stating that all losers deserve their fate, that their failure is, in the end, always their own fault: »Capable men«, he continues, »may occasionally have bad luck, but they will always manage somehow.« When his nodding listeners agree, Wendelin decides to tell his story: how he found himself one day in front of a door with two bells and by sheer luck pulled the one that led him to success, while he knew that a man who pulled the other, the left one, ended up poor and miserable. After Wendelin leaves, his cousin reveals that he had indeed spoken the truth, except for one detail: Wendelin had rung the left bell – he was the loser. The story's moral is clear – success and failure are not a question of merit and fault, but luck at the decisive moment is all. But why the detours of the narration? Why does Wendelin not tell his true story? This could be answered in a nutshell with one of Nietzsche's aphorisms from his »Fröhliche Wissenschaft«: »Kein Sieger glaubt an den Zufall.« No winner believes in chance.[7] The situation in which Wendelin's story is framed indicates that a tale told by a loser would not do to demonstrate the contingency of fate to an assembly of rich and arrogant members of the town's elite, to men who have a stake in considering their own position to be a result of their own merits. The realization that things could be different, that self-confidence based on success is an illusion, must be driven home by one of their equals, by one who made it in the world. In the end, it is suggested that Wendelin is victorious after all: after his performance by which he tricked the town's elite into understanding their self-serving error that success is merit and that failure is self-incurred, he leaves the stage without even needing to witness his adversaries' defeat.

The tension between distant vision and the immediate concerns of everyday life is formulated most explicitly in »The Spectacles« (»Die Brille«), the story that closes Herzl's collection of selected minor writings. »The Spectacles« is set up as a fictive letter written by Johannes, a forty-one year old, educated, and refined man, clearly the alter ego of Herzl himself, to his friend Franz, a former schoolmate. In this letter Johannes shares his recent experience of getting his first reading glasses and conveys to his friend the impact of this event as an inaugural moment of a new phase in his life. This narrative is accompanied by nostalgic memories and philosophical musings about the transitoriness of time and the vanity of men. Johannes' loose reflections are held together by the metaphorical extension of the story's title: the reading glasses are both real, concrete spectacles as well as a signifier for the waning capacity to see things that are close by. This oscillation between literal and metaphoric meaning corresponds to the issue at stake in the story: both tangible object and symbol of a necessary adjustment of vision, the spectacles mediate between a concrete, »literal« reality on the one hand and a generalized perception on the other. Far-sightedness, Johannes' affliction and the natural condition of an ageing man's eyesight, are equated with the loss of interest in everyday matters and the simple things of life: »The simple things lose their value. We now only see what is great and distant and this circle recedes more and more into the distance until we are finally no longer interested in what is common in life.« This loss of touch with everyday things, however, is not described as an increase in visionary power. On the contrary, the story suggests that far-sightedness without percep-

---

[7]   Friedrich Nietzsche: Die Fröhliche Wissenschaft. München: Goldmann 1959, 209.

tion of the concrete particulars is a transition towards the »end of things.«[8] The spectacles alluded to in the title are a corrective to this melancholic far-sightedness and bring nearby reality back into view. However, the price of this correction is the loss of heroic stature, of vanity, of the drive to conquer.

At the end of the letter Johannes, his glasses firmly on his nose, bids fare-well to his friend, self-consciously signing the letter as »Your far-sighted Johannes.« In the letter's last paragraphs he has graciously and somewhat humbly accepted his fate, while making it clear that far-sightedness is, for him, no longer equated with prophetic vision. Instead it signifies a handicap, the loss of the eyes' or eyesight's capacity to adapt its focus. The story implies that the eye can only remain flexible when the pragmatic adaptation to contexts and situations prevails over the mourning about the loss of one's visionary »look.«

Herzl's last philosophical tale ends on Johannes' tender farewell to his friend: »Lebe auch du wohl für heute, Franzisce.« Johannes, the New Testament's prophet of apocalyptic and redemptive visions, greets Franziscus, the humble lover of creation. It is with the simplicity of this farewell greeting, a literal »live well,« that Herzl closes his book. In some ways this story seems to point in a direction opposite from »Epaphroditus.« While the old Sulla gives up power in an act of free will, energetically plunges into the joys and pleasures of life, and outwits his enemies and, ultimately, the scandal of death itself, Johannes, in »The Spectacles,« gradually and nostalgically observes the dwindling of his former attractiveness and strength and quietly prepares for death. In »Epaphroditus,« written when Herzl was two years younger, the soldier's and the statesman's struggle for victory and glory is still replaced by another, ultimately even grander battle. As Sulla dies his happy death, he not only wins over his adversaries, but over the gods themselves. While Sulla's free choice to retreat from the public sphere and live life – and even death – to the lees can be seen as an act of resistance, even a victory, Johannes' freedom is restricted to an acceptance, an affirmation of the inevitable. However, both stories present alternatives to the heroic ideal. Respectively pointing to sensuous fulfilment and to sobered wisdom, the two stories convey different modes of leaving ambitions of glory behind, but both Sulla and Johannes replace the striving for power with a possibly even more fundamental if not daring vision, one that is to be gained in maturity alone: Leaving »Weltgeschichte« behind, they get »Leben« into sight.

Herzl's Legacy

Herzl's late »philosophical tales« convey the awareness of a tension and the change of focus occurring when youthful ideals of power, conquest, and success are replaced by the enjoyment of private life and the wisdom of maturity.

---

[8]   Ibid., 289.

The retrospective look of the two ageing protagonists Sulla and Johannes, the problematization of Bäumerle's self-serving pursuit of expansionist dreams devoid of pragmatic concerns and Wendelin's demonstration of the dictates of chance undoing heroic conceit suggest that maturity entails a changing relationship to that which, in Yehuda Amichai's poetic scene evoked at the beginning, is signified by the arch from the Roman period. In this scene, the man with the baskets of vegetables insists that man is »moving, he's moving,« that he cannot be a fixed reference for the monument of heroic triumphs because his distance to them is changing. That such a change over the course of the time – and especially with approaching maturity – is not only an individual matter but a reality concerning entire nations is what Herzl may have had in mind when, in a diary entry from July 20, 1895, he looks ahead at how a »mature« Jewish State should eventually be governed and distinguishes between different kinds of leaders for the two moments:

> Die [visionären] Monstra, die Ungeheuer, sind notwendig fürs Erschaffen, aber schädlich für das Bestehende – ob sie es nun durch Größeres ersetzen oder in den Wahnsinn hinausbauen […]. Das Bestehende, das zu Erhaltende, darf nur von mittelmäßigen Menschen regiert werden. Die Monstra verstehen die Vergangenheit, erraten die Zukunft – aber die Gegenwart […], wollen sie eilig wegräumen. Es drängt sie ja, ihre Spur zu hinterlassen. Sie haben Angst, sie könnten vorübergehen, ohne dass man merkt, sie seien dagewesen. Zur Regierung aber braucht man mittlere Menschen, weil *die* alle Bedürfnisse der Menschen: Essen, Trinken, Schlafen usw. verstehen. Das Monstrum geht über diese Bedürfnisse hinweg – bei sich wie bei anderen. (Tagebücher, 139)

> (The [visionary] monsters are necessary in order to create, but harmful for that which exists (das Bestehende) […] That which exists, which is to be maintained, may only be ruled by common men. The monsters understand the past, they envision the future – but the present […] they want to quickly eliminate. It is because they are driven to leave their mark. They fear that they could pass unnoticed. To govern [an existing state], one needs common men, because they alone understand all the simple human needs: eating, drinking, sleeping etc. The monster disregards these needs – in himself and in others.)

In what can be regarded as Herzl's most far-sighted prophecy, one that goes beyond the mere creation of a Jewish State, he envisions what Israel will really have become, what it is today: »ein Bestehendes,« »zu Erhaltendes,« something existing that needs to be taken care of and preserved. The vision that this existing State will eventually have to be governed by common men and not by heroes, is inspired by a hope similar to the one expressed in Yehudah Amichai's poetic scene. Herzl's diary entry foreshadows Amichai's utopian dream that redemption will come when the arch of triumph will be subordinated to the »simple human needs,« when the monuments of heroism and glory will lose their significance in the face of the man with the baskets of fresh vegetables. In the light of Herzl's late philosophical tales, in which he revokes his earlier shift from »Leben« to »Weltgeschichte« and reinstates the primacy of simple, everyday existence, one could possibly modify the message of a recent post-Zionist pamphlet ending on the words: »There is life after Zionism.«[9] Rather, it appears that there is more life in Herzl's Zionist legacy than meets the eye.

---

9   Tom Segev: Elvis in Jerusalem. Post-Zionism and the Americanization of Israel. Trans. Haim Waitzman. New York: Metropolitan Books, Henry Holt and Company 2001, 161.

Mark H. Gelber

The Life and Death of Herzl in Jewish Consciousness: Genre Issues and Mythic Perspectives

The various images of Theodor Herzl that have developed and established themselves in Jewish consciousness were designed, concretized, and communicated to a significant degree by published depictions of his person, including accounts of his life and death in numerous languages and in several literary genres. Following Herzl's funeral in 1904, a veritable deluge of these texts appeared, as if his death facilitated the poetical and literary expression of diverse images of him. New images and innovative formulations of them have continued to appear, alternately with greater and with lesser frequency over the course of the last century. Still, a century after his passing, it is probably the visual images and new musical references to him that dominate or overshadow the paucity of literary images in Israeli culture. Actually, most of the literary legacy regarding Herzl has been lost to Jewish consciousness for different reasons, and whether or not some of it may be recovered remains an open question.

In this paper, I would like to present briefly a few examples from the range of genres which have conveyed these images, focusing on a few texts, which have mostly been forgotten, and emphasizing the eulogistic literature in particular, in order to show ultimately how difficult it is to differentiate between the mythic Herzl and the historical figure. Almost immediately after his death, the notion appeared in Zionist literature that the nation would transform Herzl into a luminary figure in the legendary and mythological corpus of the heroes and martyrs of Jewish history.[1] In fact, Robert Weltsch remarked already in 1913 that the historical Herzl had been displaced by »the eternally living Herzl,« who would remain as the towering figure of the Jewish national movement.[2] In truth, literary and poetical depictions do not allow for easy discriminations between history and myth.

The mythic constructions of Herzl, which are the focal point of this paper, tend to glorify him or at least to place him and his career in a positive light, rather than dwell on his failures, his personal limitations, or shortcomings of character. There were obvious political reasons for this one-sidedness in the literary depictions. Still, in order to maintain a fair balance, it is important to

---

[1]   See, for example: Theodor Herzl ז״ל. In: Ost und West 4 (1904), no. 7, 502.

[2]   Cited in: Ludger Heid: »In Basel habe ich den Judenstaat gegründet.« Theodor Herzl – Wegbereiter des politischen Zionismus. (Pamphlet) Jüdisches Museum Westfalen 1998, 27.

keep in mind the negative aspects in the composite images of him, which have been largely suppressed. These include, to cite perhaps the most important ones: Herzl's imperious and condescending manner, his unfitness for military service, his illnesses, his psychosomatic and hysterical tendencies, his disastrous marriage, his extremely patriarchal or male-chauvinist tendencies, the terrible and tragic lives of his offspring, and the bitter opposition to him among Jewry and even within Zionism itself during his lifetime and afterwards.

The construction of different positive images of Herzl has served a variety of specific literary and non-literary aims. At the same time, these images may conform to the contours of a range of issues not necessarily or primarily related to Herzl at all. That is, they may construct and exploit an image of Herzl in order to accomplish a specific goal not directly concerned with him. Additionally, while we have learned from the scholarly study of autobiographical and biographical texts, just as in the case of poetical and other literary texts, that specific contextualizations will help us to categorize and thereby shed some light on what appears to be the constructed nature and aesthetic sense of the images of the subject, the images which I mention complement the common and dominating image of Herzl as a political Zionist visionary. The reason for this tendency is my contention, which I cannot dwell on at length in this paper, that Herzl, in the last so many years, has come to occupy less and less literary and cultural space in Israel and in the Jewish world and in Jewish consciousness in general. Furthermore, what is left of his image or images in Jewish and Israeli culture is no longer tied closely to the literary images, but rather to visual imagery, mostly from the realm of photography, commercialism, or kitsch. Except for his name and a few facial images, which appear to be widely or somewhat known, Herzl has been disappearing rapidly from Israeli and Jewish consciousness. Over the course of a century, he has become less and less important, paradoxically, at the very time, that is, towards the end of the 20th century, that Zionism seemed to many observers to be the dominant Jewish ideology in the world. I have already argued elsewhere that the 20th century would come to be recognized as the Zionist century in Jewish historiography. During the Herzl centennial year, the Knesset appeared to be determined to take legislative measures to establish a Herzl Remembrance Day as an official national holiday, partially as a direct result of his cultural disappearance and large-scale irrelevance.[3] Whether or not this particular remembrance day will materialize – and two years later (in 2006) it does not seem to be on its way to speedy realization – it is Herzl's image or images or what these images will be and his commensurate role in the national narrative that are ultimately of interest in this paper. These possible images or one or two dominant ones will have to be of certain interest to the educators, politicians, and

---

3   See Ariyeh Dayan: Herzl m'kabeyl yom zikaron. Ha'im zeh nakhutz umi yantziakh
    ayzo moreshet? (Herzl receives a Remembrance Day. Is it necessary and who will
    memorialize which heritage?) In: Ha'aretz, June 14, 2004, 4A.

the government, if Herzl is to be rehabilitated, when and if this remembrance day manages to establish itself in the Israeli national calendar.

Regarding the kinds of texts which one would have to take into account in order to consider fully the issue of Herzl's literary and mythic images, one might cite the following:

1) Herzl's own autobiographical statements provide a starting point for this type of consideration. For example, his autobiographical sketch, which appeared in the *Jewish Chronicle* in 1898 in London, and the self-consciously developed image of himself as an irreverent and mordant critic of the Jewish establishment need to be analyzed carefully.[4] Also, his diaries, which were edited and published well after his death, would have to be taken into account. Here one might attempt to analyze his presentation of self and measure the degree to which he himself attempted to create or exert some control on the development of his own mythic image during his lifetime and for posterity.

2) The reports, comments, and criticisms of his friends, acquaintances, colleagues, or opponents concerning their impressions of him and his work complement the image he developed himself. Here one needs to be very sensitive to the extent to which these reports serve to promote the reputations or agendas of the reporting agents. For example, there was a widespread tendency to celebrate Herzl as a towering figure in Austrian journalism and in German letters in general, during his lifetime and afterwards. Thus, an association with Herzl in this regard tended to bolster the very reputation of the observer. Felix Salten, for example, and other journalist colleagues in Vienna and elsewhere praised Herzl as a master »feuilletonist.«[5] Upon his death, virtually all of the Viennese and European newspapers celebrated him as a »genial journalist.« That was the specific formulation of his own newspaper, the *Neue Freie Presse*, in the eulogy printed there.[6] The *Wiener Abendpost* called him »eine

---

4   Theodor Herzl: Autobiographical Sketch. First published in: Jewish Chronicle (London) on January 14, 1898.

5   Felix Salten: As a Friend Knew Him. In: Theodor Herzl. A Memorial. Ed. by Meyer W. Weisgal. New York 1929, 259. See also Felix Salten: Gestalten und Erscheinungen. Berlin: S. Fischer 1913, 144. Cf. Siegfried Trebitsch: Ein Erinnerungsblatt. In: Zeitgenossen über Herzl. Ed. by T. Nussenblatt. Brünn: Jüdischer Bund- und Kunstverlag 1929, 229–232. Trebitsch wrote: »Er war allmächtiger Feuilletonredakteur der gewaltigsten Zeitung meines ausgedehnten Vaterlandes und der Weg eines jungen Dichters, der an die Öffentlichkeit wollte, führte natürgemäß in die Redaktionsstube Theodor Herzls.« (He was the omnipotent editor of the feuilleton section of the most powerful newspaper in my extended fatherland, and the path of a young writer, who wished to become known to the public, led naturally to the editorial office of Theodor Herzl.)

6   Cited in: Die Welt 8 (1904), no. 28, 8. Herzl was described in the *Neue Freie Presse* as: »[…] ein Schriftsteller von höchster Begabung, ein Künstler durch sein Darstellungsvermögen, ein genialer Journalist und ein vornehmner Mensch.« ([…] a writer of the highest talent, an artist by way of his theatrical ability, a genial journalist and a refined human being).

Zierde des deutschen Feuilletons,« and a »feinsinnger Publizist.«[7] (»an orna-
ment of the German feuillton and a subtley discriminating journalist«). Even
Karl Kraus, who mocked Zionism mercilessly, called Herzl »dieses feinsten
unter den jungen Wiener Prosaisten,«[8] (»the finest among the younger Vie-
nesse prose writers«) in his polemic against Zionism of 1898, *Eine Krone für
Zion*. Kraus and others tended to emphasize the particularly Viennese or Austrian character of his artful prose.

3) The variety of images of Herzl in novelistic literature or of characters
based on Herzl that appeared during his lifetime and afterwards add a new
dimension to the general discussion. Here the fictional framework grants authors a certain imaginative latitude in terms of fashioning the purportedly fictional figure. One of the early literary incarnations of Herzl is the character of
Dr. Geist in Friedrich Fürst Wrede's novel, *Die Goldschilds*. This work appeared serially in the chief journalistic instrument of the World Zionist Organization, *Die Welt* (which had been founded by Herzl), in 1898 and 1899.
Herzl facilitated the publication of literary work in *Die Welt*, as long as it could
be read as supportive of, or compatible with, and congruent to Zionist aspirations. Along the lines of his model Herzl, the fictional Dr. Geist had been an
enthusiastic fraternity brother who espoused German nationalist ideals during
the time he was a student in Vienna. In the novel, Geist appears as an eloquent
spokesman for Zionism, which he articulates according to the vision of Herzl,
including its modern technological orientation, the seven-hour workday, and
the universal beneficiality of Zionist activity.[9]

4) The numerous and sundry biographical accounts offer variegated images
of Herzl. These begin with Adolf Friedemann's Herzl biography of 1914, but
the biographical literature is vast by any standard. The biographical studies
attempt mostly to present, categorize, and assess his career and contribution to
Jewish history, but there is a recurrent fascination with his complex and enig-
matic personality. How Herzl was transmogrified from »a dandified littérateur
into the charistmatic, uncrowned king of the Jews« (Pawel) has fascinated
many a biographer. Here the issue is not so much the reputation of the biographer, but rather it is the question of sources, emphasis, the literary economy of
the biography, the particular image or images of Herzl which have served
individual biographers at specific junctures in time, and the implied reader-
ships at certain historical moments. Biographers who identified closely with
Zionist aspirations appear to present ideal and idealistic images of Herzl. Also,
biographies written after the establishment of the state need to be examined
with an eye towards the extent to which attitudes towards the state are reflected

---

[7] Ibid, 9.
[8] Karl Kraus. Eine Krone für Zion. Vienna: Verlag Moriz Frisch 1898, 31. Cf. Kraus's
     review of Herzl's Altneuland in: Die Fackel 5 (1903/04), no. 141, 20–21.
[9] Die Goldschilds appeared serially in *Die Welt* through 1898–99. It was published in
     its entirety by Ernst Hofmann & Co. in 1900.

in the accounts of Herzl's life. Furthermore, it would be important to try to differentiate between hagiography and biography, although the boundaries in this regard are not consistently clear.[10]

5) The images of Herzl in school textbooks, in Israel and in Jewish schools in the diaspora, as well as in children's literature in general, tend toward a certain ideological one-sidedness in terms of presenting an heroic image, while often avoiding blatant propaganda. Regarding the school texts, it is fair to say that in general there is a good amount of information and very often an attempt to promote a rather balanced view of Herzl's career.[11] One problem may very well be that teachers in Israeli schools do not always require that pupils read the school texts, almost guaranteeing their irrelevance for the pupils. On the basis of my many interviews with Israeli school children, it is fair to say that the teachers – not the history school texts – are the major factor in terms of the retention of an image of historical figures like Herzl.

Children's literature may function a bit differently. For example, here one might contrast one of Devorah Omer's books for children, *Devora Omer m'saperet al Herzl* (Devorah Omer tells about Herzl; on the inside cover, the English title is given as »The Story of Theodor Herzl«), illustrated by Yohanan Lakizevitz, which appeared in 1998, with previous examples in this genre. In Omer's book, children are presented naturally, within the framework of the reading, or being read-to experience, with the opportunity to learn the vocabulary which informed the development of early Zionism, terms like »antishemi« (antisemitic), »golah« (diaspora), and »moledet« (homeland), as well as Herzl's Hebrew cognomen, Binyamin Ze'ev. Perhaps knowing his Hebrew name might help Israeli children relate to him more personally, that is, as »one of us,« even though he really was not an Israeli by any means. In »Devora Omer misaperet al Herzl,« Herzl's own children, who serve as the identifying focal point of the text for the child reader, are exhorted by the grandfather, or by Herzl, or by the narrative voice itself to remember that they are Jewish and

---

10 Adolf Friedemann: Das Leben Theodor Herzl. Berlin: Jüdischer Verlag 1914; Ruben Brainin: Chajej Herzl (Herzl's Life) 3 parts. New York: Asaf Publishers 1919; Manfred Georg: Theodor Herzl. Sein Leben und sein Vermächtnis. Berlin, Wien, Leipzig: Ralf A. Höger 1932; Alex Bein: Theodor Herzl. Wien: Fiba-Verlag 1934; Josef Patai: Herzl. Tel Aviv 1936; André Chouaqui: Théodore Herzl. Inventeur de l'etat d'Israel, 1860–1904. Paris: Editions du Seuil 1960 (English version: A Man Alone. The Life of Theodor Herzl. Jerusalem: Keter Books 1970); Martha Hofmann: Theodor Herzl, Werden und Weg. Frankfurt a. M. 1966; Desmond Stewart: Theodor Herzl. Artist and Politician. London, Melbourne, New York: Quartet Books 1974; Amos Elon: Herzl. New York, Chicago, San Francisco: Holt, Rinehart and Winston 1975 (Hebrew edition: Tel Aviv: Am Oved 1975); Ernst Pawel: The Labyrinth of Exile. New York: Farrar, Straus & Giroux 1989; Steven Beller: Herzl. London: Peter Halban 1991; Avner Falk: Herzl. King of the Jews. A Psychoanalytic Biography. Lanham/Md.: University Press of America 1993.

11 See, for example: David Schachar: Migalut l'Komemiyut. Toldot Am Yisrael B'dorot Ha'akhronot, Perek Aleph. Idan 1990, 70–92.

thus intrinsically different from other nationalities.[12] Also, the idea is inculcated, especially following the section on the pogrom in Kishinev, that all Jews
really only wish to live in the land of Israel and nowhere else.[13]

This kind of nationalist rhetoric, which is not characteristic of Herzl at all, is
complemented by the strong fairytale element in the book. Despite the death of
their father and the tragedy which befell the family, Herzl's children in the text
express confidence that one day they will live in a sumptuous palace like roy-
alty, admired by all in the land of Israel. Perhaps the Israeli child will also
believe that this indeed happened. Certainly, the terrible fate of Herzl's children, especially from a Zionist point of view, could not be more jarringly in-
congruent to this image. But the idea of a desolate land that might be transformed into a paradise gains credibility in the minds of the young readers of
this book: »a blossoming garden of Eden, in which everyone lives happily and
in peace, without illnesses and without wars.«[14] Evidently, the premature
euphoria of the peace process in the 1990s and the anticipated successful conclusion of negotiations for a final resolution of the conflict, characteristic of
those times, exerted a strong impact on the conception of the book. It might be
said in the book's favor that it is very sensitive to, and it engenders certain
sympathy for, the situation of families and children with absentee fathers, who
love or care perhaps for their children but who are essentially workaholics like
Herzl and who thus neglect the narrowly defined best interests of their children
(and wives) in favor of the greater good of the community, or even, as here,
the nation. Thus, a concern of modern life in Israel regarding absentee fathers
is worked into the heart of a book about Herzl. I suppose the hope is that children and possibly mothers who read a book like this one to their children will
be more understanding of such fathers.

6) The images of Herzl as depicted in drama or on stage in theatrical productions add a new dimension to this discussion. Two very different examples
would be Nathan Biztritzky's trilogy, »Chevlai Gilgul« (Agonies of Reincarnation), and the fundamentally upbeat Habimah musical production, »Melekh
Hayehudim« (King of the Jews). As Gershon Shaked has noted regarding
Biztritzky, it was the saga of Herzl as a modern manifestation of the myth of
messianic redemption, of a secular Messiah, which fascinated him.[15] But the
trilogy is a parody that mocks secular messianism. Through its psychological
analysis and focus on the tragedy of the Herzl family, a message opposite to
the one in Devora Omer's book for children is conveyed. On stage, the children of Herzl are his primary victims. His psychological and personality disor-

---

[12] Devorah Omer: Devorah Omer misaperret al Herzl. (Devorah Omer tells about
Herzl). Tel Aviv: Zmora Bitan 1998, n. p.

[13] Ibid., n. p.

[14] Ibid., n. p.

[15] See Gershon Shaked: Herzl the Myth and Herzl Flesh and Blood: The Literary
Reception of Herzl in Nathan Bistritzki's ›The Secret of Birth,‹ 221–233.

ders ultimately wrecked his family life and destined his children to tragic ends. This presentation is tantamount to the total debunking of the Herzl myth. That Biztritzky's Herzl plays are virtually unknown in Hebrew literature has made this particularly infantile and negative dramatic image of him mostly inaccessible to the Israeli public. However, the Habimah musical, »Melekh Hayehudim,« is totally oblivious to this problematical and negative portrayal of Herzl. It is almost entirely optimistic, as musicals tend to be in general, and there are many good tunes. They contribute to intensify the sense of a happy, mostly uncomplicated, and successful career, despite some moments of doubt or difficult challenges.

7) The outpouring of elegiac poetry and eulogistic literature (Nachrufe) which appeared in 1904, but also on the occasions of the 5th, 10th, 25th, and 50th anniversaries of his death, or poetry composed for the occasion of the centenniel of his birth in 1960, provide a wide range of texts pertinent to our discussion. While often suffused with the tone and aura of painful leave-taking, sober reflection, and unabashed praise of the dead leader conveyed in the language of consolation and hope, the texts in this category document the tragic loss of the heroic leader for the nation. One of the most famous examples in its day, »Farewell o Prince,« a sonnet penned on the very day of Herzl's death by the English writer and Zionist, Israel Zangwill, first appeared in the commemorative (death) issue of »Die Welt,« alongside a German translation by the cultural Zionist Berthold Feiwel.[16] This poem, as many others like it, for example, Israel Auerbach's »Dem toten Fuersten,« (To the dead prince) which appeared on the front page of the Zionist newspaper, the *Juedische Rundschau* (Berlin) on July 15, 1904, emphasized the aristocratic »habitus« of Herzl and the confident view that his death was but the portal to eternal life and a call to more committed Zionist engagement. As Zangwill phrased it: »Death has but fixed him in immortal life.«[17] In this sense the great leader defies even death. Also, the poem seemed to justify the leader's death as the price for salvation of the people, expressed poetically as a form of crucifixion: »To save a people, leaders must be lost,/ By foes and followers be crucified.«[18] Or, as Auerbach put it poetically: »Der Tote aus dem Grabe ruft zum Werke. Dem toten König bangt nach seinem Land.«)[19] (»The dead calls to action from the grave, the dead king anxious for his country.«) Harry Epstein's poem »Dem Andenken Herzls« recited at the memorial service of the Zionist Union in Duisburg in July 1904 likewise emphasized in desperation and despairing hope the continued living presence of the deceased leader. The poem's concluding line reads:

---

[16] Israel Zangwill: Farewell o Prince. Reprinted in Ost und West 4 (1904), no. 8/9. Reprinted again in: Weisgal (Ed.), Theodor Herzl. A Memorial (note 5), 12.

[17] Ibid.

[18] Ibid.

[19] Israel Auerbach: Dem toten Fürsten. In: Jüdische Rundschau 3 (1904), no. 28, 1.

»Er ist bei uns, er lebt doch! Sagt: er lebt.«[20] (»He is with us, he lives. Say it, he lives!«) Also, Gertrud Krause, in a poem recited during the memorial service of the local Zionist organization in Posen, compared Herzl in a recurrent simile to »segnende Sonne,« blessed, or blessing sun.[21] The poem expressed confidence that his death would be inspirational for the determined continuation of the Zionist project. The last stanza reads: »Es schweige die Trauer, es spreche die Kraft– Wir sind seine Erben, wir halten das Gut!– Dann wirkt es weiter und blueht und reift– Und die segnende Sonne ist er uns geblieben.[22] (»Let mourning be silenced, let strength speak. We are his heirs, we possess the inheritance. It works on, it blossoms and ripens, and he, the blessed sun, remains ours!«)

Poetic and prose encomia to Herzl, as well as many of the eulogies, compare him with the Biblical figure of Moses. Herzl himself had intimated on occasion a connection with this same image of himself. Börries von Münchhausen, the North German balladier who later moved in Nazi circles, but who had collaborated productively with the Zionist artist E. M. Lilien at the turn of the century in Berlin, expressed this connection in anapestic cadences in a poem about Herzl: »Du Mose der Zeit, da das Heimweh in Israel stieg/ Du Mose unserer Tage, Gott geb deiner Sache den Sieg!«[23] (You, Moses of the time, when homesickness rose in Israel/ You Moses of our days, may God give victory to your cause!«) In Marta Baer Issacher's poem, »Moses' Prayer« (»Moses Gebet«) published shortly after Herzl's death on July 22, 1904 in *Die Welt*, the poetical voice of Moses may be read as identical to that of Herzl. Like Moses, Herzl is the loving patriarch of the people.[24] In the special Herzl issue of *Die Welt*, published on July 3, 1911, a decade after his death, M. Jardeni's prose poem, »Moses (zum zehnten Todestage Theodor Herzls)« does not name Herzl explicitly, allowing the dedication to make patently clear the resonating parallels in the lives of the two leaders. G. Sil-Vara, a political journalist and dramatist, who worked with Herzl contemporaneously at the *Neue Freie Presse*, called him in 1929 »a heaven-sent Moses, /who/ was leading the /Jews/ out of the wilderness of the Galuth into the Promised Land.«[25] The

---

[20] Harry Epstein: Dem Andenken Herzls. In: Jüdische Rundschau 3 (1904), no. 29, 313.

[21] Gertrud Krause: Theodor Herzl. In: Die Welt 8 (1904), no. 29, 26.

[22] Ibid.

[23] Börries von Münchhausen: Theodor Herzl. In his: Die Balladen und ritterlichen Lieder. Berlin: Egon Fleischel 1921, 237.

[24] Martha Baer Issacher: Moses Gebet. In: Die Welt 8 (1904), no. 30. See also: Max Viola: Theodor Herzl. In: Die Welt 8 (1904), no. 29, 26: »[...] Wie Moses hast du hingewiesen/ Auf des gelobten Landes Au'n,/ Wie Moses hast Du es gepriesen,/ Wie Moses durftest Du'es nicht schau'n/ [...].« (»[...] As Moses you pointed the way/ To the meads of the promised land/ As Moses you praised it/ As Moses you were not allowed to see it [...].«) Cf. Rabbi David Golinkin: Moses and Herzl. In: Conservative Judaism XLVIII (1994), no. 1, 39–49.

[25] G. Sil-Vara: At Herzl's Grave. In: Weisgal (Ed.), Theodor Herzl. A Memorial (note 5), 21.

linkage with a certain image of the Biblical Moses represents an effort to invest the image and legacy of Herzl as a leader and nation-builder with the credibility and authority of the Bible, for a secular as well as for a religiously oriented readership, which would likewise respect that authority. The religious dimensions and associations of these poems and related formulations are not easily ignored; they bring the secular Herzl into the orbit of the poetical rhetoric of religion.

Following Max Nordau's lead in his eulogy published in French in July 1904 in *L'Echo Sioniste*, the claim is often made that even if Herzl's death was tragically premature and historically unfair, it was only after his death that his true greatness could be comprehended by the nation.[26] Nordau, who was prone or partial to the racial-anthropological categories popular at the turn of the century, cited Herzl's physical beauty, his noble forehead, his height and well-built physique, in order to buttress his claims of the leader's innate stature. He also mentioned his unending patience. Nordau used a contrastive rhetorical device to measure Herzl's ultimate greatness. While Herzl was a distinguished poet, he was, according to Nordau, not as brilliant as Heine; although he was an impressive speaker, he was not as captivating as Disraeli; while he was a very talented writer, he was less imaginative than George Eliot; although he was an extremely competent administrator and manager, he was less accomplished than Baron Hirsch. Nevertheless, for Nordau, Herzl was greater than the others because he combined all of these qualities in his one person. Thus, by seeming to diminish or relativize Herzl's greatness in specific contrastive rhetorical formulations, Nordau accomplished the opposite; namely, he succeeded to enlarge and magnify Herzl's overall stature. Along these lines, five years after Herzl's death, Nachum Sokolow depicted him as a »Geistesaristokrat,«[27] an aristocrat of the spirit, while S. M. Melamed described him as a veritable renaissance man, recalling the towering exemplars of the Italian Renaissance of the fourteenth and fifteenth centuries.[28] Herzl had distinguished himself as a great artist, a poet, journalist, a statesman and a politician of the people, a parliamentarian and organizational genius, an expert in European law, and a man of serious and deep philosophical reflections. Thus, the comparison with the greatest and most accomplished figures in the Gentile world at the height of its cultural expression seemed to make good rhetorical sense. Other literary depictions, poems, and eulogies emphasize or combine aspects of Herzl's appearance with character traits including his native generosity, his introspection, his cheerful and kindly manner, his discretion, aristocratic gentility, love of fellow human beings, and his patriarchal encouragement of young literary talent.

---

[26] Max Nordau, cited in: Die Welt 8 (1904), no. 30, 392–393.

[27] Nachum Sokolow: Theodor Herzl. In: Die Welt 13 (1909), no. 28, 601.

[28] S. M. Melamed: Theodor Herzl. In: ibid., 602.

Sometimes, this literature focuses on aspects of Herzl's corporeal self. The Viennese poet Marek Scherlag emphasized Herzl's proud and manly figure,[29] and many others, including his friend, the Nobel Prize-winning writer and pacifist Bertha von Suttner, were effusive about his manly beauty. She thought he outwardly resembled an Assyrian monarch.[30] Heinrich Loewe viewed Herzl as the most noble, ideal type of the Jewish people (»Stamm«), whose beauty seemed to be unified in this one man.[31] A constructed unambiguous manliness with an aura of ancient lineage was a *sine qua non* of rightful ascension in the political leadership of the patriarchal culture. On the other hand, Maria Stona (Marie von Scholz, Gräfin von Stonakowski) wrote about the soft sadness around him and his alienation from Vienna. She claimed that he never felt at home there.[32] Perhaps that could help explain his turn to Zionism. His cousin, the writer Raoul Auernheimer, wrote of Herzl's magical personality, and his aura of lofty solitude and the silence of one who possesses great knowledge.[33] Hermann Struck, the German-Jewish artist, commented on Herzl's other-worldly beauty, his towering stature of perfect harmony; every movement was that of an uncrowned king.[34] Some observers, like Sil-Vara, suggested that in addition to his tall and stately appearance and elegantly dressed manner, he had an oriental aspect, which gave him an attractive, exotic air: »He was an Arabian sheikh, a prophet, a high priest, and at the same time, the elegant, cultured modern man.«[35] That he could be so many different things to a wide variety of people indicates how successful the mythopoetic process was in his particular case. But it also indicates the degree to which the poets, eulogizers, and remembrancers attempted to determine the image by drawing on their own inner resources and on images which they deemed attractive or convincing for superior heroic personalities in the new national pantheon.

Sometimes many of these positively drawn qualities were framed in a negative light. For example, Franz Servaes, a colleague at the *Neue Freie Presse,* recalled Herzl's supercilious manner and his unapproachability, the distance he maintained from his co-workers.[36] Hermann Menkes, another journalist colleague, depicted Herzl with the almost despotic gestures of a dangerous revolutionary leader. He was, to be sure, an imposing figure with fiery and dreamy eyes, but his manly energy was almost humiliating in its impatient and unmiti-

---

[29] Marek Scherlag: Der Führer. In: Nussenblatt (Ed.), Zeitgenossen über Herzl (note 5), 177.

[30] Bertha von Suttner, cited in: Ost und West 4 (1904), no. 7, 549.

[31] Heinrich Loewe: Das Jüdische Volk in Trauer. In: Sonderausgabe zum Andenken an Theodor Herzl, Jüdische Rundschau, Berlin 5665, 9.

[32] Maria Stona: A Colleague's Reminiscence. In: Weisgal (Ed.), Theodor Herzl. A Memorial (note 5), 96.

[33] Raoul Auernheimer: Uncle Dori. In: ibid., 34.

[34] Hermann Struck: As an Artist Saw Him. In: ibid., 36.

[35] Sil-Vara, At Herzl's Grave (note 25), 22.

[36] See Franz Servaes: Grüsse an Wien. Berlin, Wien, Leipzig: Paul Szolnay 1948, 28.

gated power.[37] Martin Buber, one of Herzl's most incisive critics, who never-theless tried in retrospect to form a somewhat positive image of him, wrote in *Freistatt* in July, 1904 that Herzl exercised the power of a dictator, and that he acquired the soul of a tyrant, whose despotic suppression of opinion was al-most criminal.[38] Buber viewed Herzl as a man filled with inner contradictions. He was essentially a poet with tremendous charisma, a man of action whose impressive strength was to found in providing an illusion to those who met or who heard about him. In any case, for Buber, he was not to be thought of, or categorized as, a Jewish personality.[39] He was rather an outsider who never comprehended the inner dilemma of the Jewish people or the ultimate signifi-cance of Zionism itself. Perhaps, though, this worked in his favor in practical terms, even if this designation appeared to be a definite slight.

At this point, I would like to discuss briefly two specific examples which demonstrate concretely the very complicated task of differentiating between myth and reality in the literary depictions of Herzl. The first is taken from the work of an author whose name and works have been mostly forgotten; the other example is taken from an internationally famous writer, whose reputation and fame are secure in many countries of the world, less secure in others. The first, and mostly unknown writer, is Lothar Brieger-Wasservogel; the second and better known figure is Stefan Zweig.

Lothar Brieger-Wasservogel was an impressively prolific author and art critic in the first part of the twentieth century; he was the biographer of E. M. Lilien, for example, and he was associated with Zionism for a while. He is buried in the large Jewish cemetery in Weissensee in Berlin. Brieger-Wasservogel authored the major novel of modern racialist Zionism, *René Richter. Die Entwicklung eines moderen Juden*, published in Berlin in 1906. It follows the typical Zionist narrative model – the paradigm having been estab-lished by Herzl himself in *Altneuland* (1902). In Brieger-Wasservogel's novel, René Richter, the prototype of the decadent, aimless Jewish male, eventually finds his way to purposeful activity in Jewish nationalism, signalizing com-mitment, love, regeneration, and salvation in Zionist engagement. The third section of the novel is entitled »Renaissance« and it is dedicated »to the mem-ory of Dr. Theodor Herzl in deepest reverence.«[40] René Richter's journalist colleague from Vienna, Dr. Merten, who appears in this part of the text, is patently based on Herzl. However, the historical Herzl also finds his way into the novel, when Merten decides to introduce René Richter to Herzl at the Zion-ist Congress in Basel in 1903.

---

[37] Hermann Menkes: Zwei Generationen. In: Nussenblatt (Ed.), Zeitgenossen über Herzl (note 5), 132.

[38] Martin Buber: Theodor Herzl. In his: Die Juedische Bewegung. Berlin: Jüdischer Verlag 1916, 138–152.

[39] Martin Buber: Herzl und die Historie. In: ibid., 172.

[40] Lothar Brieger-Wasservogel: René Richter. Die Entwicklung eines modernen Juden. Berlin: Richard Schröder Verlagsbuchhandlung 1906.

Despite its many aesthetic flaws, improbablilities, and fundamental lack of verisimilitude, the novel makes a strong case for Jewish nationalism founded upon racial purity and the idea of racial regeneration. The goal of Zionism, according to Merten, is to remove the degenerate Jewish race from the arena of an enervating struggle with the Aryan race in Europe and to reunify the dispersed Jewish racial strains in the ancestral homeland, in order to rejuvenate the race and build a new Jewish empire based on the principle of race. The discourse of German racialist writers like Langbehn and Chamberlain is dominant here.[41] Upon meeting the historical Herzl, the fictional René Richter is overwhelmed by the former's royal splendor and majestic beauty, as well as his leadership qualities. Here was the undisputed leader and king of the nation. On the basis of the ultimate compatibility of their aims, and their common aristocratic geneology, René Richter receives a mandate from the Zionist leadership to head a colonization project in Palestine. The denouement of the fictional text presents the protagonist, together with his supportive and racially compatible Jewish wife, Ruth, packing up and closing out their affairs in Berlin. They confidently take leave from family and friends before departure. In the last scene, the »old Europe« sinks below the horizon, as the ocean liner steams towards Zion and the Jewish future there.

What is significant about this novel is that it willfully, if perhaps recklessly, connects Herzl sympathetically to ideas and activities which he staunchly opposed during his lifetime. That Herzl could be appropriated to this degree so soon after his death testifies to the rapid pace of the mythicization process under way at that time. First, Herzl is identified in the novel with the racialist Zionist viewpoint characteristic of many cultural Zionists at the turn of the century, typical, say, of the early Zionism of Nathan Birnbaum. But, in fact, Herzl distanced himself from this stream rather consistently. He did not champion Zionism as a racial movement, and he tended to avoid the common racialist jargon. Also, the fictional characters, René and Ruth Richter, receive a mandate from Herzl and the Congress to colonize the land, something which Herzl opposed politically, as a premature move which was potentially harmful to the cause. Still, by linking Herzl in fiction to racialism and settlement politics, Brieger-Wasservogel attempted to gain credibility for those positions, which he no doubt wished to advance at the time. Luckily, this novel was never very successful; it disappeared quickly from bookstores and from Jewish consciousness, as did the racial Zionist stream altogether.

The last example is the depiction of Herzl written by Stefan Zweig in two versions, one in 1929 on the occasion of the 25th anniversary of his death, and the other, based on the first version, which appeared in Zweig's posthumously published autobiography, *Die Welt von Gestern* (The World of Yesterday). Owing to the stupendous popularity of this work, which has been translated

---

[41] Cf. Mark H. Gelber: Melancholy Pride: Nation, Race and Gender in the German Literature of Cultural Zionism. Tübingen 2004, 125–160.

into dozens of languages, many readers throughout the world have been introduced to Herzl through Zweig's depiction of him in this complicated memoir book. Also, the account of Herzl's funeral, suffused with a plethora of hyperbolic formulations, remains the most accessible account of what appears to have been a memorable occasion, even if it was not the hysterical, massive, historically significant convocation described by Zweig. Already at the time of the book's appearance in the 1940s, many observers dismissed the possible veracity of *The World of Yesterday*, noting that the work could not serve as a reliable historical source. Nevertheless, Zweig's constructed image of Herzl as the paragon of literary excellence in Vienna in his capacity as a feuilletonist and literary editor at the *Neue Freie Presse* is corroborated by many other contemporary commentators and eulogists.[42] Likewise, other accounts of the funeral attest to a large gathering of distraught mourners and they convey clearly the sense of the loss of a great personality. According to this logic, the greater the number of mourners at the funeral procession, the greater the stature of the dead leader would be.

What turns out, after careful, even painstaking, literary scrutiny of Zweig's versions of Herzl's career and his accounts of his encounter with him, in addition to consideration of much related literary and other documentation, is the following: Zweig's account in *Die Welt von Gestern* of his youthful deification of Herzl the journalist, as well as the poignant literary depiction of their first encounter, in connection with Herzl's position as editor of the feuilleton section at the *Neue Freie Presse,* are mostly fictional depictions. That is, they are largely imaginary and highly stylized accounts. First, there is solid evidence in Zweig's correspondence that as a young man he did not particularly appreciate Herzl's journalism.[43] Also, the famous encounter of the young writer with the supposedly revered editor Herzl could not have taken place in the manner described or produced the results Zweig reports.[44] The literary sequence which led to Herzl's supposedly intuitive positive appraisal of the young, aspiring writer's talents and the acceptance of one of his early prose pieces, turns out to be mostly fantasy. In the end, though, we cannot determine any more what the

---

[42] Stefan Zweig: König der Juden. In: Weisgal (Ed.), Theodor Herzl. A Memorial (note 5), 55–57.

[43] See, for example, Zweig's letter to Karl Emil Franzos, dated December 10, 1901, in which he expresses his strong dislike, even hatred, of the form of Viennese journalism practiced in the city, which presumably included Herzl's journalism as well: »Journalismus in der Form, wie er in Wien ausgeprägt ist, ist mir verhaßt, die Litteraten selbst sind nicht allzu sympathisch [...].«). In: Stefan Zweig. Briefe 1897–1914. Ed. by Knut Beck, Jeffrey B. Berlin and Natascha Weschenbach-Feggeler. Frankfurt a. M.: S. Fischer 1995, 30.

[44] See Mark H. Gelber: Stefan Zweig und die Judenfrage von heute. In: Stefan Zweig – heute. Ed. by Mark H. Gelber. New York, Berne, Frankfurt a. M., Paris: Peter Lang 1987, 164–167. See also the chapter on Stefan Zweig and Die Welt von Gestern. In: Michael Stanislawski: Autobiographical Jews. Seattle: University of Washington Press 2004.

real sequence of events might have been in this regard. That is, while Zweig did publish an early piece of prose in the *Neue Freie Presse* during the time of Herzl's editorship there, the specific depiction of how this came about cannot be truthful. The question must be asked then why Zweig – a world famous author in 1929, who had attempted over decades to project a self-image as a cosmopolitan humanist who had transcended nationalist causes and nationalist consciousness from the very beginning of his career –would depict Herzl years later in such unambiguously positive literary terms and wish to associate himself and his literary career retrospectively with him? This appears to have been the case, both in 1929 and then again during his very last years in exile, shortly before he committed suicide in desperation in 1942. In *The World of Yesterday* he presented an image of himself as a cosmopolitan humanist with certain Jewish interests, who could never embrace nationalist ideologies and who saw in Nazism, which had burnt his books and had destroyed the internationalist, pacifist world of his dreams, the worst possible expression of a nationalist ideology.

There are numerous possible answers to this question, and they all hinge on Zweig's retroactive creation of his own myth. One answer could be his wish to have it both ways. That is, he may have wished to retain his image as an internationalist and humanist who also belonged to Jewry, by affirming a variety of Zionism through Herzl, especially as a movement which might be good for the world at large. Another answer is his possibly growing but largely hidden sympathy with political Zionism, especially given virulent antisemitism in Austria after the First World War followed subsequently by the brutal reality of Nazi antisemitism after the Anschluss in 1938. A third option is that Zweig hoped in this way to hedge his bets, as it were, by claiming that he was an historical witness, one who knew Herzl and one who had been touched deeply by him, just in case it turned out that Zionism proved to be the best option for Jewry given the fateful direction European history and politics were taking in the late 1920s and 1930s.

The case of Zweig may remind us of a very similar literary fabrication found in Zev Jabotinsky's autobiography, where Jabotinsky manufactures an incident, an encounter between Jabotinsky and Herzl, which supposedly took place on the podium at the Sixth Zionist Congress and includes a totally fabricated short exchange between the youthful Jabotinsky and Herzl. As Michael Stanislawski has written convincingly, by transposing a few details, a few names and a few facts, Jabotinsky sought by including this fictional sequence to accomplish the retroactive creation of his own myth.[45] Here, though, unlike in the case of Zweig, Jabotinsky claimed vociferously that he was the true political heir of Herzl.

---

[45] Michael Stanislawski: Zionism and the fin de siécle: Cosmopolitanism and Nationalism from Nordau to Jabotinsky. Berkeley, Los Angeles, London: University of California Press 2001, 162.

In the end, it is the ideal image of Herzl which remains potentially useful, even if one cannot know anymore where to draw the line between myth and history in the literary record of Herzl's life and career. Within the vast reservoir of literary depictions and images of Herzl, there may be some which are well-suited to an Israeli and Jewish culture of the 21st century. The solution will depend on the development of new strategies to remember the past, or to construct a version of it, with a view towards an Israeli, or Israeli-Jewish identity, and the future of the state. Perhaps it will be the more patient, melancholy, pacifistic, internationalist, and compromising image of Herzl which will come to the fore, and a new collective memory may be substantiated through commemoration of this Herzl (or these Herzls). Even if these images did not appear to serve the pressing needs of the Zionist movement for a good part of the 20th century, it may be that these qualities, as embodied by a new mythic Herzl, would serve Zionism and the State of Israel well in the 21st century. As Ahad Ha-am wrote already during Herzl's »Shloshim«:

> As time goes on, and the ideal picture of the national hero attains its perfect form, he will perhaps become for our day what the old national heroes were for our ancestors in days gone-by; the people will make him the embodiment of its own national ideal […] and will derive from him strength and courage to struggle onward, indefatigably, along the hard road of its history.[46]

With a newly constructed image of Herzl in mind, perhaps the nation might be fortified in its effort to navigate that hard road of history more easily, or maybe that road may become less difficult to tread. Perhaps it could become a more easily traveled road of history, that is not as hard as it has been for a very long time, even if it avoids becoming a normal, average, or ordinary one.

---

[46] Ahad Ha-am, quoted in Leon Simon: Herzl and Ahad Ha-am. In: Weisgal (Ed.), Theodor Herzl. A Memorial (note 5), 91.

Frank Stern

Der Wandernde Jude – Herzl und der Zionismus auf der Leinwand

Die Darstellung kultureller Erinnerung hängt stets von Bildern ab, die wir in unserem Kopf tragen, die unseren Augen und unseren Sehweisen entsprechen und die in unseren Visionen und Utopien eine Rolle spielen. Personen und Orte stehen bei solchen Erinnerungen meist im Zentrum. Die jüdische Erinnerung beginnt mit Abraham, die zionistische mit Herzl. Die Bibel war und ist für Generationen eine lebendige und farbenprächtige Beschreibung von Orten, Landschaften, Völkern, Frauen und Männern in ihrer Zeit, die nach wie vor die spirituelle und visuelle Phantasie anregt. Malerei, Literatur, Fresken und Darstellungen auf dem Theater schufen seit der Antike Bilder der biblischen Heldinnen und Helden, die für Generationen unvergessen blieben. An der Wende vom 19. zum 20. Jahrhundert wurden die biblischen Erinnerungen durch zionistische Visionen und Träume nicht nur schriftlich oder mündlich ergänzt, sondern abgebildet in Büchern, Zeitungen, Zeitschriften, Postkarten, Fotographien und zunehmend auch Spiel- und Dokumentarfilmen.

Doch wie sahen diese Bilder aus, was sahen die frühen Zionisten, was hatten sie vor Augen, wenn sie um 1900 über Zionismus sprachen und schrieben? Orangen, Altertümer, die Klagemauer, die Wüste, Kamele und die orientalische Silhouette von Jerusalem? Was sieht jemand vor Augen, den man heute nach Israel fragt? Modeboutiquen in der Shenkin Straße in Tel Aviv, orthodoxe Juden in frühneuzeitlichen Kaftanen und mit Schläfenlocken, bewaffnete Siedler, palästinensische Terroristen, die Salzsäule am Toten Meer, Mittelmeertourismus oder arabische Dörfer und romantische Beduinen am Wüstenhorizont?

Zwischen dem heutigen positiven oder negativen, zionistischen oder jüdischen, christlichen oder islamischen Blick auf den Nahen Osten und dem Blick der Zionisten vor mehr als hundert Jahren liegen mehrere Kriege, die Shoah, die Staatsgründung und die Medienbilder eines krisengeschüttelten Staates Israel im Konflikt mit den Palästinensern. Hinzu kommen inzwischen unzählige Spiel- und Dokumentarfilme über Israel, Judentum, die Shoah und Palästina.

Der Blick und die Visionen um 1900 waren ohne Zweifel primär geprägt vom christlich-jüdischen Selbstverständnis der Wiener oder Berliner Moderne und den Interessen derjenigen, die sich überhaupt mit Themen wie Zionismus oder Antisemitismus, jüdischer Identität oder dem Problem einer jüdischen Heimstatt außerhalb der Wiener und Berliner Kaffeehäuser befassen wollten. Das Judentum historisierende und auch romantisierende Debatten waren ge-

nauso an der Tagesordnung wie die ironische Infragestellung solcher Orientierungen durch liberale, sozialdemokratische, sozialistische und deutschnationale jüdische Kreise. Erinnert sei nur an Martin Buber und Franz Rosenzweig auf der einen und Kurt Tucholsky, Karl Kraus und Rosa Luxemburg auf
der anderen Seite. Der Kunst- und Kulturhistoriker Ernst Gombrich betont
rückblickend, wie wichtig die deutsche Sprachkultur in den ersten Jahrzehnten
des 20. Jahrhunderts für die in Wien ansässigen jüdischen Familien war und
welche Scheidelinie zu den des Deutschen nicht mächtigen jüdischen Migranten aus Osteuropa bestand.[1] Doch die visuelle Kultur kannte im Gegensatz zur
literarischen Kultur solche Schranken kaum.

In der literarischen und kinematographischen Popularkultur spielten zwar
die intellektuellen Debatten keine Rolle, es gab aber Anfang der 20er Jahre
eine kulturelle Welle der Beschäftigung mit der Antike, Ägypten und damit
auch mit den biblischen Geschichten, die durch archäologische Ausgrabungen
und dem Fund des prächtigen Grabes von Tut-Ench-Amon ausgelöst worden
waren. Es liegt daher nahe, zu fragen, wie sich derartige kulturelle Entwicklungen mit der christlich geprägten Gesellschaft und den christlich-jüdischen
Erwartungen an die visuelle Kultur verbanden. Gleichzeitig ist aber auch danach zu fragen, welche Rolle im christlich-jüdischen Selbstverständnis Kenntnisse über die biblischen Wanderungen der hebräischen Stämme oder über die
Probleme und das Leiden von Teilen der jüdischen Bevölkerung in Osteuropa
spielten. Die innerjüdischen Debatten wiederum sind auch kaum vom kulturellen Zeitgeist der konfliktreichen Moderne zu trennen.

War das jüdische Selbstverständnis von Tradition und Religion nicht hochgradig säkular geworden? Seit Moses Hess, der aufgeklärten Religionskritik
und den nationalen Bewegungen des 19. Jahrhunderts war den zionistischen
Vordenkern und Publizisten deutlich, dass eine moderne Variante der Heiligen
Schriften popularisiert werden musste, die Antworten auf Antisemitismus,
Pogrome und die neue nationale Idee in Mittel- und Osteuropa geben sollte.
Das religiöse Gebet reichte nicht, der Traum vom Messias beschäftigte mehr
die Orthodoxie. Große Teile des westeuropäischen Reformjudentums hatten im
Bunde mit der Wissenschaft vom Judentum den geistig-kulturellen Schritt in
die jüdische Moderne dadurch vollzogen, dass jüdische Überlieferung und
Tradition historisiert wurden, und die zeitlosen Mythen sich in Zeitgeschichte
verwandelten. Nicht religiöser Glaube oder das Ringen um die Wahrheit in der
Seele des Gläubigen standen im Zentrum jener modernen jüdischen Renaissance, sondern das Schicksal der Wanderungen, der auf einen Staat orientierten Bemühungen und Kämpfe in der Antike, die nationalen Ambitionen und
Identitätsbewahrungen in der Geschichte und die Durchsetzung der Gleich-

---

1 Vgl. Ernst Gombrich: »Niemand hat je gefragt, wer jetzt gerade ein Jude oder ein
   Nichtjude war«. Ein Interview von Hermine Koebl. In: Gerhard Botz/Ivar O-
   xaal/Michael Pollak/Nina Scholz (Hg.): Eine Zerstörte Kultur. Jüdisches Leben und
   Antisemitismus in Wien seit dem 19. Jahrhundert. Wien 2002 (2. Aufl.), 88.

heits- und Demokratievorstellungen des modernen Liberalismus. Das Leiden und die Not jüdischer Bevölkerungen seit dem Mittelalter durch Ritualmordbeschuldigungen, Zwangskonversionen, religiösen, wirtschaftlichen und politischen Antisemitismus bis zur Dreyfus-Affäre prägten die Visionen der ersten Zionisten genauso wie ein – wenn auch oft unklares – Verständnis der Unterschiede zwischen osteuropäischer jüdischer Tradition und dem akkulturierten, weitestgehend verbürgerlichten westeuropäischen Judentum. Wien, die Metropole Mitteleuropas, war die geistige Grenze und der intellektuelle Sammlungsort von beidem.[2]

Das Volk des Buches hatte viel Geschichte, eine globale Geographie, aber wenig eigenen Raum, so schien es, seit den antiken jüdischen Helden König David, Jehuda Makkabäus und Bar Kochba zugejubelt worden war, und seit das Imperium Romanum mit den Aufsässigen monotheistischen Stämmen im Nahen Osten kurzen Prozess gemacht und die Träger jüdischer Souveränität aus Jerusalem verjagt hatte. Vor dem Hintergrund nationaler Bewegungen und antisemitischer Exzesse wurde um die Jahrhundertwende daher immer deutlicher, dass es nicht um ein religiöses Schicksal ging sondern um eine historisch zu definierende soziale und politische Identität. Nicht nach dem künftigen Schicksal sondern nach der künftigen Geschichte fragten die unruhigen Zionisten. Insofern war die Jahrhundertwende auch eine Wende in der Auffassung jüdischer Überlieferung. Vom religiösen messianischen Traum zur konkreten geschichtlichen Utopie verschob sich die Betrachtung bei zahlreichen jüdischen Intellektuellen, allen voran den zionistischen Vordenkern; denn es ging nicht mehr nur um europäische, russische, deutsche oder österreichische Geschichte, es ging nun um jüdische Geschichte im engeren Sinne als Geschichte eines Volkes umgeben von anderen Völkern.

Die Erzählungen und farbenfrohen Bilder der Bibel, die Geschichte der Juden in Europa bekamen einen aktuellen Rahmen im zionistischen Denken, aber auch generell in der europäischen und amerikanischen Kultur, da sich ihnen das neue Medium des 20. Jahrhunderts annahm: der Film. Das Buch der Bücher wurde zum Drehbuch für unzählige Filme, und die Menschen der Bibel wurden zu Schauspielerinnen und Schauspielern, zu Komparsen der Moderne. Jahrhunderte nach den Bibelübersetzungen und dem Beginn der mündlichen Überlieferung von Abraham und Sarah, von Joseph und Osnat, von Moses und den Propheten wurde die Visualisierung von jüdischer Geschichte und Kultur erneut Bestandteil der westlichen Moderne, der modernen visuellen Kultur. Die ersten dreißig Jahre des Filmschaffens sind voll von biblischen Themen, Geschichten und Kostümfilmen mit den Helden aus der hebräischen Bibel, so wie sie in der christlichen Gesellschaft überliefert und adaptiert wurde.

---

2 Vgl. Frank Stern: Moses in Wien und Freud in Sodom. Jüdisch-christliche Visualisierungen im Wiener Film. In: transversal. Zeitschrift für jüdische Studien 1 (2004), 18–32.

Visueller Zionismus

1896, als Herzl den *Judenstaat* schrieb, fanden auch die ersten Kinovorführungen in Wien statt. Das erste Jahrhundert des Films ist untrennbar mit 100 Jahren Zionismus verbunden. Doch die Teilnehmer der Zionistischen Weltkongresse gehörten nicht immer zu den aufgeschlossenen und der Moderne zugewandten Köpfen ihrer Zeit. Versuche, Beschlüsse durchzusetzen, die das neue Medium Film zu einem wichtigen Instrument der zionistischen Aufklärung hätten machen können, scheiterten oder wurden solange vertagt, bis keiner mehr wusste, dass es sie gab. Nicht zufällig gibt es nur Legenden über ausführliche Filmaufnahmen von Herzl und die Hoffnung, irgendwann in einem Archiv fündig zu werden: Wort und Bild hatten in der Arbeit der zionistischen Institutionen noch nicht zu den bewegten Bildern gefunden.

Verschiedene Versuche der Film- oder Studioförderung scheiterten, doch gab es immer wieder örtliche oder regionale zionistische Institutionen, die sich der Filmarbeit auch finanziell annahmen, etwa durch die Förderung von Vorführungen. Selbst der Herzl-Film wurde von den zionistischen Behörden zuerst aus inhaltlichen und finanziellen Gründen abgelehnt. In Großbritannien fanden die dortigen zionistischen Institutionen Gefallen am Film, allerdings mussten einige Veränderungen am Inhalt vorgenommen werden.[3] Doch die unruhigen Wiener jüdischen Filmgeister hatten aufgrund der bewegten Filmverhältnisse und der expandierenden Filmproduktionsfirmen in Wien nicht auf schwerfällige Bürokratien zu warten. Jüdische und zionistische Filmstoffe lagen einfach in der Luft. Joseph Roth, Anfang der 20er Jahre ein ungestümer und innovativer Journalist, schrieb in *Die Filmwelt* am 21. März 1919:

> Und so ist mit Kaiser und Hofstaat auch eine Anzahl von Filmen unbrauchbar geworden. Der Film muß Schritt halten mit dem Galopp der Weltgeschichte [...] Die Revolution ist die künftige Beherrscherin der Kinowelt. Wie die Phrase aus Zeitungen, so wird die verlogene Gebärde aus dem Kino verbannt.[4]

In Wien produzierte Spielfilme mit jüdischen Themen hatten ihre Wurzeln in der Literatur, im Theater, in den erfolgreichen Stücken am Volkstheater, dem Theater in der Josefstadt. Einige Schauspielerinnen wie Gisela Werbezirk und andere waren auch dem Jiddischen Theater verbunden. Dies war oftmals, wie der erste Herzl-Film zeigt, nicht zu übersehen. Die jungen Filmschaffenden wechselten vom Theater auf die Leinwand und zurück. Die Regie, Drehbuch und intendierte Botschaft konzentrierten sich auf die expressiv eingesetzten Körper, die Begleitmusik und je nach Finanzen auf die mise-en-scène in grandiosen Kulissen und mit tausenden Wiener Arbeitslosen – darunter nicht weniger Wiener Juden aus der Leopoldstadt – als Komparsen.

---

3 Vgl. zum jiddischen Film: J. Hoberman: Bridge of Light. Yiddish Film Between Two Worlds. Philadelphia 1991.
4 Ebd., 65.

Parallel zu den zionistischen Strategien entwickelten sich auch die filmischen und narrativen. Die inhaltlichen und narrativen Aspekte jener frühen Filme sind in einem doppelten Kontext zu sehen. Zum einen sind diese Filme – auch mit zionistischen oder religiösen Themen – stets geronnene Kultur- und Filmgeschichte. Zum anderen ist der Kontext der Entstehung und der Wirkung eines Films bisweilen bedeutsamer als die Geschichte, die der Film erzählt. Wie beim historischen Film insgesamt, so sind auch hinsichtlich der zionistischen Dokumentar- und Spielfilme der Kontext der Filmproduktion und die aktuell beeinflusste Filmerzählung oft aufhellend und weisen auf deren Rezeption unter den Zuschauern und Kritikern hin.

Kontext und Narration: »Theodor Herzl – Bannerträger des Jüdischen Volkes«

»Theodor Herzl – Der Bannerträger des Jüdischen Volkes«, so lautete der Titel des Dokudramas, das – 1920 produziert – im Februar 1921 in die Wiener Kinos kam. Regie führte Otto Kreisler, die bewegende Kraft hinter den Kulissen waren der Schauspieler Rudolph Schildkraut und sein Sohn Joseph. Rudolph Schildkraut hatte bereits mit Max Reinhardt und anderen Regisseuren in Wien und Berlin gearbeitet. Produziert wurde der Film von der Helios-Film. Der Film hat vier erzählerische Ebenen.

Erstens geht es um ein Bio-Pic, eine Herzl-Biographie von seiner Kindheit bis zu seinem Tode, die in 56 Minuten den Zionismus in bewegten Bildern als Erfolgsgeschichte darstellt, in der Herzl bei Baron Hirsch, bei der Züricher Bevölkerung aus Anlass des ersten zionistischen Kongresses, beim türkischen Sultan, bei Papst Leo XIII. nur auf positive Zustimmung stößt. Der Film gibt so eher Herzls Vision und Träume wieder als die Skepsis der Audienz-Gewährenden hinsichtlich der vorgestellten Pläne der Gründung einer jüdischen Heimstatt in Palästina.

Zweitens liefert der Film in monumentalen Szenen einen kurzen Abriß der jüdischen Geschichte, allerdings zunächst der Glanzepochen: König David, Makkabäer, Bar-Kochba. Dem folgen Inquisition, Pogrome, Dreyfus-Prozess. Damit werden wichtige Aspekte des jüdischen historischen Bewusstseins aus der zionistischen Perspektive dargestellt.

Drittens visualiert der Film die jüdische Säkularisierung, indem Herzls Bewusstwerdung und historisches Bewusstsein, das durch eigenes Erleben und Erzählungen von Pogromen befördert wird, wesentlich auf seiner Lektüre der »Geschichte des jüdischen Volkes« basiert, womit zweifelsohne Heinrich Graetz epochales Werk gemeint ist, dass damals in jede Wohnung des aufgeklärten und Deutsch lesenden jüdischen Bürgertums gehörte. Gleichzeitig haben Film und Texttafeln religiöse Konnotationen, erscheinen Engel, Boten Gottes und wird Herzl mit Moses verglichen, der ebenfalls nicht ins Land Israel ziehen konnte, sondern vorher verstarb.

Viertens wirft der Film durch seine narrativen Schwerpunkte Licht auf die
frühen 20er Jahre, die Erfahrungen der in Wien lebenden Juden und blickt in
die Zukunft, nach Amerika und auf künftige führende Persönlichkeiten der
jüdischen Welt wie Einstein und Weizmann. Der Film zeigt Herzls Begegnung
mit dem Antisemitismus als Kind in Ungarn, als Student in Wien und im
Staatsdienst, seine im Film zentrale Begegnung mit Vater Abraham, einem
Überlebenden der Pogrome in Russland und Polen, dessen Erzählungen sein
zionistisches Engagement stark beeinflussen. Herzls Ringen um ein einheitli-
ches Vorgehen der Zionisten klammert auch seine Option für den britischen
Vorschlag, Uganda als Heimstatt in Erwägung zu ziehen, nicht aus.

Der Herzl-Film in seiner Zeit

Herzl starb 1904, der Film wird 1920 produziert. Der erste Weltkrieg brachte
zahlreiche Begegnungen der österreichischen und deutschen Juden mit der
jüdischen, Jiddisch sprechenden Bevölkerung Osteuropas. Die zionistische
Bewegung hatte praktisch und propagandistisch das Altneuland zum zentralen
Fokus gemacht. Und der britische Außenminister Balfour hatte in einer schrift-
lichen Erklärung die Errichtung einer jüdischen Heimstatt im britischen Man-
datsgebiet Palästina zugesagt. Diese internationale Entwicklung gehört ohne
Zweifel zum Hintergrund des 1920 fertig gestellten Herzl-Films.
    Der filmische Blick Herzls auf Pogrome und Fluchtbewegungen aus dem
Shtetl, die sich auf das 19. und das beginnende 20. Jahrhundert beziehen, die
die Not der osteuropäischen Volksmassen anschaulich machen, die Herzen
potentieller Sponsoren erweichen und möglichst jüdische Unterschichten zur
Weiterwanderung nach Palästina bewegen sollen, hatten allerdings nicht allein
historische sondern 1920 auch ganz aktuelle Konnotationen. Zu Beginn des
Ersten Weltkriegs wackelte die k.u.k. Ostfront erheblich, in den Dörfern und
Kleinstädten Galiziens vermischten sich nun Erinnerungen an die Pogrome
und Überfälle der Kosaken mit den Berichten über Kriegsgreuel, die auch
damals munter überall über den jeweiligen Gegner verbreitet wurden. Im
Herbst und Winter 1914 erreichten ungefähr 150.000 Flüchtlinge Wien, davon
die meisten Juden. Fotographien vergangener Fluchtbewegungen sind im Film
nahezu dokumentarisch nachgestellt, doch werden die dann für die Flüchtlinge
sich ergebenden Probleme in Wien ausgeklammert. Der filmische Zusammenhang setzt die aktuelle Erfahrung mit Bildern der Vergangenheit, mit Berichten
über andere Perioden, in Szene. Die Spielfilmhandlung appelliert an die konkreten Erinnerungen der Zuschauer an die Kriegsjahre, doch werden diese, da
Herzl ja 1904 starb, nicht dargestellt.
    Filmisch wird hier mit doppelter Erinnerung gearbeitet. Zum einen die Ge-
schichte Theodor Herzls vor dem Hintergrund des Antisemitismus in Osteuropa und Wien und zum anderen die Erinnerungen an die unmittelbar zurücklie-

genden Kriegsjahre mit der starken ostjüdischen Migration nach Wien. Dadurch konnten die Filmemacher davon ausgehen, dass ihre gesellschaftliche und nicht allein biographische Filmerzählung auf Zustimmung stoßen würde.

1916 gab es noch 20.000 jüdische Flüchtlinge in Wien. Die Zahl wuchs dann auf 40.000 an, 1918 waren es aber nur noch etwa 17.000. Doch das waren nur die offiziellen Zahlen.[5] Mit Blick auf die Rezeption des Publikums befasste sich der Film implizit damit nicht allein mit dem Schicksal der Juden in Osteuropa sondern mit dem in Wien lebenden und aus Osteuropa kommenden Teil der jüdischen Wiener Bevölkerung. Der Film verbindet durch die zentrale Darstellung der Begegnung Herzls mit dem Buchhändler Vater Abraham – der Name ist kein Zufall, da dieser Charakter durch seine Flucht-Wanderungen bestimmt ist – das aufgeklärte säkulare Wiener Judentum mit dem traditionsverbundenen ostjüdischen Judentum. Die säkulare und die religiöse jüdische Welt scheinen filmisch hier im Zionismus zusammenzufinden. Damit werden unterschwellig und visuell zentrale Themen des Zionismus zu dieser Zeit repräsentiert. Wien war vielen in Osteuropa aus der Ferne als eine Art »irdisches Jerusalem« erschienen, ein Topos, der in den Erinnerungen von Elias Canetti und Manes Sperber erwähnt wird.

Nach ihrer Ankunft in Wien wurden die ostjüdischen Migranten allerdings mit der sozialen und wirtschaftlichen Wirklichkeit konfrontiert, und die Wiener Leopoldstadt erwies sich nicht wirklich als Paradies. Die meisten Flüchtlinge lebten nicht im Wohlstand, sondern in Armut und Not und hingen von der jüdischen Wohlfahrt ab. Staatliche und private Hilfe konnten die Not kaum lindern, das zionistische Hilfswerk konzentrierte sich auf die Kinder der Flüchtlinge und auf deren Bildung, immer mit der Hoffnung, die politische Arbeit hier voranzutreiben.

Dieser soziale und politische Kontext des Films über Theodor Herzl wiederum ist im Zusammenhang mit anderen Spielfilmen zu sehen, die zur gleichen Zeit produziert wurden. So schildert ein Stummfilm aus dem Jahr 1920 die Arbeit des »Jüdischen Hilfswerks« ohne zentrale zionistische Bezüge.

Dieser Film »Opfer des Hasses. Die Tragödie eines russischen Fabrikanten«, Regie Hans Marschall, 1920, beschreibt die Geschichte eines russischen Flüchtlings, allerdings vor den Bolschewiki, und seiner Kinder, sowie die Arbeit des Hilfswerks, also Wiener jüdischer Wohlfahrtseinrichtungen, die diese Familie retten. Die filmische Repräsentation jüdischen Schicksals war nach 1918 auf der aktuellen Wiener Tagesordnung. Der Zionismus war nur eine der kulturellen und sozialen Optionen, die der ostjüdischen Bevölkerung angeboten wurden. Allerdings regte sich bereits 1915 der Widerstand der Wiener Gemeinde, die nicht daran interessiert war, dass die Flüchtlinge Arbeit fänden und sich als Folge ansässig machen würden. Die Gemeinde befürchtete,

---

5   Vgl. die genauen Angaben in Beatrix Hoffmann-Holter: »Ostjuden hinaus!« Jüdische Kriegsflüchtlinge in Wien 1914–1924. In: Guntram Geser/Armin Loacker (Hg.): Die Stadt ohne Juden. Wien: Filmarchiv Austria 2000, 314f.

dass die Stadt Wien dadurch »das ihr charakteristische Gepräge und ihre Eigenart« einbüssen würde.[6] Ablehnung der jüdischen Migranten aus dem Osten war nicht allein ein Problem der Antisemiten.

So gab es in Wien gegen die grassierende Feindschaft gegenüber Ostjuden z. B. am 27. November 1918 »Massenkundgebungen des Jüdischen Nationalrats« im 1. Bezirk im Hotel Post am Fleischmarkt, im 2. Bezirk in der Unteren Augartenstrasse im Beisl mit dem schönen Namen »König Dawid«, allerdings mit w geschrieben, und im 20. Bezirk im Brigittasaal in der Wintergasse. Für ortskundige Leser sei angemerkt, dass zumindest hinsichtlich des gemütlichen kleinen Saales im Hotel Post von Massen bei diesen Versammlungen kaum die Rede sein konnte. Unter den Rednern waren der Oberrabbiner Dr. Chajes und auch ein angereistes Gemeindemitglied aus Krakau. Die öffentliche Diskussion über, wie es damals in den Zeitungen genannt wurde, das »Ostjudenproblem« versiegte jedoch 1922–23.[7] Es kann aber davon ausgegangen werden, dass dieser zeitgenössische antijüdische Hintergrund in den Köpfen der Zuschauer vorhanden war genauso wie die große weite Welt der Spielfilme aus Frankreich, den USA, in denen es von romantischen Affären, Helden und lieben Mädeln, Historien, Kämpfen und Niederlagen nur so wimmelte.

Die Regisseure Michael Kertész und Alexander Korda produzierten in Wien historische Monumentalfilme mit biblischen Geschichten, jüdischen Heldinnen und Helden, in denen das neue jüdische Selbstbewusstsein genauso visualisiert wurde wie die christlich-jüdische Ambivalenz der Wiener Gesellschaft.

Insofern ist der den Zionismus propagierende Herzl-Film nicht aus dem filmischen Kontext zu lösen. Das Publikum sah Filme, die sich mit Ägypten und dem biblischen Exodus befassten, so in den folgenden Jahren »Die Sklavenkönigin« oder auch einen Spielfilm wie »Stadt ohne Juden«, der sich in utopisch-konkreter Form vehement mit dem Problem des Wiener Antisemitismus auseinandersetzte und ebenfalls in einer Sequenz eine liebevoll ironische Darstellung des Zionismus anbot.[8]

Kulturelle Erinnerungen, utopische Visionen, Unterhaltung pur und Starkult verbanden sich in der jungen Filmkunst mit der jüdischen Moderne. Der Film visualisierte und schuf kreativ die modernen Ikonen der jüdischen und christlich-jüdischen Traditionen, der westlichen Erinnerung und Kultur. Die zionistische Bilderwelt entwickelte sich folglich in einer kreativen kulturellen Spannung zwischen den sozialen und politischen Realitäten einerseits und der visuellen Welt imaginierter Mythen und scheinbar dokumentarischen Repräsentationen der Vergangenheit und des Nahen Ostens andererseits. Dadurch enthielten die kulturellen Visualisierungen beides – die biblischen jüdischen Narrative und die phantastischen und romantischen Bilder der jüdischen Kolonialisierung Palästinas. Der Orientalismus des beginnenden 20. Jahrhunderts war extrem roman-

---

6 Ebd., 325.
7 Ebd., 340.
8 Ebd.

tisch, abgesehen davon waren ja die Wiener und Berliner jüdischen Kinder alle mit Karl May aufgewachsen.

Das frühe Filmschaffen ist voll von Sequenzen mit orientalischen Bildern und Ambitionen. Nach dem kolonialen und imperialen begann nun überall in Europa ein visuelles »scramble for Africa«. Die Bilder beflügelten die imaginierte Welt des Nahen Ostens vom Euphrat bis an den Nil. Mit dem Zusammenbruch des Ottomanischen Reiches Ende des Ersten Weltkrieges, auf das Herzl sich mit dem Besuch beim Sultan noch beziehen musste, wurde Großbritannien zum Ansprechpartner des Zionismus. Herzls Versuch, den deutschen Kaiser zu gewinnen, wurde im Film ausgeblendet, schließlich war es ja eine Wiener Produktion, und außerdem ging es nach Versailles darum, Deutschland möglichst fern von allen kolonialen Ambitionen zu domestizieren. Angesichts der antideutschen Stimmungen u. a. in Polen und den USA verzichteten die Filmemacher auf die deutsche Episode in Herzls Biographie.

Die filmische Argumentation hatte sich stärker an den generellen kolonialisierenden Trend anzupassen. Zionismus und Kolonialismus verbanden sich nicht zuletzt durch die Bilder, die in den europäischen Kinos über die Leinwand liefen, und es ist nicht zu übersehen, dass ein populärer Orientalismus im Wiener Zeitgeist und auch im Jugendstil vorhanden war. Die Illustrationen von E. M. Lilien sind dafür ein Beispiel.[9] Die zionistischen Visualisierungen schwankten zwischen staatspolitischen Orientierungen, Kulturzionismus und der durch Wohlfahrt und zionistische Bewegungen beförderten Migration. Kurz, der visuelle Zionismus modernisierte den klassischen Orientalismus.

Zionistischer, jüdischer und jiddischer Film

Ein Anfang der 20er Jahre in Palästina produzierter dokumentarisch angelegter Film, »Rückkehr nach Zion/Shivat Zion« präsentierte umfassend Bilder einer sich entwickelnden neuen Gesellschaft mit Bildern des Aufbaus und Bildern der Wüste mit Kamelen. Ein alter Traum schien Wirklichkeit, »Altneuland« nur eine Schiffsreise entfernt. Der Regisseur des Films, Jakov Ben-Dov, kann als Vater des hebräischen Films bezeichnet werden. Er schuf in der jungen palästinensischen Filmindustrie die grundlegenden Bilder, die visuellen Ikonen der nationalen jüdischen Renaissance, die sowohl das Wiener Filmschaffen als auch bis heute alle visuellen Repräsentationen Israels und Palästinas prägen. Der Film überlebte das Jahrhundert in einem Prager Filmarchiv. Dort, in Prag, hatte Franz Kafka 1921 den Film gesehen. In seinem Tagebuch vermerkte er am 23. Oktober 1921: »Nachmittag Palästinafilm.« Am 19. Oktober hatte er

---

9 Vgl. Morris Rosenfeld: Lieder des Ghetto – mit Zeichnungen von E. M. Lilien. Berlin 1902 und Oz Almog/Gerhard Milchram: E. M. Lilien. Jugendstil, Erotik, Zionismus. (Hg. im Auftrag des Jüdischen Museums der Stadt Wien und des Braunschweigischen Landesmuseums). Wien 1998.

nach der Lektüre der biblischen Geschichte von Moses das Ende im Tagebuch
gelobt, nämlich dass Moses nicht über den Jordan ins Gelobte Land zieht.[10]
Prag, Wien, Berlin, New York, Chicago – die Leinwand wurde zu einem Medium visueller Aktualisierung der biblischen Mythen, der neuen Realitäten,
eines imaginären jüdischen Tourismus, der von Wien ausging und der sich um
die emotionale Identifizierung mit jenem kleinen Landstrich an der östlichen
Küste des Mittelmeeres bemühte. Neben professionellen Filmemachern hatten
aber bereits seit 1911 jüdische Reisende Filmaufnahmen gemacht, darunter
Murray Rosenberg, dessen erste Bilder jüdischen Lebens in Palästina heute im
Steven Spielberg Jewish Film Archive in Jerusalem lagern.

An solchen Bildern und Vorstellungen setzte der Herzl-Film an, indem er die
Geschichte des Jüdischen Volkes als antike Erfolgsgeschichte und moderne Leidensgeschichte, zumindest was Osteuropa anbetraf, visuell, narrativ und monumental in Szene setzte. Darüber hinaus sollte der Film insbesondere in seiner
amerikanischen Fassung von 1921 aufklärenden Charakter haben, die Quellen des
Zionismus aufzeigen und unter den jüdischen Zuschauern Identität stiften.

Die filmische Herzl-Biographie gehört folglich zu einem größeren Kontext
jüdischer Filmstoffe. Jüdische Themen waren nach dem Ende des Kaiserreichs
in der Wiener Kultur einfach »in«, was sich kurzfristig nach 1945 wiederholte!
1918 verfilmte die Wiener Kunstfilm Eugene Scribes Theaterstück »Die Jüdin«. 1919 drehte der Schauspieler Otto Kreisler eine filmische Langfassung
von Franz Grillparzers Stück »Die Jüdin von Toledo« und nach den Erfolgen
dieser Filme drehte Kreisler das Epos »Theodor Herzl. Bannerträger des Jüdischen Volkes« nach einem Drehbuch von Heinrich Glücksmann. Noch im
selben Jahr ließ Kreisler dem männlichen Helden Herzl eine bezaubernd komische, attraktive Heldin folgen. Der Film hieß »Das Judenmädel« mit der
22jährigen amerikanischen Molly Picon in der Hauptrolle. Sie hatte trotz Lower Eastside and Vaudeville-Erfahrung längere Wiener Engagements, da ihr
Ehemann und Manager Molly das, wie er meinte, schlechte Lower Eastside-
Jiddisch zugunsten eines gehobenen Wiener jiddischen Akzents austreiben
wollte. Als beide Wien verließen, zollten sie dem Zeitgeist Tribut, indem sie
vor der Presse verkündeten, dass sie in Palästina ein Filmstudio aufbauen wollten, in dem nur biblische Stoffe verfilmt würden.[11] Solcherart der allgemeinen
Zustimmung gewiss, konnten sie dann Mollys Karriere in den USA erfolgreich
fortsetzen. Doch bis dahin hatte sie auch in zwei weiteren Wiener jiddischen
Filmen gespielt. Der Wiener jüdische Regisseur Sidney M. Goldin und seine in
Wien produzierten jiddischen Filme waren erfolgreich und gehörten zu den
Wiener Filmverhältnissen Anfang der 20er Jahre. Die Antisemiten vergeiferten
sich zwar bei jedem neuen Film, doch das Publikum liebte die Filme, so wie es
auch Herzls trübsinnig-forschen-zionistischen Blick von der Leinwand bewun-
dert hatte. Zudem war der Filmheld Herzl erheblich stattlicher als der echte

---

[10] Ebd.
[11] Hoberman, Bridge of Light (Anm. 3), 65.

kränkelnde Theodor Herzl. Im folgenden Jahr verfilmte Kreisler die Geschichte eines anderen österreichischen Helden unter dem Titel »Mozarts Leben, Lieben und Leiden«, und der starb dann auch wie Herzl den Filmtod im Bett.

Die filmische Herzl-Biographie unterscheidet sich von allen späteren Versuchen, die Person Theodor Herzl, hier gespielt von Ernst Bath, auf die Leinwand zu bannen. Es ging nicht um das wirkliche Leben des Helden, sondern um einen jüdischen Bildungs- und Entwicklungsstoff, der, so die zeitgemäße Werbung, als historischer Monumentalfilm angekündigt wurde und als »zionistische Intoleranz«, also »Intolerance«, jenem grandiosen Monumentalfilm von Griffith aus dem Jahr 1916 vergleichbar, die jüdische Universalgeschichte in ein dramatisches Kunstwerk gießen sollte.[12] Der Film sollte Herzls Entwicklung zeigen, das gutbürgerliche Elternhaus, die Lektüre von Heinrich Graetz' Jahrhundertwerk der Geschichte des Jüdischen Volkes, den Einfluss der russischen Beilis-Affäre, des ungarischen Tiszaeszlarer Ritualmordvorwurfs, kurz: des europäischen Antisemitismus, der auch bösartig die junge Erste Republik heimsuchte, was daran ablesbar war, dass in der Wahlpropaganda der jungen Republik Ostjuden mit Korruption gleichgesetzt wurden. Insofern hat der Film zahlreiche der genannten aktuellen Wiener Konfliktstoffe in visuelle Konnotationen umgesetzt.

Herzls Lektüre der Geschichte des Jüdischen Volkes wird in historischen Episoden monumental in Szene gesetzt. Der Film als Dokudrama ist, heute betrachtet, ein offener filmischer Diskurs. Seine Ankündigung lautete »ein Film, den jeder Jude sehen muss«.[13] Daher sollte der Film auch wie viele andere historische Filme der Wiener Kinowelt ein Exportschlager werden. Dem Export ist es zu verdanken, dass wir den Film überhaupt heute noch sehen können. Das Jewish Film Archive in Boston fand die verstaubten Rollen der amerikanischen Fassung und restaurierte den Film.

Für europäische oder amerikanische Bedürfnisse konnte der Film damals jeweils ein wenig umgeschnitten werden. Die Filmmoderne dekonstruiert sich oft gern selbst, die amerikanischen jüdischen Zuschauer sollten schließlich nicht nach Palästina gehen, sondern einen zionistischen Obolus entrichten. Der Film blickt auf Zion, das biblische, das geographische Zion, indem er sich der jüdischen Erfolgs- und Leidensgeschichte vergewissert. Der cineastische Stummfilmblick ist aber auch auf das humanistische, das nicht-antisemitische Zion der Neuen Welt gerichtet. Optionen, die die Wirklichkeit der jüdischen Migration nach der Jahrhundertwende widerspiegeln. Wie viele Zuschauer des Films sich entschieden, nachdem der Film zu Ende war, eine Schiffspassage nach Palästina zu erstehen, wissen wir nicht. Was wir allerdings wissen, ist, dass der Darsteller des wandernden Juden und russischen Pogromflüchtlings, späterer Besitzer der Buchhandlung am Praterstern, Rudolf Schildkraut, und sein Sohn Joseph, die treibenden Kräfte der Filmproduktion, bald Schiffspassagen nach New York buchten und dort im beeindruckenden jiddischen Theater in der Lower East Side nun mit dem richtigen Wiener Jiddisch neue Erfolge

---

[12] Ebd.
[13] Zitiert nach ebd.

feierten. Rudolph und Joseph Schildkraut waren bald gefragte und populäre
Filmdarsteller in Hollywood. Zion in der Hester Street in New York...[14]

»Theodor Herzl – Bannerträger des Jüdischen Volkes« kam ab 11. Februar
1921 in die Kinos, zunächst in Wien in der Leopoldstadt – in der Taborstrasse,
dann in der Praterstrasse und anderen Kinos. Der Film im H. Engel Filmver-
leih hatte in Österreich Schulverbot und wurde in Filmzeitschriften als tenden-
ziös beschrieben.[15] »Die Neue Freie Presse« schrieb am 11.2.1921, dass der
Film »mit Ahasver, dem ewigen Juden« beginne und die »unvergleichliche
Darstellung« dem Film ausverkaufte Häuser sichere. Das Ferdinands-Kino in
der Taborstraße warb noch mit dem Namen Ahasver, was in späteren Be-
schreibungen nicht mehr auftauchte, weil dem einen oder anderen Wiener
Juden vielleicht die christliche Konnotation des Namens Ahasver aufgefallen
sein dürfte. Allerdings liefen im Februar 1921 in Wien zahlreiche abenteuerli-
che und dramatische Liebesfilme an, darunter der hochbeworbene Film Car-
men mit Pola Negri unter der Regie von Ernst Lubitsch.[16]

Im September wurde eine Sonntags-Matinee im Kino des Zirkus Busch mit
2000 Sitzen zugunsten der Opfer ukrainischer Pogrome veranstaltet. Und danach trat der Film seine Reise nach Amerika an, um ein größeres jüdisches
Publikum zu erreichen und für das zionistische Projekt zu gewinnen. Die ur-
sprüngliche Fassung des Films, damit auch möglicherweise heute fehlende
Szenen, ist bisher nicht bekannt, doch die amerikanische Fassung hat überdau-
ert, ist restauriert worden und zeugt von der ersten und bleibenden Visualisierung des zionistischen Gedankens, die in den Wiener Filmstudios entstand.

Allerdings wissen wir auch um die Reaktionen des Publikums bei der Wiener Premiere. Der Wiener Korrespondent des New Yorker »Forwerts« beschreibt ein alters- und herkunftsmäßig gemischtes Publikum, das mit herzer-
weichenden Rufen auf Herzls Schicksal und seine Suche nach Antworten rea-
gierte. Erst als im Film der alte russische Jude und Überlebende der Pogrome
Herzl aus ganzem Herzen die Perspektive Zions erleuchtet, atmeten die Zuschauer auf. Nach Ende des Films, so vermerkt der Korrespondent:

> There was great joy and happiness. Jews and Gentiles shook each others' hands [...]
> And so it happened that I also embraced the neighbors in my row – two beautiful
> Viennese shikslekh. We kissed and we hugged each other with great enthusiam. Ap-
> parently that is how God made good on the tears I had just shed.[17]

---

[14] Zu Rudolph und Josef Schildkraut vgl. Julius Bab: Schauspieler und Schauspielkunst. Berlin 1926, 181f.; Joseph Schildkraut: My Father and I. New York 1959;
Patricia Erens: The Jew in American Cinema. Bloomington 1984, 85f.
[15] Paimanns Filmliste Nr 237, 15.–21. Oktober 1920.
[16] Filmwelt 7.2.1921.
[17] Zitiert nach Hoberman, Bridge of Light (Anm. 3), 65.

Na'ama Rokem

Making Use of Prose: The Politics of Genre in Theodor Herzl and H. N. Bialik

Prose is a term that has had a surprisingly modest career in literary theory, perhaps because it seems to say at once too much and too little. Attempting to define prose, one is left with frustrating generalities (»words that go to the end of the page«) or with negative definitions (prose as *un*bound language, or as that which is not verse). What remains under-theorized is the density of this concept, which denotes a literary mode (prose as a type of text) as well as a modality (the prosaic, the mundane, the contingent): both a thing in the world and a way of looking at the world. In other words, prose and the prosaic are concepts that invite us to bridge form and history, and think about the politics of form. In his lectures on aesthetics, Hegel refers to the »current prosaic conditions« facing art in the present, using the term to refer to the historical nature of art and to a perceived antinomy between modernity and art. In the century that follows those lectures, the idea that prose is a historical marker through which art confronts the present conditions surfaces in many different contexts; one of these is the work of Zionist authors, who use prose as a prism through which to present the role of literature within the revolutionary transformation of Jewish life. Haim Nahman Bialik and Theodor Herzl both turned to prose – as an object to be studied and contemplated and as a tool to be used – in exploring the powers of literary language to do political work. Both of them produced a body of reflection on prose, through which they grappled with a set of very similar questions: What is the relation of Zionism to the past? How does it break with history, and how does it build on it? What is the place of law in the Zionist imagination, and what tradition is this law to be founded on?

I   »The shirt came into being!« – Herzl's Generic Hesitations
        and the Emergence of Prose in *Die Glosse*

From the earliest of his feuilletons to the literary works he penned as a Zionist, Herzl often explicitly reflects on questions of genre. The subject matter of his very first published feuilleton, dating to his gymnasium days in Budapest, is the feuilleton itself as an art form and the question of how to excel in it.[1] In-

---

[1] The manuscript, dated to the mid 1870s, is available in: Central Zionist Archive (henceforth: CZA), H-3084. See also Ernst Pawel: The Labyrinth of Exile; a Life of Theodor Herzl. New York: Farrar, Straus & Giroux 1989.

deed, to begin with, the feuilleton and the theater were the two genres that most prominently vied for his attentions and his creative powers, and in his early correspondence and journalistic publications he repeatedly renounces either the one or the other in ceremonious terms, vowing to become exclusively either a playwright or a journalist.[2] In his feuilletons, Herzl also often ironically renounces the possibility that he would write a novel.[3]

In fact, plans for a novel were never far from his mind. Several manuscripts indicate that he was particularly eager to write a novel that would bring to life, in a naturalist style, the city that had become his home at the age of 18, Vienna. The young author planned research visits to the city's poorer quarters, and prepared character sketches of members of different social groups.[4] But these were not to come to fruition. Instead, Herzl specialized in a branch of journalism that turned away from social reality and inhabited a self-fashioned cultural space which consisted of Viennese high society and the theatre, and adhered to strict social mores and rules of good taste.[5] It was only as a Zionist that Herzl could finally pen a novel, turning to utopia rather than naturalism, and offering his 1902 novel *Altneuland* as a model for the Jewish state.[6]

To understand how Herzl's Zionism was to give birth to novelistic prose, or how prose became a useful tool for Herzl the Zionist, it is useful to consider his staging of the philological event of the emergence of prose in his play *Die*

---

[2] Theodor Herzl: Briefe und Tagebücher. Ed. by Alex Bein, Hermann Greive, Moshe Schaerf and Julius Schoeps. Berlin: Propyläen Verlag 1983, I, 72. Theodor Herzl: Das Buch der Narrheit. Leipzig: F. Freund, Buch und Kunst Verlag 1888, 150. Leon Kellner, one of Herzl's earliest biographers, seems to take these statements very seriously, and names an entire chapter »Das Verzicht auf das Theater,« emphasizing that this was a necessary step in Herzl's political maturation. He does not explain the fact that Herzl continued to pen texts for the theater well into his career as a Zionist leader and almost to the end of his life. Leon Kellner: Theodor Herzls Lehrjahre 1860–1895. Berlin: R. Lowit Verlag 1920, 107ff.

[3] For Herzl's disavowals of these attempts, see disparaging statements about writing a novel in Herzl, Das Buch der Narrheit (note 2), 164.

[4] See notes for a ›Wiener Roman‹ CZA H-8034. Other novel manuscripts are available in: CZA H-8034, H-3086, H-70.

[5] The greatest critic of this journalistic genre was Karl Kraus. Paul Reitter: Karl Kraus and the Jewish Self-Hatred Question. In: Jewish Social Studies 10.1 (2003).

[6] The idea of a novel is tightly woven into Theodor Herzl's political plans from the start. His early plans and drafts for a Zionist manifesto are firstly articulated as drafts for a Jewish novel; even after the political tract – his *Der Judenstaat*(1895) – initially wins over, it must be explicitly differentiated from the novel. Shlomo Avineri: Theodor Herzl's Diaries as a Bildungsroman. In: Jewish Social Studies 5.3 (1999); Gisela Brude-Firnau: 1895: The Author, Feuilletonist, and Renowned Foreign Correspondent Theodor Herzl Turns toward Zionism and Writes the Manifesto *The Jewish State*. In: Yale Companion to Jewish Writing and Thought in German Culture, 1096–1996. Ed. by Sander L. Gilman and Jack Zipes. New Haven, London: Yale University Press 1997; Michael Gluzman: The Yearning for Heterosexuality. In: Theory and Criticism 11 (1997) [Hebrew].

Glosse (1895). This will allow us to read the novel as an experiment with prose as a medium among others, and to articulate the importance of this experiment for Herzl's political Zionism. The plot of the play, situated in 13th-century Bologna, is simple: Philippus von Montaperto has given up his vocation as a troubadour and is busy writing a glossary of the Roman Law; his wife, Regina, feels neglected and is hence susceptible to the advances of an old friend of Philippus, Aimeric von Péguilain, who still produces chivalric songs; at the last moment Philippus saves his marriage by reciting his commentary on the Roman marriage code, which turns out to be a performance even more poetic than his rival's.[7] This text – and even more so Herzl's choice of subject matter and the preparations made for writing about it – are an interesting key to understanding Herzl's views on the relation of literature and history.

Herzl's view of the past, as expressed in *Die Glosse* and elsewhere, posits a radical difference between the past and the present; this is a concept of history structurally parallel to Hegel's »prosaic conditions of the present,« the category used in his lectures on aesthetics to posit the historical transformations that present a challenge to modern art.[8] As my reading of the play shows, Herzl follows Hegel not only in positing that the transformation of possibilities for human action has altered the possibilities open to literature, but also in offering *prose* – and ultimately his own novelistic prose – as the answer to this transformation. Recognizing this ›prosaic‹ element in Herzl's literary works, most readers of which have focused on what seem to be conspicuously un-»prosaic« matters such as the great importance given to honor and the pathos of his Zionist discourse,[9] will allow us better to understand *Altneuland* and its place in the Zionist tradition. In other words, previous readers have often been interested in Herzl's aspirations to restore honor to the Jews, to make them *Satisfaktionsfähig*, worthy of participating in a duel; I suggest that as he continued to work on his Zionist plans and returned to his idea to write a novel he

---

7 Theodor Herzl: Die Glosse. Vienna 1895. The play, like most of Herzl's other theatrical productions, was received coldly by the theater directors to which it was sent. Joseph Fränkel: Theodor Herzl: Des Schöpfers Erstes Wollen. Wien: Fiba Verlag 1934. Oskar K. Rabinowicz: Herzl the Playwright. In: Jewish Book Annual 18 (1960–1961). This cold reception continues in later scholarship, where it is mostly mentioned only fleetingly, if at all, as another example of Herzl's complete failure as a playwright. An exception to that is Klaus Dethloff, who reprints the play and comments on it. Dethloff: Theodor Herzl oder der Moses des fin de Siècle. Wien: Böhlau 1986.

8 G. W. F. Hegel: Vorlesungen über die Ästhetik. Frankfurt/M.: Suhrkamp 1970, I, 253–255.

9 For example: Daniel Boyarin: The Colonial Drag: Zionism, Gender, and Mimicry. In: The Preoccupation of Postcolonial Studies. Ed. by Fawzia Afzal-Khan and Kalpana Seshadri-Crooks. Durham: Duke University Press 2000; Gluzman, The Yearning for Heterosexuality (note 6); Carl E. Schorske: Fin-De-Siècle Vienna: Politics and Culture. New York: Knopf 1980, 160ff.; Shmuel Almog: Zionism and History: The Rise of a New Jewish Consciousness. New York: St Martins Press 1987.

found that it was even more important to become »*prosafähig*,« that is, capable of using prose and the novel in the service of a political plan.

The medieval commentator Philippus is of interest to Herzl, who had studied law in the emphatically historicist atmosphere of the University of Vienna in the early 1890s, with scholars such as the Hegelian Lorenz von Stein, because he stands for a transformation in the world of law.[10] The events take place in Medieval Bologna, where the study of Roman Law was revived from the eleventh century onward, and from where it spread to the rest of continental Europe to form one of the foundations of civil law, and hence one of the instruments that formed the emergence of vernacular prose.[11] Earlier readers of this text have also identified the element of change and transformation as central to the text, reading it as an allegory of Herzl's biographical transformation into a Zionist leader.[12] I agree that *Die Glosse* should be read in connection to the development of Herzl's political thought in the 1890s and his »discovery« of Jewish nationalism. However, I suggest that the historical transformations at the center of *Die Glosse* are important to Herzl not only as an allegory of the present but precisely because of their difference and separation from the present. To return to the terms of Hegel's aesthetics, this text is an opportunity in which Herzl develops his prosaic historical consciousness: an interest in the past as essentially different from the present, and in the past transformations

---

[10] On Herzl's education in Viennas see Julius H. Schoeps: Theodor Herzl and the Zionist Dream. London: Thames and Hudson 1997, 29. Schoeps suggests that this Hegelian schooling laid the ground for Herzl's political Zionism and his hopes for a Jewish state, which – as he translates Herzl's program into the language of Hegel's political philosophy – would fulfill the spirit of the Jewish people (15). For a detailed analysis of von Stein's use of and divergence from Hegel's Philosophy of Right see Herbert Marcuse: Reason and Revolution: Hegel and the Rise of Social Theory. Boston: Beacon Press 1960, 374–388. In a very different tone, Reinhart Koselleck describes von Stein as an embodiment of the nineteenth century's Janus-faced interest in both historicism and progress. Reinhart Koselleck: Historical Prognosis in Lorenz Von Stein's Essay on the Prussian Constitution. In: Futures Past: On the Semantics of Historical Time. New York: Columbia University Press 2004.

[11] Marc Bloch: Feudal Society. Chicago: University of Chicago Press 1961, 109–120. As Bloch explains, the legal scholarship of Bologna also laid the ground to legal codification in the vernacular (117ff.). For the tie between legal writings in the vernacular and the emergence of prose see Wolf-Dieter Stempel: Die Anfänge der romanischen Prosa im XIII. Jahrhundert. In: Grundriss der rom. Literaturen des Mittelalters I (1972).

[12] Alex Bein interprets the play as a renunciation of Herzl's earlier male ideal – the dueling aristocrat – in favor of the lawyer and statesman. Bein: Theodor Herzl. Biographie. Wien: Fiba Verlag 1934, 136. This position is hard to defend in face of Michael Gluzman's important analysis of Herzl on masculinity. Gluzman: The Yearning for Heterosexuality (note 6). In his fascinating commentary on the »Die Glosse,« Klaus Dethloff, suggests that it articulates a crucial question with which the author of *The Jewish State* had to contend: whether jurisprudence could be the basis for action. Dethloff, Theodor Herzl oder der Moses des fin de Siècle (note 7).

that have produced the present. Thus, the historical past of the troubadours and legal scholars that appear in the play is of interest to him because of its anterior relation to the present, that is, for the causal relations between the past, and the transformation that occurred in it, and the present, which is seen as existing beyond this transformation and hence fundamentally different than the past.[13]

Of course, it is not unusual for a budding national leader to be engaged with the past: looking back for cultural roots and models in the past is one of the basic gestures of the modern national movements.[14] But all of Herzl's choices in making this gesture are interesting. He is not interested in constructing a stable picture of the Jewish past, which would then serve as a possible source for renewed Jewish national culture.[15] Instead, he portrays a cultural space that is in flux and dialogue: between the Roman past on the one hand and a future of the European civil law on the other, between Provence with its troubadours on the one hand and Bologna with its scholars of the law on the other. Furthermore, Herzl's literary representation of the troubadours is far from conventional, highlighting and valorizing not their image as great lovers or creative poets, but rather the marginal position of the troubadour turned legal scholar. The conflict between the two troubadours, Philippus and Aimeric, can be read as a paraphrase of Richard Wagner's historical opera *Die Meistersinger von Nürnberg*.[16] In act I, scene III of the opera, and then again in its closing scene,

---

[13] I build here on Reinhardt Koselleck's description of the transformations in the perception of historical time after the French Revolution: »Space of Experience« and »Horizon of Expectation«: Two Historical Categories. In: Futures Past: on the Semantics of Historical Time (note 10).

[14] Prominent examples from the vast literature on nationalism and national cultures: Benedict Anderson: Imagined Communities: Reflections on the Origin and Spread of Nationalism. Revised and extended edition. London, New York: Verso 1991; Liah Greenfeld: Nationalism: Five Roads to Modernity. Cambridge/Mass.: Harvard University Press 1992. On the complexity of Zionism in its relation to the past see: Almog, Zionism and History: The Rise of a New Jewish Consciousness (note 9) and Yael Zerubavel: Recovered Roots: Collective Memory and the Making of Israeli National Tradition. Chicago: The University of Chicago Press 1995.

[15] One might, for example, expect a Jewish thinker who is writing about Roman Law and its medieval revival to reflect upon the fact that the Romans had sacked the temple and sent Jews into exile and that the codex that was being revived was the earliest source of Anti-Jewish legislation in Europe. Menahem Stern: Antisemitism in Rome. In: Antisemitism Through the Ages. Ed. by Shmuel Almog. Oxford, New York: Published for the Vidal Sassoon International Center for the Study of Antisemitism, the Hebrew University of Jerusalem, by Pergamon Press 1988, 13–27. Herzl does (excitedly?) mention the Jewish troubadour Süsskind von Trimberg in the notes for the play, but does not choose to write about him (CZA, H-522).

[16] Herzl's relation to Wagner was anything but neutral. His first public conflict with antisemitism is not in the context of the Dreyfus trial in Paris (as some Israeli schoolbooks would have it) but rather as a student in Vienna when he withdrew his membership from the nationalist student »Burschenschaft« *Albia* in the context of a ceremony in commemoration of Wagner's death in 1883. Pawel, The Labyrinth of

the young and enthusiastic Walther von Stolzing performs a song that fails to conform with the rules and regulations of the guild of mastersingers, and this is precisely its success. Wagner ridicules the men who constantly refer to their law books and obsessively count the feet of Walther's verse, and he valorizes the Romantic individualism and spontaneity of his song as a revolt against oppressive rules. Herzl presents a mastersinger that has turned to a different kind of law book, the glossary, and his conception of the relations between the troubadour's song and law is quite different from Wagner's and much more interesting. In *Die Glosse*, the law is the source for a new literary language which replaces the song of the troubadour.

From the remaining notes and manuscripts, we learn that Herzl took the historical background of the play very seriously, studying not only philological sources but also legal history, in particular Roman marriage law, and the history of costume. »Clothes became more complex« he notes, »the shirt came into being!«[17] In his philological preparations to write the play Herzl was most

---

Exile; a Life of Theodor Herzl (note 1), 69ff. More detailed information, as well as reproduction of the relevant documents, can be found in Harald Seewann: Theodor Herzl und die akademische Jugend: Eine Quellensammlung über die Bezüge Herzls zum Korporationsstudententum. Historica Academica Judaica. Graz 1998. At the same time, it is important to remember that Herzl was a self-professed enthusiast of Wagner, and often referred to him as a model. See Mark H. Gelber: Heine, Herzl and Nordau. Aspects of the Early Zionist Reception. In: The Jewish Reception of Heinrich Heine. Ed. by Mark H. Gelber. Tübingen: Max Niemeyer 1992, 145; Herzl, Briefe und Tagebücher (note 2), II, 74.

[17] CZA, H-522. On the history of costume, Herzl read Jules Etienne Quicherat's *Histoire du costume en France depuis les temps plus recules jusque a la fin du XVIII Siecle* (1876). His source on history of the law was Friedrich Karl von Savigny's *Geschichte des Römischen Rechts im Mittelalter* (1815–1831). Herzl's relation to Savigny should be considered along the lines of the work of Karl Dethloff quoted above. On the one hand, Herzl seems to adopt the principles of Savigny's historical approach to the law, in particular his meticulous engagement with the Roman law. On the other hand, his concept of rational legislation and constitution-making seems at odds with Savigny's romantic sensibility, which maintained that the law cannot be made rationally but rather develops as part of the *Volksgeist*. (Savigny, Friedrich Karl von. In: Meyers Enzyklopädisches Lexikon. Mannheim: Bibliographisches Institut 1977.) The details that Herzl culls from Savigny are also interesting: his notes mention »proud students« and the loud reading of legal manuscripts by students of the law (a kind of prosaic performance, as it were). His main philological sources are François-Just-Marie Raynouard's *Choix des poésies originales des troubadours* (1816–1821) and Claude Charles Fauriel's *Histoire de la poésie provençale* (1846). The former is particularly interesting, because it is essentially the first philological, linguistically oriented work to be done on the troubadours. John M. Graham: National Identity and the Politics of Publishing the Troubadours. In: Medievalism and the Modernist Temper. Ed. by Howard Bloch and Stephen G. Nichols. Baltimore: The John Hopkins University Press 1996, 59. The choice of such an early source, that had since been antiquated and challenged (to a great extent by German philology) seems to reflect mainly on the ignorance of Herzl, who had no formal educa-

interested in the transformations undergone by the different genres of troubadour poetry, which lead to the rise of a new discourse, embodied in his play by
Philippus's commentary on law. In particular, Herzl is interested in moments
in which the poetry of the troubadours comes into contact with other modes of
discourse through contemporary (that is, medieval) commentaries. Thus, he
reads Raynouard and gathers quotations that refer to the matter of texts with
commentaries, noting with interest commentaries in *prose*. Herzl constructs a
continuum between these commentaries – specifically the prose commentary
on one of Ramband d'Orange's songs – and the legal commentary with which
his protagonist is busy. In other words, he thinks of the medieval legal gloss
primarily in literary terms, as a mode that competes and interferes with the
song of the troubadour, and which has its likeness in other interfering modes,
such as the prose commentary on Ramband.[18]

When Philippus has finally had enough of his rival's flirtation with his wife,
he produces an interesting hybrid between the discourses of love and law and
claims Ramband d'Orange as his model:

PHILIPPUS: I strike my chords/ upon the corpus iuris – and my understanding of it/
I sing a song of the law… *reads*: marriage/ *Prose*. Nupitae sunt coniunctio maris et
feminae, consortium omnis vitae, divini et humani iuris communicatio…/*takes his
harp*/ My song is a glossary, like Ramband/ D'orange often sang/ AIMERIC: he

---

tional background in philology, and who after all was in France when he wrote the
play. However, perhaps the choice to circumvent later scholarship was made consciously, in what Herzl perceived as a return to the sources, choosing to focus on the
philological resources in Raynouard's work rather than the more ideologically bi-
ased works that came from Germany following A. W. Schlegel's reception and critique of Raynouard. As Graham explains, Raynouard's theory, which did not attract
the German scholars and was quickly refuted by them, was that the troubadours of
the 11th century all spoke and sang in one language, the »langue romance primitive.«
One might speculate that Raynouard's position was more attractive to Herzl as a
kind of antidote to nationalist appropriations of the troubadours, depicting them as
members of a pan-European (or, more accurately, pan-south-west-European) group,
which, like the Jews, moves around and is not associated with one place or national
culture only. See also: Hans Ulrich Gumbrecht: Un Souffle D'allemagne Ayant
Passé: Friedrich Dietz, Gaston Paris and the Genesis of National Philologies. In:
Romance Philology 40.1 (1986). He describes Raynouard's work as an exception in
relation to the dominant atmosphere in France at his time: »Although he writes in a
strictly classical form Raynouard's concern is – viewed typologically – quite Romantic: he wishes to rehabilitate the French Knights Templar. […] In an era of revolutionary and post-revolutionary centralization his interest in the cultural past was
motivated by a crisis – similar, if not altogether analogous, to the interest out of
which German national historiography took shape« (14).

18 Ramband is an interesting choice that highlights Herzl's unique, not to say idiosyn-
cratic, view of the Troubadours. On this unusual troubadour see: Walter Thomas
Pattison: The Life and Works of Troubadour Raimaut D'Orange. Minneapolis: University of Minnesota Press 1952.

grabs the emptiest straw/ PHILIPPUS: *plays some opening chords. Speaks:*/ Conjunctio maris et feminae/ *recites*: May in the country/ young May![19]

Herzl's instructions to the actor are the most interesting part of this passage. As Philippus draws his sword and later his harp the verbs *lesen, sprechen,* and *rezitieren* – read, speak, and recite – apparently refer to significant modulations in the performance; they draw our attention to the different modes or discourses through which Philippus's speech moves: quotation from the law (*liest*), commentary on his own performance (*spricht*) and the performance of the song itself (*rezitiert*). To these Herzl adds the noun *Prosa* before the Latin phrases from the law. It is hard to assume that Herzl thought it necessary to warn the actor that he here momentarily abandons the clumsy and heavy-handed rhymed verse to which he sticks more or less throughout the play. Rather, prose is mentioned here because it represents the limit of the range of discourses or modes available to Philippus, as well as to Herzl. The explicit reference to prose amplifies the act of reading and suspends the troubadour's performance, as well as the theatrical performance within which the troubadour appears. By mentioning prose at this moment Herzl turns it into a literary crossroad: through the linguistic practice in which he is engaged, Philippus opens the road to prose, and ultimately the novel.[20] But at this point, and within the medium that Herzl has chosen for his reflection, prose can only make a short appearance, and Philippus ends up performing a kind of literary alchemy by which prose turns into poetry and by which he wins back his wife.

Herzl imagines Philippus as the agent who embodies various interrelated evolutions, ranging from the development of the modern shirt through the laying of the foundations of the civil law in Europe, and to the transformation of literary language and the emergence of prose. In this last sense, *Die Glosse* is written not only in preparation for Herzl's entrance into the world of law, of politics and of diplomacy, but also as an exercise necessary in preparation for the writing of *Altneuland*, that is, in preparation for the conscious and strategic use of novelistic prose. Herzl writes *Die Glosse* – and, equally importantly, he carries out the studies necessary for this writing – in order to make clearer to himself the conditions of writing prose and to situate that practice historically. But *Die Glosse* is a play, and as such it can only refer to written prose but not offer the space of experimentation with this tool that exists in the novel. This, in fact, is the key lesson that Herzl »learns« from *Die Glosse*: that prose does not lend itself to performance. It is the replacement of one space – the stage of performance – by another, prosaic space that Herzl carries out in *Altneuland*.

---

[19] Herzl, Die Glosse (note 7), 42.
[20] On the role of legal commentary in the emergence of prose as a literary language in the Middle Ages, see Stempel, Die Anfänge der romanischen Prosa im XIII. Jahrhundert (note 11).

II   *Altneuland* – Engineering on the Page

In his novel, Herzl sends his young protagonist to the location of the original Utopia, a remote island, cut off from civilization.[21] However, he chooses to build his Utopia not on an island, not on *terra incognita*, but in the overdetermined space of the *terra sancta*. As they return from the island for a visit in Europe in 1920, the two protagonists visit Palestine, which has – in the idealized projection into the future of Herzl's novel – been transformed by Jewish settlers and is now the Old-New Land. With every surprising new feat of technology or engineering that they encounter, the two guests are reminded that the means to produce it were already available around 1900, when they left Europe, and when the novel was written. Kingscourt finally understands the principle when he exclaims: »It's a mosaic – a Mosaic mosaic.«[22] Herzl transposes history, which is laboriously undone by the insistence that everything that was produced in twenty years of work on the new society was already there in Europe before the work began, into space. It is the technologically transformed landscape, a human-made space, which carries the burden of the narrative.[23]

Nevertheless, one thing about which the text, which gives such prominence to the description of land and cityscapes and lingers most of all on human-made spaces, is remarkably vague, are the borders of *Altneuland*. Herzl chooses never to draw a map, and the different characters who host the two visitors are consistently vague about the issue of borders.[24] In other words,

---

[21] See the introduction and chapter on Thomas More in Frank Edward Manuel/Fritzie Prigohzy Manuel: Utopian Thought in the Western World. Cambridge/Mass.: Belknap Press 1979. As Fredric Jameson notes, More's Utopia turns into an island in a feat of engineering, »an extraordinary anticipation of the great public works projects of modern or socialist times.« Jameson: Morus: The Generic Window. In: New Literary History 34 (2003), 447. In this sense, More also anticipates the engineering operations that were of interest to Herzl in *Altneuland*. See also Louis Marin: Utopics: The Semiological Play of Textual Spaces. Amherst: Humanity Books 1984; Philip E. Wegner: Imaginary Communities: Utopia Narration, and the Spatial Histories of Modernity. Berkeley: University of California Press 2002.

[22] Theodor Herzl: Altneuland. Wien: Benjamin Harz 1911, 301. In German: »Es ist 'ne Mosaik – eine mosaische Mosaik.«

[23] On Space in Utopia see Marin, Utopics: The Semiological Play of Textual Spaces (note 21). For a different perspective on the construction of space in *Altneuland* see Yigal Schwartz: ›Human Engineering‹ and the Construction of Space in the New Hebrew Culture. In: Mikan: A Journal for the Study of New Hebrew Literature 1 (2000) [Hebrew].

[24] The vagueness is not an oversight of Herzl's, nor is it a deliberate tactic of leaving options open on an issue that will later be decided. Rather, the topographical vagueness is inherent in the political system that Herzl's novel describes. The »New Society« that the Jews have founded in Palestine is – emphatically – not a nation state, but rather a society (*Gesellschaft*) in the tradition of the Zionist socialism of Moses Hess and Nachman Syrkin or, more accurately, a federation of cooperatives. These cooperative villages and factories vary in the extent of ownership exercised by their

Altneuland maintains a complex relation to territory; the novel is written to make plausible the habitation of a geographic space within the Ottoman Empire by Jews, but at the same time it hesitates to define the space too concretely, and leaves the matter of ownership of the land open-ended and permutable.[25] In place of a map that would draw the borders of a state and make a claim for a certain territory, Herzl allows the new society to own space insofar as it makes it or transforms it technologically. In other words, the human-made landscapes through which the narrative moves belong to the new society as a matter of copyright, and only as derivative of that, of territorial conquest; the landscape thus turns into a text, and for this text to be inscribed in his novel, Herzl turns to his own technology, a technology which he now finally knows how to put to work, prose.

Following the conventions of the genre, Herzl constructs his utopia as a guided tour, in which his protagonists, and through them his readers, are introduced into the Old-New Land, its history and politics. The longest lecture presented to the two visitors in the novel is a gramophone recording of one of the founders of the »New Society for the Colonization of Palestine,« Joseph Levy. Herzl describes the machine that allows the guests to hear the speaker in his absence at length, and takes several opportunities to pause the recording and restart it, demonstrating how technology has supplanted the performance of the human body.[26] The gramophone represents an intermediate position, between the performance of the bard, to which Philippus the commentator on the law is still tied, and the descriptive prose of the novel. The absent speaker

---

members, who in some cases are described as shareholders, and lease the land from the association, or the New Society, which functions as a landlord and regulating body whose most important task lies in the past: to organize the mass immigration of the Jews to their new land, and to buy up the lands which would be leased to these immigrants.

[25] Herzl, Altneuland (note 22), 134 and 218ff. As Joseph Massad shows, Herzl, like other early Jewish nationalists, explicitly described Zionism as a branch of the Western colonial project. In his negotiations first and foremost with the British government, but also with representatives of Italy and Portugal, Herzl represented the Jews as emissaries of the enlightened west, whose presence in the colonies would be in Europe's interest. This, Massad claims, was the dominant rhetoric of the Zionist movement until the 1930s when the attempt was made »to rehistoricize the new Zionist era as a postcolonial one.« Joseph Massad: The ›Post-Colonial‹ Colony: Time, Space, and Bodies in Palestine/Israel. In: The Pre-Occupation of Postcolonial Studies (note 9), here 318. For an opposing view of the relation between Zionism and European colonialism see for example: Anita Shapira: Zionism in the Age of Revolution. In: Modern Judaism 18.3 (1998). Shapira claims that the success of Zionism in the twentieth century depended on the decline of the great colonial powers, and hence implicitly makes an essential differentiation between the two phenomena.

[26] Herzl, Altneuland (note 22), 207ff. As Friedrich Kittler put it: »Ever since the invention of the phonograph, there has been writing without a subject. It is no longer necessary to assign an author to every trace, not even God.« Friedrich Kittler: Gramophone, Film, Typewriter. Stanford: Stanford University Press 1999.

devotes large parts of his discourse to various aspect of the relationship between technology and space. This starts with the elaborate system of maps that were used by the New Society to organize the buying of lands, the transportation of masses of immigrants, and the procurement of raw and processed goods from the entire globe, a technology used by the Zionist pioneers described in the novel to regulate and rationalize space,[27] and reaches a climax with the monumental project of building a canal between the Mediterranean and the Dead Sea, a radical transformation of topography.[28]

The description of the canal is one of the moments in which Herzl's novel draws most directly on the historical reality of the Zionist movement. In the recording, the fictional Joe Levy mentions »a Swiss engineer, a Christian who enthusiastically converted to Judaism and assumed the name Abraham,« and credits him with the idea of building the canal.[29] This, in fact, is Abraham Bourcart, a Christian Swiss engineer who in his enthusiasm for Zionism converted and embarked on a journey to Palestine to make plans for a canal between the Mediterranean and the Dead Sea.[30] During the late 1890s, Bourcart was in close contact with Herzl, sending him detailed maps and notes about the construction of the canal. These – along with other technical information, such as a brochure of a French construction company that sold ready-made houses – found their way to the files that Herzl used when writing *Altneuland*.[31] Herzl's reference to the converted engineer in the recorded narrative is a superfluous detail of the order of what Roland Barthes calls the »reality effect,« an »irreducible residue of functional analysis [...which] denotes what is ordinarily called ›concrete reality‹«.[32] But the potential for realism cannot be realized as long as Herzl's narrative is mediated through the gramophone recording.

The recorded voice of the gramophone is a medium essentially differentiated from the written prose within which it is represented, and Herzl emphasizes the differentiation by allowing the two technologies to touch upon one and the same space: the canal. Thus, Joe Levy is a successor of *Die Glosse*'s Philippus: both are characters that represent a step on the way to novelistic prose, a performance that is on the verge of undoing the space of performance

---

[27] Herzl, Altneuland (note 22), 219.

[28] Ibid., 229.

[29] Ibid.

[30] Herzl refers to him in a personal letter: »Ich kann mir vorstellen, daß ein Christ Jude wird, um an der herrlichen Sache mitarbeiten zu können. Ja ich kenne solche Menschen. Einer heißt Abraham Bourcart, ein Schweizer Christ, der sich sogar beschneiden ließ, um wie er meinte, allen Anforderungen zu genügen. Armer Kerl, das Schneiden war überflüssig. Er ist aber nicht wahnsinnig [...] Von ihm rühren die Pläne zu elektromagnetischer Ausnutzung der vorhandenen Wasserkräfte her. Ich will sie in meinem bald vollendeten Programmroman ›Altneuland‹ anbringen und werde sie vielleicht dereinst zwischen Hermon und Totem Meer verwirklichen.« Herzl, Briefe und Tagebücher (note 2), VI, 276.

[31] CZA, H-460.

[32] Roland Barthes: The Rustle of Language. New York: Hill and Wang 1986, 146.

in favor of the construction of space that is carried out by prose. At the end of Levy's recorded non-performance, Kingscourt refers to the uncanny bodiless voice, and takes up one element from the many projects and places that it had described, as if underscoring the fact that this medium had not managed to make the space present: »There's one thing of which he made me really curious: the Dead Sea Canal. Seems to be some kind of wonder of the world. When will we get to shine our eyes on this mythical canal?«[33] The description of the canal, as presented through the medium of the gramophone, leaves something to be desired. For Herzl's character, the solution is to visit the location itself and view the canal. But on the level of Herzl's meta-medial, or meta-technological reflection, Kingscourt's dissatisfaction signals the difference between the performance carried out by the gramophone and the construction of space of which prose is capable. Kingscourt thus prepares the reader to encounter a space engineered by prose.[34]

Michel de Certeau draws a parallel between several modes of constructing space:

> In front of his blank page, every child is already put in the position of the industrialist, the urban planner or the Cartesian philosopher – the position of having to manage a space that is his own and distinct from all others and in which he can exercise his own will.[35]

With the description of the canal Herzl joins this list, becoming an industrialist, an urban planner, a Cartesian, or an engineer on the page:

> Before them spread the deep blue mirror of the Dead Sea. A roaring noise was felt – the water of the canal, brought here by tunnel from the Inland-Sea, dropping into the deep. As far as the eye could see around the sea and the mountains on its shores, one could see huge factory plants. The source of power had drawn all the different kinds of industry. The canal had woken the Dead Sea to life.[36]

This descriptive voice is the core of Herzl's prose, and its ultimate *raison d'être*: it carries out the task of the novel, to make the Jewish state imaginable as a real space, fully designed, engineered, and habitable. The famous epigraph of the novel – »Wenn ihr wollt, ist es kein Märchen,« »If you will, it is no legend« – can be read in this light as a comment on the mutable genre of the novel. If the reader lacks will, it is nothing but a legend; if, on the other hand, the reader is inspired into action, it will turn into descriptive prose.

---

[33] Herzl, Altneuland (note 22), 231.

[34] Herzl's literary style is thus realistic in the sense elaborated by Frederic Jameson: a discourse with programmatic ambitions, which takes it upon itself »in a virtual or symbolic way to produce [a] whole new spatial and temporal configuration.« Jameson: The Realist Floor-Plan. In: On Signs. Ed. by Marshall Blonsky. Baltimore: Johns Hopkins University Press 1985, 374.

[35] Michel de Certeau: The Practice of Everyday Life. Berkeley: University of California Press 1984, 134.

[36] Herzl, Altneuland (note 22), 268–270.

III   The Work of Prose in H. N. Bialik

Like Herzl, H. N. Bialik follows Hegel in attributing to prose a key role in the dialectical transformations that condition literary form, using it as an index of the revolution in Jewish life of which Zionism was part. However, in Bialik's case, tradition and continuity occupy a far more important position in the dialectic, consequently changing his view of the function of prose within the historical transformation. Bialik was concerned first and foremost with the construction of a language, a quotidian idiom for the new Jewish society. In other words, he looks to prose as a language-generating, rather than space-generating, genre. In his work, he thinks of prose both as a formal literary challenge to Hebrew writers and as a modality, embodied in the prosaic nature of Jewish law. And it is in both of these capacities that prose is used to address the need to forge a new language.

Beyond his literary work, which encompasses poetry, short narrative fiction, and essays, and through which Bialik participates in the forging of the modern Hebrew vernacular, the central cultural activity through which he furthers his historical view of Zionism is the ingathering and canonization of Jewish texts, most notably in the *Book of Legends* (»Sefer ha'Aggadah«) edited and translated in cooperation with Yehoshua Hana Ravnitsky and first published in Odessa in 1908–1911.[37] By translating the best of the Aggadah, the two sought to recover a tradition which, in their perception, was quickly disappearing as Jews abandoned religious schooling in favor of western, secular education. Their anthology is thus a reaction to the process of Jewish enlightenment (Haskalah), of which they themselves were active proponents. Aggadah, an integral part of the traditional education that young men like Bialik and Ravnitsky were leaving behind in increasing numbers, is a mixed genre, comprising all Rabbinic texts that are not part of the system of Rabbinic law (Halakhah).[38] The editors extract pieces of Aggadah from their original, varied contexts, isolating the legend from the law; they translate the many Aramaic narratives into Hebrew, explicating difficult words when needed. In order to highlight the epic nature of Aggadah, they piece various fragments together into larger narratives, and unite materials from different Talmudic sources according to themes such as »The Creation of the World« or »The Birth and Growing up of Moses.«[39]

---

[37] I use here the English translation: Hayim Nahman Bialik/Yehoshua Hana Ravnitsky (Ed.): The Book of Legends – Sefer Ha-Aggadah: Legends from the Talmud and Midrash. Trans. by William G. Braude. Introduction by David Stern. New York: Schocken Books 1992.

[38] David Stern: Introduction. In: The Book of Legends (note 37), xvii.

[39] Yoseph Heinemann: On Bialik's Way with the Talmudic Aggadah. In: Molad 1.31 (1974), 83–92 [Hebrew].

Over the years, the anthology has met with a wide range of critical responses. At the time of its publication, *The Book of Legends* became an »instant classic«[40] and a »phenomenal bestseller,«[41] although not all contemporary readers saw it in a purely positive light. The younger generation of Hebrew poets, prominently represented by Avraham Shlonsky, were highly critical of Bialik for the reactionary nature of his work, on the grounds that the labor of Zionism required revolutionary poetry rather than reminders of traditions past.[42] Scholars of Rabbinic literature have since criticized the editors for their creative freedom in editing and reworking the sources.[43] Another line in the scholarship traces not the relationship between the source materials and the end product, but the connections between the anthology and other parts of Bialik's oeuvre, comparing Bialik's editorial and pedagogical relation to the Aggadah to his dialogue with these same texts as a poet.[44] In this essay, I consider how the work on the anthology provided an opportunity for Bialik to reflect on questions of form and genre and, in particular, to articulate his ideas about prose as a literary language, a matter that also preoccupied him as an essayist.

Bialik and Ravnitsky perceived the varied traditions of the Aggadah – whose roots in oral tradition are indicated by the relation of its name to the Hebrew root for speaking or saying – as »one of the greatest expressions of the spirit of the nation and its people.«[45] As a collection of folk narratives that express the Jewish people's heritage and genius, the project was clearly rooted

[40] Stern, Introduction (note 38), xvii.

[41] Mark W. Kiel: Sefer ha'aggadah: Creating a Classic Anthology for the People and by the People. In: Prooftexts 17.2 (May 1997), 177. In the final page of his critique of the anthology, Yoseph Heinemann defines it as a classic and claims that no other anthology of Aggadah will ever assume a similar importance in Hebrew culture. Heinemann, On Bialik's Way with the Talmudic Aggadah (note 39).

[42] Monty Noam Penkower: The Silences of Bialik: Zionism's Bard Confronts Eretz Israel. In: Modern Judaism 26.3 (2006), 240–273. See also Zippora Kagan: Halakhah and Aggadah as a Code of Literature Jerusalem: The Bialik Institute 1988, 95ff. [Hebrew]. As Gershon Shaked intimates in the opening pages of his five-volume history of modern Hebrew prose, one of the central bones of contention in the early phase of historiography of modern Hebrew literature was the question of breaks and continuities: in what sense is modern Hebrew prose an entirely new phenomenon, and to what extent does it build on earlier Jewish traditions? Gershon Shaked: Hebrew Narrative Fiction: 1880–1970. Vol. I: In Exile. Tel Aviv: Hakibbutz Hameuchad 1977, 19ff. [Hebrew].

[43] Heinemann, On Bialik's Way with the Talmudic Aggadah (note 39).

[44] See for example: Ephraim Urbach: Bialik and the Legends of Haza''l: Appreciation and Inspiration. In Urbach: On Judaism and Education. Jerusalem: The Hebrew University of Jerusalem 1966, 140–161 [Hebrew]. Dan Miron: Taking Leave of the Impoverished Self: Ch. N. Bialik's Early Poetry, 1891–1901. Tel-Aviv: Open University Press 1986, 34–39 [Hebrew].

[45] Bialik/Ravnitsky: Introduction. In: Bialik/Ravnitsky: Sefer Ha-Aggadah. Berlin: Moriah 1922, vii [Hebrew].

in a European Romantic tradition, going back to Herder and the Grimm brothers.[46] But this tradition was too foreign and distant (indeed, it was often openly
hostile to Jews) to make the work of ingathering into a procedure that does not
require explanation, nor was the model of the fairy tale usable to bring coher-
ence to the materials gathered in the anthology. At the root of the anthology is
the process of selection, and the differentiation between legend and law (Aggadah and Halakhah).[47] Interestingly, Bialik questions this very distinction in
other texts, notably the essay »Halakhah and Aggadah,« published in 1916, in
which he presents a dialectical view of the very two modes of thought which
the anthology ostensibly makes such an effort to divide.[48]

Bialik's view in this essay – that law and legend, Halakhah and Aggadah,
are complementary in nature, one begetting the other in an ever-evolving process – places him in dialogue with the sources collected in the anthology. The
first two sections of *The Book of Legends* are concerned with the definition of
Aggadah, which is approached contrastively: Aggadah and Parable, and Aggadah and Halakhah. Under the second rubric, Bialik and Ravnitsky collect
references to the differing natures of these two elementary genres that form the
Talmud: the narrative legends and the discussions of Jewish law. Referring to
the first verse of Isaiah III – »the Lord of Hosts removes from Jerusalem and
from Judah a support and a stay, every support of bread and every support of
water« – one of the quotes explicates: »Every support of bread – these are the
masters of the Talmud [whose halakhic teachings are as essential as bread] –
and every support of water – these are the masters of the Aggadah, who draw
men's hearts with Aggadah as easily as one draws water from a well.«[49] An-

---

46 Kiel, Sefer ha'aggadah: Creating a Classic Anthology for the People and by the
    People (note 41). On Bialik and the tradition of Romanticism see also Ariel Hirsch-
    feld: On Bialik's Relation to his Sources. In: On »The Explicit and the Allusive in
    Language« – Studies on Bialik's Essay. Ed. with an introduction by Zvi Luz and
    Ziva Shamir. Ramat Gan: Bar Ilan University 2001, 130–144 [Hebrew]. On the
    roots of Bialik's project of ingathering in the German ideal of Bildung, see Paul
    Mendes-Flohr: Cultural Zionism's Image of the Educated Jew: Reflections on Creat-
    ing a Secular Jewish Culture. In: Modern Judaism 18.3 (1998), 227–239.

47 In using legend for Aggadah, I am not making a statement about the nature of the
    historic text, but attempting to capture Bialik's understanding of it.

48 As Pinkhas Ginosar describes, the essay had a very wide reception, and was read
    with interest and adopted by audiences as different as the orthodox »admirers of the
    Halakha« and Zionist-Socialist Berl Katznelson. Pinkhas Ginosar: Bialik's ›Halakha
    and Aggadah‹ and Brenner's Reaction. In: Iton 77 (June–July 1984), 54–55 [He-
    brew]. Gershom Scholem translated the essay (as well as Y. H. Brenner's critique,
    though the latter was never published) for Martin Buber's *Der Jude* shortly after it
    was published in Hebrew. Gershom Scholem: From Berlin to Jerusalem. Tel Aviv:
    Am Oved 1982, 74–75 [Hebrew]. The translated essay is mentioned several times in
    the correspondence between Scholem and Benjamin, in the context of their discus-
    sion on Kafka. Walter Benjamin, Gershom Scholem: Briefwechsel, 1933–1940. Hg.
    von Gershom Scholem. Frankfurt/M.: Suhrkamp 1980, 157, 166, 172.

49 The Book of Legends (note 37), 5 (translation modified).

other excerpt describes Halakhah and Aggadah, the law and the legend, as competing performative modes:

> R. Abbahu and R. Hiyya bar Abba happened to come to a certain place where R. Abbahu lectured on Aggadah and R. Hiyya bar Abba lectured on Halakhah. All the people left R. Hiyya bar Abba and went to hear R. Abbahu, so that R. Hiyya bar Abba was greatly upset.

The passage continues with an explanation of the charisma of Aggadah in contrast with the law:

> To comfort [R. Hiyya bar Abba], R. Abbahu said: May I tell you a parable to illustrate what each of us represents? Two men came to a certain city, one to sell precious stones and pearls, and the other to sell different kinds of small [or cheap] things [minei sidqit] To whom will people run? Will they not run to him who sells the small things?[50]

The parable embodies the complexity that interested Bialik in his own writing on Halakhah and Aggadah. Referring to the prestige and seriousness of the law, Rabbi Abbahu likens it to precious stones, and, by comparison, denigrates the legend as »minei sidqit,« a very vague term that the editors interestingly neither translate nor explicate.[51] But the parable is open to the opposite set of comparisons as well: Aggadah is embellished like precious stones, whereas the Halakhah is preoccupied with the minutiae, the small things for which people have use in their daily lives. In this case, the open-ended parable, which suggestively ends with a question rather than an assertion, carries out a deconstruction of the terms Halakha and Aggadah, setting up an opposition and a hierarchy only to question them.[52] Or, to use the terms of Bialik's essay »Ha-

---

[50] Ibid., 5 (translation modified) The story is from bSotah, 40 a, and it originally follows a discussion of Rabbi Abahu's modesty in relation to Rabbi bar Abba.

[51] The medieval commentator Rashi translates sidqit as »working tools of the poor and of women, such as weaving tools, needles and weights.« Yonah Fraenkel translates »sidqit« (to Hebrew) in this same passage as »cheap wares in the marketplace.« Fraenkel: The Ways of Aggadah and Midrash. Jerusalem: Yad LaTalmud 1991, I, 325–326. Interestingly, the word does not appear at all in the concordance of Bialik's work; however, the concordance covers only the poetry, so it is not clear whether Bialik found use for this word – which is »foreign« to Biblical Hebrew, and hence associated with the style of Hebrew prose initiated by Mendele and celebrated by Bialik in the essays on Mendele to which I refer below – in his own prose. A. Even Shoshan/Y. Segal: Concordance of Bialik's Poetry. Jerusalem: Kiryat Sefer 1950 [Hebrew]. For an exposition of the differences between Bialik's use of Biblical and Post-Biblical Hebrew in his poetry and in his prose, see Jacob Fichmann: Bialik's Poetry. Jerusalem: Mosad Bialik 1947, 111ff. [Hebrew].

[52] I use the term deconstruction as outlined, for example, by J. Hillis-Miller: The Critic as Host. In: Critical Inquiry 3 (1976). As Fraenkel notes, this is an interesting case of a parable that fails, since Rabbi Hiyya Bar Abba is not convinced. Fraenkel, The Ways of Aggadah and Midrash (note 51), I, 326, and II, 645, note 17. Neither the original context of the tension between the two rabbis, as described in the Talmud,

lakhah and Aggadah,« neither of the metaphors – the gems and the inconsequential objects – can exhaust the nature of the two modes. If Aggadah is more popular, more readily available to a listening audience than the intricacies of the Halakhah, the latter injects itself into the space of lived experience and becomes the stuff of new parables.

The essay opens with a stark differentiation of the two modes:

> Halakhah wears a frown, Aggadah a smile. The one is pedantic, severe, unbending – all justice; the other is accommodating, lenient, liable – all mercy. The one commands and knows no half-way house; her yea is yea and her nay is nay. The other advises, and takes account of human limitations; she admits something between yea and nay. The one is concerned with the shell, with the body, with actions; the other with the kernel, with the soul, with intentions. On one side there is petrified observance, duty, subjection; on the other perpetual rejuvenation, liberty, free volition. Turn from the sphere of life to that of literature, and there are further points of contrast. On the one side is the dryness of prose, a formal and heavy style, a gray and monochrome diction: reason is sovereign. On the other side is the sap of poetry, a style full of life and variety, a diction all ablaze with color: emotion is sovereign.[53]

This differentiation echoes the differentiation between prose and poetry as Bialik had articulated it in an essay on the philosophy of language published two years earlier, »Revealment and Concealment in Language«:[54]

> There is a vast difference between the language of the masters of prose and that of the masters of poetry. The former, the masters of exposition, find their sanction in the principle of analogy, and in the elements common to images and words, in that which is established and constant in language, in the accepted version of things – consequently, they walk confidently through language. To what may they be compared? To one who crosses a river walking on hard ice frozen into a solid block. Such a man may and can divert his attention completely from the covered depths flowing underneath his feet. But their opposites, the masters of allegory, or interpretation and mystery, spend all their days in pursuit of the unifying principle in things

---

nor the fact that the parable fails are mentioned in *The Book of Legends*, a telling example of the editing work for which Bialik and Ravnitsky were criticized (see note 38 above). Another editorial intervention in this case is the insertion of question marks, which are not an element of the Talmudic text, that can formulate a question but not mark it typographically.

53 Bialik: Halakha and Aggadah. Trans. by Leon Simon. In: Revealment and Concealment: Five Essays. Jerusalem: Ibis 2000, 45.

54 I use the terms »gilui« and »kisui« as translated by Jacob Sloan, and republished in *Revealment and Concealment: Five Essays* (note 53). Others have translated the terms as »explicit« and »implicit«, or as »explicit« and »allusive«; while this is not inaccurate, I prefer the former translation emphasizing the concreteness of Bialik's terms. This is the only one of Bialik's essays (indeed, more or less the only one of Bialik's prose texts) that does not refer to Judaism or Jewish culture explicitly in any way. On this interesting exception see Ziva Shamir: Much has Happened in the Land: The Essay ›The Explicit and the Allusive in Language‹. In: Shamir/Luz (Ed.), On »The Explicit and the Allusive in Language« – Studies on Bialik's Essay (note 46), 151–170 [Hebrew].

[…] And to what may those writers be compared? To one who crosses a river when it is breaking up, by stepping across floating, moving blocks of ice. He dare not set his foot on any one block for longer than it takes him to leap from one block to the next, and so on. Between the breaches the void looms, the foot slips, danger is close […][55]

A striking element of Bialik's image of the frozen river of prose, and the contrast with the poet who jumps from one block of ice to the next, is the implication that both modes ultimately allow a passage across the abyss.[56] This is, perhaps, a first intimation of the complementary relation that will emerge in the later essay.

As »Halakha and Aggadah« unfolds, Bialik offers a dialectical model to replace the stark opposition with which he opens the essay in the passage I quote above. This dialectical model is encapsulated in the metaphor of a flower and a fruit:

As a dream seeks its fulfillment in interpretation, as will in action, as thought in speech, as flower in fruit – so Aggadah in Halakhah. But in the heart of the fruit there lies hidden the seed from which a new flower will grow. The Halakhah which is sublimated into a symbol – and much Halakhah there is, as we shall find – be-

---

55 Bialik, Revealment and Concealment (note 53), 24–26. This essay too had a remarkable reception history in Hebrew letters, which deserves a more detailed study. Robert Alter suggests that Bialik's description of the abyss, above which language precariously floats, deeply influenced Gershom Scholem's thought and the image of the abyss in his description of Jewish mysticism. Robert Alter: Scholem and Modernism. In: Poetics Today 15.3 (Fall, 1994). For a synoptic view of the critical reception, see Shamir/Luz (Ed.), On »The Explicit and the Allusive in Language« – Studies on Bialik's Essay (note 46).

56 Bialik's image is echoed in Georg Lukacs's remarks on prose in his *Theory of the Novel* (the first draft of which was also written in 1914), though the implied value judgment is here reversed: »Verse itself […] can only tentatively encourage the bud to open; verse can only weave a garland of freedom round something that has been liberated from all fetters. If the author's action consists in disclosing buried meaning, if his heroes must first break out of their prisons and, in desperate struggles or long, wearisome wanderings, attain the home of their dreams, their freedom from terrestrial gravity – then the power of verse, which can spread a carpet of flowers over the chasm, is not sufficient to build a practicable road across it. […] Only prose can then encompass the suffering and the laurels, the struggle and the crown, with equal power; only its unfettered plasticity and its non-rhythmic rigor can, with equal power, embrace the fetters and the freedom, the given heaviness and the conquered lightness of a world henceforth immanently radiant with found meaning.« Georg Lukacs: The Theory of the Novel; a Historico-Philosophical Essay on the Forms of Great Epic Literature. Cambridge/Mass.: M.I.T. Press 1971, 58–59. Bialik's contrastive use of »poetry« and »prose« in this essay is based on the work of Russian linguist A. A. Potebnya (1835–1891). Fichmann, Bialik's Poetry (note 51), 140. Rina Lapidus reviews references in Hebrew scholarship to Bialik's reading of Potebnya, and systematically compares their views on language. Lapidus: On Bialik's Essay ›The Explicit and the Allusive in Language‹ and its relation to A. Potebnya's Linguistic Theory. In: Shamir/Luz (Ed.), On »The Explicit and the Allusive in Language« – Studies on Bialik's Essay (note 46), 129–144.

comes the mother of a new Aggadah, which may be like it or unlike. A living and healthy Halakhah is an Aggadah that has been or that will be. And the reverse is true also. The two are one in their beginning and their end.[57]

The essay is a vindication of the prosaic mode of the law, arguing that a culture that turns exclusively to the poetic mode of legend cuts itself off from a rich resource. To make this point, Bialik returns to the image of the frozen river, but here the river is observed from the safety of the shore; instead of the practical question of passing safely to the other bank, the author here addresses the theoretical question of the nature of water and ice:

> Those who so conclude [that Halakha and Aggadah – and by extension prose and poetry – are irreconcilable opposites] are confusing accident and form with substance; as who should declare the ice and the water in a river to be two different kinds of matter.[58]

Ironically, the image is subjected to this transformation in the service of an argument for the role of daily life and the mundane in the literary imagination.

For this is the heart of Bialik's argument for Halakhah as material for literature: the law is rooted in lived experience, and this is why it is a valuable literary source. After all, Bialik himself was an agnostic, a thoroughly secular Jew. Clearly, in constructing his apology for the Halakhah he did not intend his readers to understand that its laws are to be followed by the letter.[59] Halakhah here stands not for a natural law that is derived from a transcendental order, but for law in the sense of a system regulating daily life, and confronting the richness of this life. This is why the Halakhah – and the prose associated with it – is described as an invigorating force within the project of the revival of Hebrew. This argument is completed in Bialik's essays on Mendele Mokher Sforim (pseudonym of S. Y. Abramovitch, 1836–1917), whom he described as the creator of the »nusakh.«

This term, borrowed from Jewish liturgy and from the medium of oral performance, is used by Bialik to describe Mendele's great innovation, his achievement in creating a unified style for modern Hebrew literature.[60] Bialik fashions Mendele as the first Hebrew author to liberate literary language from Biblical quotations and to unify all the different sources from which a Hebrew author could borrow into one viable language. This feat is formulated in the terms of novelistic realism:

---

[57] Bialik, Halakha and Aggadah (note 53), 47.

[58] Ibid., 46.

[59] As noted by Paul Mendes-Flohr, Cultural Zionism's Image of the Educated Jew (note 46), 234–235.

[60] As Bialik explains the term »nusakh« in a footnote to one of the Mendele essays: »In Volin, this is how they call the tradition of liturgical melodies common to the people, and by extension any trodden path or accepted chablon in one of the occupations.« Bialik: The Collected Writings of Haim Nahman Bialik. Tel Aviv: Dvir 1984, 167 [Hebrew].

Just as Mendele was the first to offer artifice and illustration in Hebrew literature, so he was the first to produce a Hebrew style, a realistic and complete style. Before Mendele we had language games, or language trickery, prances of language and patches of language; Mendele gave us one whole language, a »human language.« Mendele put an end to all child-play of the Hebrew language and to all its monkey faces. He is practically the first of the new authors to cease from imitating the book – he imitates nature and life. Mendele imitates neither the Bible nor the Mishna and the Midrash, he creates a likeness and an image, according to the inner nature and the proper spirit of the language.[61]

The implicit assumption made in Bialik's comments on Mendele is that his achievement, the forging of the new style in Hebrew literature, could only be made in prose.[62]

Unlike Herzl, Bialik did not channel his interest in the poetics and politics of prose into writing a novel.[63] But, as I have shown, both used prose to investigate the historical-philosophical underpinnings of their work. Through prose, both authors reach back to the past, but also formulate the essential difference between their own time and the past; both used this constellation in order to meditate on the relations of law and literature, and on the potential uses of literature in the service of Zionism.

---

[61] Ibid., 189.

[62] On Mendele/Abramovitch and the nusakh in Hebrew literature see Robert Alter: The Invention of Hebrew Prose: Modern Fiction and the Language of Realism. Seattle, London: University of Washington Press 1988; Shaked, Hebrew Narrative Fiction: 1880–1970 (note 42), I.

[63] It is beyond the scope of this essay to discuss the generic choices that he did make in light of his views on prose. In future work, based on a dissertation I am currently completing at Stanford University, I plan to expand on this.

Gershon Shaked

Mythic Figure or Flesh and Blood?
The Literary Reception of Herzl in Hebrew Poetry and in Nathan Bistritzki's »The Secret of Birth«

I

Nathan Bistritzki (Agmon) was born in Zunigrodka (Ukraine) in 1896. He immigrated to the land of Israel in 1920 and was part of the third immigration wave, which was made up of Socialist pioneers from Eastern Europe. He died in Jerusalem in 1980. As soon as he arrived in Israel, he joined the Bitaniya group, a commune of young Hashomer Hazair members in the Lower Galilee. There, from 1922 on, he edited an anthology of personal reminiscences and memoirs. These were combined and merged into what might be called a communal diary, entitled *Our Community* (*Kehiliyatenu*). In 1927 he published his major work, the expressionistic novel *Days and Nights*. This fictionalized narrative made extensive use of the collective diary and of the several months Bistritzki spent in Bitaniya.[1] Following this novel he published mostly expressionistic historical plays. They centered around various topics, including Judah Iscariot, (*Jehuda Iskariyot*, 1930), the destruction of the second temple, *This night* (*Beleil Ze*, 1934), *Josephus Flavius* (1939), *Jerusalem and Rome* (1939), *Jesus of Nazareth* (1951),[2] and *The Secret of Birth – The Legend of Herzl* (1955). Somewhat later he wrote the trilogy, *Agonies of Reincarnation* (לוגלג ילבח), which was included in his *Collected Dramas* (1960).

The thematics of destruction and redemption, of messianic hopes and the disappointment of these hopes, fascinated Bistritzki, and he found in Herzl's story a point of departure for reactivating these subjects in the context of the 20th century. For him, the birth of Zionism was a modern manifestation of the myth of messianic redemption. The theme of his drama might have been the Herzl story as a secularization of the Messianic idea. In this play, Herzl's friend Schiff compared him to Shabbetai Zevi. He thought that society would ridicule him because the idea of a Jewish State was so irrational and ludicrous.[3] Schiff told him the story of Shabbetai's rise and fall, which ended in his conversion to Islam; Herzl's reaction was that he ended up where Herzl

---

[1] Gershon Shaked: Modern Hebrew Fiction. Bloomington 2000, 123–125.

[2] Gershon Shaked: The Hebrew Historical Drama in the Twentieth Century. Jerusalem 1970, 189–199 (Hebrew).

[3] Nathan Bistritzki: Agonies of Reincarnation. In: Dramas. Tel-Aviv 1960, vol. 2, 670.

himself wanted to start.[4] In fact, in the collective memory of his generation and of the following one, Herzl himself became a mythical messianic figure.

The reaction of the Hebrew poets to Herzl was initially ambivalent, but after the first Zionist Congress he was widely admired and even adored. In 1897, the poet laureate of Hebrew Poetry, Chaim Nachman Bialik, wrote a poem titled »In the Cities of the Sea« (מי יכרכב). Ahad Ha-am, editor of *Hashiloach*, refused to publish it because of the poem's sharply sarcastic tone. I quote two stanzas:

מי יכרכב

,מלכ המה תואלפ ישנאו
,אלפי אל רבד לכ מהם
,הנידמ ושעי הנטק עבצאב
....אלמ םלוע - םדח והבבו

!םיזירכמ אל ,-םירמוא התע מג
– ,אניוב םש לכה ןכומ רבכ
– השימחו םיקדו םיעגר ינש קמק
...!הנידמ ,בוט לזמל ,יהתו[5]

(In the Cities of the Sea

They are all miraculous people,
There is nothing they can't achieve,
With their little finger they will create a state,
And with their big toe – a whole world...

And even now they say – no, declare!
Everything is ready there in Vienna –
Two minutes and five seconds later –
there will be, Mazal Tov, a state!.)

After the first Zionist Congress, Bialik published the following ode to the Congress and to the people who had participated in it. The tone was extremely different from »In the Cities of the Sea«; Ahad Ha-am, who did not accept Herzl's agenda but admired its initiator, agreed this time to publish the ode. Here follows the first stanza:

וויצ יארקמ
(האיליזוב סרגנוקה רכזל)

,הלוגה תונפמ םכצבק םכמע די א
–המיקה םכלכ תא הרמה ותרא-נ

---

4   Ibid., 670–671.
5   Chaim Nahman Bialik: Shirim Genuzim. Tel-Aviv 1971, 131. (The poem was offered to Ahad Ha-am and not published in 1897).

הלודגה הארמה התיהנ הנהו
העמדה ןמאנה הרוקממ ןורפתתן
המחה ,הריהבה ,המיענה ,הלודגה
6...המכ הז ללפתנ הילא

(Called in for Zion.
[In memory of the Congress in Basel]

The agonies of your people have assembled you from all corners of the Diaspora,
Its bitter groans prompted you all to rise–
And here the great sight was revealed
and from its loyal source
a great, pleasant, lucid and warm tear broke through,
a tear for which we have long prayed…)

Elsewhere in the poem the poetic persona expresses despair regarding life in the Diaspora and the hope for redemption that the congress has awakened. These two poems appear to be direct historical reactions to the ideas of Jewish independence and statehood promoted by Herzl and his followers. They do not refer to Herzl's personality or to his individual role as leader of the nation. It was only later that reactions to Herzl lost their grounding in historical fact and became a myth. These types of reactions do not refer to his ideas and his human, all too human life, but to the reception of his mythical image.

This trend begins with Saul Tchernichovski, who in 1929 published a poem in Herzl's memory, called »To the Son of the Legend« (הדגאה ןבל). The poem opens with the following line: »You have become a poem for us« (ריש ונל תייה), and it mythicizes Herzl as the hero of his time.[7] Another interesting example of this kind of reception can be found in a poem by Abraham Ben Yitzchak Sonne, a Jewish-Viennese intellectual and one of the first modernist poets (Przemysl, 1883–Tel Aviv, 1950). The poem was dedicated to Herzl's memory, and here follows a literal translation of it:

ןראל ןעה םייח יכ

לצרה םש ןוני םלוע רכזל
תועיטנב והובגש
ולצב הלוג-יבש ויחי
לארשי-ןרא הרפות
8היחו הויחה

---

6   Chaim Nahman Bialik: Kol Shirei. Tel-Aviv 1957, 71. (First published, 1898).
7   Saul Tchernichovski: To the Son of the Legend. In: Poems. Tel-Aviv 1966, 340. (First published, 1929).
8   Abraham Ben-Yitschak: Kol HaShirim. Ed. by H. Hever. Tel-Aviv 1992, 51.

(The tree will be life for the soil

Herzl's name will live forever
exalt him by planting trees
in his shadow the returnees from the Diaspora will live
The land of Israel will be fertilized
revive it and live!)

Herzl is portrayed by the poet in the high mimetic mode as a figure beyond human mediocrity, who has become to many people – as Bistritzki indicated in his cycle of messianic dramas – a secular Messiah, or a sanctified political leader.[9]

Another interesting poetic response to the Herzl myth was written by the Hungarian-Jewish poet Joseph Patai (G'eng'esh-Pata, 1882–Givatayim, 1953) and published in his collection *On the Rivers of Babylon and the Gates of Jerusalem*. Patai composed a poetic elegy lamenting the deceased leader, who in a metaphorical sense passed away without building his own house. This is an allusion to the tragic fate of the house of Herzl: two of Herzl's three children committed suicide, and the third was killed by the Nazis as part of the euthanasia program. (However, it is also possible that I am misinterpreting Patai, and that by »house« he meant the Jewish homeland.)

עַל בֵּית הֶרְצֵל שֶׁאֵינֶנּוּ

אוֹב יְבוֹאוּ יְמֵי סְתָו, כְּפוֹר וְצִנָּה
וּבַקְּשׁוּהוּ וְהַמְכֵי זִיו וְרָק לְךָ וֹרְפוּנְה
הַאֲהָל יֶלֶד מִיאַבְרָמוּנֹת שִׁיש
וְהוּ... יוּ, וְל, אֵל בְּנִינוּ בֵּית [10]

(To the House of Herzl that Exists No More

The days of autumn's frost and chill will come
And those who desire brightness will look for him in every corner
in the tents of the poor and in marble mansions
But lo! for him we have still not built a home!)

Bistritzki did not follow in the footsteps of those who mythicized Herzl. His interpretation/reception of Herzl follow another direction entirely.

---

9   Franz Rosenzweig argues that Herzl proves that Moses was an historic character. Martin Buber said that he was a monument without any flaw, a face lightened by the eyes of the Messiah. The painter Lillian painted him as half Moses and the other half as the Germanic God Wotan. Amos Elon: Herzl. Tel-Aviv 1977, 22 (Hebrew).

10 Raphael Patai: Shirim, On the Rivers of Babylon and the Gates of Jerusalem. Tel-Aviv 1946, 166. (Patai wrote also a Herzl drama.)

II

The three parts of Bistritzki's dramatic Herzl trilogy were written and published at different times, and they appeared in his collected plays under the title *Agonies of Reincarnation* (לוגלג ילבח). The first part is devoted mostly to Herzl as a son and husband, the second to his political enterprise, and the third to the fate of his descendants after his death. Bistritzki attempted to link dramatically Herzl's family life to his ideological mission and to the crystallization of his national awareness. The materials of his plays are Herzl's diaries and his life story, as reflected in the work of his most prominent biographers: Leon Kellner, Martha Hoffman, and Alex Bein.[11]

In the first two parts of the trilogy, Bistritzki attempted to combine biography and history and to understand historical decisions through their biographical-psychological motivation. The third part is much more of a poetic invention, portraying the tragic fate of Herzl's son, Hans.

In the first play of the trilogy, the first two acts are mostly biographical; the last one is much more historical, and the final scene is an attempt to return from history to biography. The fusion does not always succeed, and the mixture of these two elements, biography and history, often seems quite artificial.

The plays' *dramatis personae* include Theodor Herzl, Jacob, Jeanette and Julia Herzl, Goldsmith, Montague, Rabbi Singer, Hechler, Benedikt, Bacher, Ish Kishor, and in the last part of the trilogy, Nelly, Dr. Gross, and Hechler again. Each play is mostly what the Germans called a »Konversationsstück« (conversation play), a genre that was promoted by playwrights like Oscar Wilde and George Bernard Shaw.

The real-life historical plots do not take place onstage, but rather in the background; they are foregrounded to the stage as gossip, hearsay, and through the speeches Herzl gives while on his self-created mission. His diplomatic efforts in Turkey are conveyed to the addressee (that is, the spectator) through the story of Benedikt, who explains to the Herzl family what happened behind the scenes of the editorial board of the »Neue Freie Presse,« apologizing for the anti-Turkish editorial the paper published, an editorial that undermined Herzl's Turkish agenda.[12]

Until its last part, the drama has no new point of view, no de-automatization of the conventional approach of Herzl biographers, and nothing beyond a very conventional interpretation of the primary sources, letters and diaries.[13] Bis-

---

[11] Leon Kellner: Theodor Herzl's Lehrjahre. Löwitt 1920; Alex Bein: Theodor Herzl – Biographie. Wien 1936;
סילשורי .ריעצה לצרה :זמפוה התרמ 1491.

[12] Bistritzki, Agonies of Reincarnation (note 3), 772–773.

[13] From the biographical point of view, his main concern was the tension between Theodor and his wife Julia, on one side, and his deep devotion to his mother, on the other. His mother was his major support; his wife was rather skeptical and did not believe in his grandiose political visions and plans. (Alex Bein, 106–109; Martha

tritzki's dialogue is neither sharp nor witty, so that the conversations on ideological issues are, frankly, quite boring. The only source of wit is Julia's ironic comments about Theodor's bombastic speeches.

The play is composed of a family plot – love, divorce, and resignation in order to keep the family together – and of ideological issues, such as antisemitism, religious conversion, and Zionism. It is a typical ideological melodrama,[14] that is, a play of action and ideas that tries to present lofty concepts through the use of conventional melodramatic scenes. From the melodramatic point of view, the plot follows the conflict between mother-in-law and daughter-in-law, who have different ideas about the life and future of the son/husband; but the melodramatic plot is also part of Herzl's effort to gain support for his ideas and mission from his nearest relatives.[15] We can also understand these dialogues as depicting the attitude of the Jewish middle-class towards the political issues of their time. They also contain references to real-life figures, who become, through the literariness of the drama, fictitious dramatic characters. As part of the family intrigue, Herzl's father, Jacob, thinks that his son is insane. Even when Herzl's parents recall hearing from a Russian Jew about Jewish colonies being established in Palestine – a story that indicates that they understand the direction of their son's ideas – they are still not convinced that their son and his cause are rational.[16] I will not discuss here the ideological aspect of the drama, since it is very obvious and conventional; instead, I wish to concentrate on the play's psychological aspects.

The last part of the trilogy, called »The Verdict,« is the most melodramatic and interesting of the three. It is the pathetic melodrama of Hans, Herzl's son, who hates his father, is suicidal, and, after a long, agonizing dialogue with a Jewish prostitute (the survivor of a pogrom), finally carries out the act of suicide he has been planning ever since his sister, Paulina, took her own life.

Hoffman, 36; Leon Kellner, 8–9) Benedikt, the editor of the »Neue Freie Presse«, mediates between the two. Benedikt is one of the major characters in Herzl's diary (Theodor Herzl's Tagebücher. Berlin 1922, 275, 281, 285, 294, 300, 302, 333). Against him and the anti-Zionist trends in Herzl's immediate surroundings he represents Herzl's fight (ibid., 547–548). In several passages Bistritzki quotes memories and ideas of Herzl from his diaries in order to depict his character as authentically as possible, but his originality breaks through in the third part, when he leaves the biographical material behind and allows his poetic fantasy to take over (ibid., 411). The historical part is dedicated to the process of writing »Der Judenstaat« and to the events surrounding this enterprise (ibid., 127, 130–131). He depicts Herzl's meetings with the Christian parson Hechler, his frustrating confrontations with the leaders of the Jewish community in England (ibid., 356, 355, 463), his view of Bulgarian Jewry and Zionism and the positive attitude of the Eastern European Jewish masses (represented by the character of Ish- Kishor) towards the Zionist idea.

[14] Gershon Shaked: The Hebrew Historical Drama in the Twentieth Century. Jerusalem 1970, 144–156.

[15] Bistritzki, Agonies of Reincarnation (note 3), 644–645.

[16] Ibid., 682–683.

Suicide, agony, and the love-hate relationship between father and son are intense melodramatic components, and the play of conversation is transformed
into an authentic drama.

III

Politics are an integral part of the Herzl family conversations. For example, the
Dreyfus case was a frequent topic of family discussion. It is the naïve, bourgeois father, Jacob, who defines it as a blood libel.[17] These intellectual and
social disputes are driven, according to Bistritzki, by psychological motives.

The root of Herzl's genius and the source of his successes and failures lie in
the dynamics of his nuclear family. The discussions between his parents are a
reflection of his own inner conflict. The conflict between his father (Jacob) and
his mother (Jeanette) is basically a clash between the conventional, Westernized liberal Jewish thinking of Jacob and the more daring ideas of his wife.
She, influenced by her son, understands and accepts the idea that Jews should
have a state of their own.

This view is unacceptable for her husband, and it threatens to destroy all of
his conventional ideas about Jews and nation-states.[18] The conventional
thought of the father is the norm for his time and place in life (»Sitz im Leben«). He represents the typical assimilated, middle-class Jew, who attempts to
repress the existence of antisemitism and deny his own reaction to the hatred.
Liberalism, claims Jacob, will not disappoint the Jews.[19] As he sees it, his
son's program is appropriate for poor Eastern European Jews, not for the advanced and sophisticated Western Jews.[20] According to Bistritzki's drama, the
father was more or less irrelevant in young Theodor's life.[21] Herzl's revolutionary thoughts gain meaning from the background provided by his father and
his social context, represented mainly by »Die Neue Freie Presse.«[22]

The major figure in Herzl's life is his mother. In one of the episodes of Bis-
trizki's drama, he confesses on his knees that he wants to die in her lap. The
Oedipal relationship with her is depicted in a very obvious, even primitive
way; Bistritzki has, so to speak, »Freudianized« his biographical drama. The

---

[17] Ibid., 623.
[18] Ibid., 685.
[19] Ibid., 624.
[20] Ibid., 683.
[21] Ibid., 656–657. The clash between the Diamant family (the mother's family) and the
Herzl family (his father's) is essential here. Herzl's biographical roots are not only
to be understood in terms of his nuclear family, but also in the conflict between the
romantic clan of his mother and the realistic merchant clan of his father (ibid., 687).
[22] A comic misunderstanding of the idea of »Altneuland« (Old New Land) is presented
in the play. The parents interpret it as Atlandida, the lost continent. They maintain
that he is writing a utopian novel about a lost continent (ibid., 677).

mother is the only one who believes in Herzl; his wife is skeptical, and his father only wants him to be a good bourgeois citizen. From this point of view, the play is about an infantile, Oedipal »mama's boy,« a neurotic with literary pretensions, whose marriage is in crisis and who speaks to his mother about projects that even he does not quite understand. In fact, there is a gap between Herzl's persona as a nice bourgeois boy and the Herzl anima, with its contradictory blend of superiority complexes and suicidal impulses. Herzl, according to Bistritzki, is an Oedipal mama's boy full of frustration and low self-esteem, who dreams of achieving something great and leaving his mark on world history.

The mother's antagonist is her daughter-in-law, Herzl's wife Julia. This conventional triangle, which places the son between the two women in his life, was modified and in a way renovated by the playwright. Julia is the psychological brute and the sober interpreter of Herzl's life: She functions mostly as the ironic, skeptical *eiron* who bursts the bubble of Theodor's vanity and pomposity.[23]

Bistritzki uses Julia as the major *eiron* for Herzl, the *alazon* of history. She undermines his ideological philosophy and his philanthropic pretensions by interpreting his idealism as a psychological outlet for his megalomania. Speaking to Benedikt, she claims that her husband's hallucinations about a Jewish state are absurd, and that he has invented them because of his superiority complex or as an obsessive idea (*idée fixe*). Ironically, she claims that Theodor thinks that he is going to invent a hot air balloon, or that what he envisions is a state of gypsies.[24] Julia's metaphors may actually represent the possible realistic reactions to Herzl's visionary ideas. As a result, the political discussion becomes a family affair between Theodor and Julia. He argues that he is committed to the Eastern European Jewish masses, to whom he brought immense hope. These people, he claims, believe in his message ever since they met with him in the London East End, and he cannot let them down.[25] Julia is very skeptical of her spouse and she exposes what she thinks are the real motives for his actions. Herzl tells her that he asked the capitalist leaders of the Jewish community (Hirsh, Montague, Goldsmith, and Rothschild) to take over his plans and dreams and to carry them out; Julia reacts by saying that he hopes, consciously or not, to be turned down by them, so that he might remain the one and only prince of the Jews. Bistritzki allows her to voice her skepticism with certain irony. For example, she states that Herzl enjoys his meetings with kings and ministers, and that his main goal is to make his life into a novel and to enjoy living it instead of merely writing it. In the end, she imagines, he will be the scapegoat and fool of his peers. She recommends that he shave his beard,

---

[23] Ibid., 691, 693.
[24] Ibid., 691.
[25] Ibid., 778–779.

put on sunglasses, and avoid walking in public places, because everyone will laugh at Mr. Gross-Herzl, the pompous Jewish duke.[26]

Bistritzki employs Julia as the major debunker of the Herzl myth. She also, however, professes her love for her husband, saying that she loves him more than her children, and that she fears for his health and reputation. She wants him to be a normal human being and father, but he prefers to be the king of paupers and to bring happiness to strangers rather than to his own family. Herzl, she says, is not satisfied with the position and status of an ordinary writer and journalist. Over and over she claims that his ideology is driven by megalomania.[27]

The play's main original turn and de-automatization occur in a dialogue in which Julia threatens to turn Hans against his father, so that his favorite child, the one he hoped would be his heir and successor, will erase him from memory. In the nursery, she promises that she will create a different Herzl legend, nothing like the legend he has spent his life trying to shape: »You are shnorrering a beggar's princedom for your beggars in order to create your own legend, but I dominate the nursery, and in the nursery I will introduce a different legend.«[28] In the third part of the trilogy, the son, Hans, indeed fulfills his mother's curse.

IV

According to Bistritzki, Herzl's infantile behavior, his vanity and idealization of his uncle – the genial »shlemazel« who wanted to invent a so-called »flying balloon« – are the essential components of Herzl's character. The uncle's theory of the hot air balloon, thought to be a daydream and delusion, was later examined by specialists and found to be more solid than anyone had imagined. To a certain extent, his grandnephew identifies with him.[29] In the play, there is no transition from the infantile Herzl with megalomaniac ideas to the Herzl who is striving to solve the »Jewish Question.« He describes his ideas to his friend Schiff and to his wife; the ideas seem to Schiff to be the nightmares of a lunatic, and he suggests that Herzl see their mutual friend, Dr. Max Nordau, who happens to be a psychiatrist. Herzl declares that he will not go to Nordau as long as his vision is only a mystic dream; if he wants to convince Nordau, he says, his vision must be ripe and rational.[30]

Bistritzki reflects Herzl's megalomania through another character trait: he lectures to his followers, but does not talk to people. He preaches his beliefs in

---

[26] Ibid., 689.
[27] Ibid., 781–782.
[28] Ibid., 784.
[29] Ibid., 703–704.
[30] Ibid., 667.

numerous monologues and monodialogical responses, but real dialogue with his colleagues is rare. The ongoing problem is the clash between the realistic, down-to-earth approach of his family and colleagues and the idealistic, high-register speech of Herzl himself.[31]

The character of Herzl in the play is quite complex. He is on the verge of suicide. But his suicidal inclinations can be understood as the *thanatos* aspect of the prophet of revival. His character oscillates between an urge for life and the death wish, between daydream and the reality principle, between fiction and reality. He seems sometimes like a character in a drama of his own fantasy, as if his actions were elements in a novel or a drama he is now writing or will write in the future. The dreamy, fictional atmosphere is characteristic of the main character and of the development of his so-called vision. Herzl calls it a dream while being awake. Some characters in this dream are very real: Bismarck, Rothschild, Hirsch, the German Kaiser. Only a dreamer and visionary could imagine, in his wildest hallucinations, that the meetings with these historical figures could become real. Sometimes he announces that if his dream or novel does not become reality, then the ideas of reality will be transformed into a novel. [32]

V

The discussion up until this point leads to the following question: If we did not have historical information about the material of the drama – including Herzl's biography, Zionism, Europe at the *fin de siecle* – and read the text on its own merits, what major impression would a reader or a common theater spectator form of Herzl's character? If we return to the knowledge we have, as implied readers, will there be an enormous gap between the inherited myth of Herzl and its realization in Bistritzki's dramatic trilogy? In other words, what will be the extent of the gap between the horizon of expectations and the literary realization of the theme?[33]

---

[31] Ibid., 730–731. In this play the long speeches about the age of technology and the future of Jewish capitalism, dialogue about the future of the Zionist movement and its diplomatic manipulations, and the long sermons and speeches of Herzl are quotations from his diaries and essays (ibid., 733).

[32] Ibid., 709.

[33] Hans Robert Jauss: Literary History as a Challenge to Literary Theory. In: New Directions in Literary History. Ed. by R. Cohen. London 1974, 11–41; Wolfgang Iser: The Reading Process: A Phenomenological Approach. In: ibid., 125–145. Herzl's demythification starts with the fact that his entire encounter with the Dreyfus affair is described as a journalistic success, well-written reportages and no more. In the beginning it seems that he wants to become partner of the paper as a reward for his successful feuellitons. The national and ideological impact of the affair is still minor and not even mentioned (ibid., 628–629).

The major problem of the literary reception of Herzl is the contrast between Herzl the myth and Herzl the man, the flesh-and-blood human being. It is the demythification of a myth, or the humanization of a character who has become a symbol and myth. Telling the story of Herzl seems quite easy, because his biographers and those who sought to create his artistic profile have excellent material a their disposal– his diaries, which revealed the human aspect of the great leader, and his ideological manifestos *Altneuland* and *Der Judenstaat*. Demythification means using the diaries as human and psychological background for the ideology and as a source of insight into the hero's psychological motivations as a human being. It is a way of playing with a character who has become a hero in the high mimetic mode, and of debasing him into the low mimetic mode. No longer the heroic leader of a nation, he becomes a frustrated, humiliated human being, whose wife scorns him and who seems himself to be an inflated *alazon*, but is no more than a petty victim of his family and his time.

The third part of the trilogy is the most original. Herzl is now depicted from the perspective of his son. The parson Hechler convinces Hans that his only way to redemption is to convert to Christianity. Then he can find the redemption his father failed to achieve. Hans thinks that the appearance of Nelly, a Jewish girl who was converted by the family that both rescued and raped her, is a kind of sign for him. Nelly, formally Christian but still Jewish, opens the way for Hans. She presents the option of converting while remaining Jewish. Hans gives Father Hechler his consent to the conversion, and Hechler leaves to tell the story of this [in his view] historic event to the people.[34] The Hechler program, carried out through Hans's conversion, is a kind of synthesis of Theodor Herzl's first and last plans. Actually, from the political and social point of view, it is altogether meaningless; in the context of the tragic destiny of Herzl's family, however, it is the final climax and catastrophe.[35] But the main point of the third part of the play is the assumption that the descendants are the victims of their fathers. Hans hates his father because he was a visionary who lived for the masses instead of being an active father to his children. What Herzl sacrificed for the future of the Jewish people was his own personal future. Herzl has sacrificed his children and his wife on the altar of his utopia. All four of them are victims of his personal ambition or of his so-called vision.

Hans tells the story of his family to Nelly, a Jewish prostitute he meets, who was a victim of an Ukrainian pogrom. His oldest sister was behaving like a prostitute, even if she did not do so for money, and she died a lonely death in Lyon, probably by her own hand. His younger sister is also on the verge of a

---

[34] After he leaves, Hans maintains that he can give up his suicide plans and empties the bullets from his gun, but for unexplained reasons (that have, of course, unconscious sources) he leaves one bullet in it.

[35] Ibid., 916–920.

breakdown, and he himself is lonely and in despair. He blames his father for
the desperation of his mother, for his sisters' and his own mental state:

> Hans: ›They killed her soul.‹
> Nelly: ›Who?‹
> Hans: ›He who killed the soul of my mother, and left nothing to her but the grief of
> loneliness. He who killed the soul of my youngest sister and left her only insanity.
> He who killed the soul of my older sister and left her no choice but desperate pro-
> miscuity.‹[36]

Hans hates the concept of redemption, and when the prostitute, who learned it
from her late murdered father, a Herzl follower, mentions it, he responds: »I
hate saviors... Those saviors! They don't save anything but themselves, the
glory of their personality, the splendor of their greatness and the grandeur of
their mission.... [...] they grab everything in the name of redemption, everything is given to them by grace of redemption... [...] They make everyone
empty to fulfill their own soul.«[37] Hans wants to have his own agenda. He
gives Nelly, whose Jewish name was Batya, his ring and marries her formally.[38] She makes a Zionist speech, trying to convince him to immigrate to
Palestine/Eretz-Israel. After this monologue he goes to another room and
commits suicide. Nelly-Batya demands to have her amulet back – a picture
of Herzl that she inherited from her father – and swears that she is leaving
for the promised land. Hechler ends the scene by saying that his great friend
Theodor has not even one loyal descendant left.[39] The end of the play is the
epitome and climax of the Herzl family tragedy, set in motion by the father's
absolute, fatal dedication to his ideology. In a way, it also marks on a symbolic level the positive result of this sacrifice. Nelly-Batya – the victim of an
Ukrainian pogrom who was humiliated and raped, became a prostitute, and
symbolically married Herzl's son – decides to find a remedy for her personal
suffering, which is the result of the Jews' historic persecution, by immigrating
to Eretz-Israel.

VI

The skeptical irony of Herzl's wife was confirmed by the personal history of
his descendants. She was right on the personal level, but probably wrong on
the public one. The paradox of Herzl's heritage, in this sense, is the main message of Bistritzki's drama.

---

[36] Ibid., 856.
[37] Ibid., 864.
[38] The ring of Paulina.
[39] Ibid., 947–948.

The playwright's approach is not very positive. The play not only depreciates and debunks a symbol and myth; it also sometimes becomes a parody that mocks secular messiahs. Reading Bistritzki's play, one can come to the following conclusion: fifty years after Herzl's death, a Jewish-Zionist playwright living in Israel more or less believed that the source of the Zionist ideology was the mind of a neurotic, a disturbed man who escaped from his domestic problems into his mission, who wanted to prove to his mother what an important and wonderful son she had, and who sacrificed his wife and children on the altar of his vision. The exposure of psychological motivations is, in this play, a means of reducing the mythical figure of the national hero to the stature of a neurotic mama's boy, a megalomaniac who uses ideology as an outlet for his depressions and repressions. A vicious question that could be asked is whether or not the neurotic inclinations and the megalomania of this neurotic person are the sources of Zionism. Bistritzki's use of psychology to explain historical events and ideological attitudes is a way of belittling the figure of Herzl and the roots of the Zionist revolution. Perhaps this was not the playwright's conscious intention; but one can also assume that Herzl's neurosis was essentially that of his people, and that the source of his impact was their common »mental disease.«[40]

---

[40] See Lionel Trilling: Art and Neurosis. In: The Liberal Imagination. New York 1953, 176–177.

Anat Feinberg

Mein Kampf: George Tabori's Subversive Herzl Variation

»Ausgerechnet Hitler und Herzl. What a perverse idea! Tabori shies away from nothing, and nothing is holy to him.« I overheard this remark, made by a dismayed spectator, as I was attending a production of George Tabori's play *Mein Kampf*. Tabori would have loved it, I thought, well-aware of how distrustful, how disparaging he is of anything sanctimonious. »Surely, art is not allowed everything, and yet it does. Artists are professional sorcerers,« he maintains.[1] I propose to construe Tabori's play *Mein Kampf* as a provocative, indeed subversive take on Jewish nationalism, exemplified in the figure of the founding father of Zionism, Theodor Herzl. Tabori's dramatic figure, Shlomo Herzl, is to my mind Tabori's response to the so-called New Jew, the self-assured, assertive, pugnacious ideal protagonist of the Zionist narrative, who sought to break away, once and for all, from the doleful Jewish history of humiliation and persection.[2]

»It's a banal story, in the Hollywood sense of the word. A Great Love Story – Hitler and His Jew. A horrible case,« Tabori said about his play,[3] which premiered in Vienna in 1987. At the time Austria was conflicted about the controversial election to the presidency of the Nazi-collaborator and former UN-Secretary General, Kurt Waldheim. The play was an instant hit, and is up to this day Tabori's most performed play.[4] The drama brings together the Jewish »Überlebenskünstler« (survival-artist) Shlomo Herzl and the young Adolf Hitler in a dismal flophouse in Vienna, sometime round 1908.[5] Shlomo Herzl,

---

[1]   George Tabori: Betrachtungen über das Feigenblatt: Handbuch für Verliebte und Verrückte. Trans. by Ursula Grützmacher-Tabori. Munich and Vienna 1991, 78.

[2]   The article is based on the chapter »Mein Kampf« in my book: Embodied Memory. The Theatre of George Tabori. Iowa 1999.

[3]   Cf. R. Palm/U. Voss: ›... So viele ichs, so viele Figuren‹. In: Programme to Mein Kampf, Burgtheater, Vienna, May 6, 1987, 128.

[4]   The play which won the annual accolade of ›Production of the Year‹, Theater Heute 13 (1987), enjoyed innumerable productions in German-speaking theatres as well as performances in Britain, France, and USA. There were some 1,729 performances of the play on German-speaking stages between the 1987/88 season and 1993/94, according to the statistics of the Deutscher Bühnenverein.

[5]   The text mentions no year. It reads »Vienna. Winter 19 - .« Hitler's unsuccessful attempt to be admitted to the Akademie für Bildende Künste (Academy of Art) in Vienna dates back to autumn 1907, followed by another application, similarly unsuccessful, in September 1908. For historical account I have relied on Alan Bullock:

a spirited storyteller and bookseller (selling the Bible as well as the Kamasu-tra), lovingly mothers the newly arrived Adolf Hitler, an egocentric, spoiled brat, who has never matured. Herzl darns Hitler's socks, gives him the famous mustachoid Führer look, lends him a winter coat and teaches the capricious, forlorn hobo how to behave. All this is done much to the amazement and re-monstrance of inmate Lobkowitz »the Loon,« a former kosher cook who plays at being God. Shlomo Herzl painstakingly grooms the aspiring candidate for his fateful interview at the Academy of Art and consoles him when he fails, all the while advising his frustrated roommate to go into politics: »You will be a king, who walks over a blanket of bones,« he assures the ambitious young Hitler.[6] Admittedly, we, spectators, recoil, shrink back, fully aware of the course history was to take. Indeed, Tabori seeks to shock the spectator, and more follows: Frau Death pays a visit to the home of the destitute in the Blut-gasse, looking for a certain Adolf Hitler. Trying to help his roommate out of trouble, Shlomo Herzl chats her up while his chum, Hitler, hides in the toilet; towards the end of the curious visit, he finds out that the lady in black, Frau Death, a baroque allegorical impersonation, was not interested in Hitler as a corpse, as she puts it, but rather meant to recruit him »as a criminal, as a mass murderer, as an exterminating angel.« (MK, 77)

Perhaps it is »A Great Love Story« but it has no happy ending. Accompa-nied by his ardent supporters, the »Tyrolean Leather Freaks« and his »bosom-buddy« Himmlisch (clearly a reference to Heinrich Himmler), Hitler prances in during the last scene, demanding to see Herzl's long-expected masterpiece entitled »Mein Kampf.« Exposed, Shlomo is forced to admit that the book exists only in his imagination. A gruesome punishment follows: Himmlisch, as master of ceremonies, offers a mock-religious sacrifice, and Shlomo Herzl is forced to witness his beloved chicken Mitzi being dismembered, disemboweled, and fi-nally flopped into a frying pan. This mock-religious sacrifice occurs on the Day of Repentance (The Jewish »Yom Kippur«), alluding to the traditional expiatory sacrifice of the rooster (»tarnegol kaparot«). And yet there is a crucial differ-ence: In Tabori's play the chicken is no surrogate for the repenting believer, but the herald of future calamities: »If you start burning birds, you'll end up burning people,« warns Herzl, paraphrasing Heine's dictum. Shlomo Herzl realizes his miscalculation as he is saying Kaddish over Mitzi's remains: »I was too dumb to know that some people can't take love.« The ever-present, would-be God Lobkowitz, the kosher cook, emerges from a dark corner with a macabre piece

---

Hitler. A Study in Tyranny. Harmondsworth 1952, rev. ed. 1962, and on Brigitte Hamann's study of Hitler's »formative« years in Vienna: Hitlers Wien. Munich 1996. All English quotations from Tabori's »Mein Kampf« are taken from the origi-nal English text as reprinted in Carl Weber's anthology DramaContemporary: Ger-many. Baltimore 1996, 37–83. References and quotations from the German version of the play, trans. by Ursula Grützmacher-Tabori, are from George Tabori: Theater-stücke II. Munich, Vienna 1994, 143–203.

6   Only in the German version, 182.

of advice for his friend Shlomo: »Eat, my son, not in hunger, but in the hope to ingest the martyr's strength you will need in all the years to come.« (MK, 83) Shlomo follows his advice, choking with tears as he swallows.

Adapted from a short story published in 1986,[7] the German version of the play is defined as a farce.[8] Yet unlike classical farces, Tabori's play does not seem to focus upon situations and actions at the expense of character development, nor are its characters stereotypes. Truly, *Mein Kampf* is best understood in the context of avant-garde experimentations with the farce mode, which seek to invert generic expectations. Drawing together notions of black humor, elements of the grotesque and absurd situations,[9] these experiments produce a bleak spectacle of the human predicament, oscillating between horror and the ridiculous. They constitute a farce en noir, as Jessica Davis calls them in her study.[10] Tabori's farce is, like so many of his works, a collage, which works by hybridization and disjunction, by entwining fantasy with drab reality. The plethora of Christian images and innuendoes is ingeniously interlaced with undertones, quotations and misquotations from the Old Testament, Midrash Literature and Jewish liturgy. The text teems with quotes and references echoing literary, dramatic, and cinematographic texts – from Samuel Beckett, Buster Keaton, the Marx Brothers, and Charlie Chaplin, to Humphrey Bogart's *Casablanca*.[11] It merges high-brow repartee with »low« farcical knockabout and the sinister, mesmerizing tragic shading of the grotesque.

---

[7] The story, in German translation by Ursula Grützmacher-Tabori, is contained in George Tabori: Meine Kämpfe. Munich, Vienna 1986, 1–99. The original English prose ms. is at the George-Tabori-Archive, Stiftung Archiv der Akademie der Künste, Berlin (SAdK). For a comparison of the prose version and the play see Sandra Pott: Ecco Schlomo: Mein Kampf – Farce oder theologischer Schwank? In: Hans-Peter Bayerdörfer/Jörg Schönert (Eds.): Theater gegen das Vergessen. Tübingen 1997, 248–269.

[8] See title page in Tabori, Theaterstücke II (note 5), 143. I could not find a parallel subtitle in the various English drafts of the play. Nor does it appear in Carl Weber's edition. Tabori speaks of his play as a »theologischer Schwank«. Cf. Palm/Voss, ›... So viele‹ (note 3), 125. The German terms *Farce*, *Schwank* and *Posse* approximate the English farce, whereby *Schwank* is primarily associated with simple and brief peasant romps, involving cuckolding and lacking realistic motivation. Cf. Hans-Peter Bayerdörfer: Die Einakter-Gehversuche auf schwankhaften Boden. In: Walter Hinderer (Ed.): Brechts Dramen. Neue Interpretationen. Stuttgart 1984. Peter Höyng addressed this problem in: Immer spielt ihr und scherzt? Zur Dialektik des Lachens in George Taboris Mein Kampf. Farce. In: Peter Höyng (Ed.): Verkörperte Geschichtsentwürfe: George Tabori Theaterarbeit. Tübingen 1998, 129–149.

[9] Christopher Balme: Grotesque Farce in the Weimar Republic. In: James Redmond (Ed.): Farce. Cambridge 1988, 181. Prominent among these avantgarde experimentations with »farce« are plays by Ionesco, Beckett, Pinter, and other dramatists who are associated with Esslin's notion of the Theater of the Absurd.

[10] Jessica M. Davis: Farce. London 1978, 93.

[11] Frau Death and Hitler depart at the end of Tabori's production climbing the staircase arm in arm, as she refers to »The beginning of a wonderful friendship« (MK, p. 82).

Shlomo and Hitler are a peculiar pair, reminiscent at times of Beckett's homeless tramps in *Waiting for Godot*. The two play-act in a dream, a kind of directed dream, in the words of George Tabori, who is undoubtedly one of the foremost figures in contemporary German theater.[12] Like the father of Zionism, Tabori was born and brought up in Budapest, speaking Hungarian and German.[13] Growing up in an acculturated environment, Theodor Herzl nonetheless experienced some of the Jewish feasts and rituals;[14] Tabori celebrated neither the Jewish holidays nor his own Bar Mitzwa; in fact, his mother converted to Catholicism, his father was a declared agnostic, and he – like his brother – was baptized, albeit circumcised, and went regularly to confession. Like Theodor Herzl, Tabori developed a true passion for the theater at a very young age. He wrote his first play (*The Goat and the Cabbage*) at the age of twenty, but – unlike Herzl, who persisted in writing stage scripts which time and again were turned down – Tabori embarked upon a career as a novelist and author of filmscripts before he returned to his initial passion, the theatre.

The play with the perturbing title *Mein Kampf* should be seen as a wild, carnivalesque flight of fancy, in which the imaginary and the chimerical are substantial and veritable. Indeed, Tabori made it quite clear that he was not concerned with historical accuracy; nor did it make any difference to him that Hitler never encountered a certain Shlomo Herzl. His play consciously ignores the historical-political repercussions or implications of such an encounter. By taking up characters and events from history, distorting and fictionalizing them, he exposes as it were the fictionality of history itself. This »acted dream« of Tabori, whose father Cornelius was murdered in Auschwitz, was his own personal encounter with Hitler, the man who »changed my life, poisoned my dreams.«[15] Tabori admits that it is a fabricated episode with a cathartic function. »It's my Hitler. Hitler in me. It's an exorcism, like everything else I write,«[16] Tabori said, shocking a complacent, self-righteous public by suggesting that one can only overcome Hitler once recognizing his traits in oneself. Many Jewish viewers in particular found this idea to be morally repulsive. There is in Tabori's Weltanschauung no clear dichotomy of »good« and »bad« people. Herzl and Hitler, victim and victimizer, inseparable partners in an unholy symbiosis,[17] are like two poles drawn to one another, two antipodes of the Self: The one, Herzl, a born artist, master of tears and love; the other, Hitler, an anti-artist,[18] incapable of weeping and loving. As in all of his works, the

---

[12] For Tabori's biography, see Anat Feinberg: George Tabori. Portrait. Munich 2003.

[13] Cf. Palm/Voss, ›... So viele‹ (note 3), 130.

[14] Cf. Alex Bein: Theodor Herzl. Vienna 1974, 19.

[15] George Tabori: Ich habe ihm besiegt. In: Der Spiegel, Special Issue 2 (1989), 76.

[16] Andres Müry: Es ist mein Hitler. Ist Hitler in mir. In: Rheinischer Merkur, April 29, 1988.

[17] Carl Weber: Editor's Note, DramaContemporary, 40.

[18] Cf. Gundula Leni Ohngemach: Die Wahrheit des Drehorgelspielers. In: Richard Weber (Ed.): Deutsches Drama der 80er Jahre. Frankfurt/M. 1992, 107–119.

oppressor and the oppressed, the victimizer and the victim are inextricably bound in a symbiotic relationship. »When I think about the German-Jewish love-hate relationship, I sometimes see Laurel and Hardy, or Cain and Abel. Cain loved Abel, that's why he murdered him. Man, say the sages, wants to kill what he loves most,« maintains Tabori,[19] and it is indeed as a taboo-breaker that he sets out to debunk the mythologized arch-villain and depict the banality of evil.

Comparisons and contrasts play a significant role in Tabori's writing. Hitler planned the final solution to the Jewish problem, as he euphemistically termed it; Theodor Herzl, the founder of the Zionist movement, envisioned an end to the anomaly and misery of Jewish existence as a diasporic minority by advocating the national solution. The constructed fictitious Hitler of the play bears the forename and surname of the real person, relying partly at least on historical facts (i.e. Hitler's unsuccessful application at the Viennese Academy of Art, 1907–1908). The Jewish protagonist, in contrast, is not Theodor, but Shlomo Herzl, who shares nothing with the biography of his namesake. And yet, recounting his family history to the newly arrived tramp, Shlomo Herzl mentions a distant cousin, Löw Pinsker from Odessa. This, of course, is no mere coincidence, for Yehuda Leib Pinsker, leader of the »Hibbat Zion« movement and author of *Autoemancipation*, similarly argued that the only way of eliminating what he named Judeophobia, was by following a national-territorial trajectory.

But the name Herzl, as Shlomo himself points out, is also the diminutive of Herz, heart in Yiddish as well as in Viennese dialect. Herz, he continues, »rhymes with Schmerz, or Scherz (jest)« (MK, 49), which epitomizes the gist of his philosophy of survival. It is the heart which time and again blunders. Shlomo, a hapless gull with »a broken heart [...], a bleeding heart« (MK, 43), convinces himself that he can teach his disciple love and compassion. At the end of their tempestuous relationship, he realizes that Hitler, callous and unable to shed a genuine tear, is a man who »can't take love.« (MK, 82) This is but another instance in a life-long series of miscalculations. Shlomo Herzl is a self-confessed loser whose vulnerability and misfortune earn our sympathy. Bearing the Hebrew name of the Biblical King Solomon, »wiser than all men«, Shlomo is ironically enough an exemplary ›Schlemazel‹ whose never-ending misfortunes illustrate Tabori's contention that »to the Jew disaster is a way of life.«[20]

Who then is Tabori's protagonist, his idiosyncratically constructed Herzl? Certainly no secular messianic figure, he is in fact the antithesis of the much applauded New Jew. He is a homeless daydreamer, who for a while worked in a morgue, washing corpses. Later, he is a poor and incompetent bookseller. He

---

[19] George Tabori: Der Sollyjupp unter uns. In: Profil, 13, March 23, 1992, 94.
[20] George Tabori: Hamlet in Blue. In: Theater Quarterly 20 (December 1975– February 1976), 117.

is clearly the opposite of the canny, avaricious usurer, whom we encounter in anti-Jewish literature, or even for that matter in Theodor Herzl's play *Das neue Ghetto*, in the despicable figure of the repulisve stock-exchange speculator Wasserstein. In line with the essential trope of antisemitism, with the long tradition of the Jew's maligned, devious, degenerate, and grotesque body,[21] Tabori's Jew is old, weak, and ugly, resembling »an animal« that needs to be »deloused.« In his 1987 premiere Tabori emphasized the Jew's ugly features, calling to mind savage anti-Jewish depictions. Shlomo Herzl was a stooped-over man with red ears and a protruding false nose (which Hitler mistakenly pulls). He wore scummy rags and shuffled along nervously. Too old for Romeo-like fiery love-making, all he can offer his blonde, fair-skinned Madonna-»Shikse«-Gretchen – modeled on the innocent maid who falls prey to Faust's lascivious dreams[22] – are stories, anecdotes, and gumdrops. Shlomo eulogizes his beloved in Biblical style, quoting and paraphrasing from the Song of Songs, which is attributed to King Solomon, a renowned womanizer. While Jewish tradition takes a dim view of needless talk, Tabori's Jew is a spellbinding word-spinner, whose only weapon is as insubstantial as words. For Tabori, words are powerful tools, and he associates them with the Jewish way of surviving. Tellingly, he has rejected the use of arms against antisemitic attacks. Militancy, which is invariably one of the attributes of Jewish nationalism, is alien to Tabori's notion of the Jewish ethos: »The Jews have been long armed, with word and writing. I still find these more powerful than the sword.«[23]

A born loser and a »Luftmensch,« Shlomo Herzl's métier is language. A master of quick-fire questions and answers, of epigrammatic wit, he relies on rationality and realism, as Jewish humor habitually does.[24] In the vein of diasporic Jewish humor, his joke often expands into an anecdote. But perhaps most striking is his Talmudic disquisitional style, his hair-splitting mode of logical argumentation known as pilpul, the best example of which is the quibbling about the twins who fall through a chimney, with which he confronts Hitler.[25]

---

21 The topos of the ugly Jew, the infector, is prominent in antisemitic literature. See Sander Gilman: The Jew's Body. New York, London 1991, and John Efron: Der reine und der schmutzige Jude. In: Sander Gilman/Robert Jütte/Gabriele Kohlbauer-Fritz (Eds.): Der schejne Jid. Vienna 1998, 75–85.
A soul mate to Shlomo Herzl is Master Zvi, a »Talmid chacham«, Tabori's alter ego in Babylon Blues. Cf. Prologue to the play, Theaterstücke II (note 5), 245–248.

22 Peter von Becker speaks of »Mein Kampf or Mein Faust« in his critique of the production: Herzl und Hitler. In: Die Zeit, May 15, 1987. Albert Goldman recognizes the infatuation of the Schlemiel Jew with the blonde American as a topos in Jewish American comedy. See his essay Laughtermakers. In: Sarah Blacher Cohen (Ed.): Jewish Wry: Essays on Jewish Humor. Bloomington 1987, 81.

23 George Tabori: Die Macht des Wortes. In: Süddeutsche Zeitung, November 28/29, 1992.

24 Cf. Joseph Boskin: Beyond Kvetching and Jiving: The Thrust of Jewish and Black Folkhumor. In: Blacher Cohen (Ed.), Jewish Wry (note 22), 60–61.

25 Cf. Salcia Landmann (Ed.): Jüdische Witze. Munich 1963, Rpt. 1994, 70–71.

»The content of every joke is catastrophe,« says Tabori.[26] He as well as his alter ego Shlomo Herzl belie the artificial barriers between the tragic and the comic, and many of his scenes are played for a laugh; yet the gaiety springs out of despair,[27] or, conversely, is a way of warding off despondency. Tabori repeatedly uses the image of the lifebelt (»Rettungsring«) to describe the function of the joke, though he insists that the jest is never a means of escaping reality, but »reality itself.« »Must you forever be playing and jesting? You must, oh my friends, which sickens my soul. For only the desperate must.« Hölderlin's epigram serves Tabori as the motto for his play, suggesting that it conveys precisely the awareness that playing and jesting originate in despair.[28]

Indeed, like Sigmund Freud, Tabori maintains that the best jokes come from Jews,[29] for whom, one may add, humor's topsi-turviness is a mode of survival, or, to use Tabori's dictum, the principle of hope. Freud maintains that humor serves an aggressive purpose and he speaks of the tendentious joke as a means of exposing and countering obstacles. »By making our enemy small, inferior, despicable, or comic, we achieve in a roundabout way the enjoyment of overcoming him – to which the third person, who has made no efforts, bears witness by his laughter.«[30] This is precisely what Jewish humor has done for generations, scoffing at Haman, deprecating the oppressive goy in the »Shtetl,« bantering during the Holocaust against the arch-fiend Hitler. An heir to this tradition, Tabori imagines Hitler derided by the subaltern Jew. Hitler is the butt of Tabori's mordant humor, exposing the monster as a pathetic bloke who hides in the toilet.

But Jewish gallows humor does more than wryly deprecate the oppressor by way of celebrating a temporary and often moral victory over him. Martin Grotjahn sees aggression against the self as the main dynamics of Jewish wit,[31] and in truth, there is no shortage of self-critical quips and self-mockery in Tabori's play. In fact, Tabori's humor is characterized by the fusion of elements of Jewish humor with a variety of other comic essentials: the humor of misunderstanding (Herzl: »It's Talmud«, to which Hitler replies: »Another cousin?«; MK, 50), farcical cinematic topoi, wordplay, and equivocations (e.g., the

---

[26] George Tabori in an interview with Peter von Becker: Zeuge des Jahrhunderts. In: Andrea Welker (Ed.): George Tabori: Dem Gedächtnis, der Trauer und dem Lachen gewidmet. Weitra 1994, 254.

[27] So reads the original, English title of his article: Die Heiterkeit der Verzweiflung. In: Theater Heute 4 (1991), 71.

[28] Cf. Palm/Voss, ›... So viele‹ (note 3), 128.

[29] Sigmund Freud: Jokes and Their Relation to the Unconscious (1905), and George Tabori in: Welker (Ed.): George Tabori (note 26), 303. Tabori suggests elsewhere (Unterammergau oder die guten Deutschen. Frankfurt/M. 1981, 22) that humor is the Jewish contribution to civilization.

[30] Sigmund Freud: Jokes and Their Relation to the Unconscious. Trans. and ed. by James Strachey with a biographical introduction by Peter Gay. New York, London 1989, 122.

[31] Martin Grotjahn: Beyond Laughter. Humor and the Subconscious. New York 1957.

search for the title of Shlomo Herzl's book – »Shlomo in Wonderland,«
»Shlomo and Juliet,« »Ecce Shlomo,« etc.; MK, 45), or delicious puns, such as
the corruption of Hitler's name. Also, there is the slapstick and knockabout
humor reminiscent of Buster Keaton or Laurel and Hardy as well as Chaplinesque sequences. Two examples are Herzl pouring water into Hitler's ear to
wake him up and the offer of gumdrops to his beloved Gretchen, as she is
cutting his toenails.

Last but not least, there is Tabori's iconoclastic and subversive humor, the
sense of the macabre when all comic mayhem is seen in hindsight. »When my
time comes,« says Hitler to Herzl, »I shall reward you suitably. I'll buy you an
oven, [...] I'll find you a solution.« (MK, 55) Tabori's fabricated narrative of
the »Great Love Story – Hitler and His Jew,« which plays against our knowledge of history, opens up the possibility for terrifying irony and hideous gro-
tesquerie. »If the ending cannot be happy, let it at least be laughable,« argues
Shlomo Herzl. (MK, 81)

In vain does Herzl try to educate his protégé in the light of Leviticus 19:18,
»ve'ahavta lereacha kamocha« (»Thou shalt love they neighbor as thyself«).
The story of the »Great Love« that has gone awry corroborates Tabori's belief
– the 11th commandment of his alter ego Shlomo Herzl – »Better be choked,
than a choker,« »Better be hunted than a hunter« (MK, 57 and 60). This is a
heretical commandment, which a Zionist would normally find intolerable and
unacceptable. Ironically, the subaltern Jew becomes almost a Christ-like figure, instructing Hitler, the Anti-Christ in the vein of the New Testament's
»Love thy enemy as thyself.«

Two questions remain to be asked and both are not easy to answer. The first
addresses Tabori's relationship to Zionism as a political solution for diasporic
suffering in general, and to Israel as the Jewish homeland in particular.[32] In
other words: why is there such a subversive take on Jewish nationalism in the
shape of a fictitious Jew, who is so different from the muscle-Jew propagated,
for instance, by Max Nordau? A possible answer may be found in a letter Tabori wrote to a friend less than a month after the euphoria following Israel's
1967 victory: »Auschwitz was in a way the last Judaic gesture,« he wrote. It is
»salvation through suffering [...] the alternative is what Israel is doing now. It
is all very admirable and practical, but it may also be the end of Jewishness.«[33]

Matters were complicated from the outset. Like the vast majority of Hungarian Jews and his own father, Cornelius, a convinced liberal cosmopolitan,
George Tabori was never attracted to Zionism. This is all the more perplexing
in view of the fact that he spent the year 1942 in Palestine. The letters he sent

---

[32] For Tabori's attitude to and writings on Israel, see Anat Feinberg: Das israelische
Kapitel: Über zwei unveröffentlichte Manuskripte von George Tabori. In: Hanna
Liss (Ed.): Yagdil Tora we-Ya'adir. Gedenkschrift für Julius Carlebach. Heidelberg
2003, 159–168.

[33] George Tabori, Letter to Mr. Handman, July 4, 1967, SAdK.

from Jerusalem reveal his indifference to Jewish life and to the zealous Zionist activities that were sweeping the country overtly and covertly. They show not the slightest interest in, let alone sympathy for, the Jewish or Zionist struggle. The playwright who came to be the honoric Jew for many admirers in Germany, an Alibijude, admits: »I have suppressed the Jewish in me up to a certain point in time. I wanted to determine myself, when I felt a Jew, and when not. After Auschwitz, at the latest, I had to face the fact that I am Jewish.«[34] Shlomo Herzl is Tabori's construction of the anti-nationalist Jew, the Jew who is associated with the traditional Jewish ethos. Tabori maintains that the Jewish self-image has undergone a far-reaching metamorphosis in the sovereign Jewish state: »The Jews are no longer victims, they now have power. But power corrupts.«[35] His fictitious Herzl is thus a response to the self-assured, assertive ideal of the Zionist narrative, a melancholy euology to a world that is lost.

No less complex is the other issue, namely the reception of the play in Germany and Austria. »Is one allowed to laugh?« – I have often been asked by perplexed and uneasy spectators of *Mein Kampf.* Significantly, this was more than ten years before Roberto Benigni's film *La vita è bella.* Others expressed their dilemma somewhat differently: »Is it legitimate to laugh at a ludicrous Hitler in full knowledge of what really happened?«[36]

Tabori never made a secret of his wish to defy mystification, to shock spectators out of their lethargy, their consternation or affected piousness. Ever since the German premiere of his play *Cannibals* in 1969, criticism has been leveled at his callous bad taste, his disgusting »chuzpah.« He was attacked time and again for being unscrupulously outrageous and for his dangerous playing down of the Nazi malaise. Still, over thirty years have elapsed since the storm over *Cannibals*, his first production in Germany. Tabori's respected status in the German-speaking theater, his credit as the honorific Jew, or »Versöhnungsjude,« along with his by-now well-established reputation as a taboo-buster have done their share. Thus the answer to the question raised in so many critiques of the play – »Is one allowed to do that?« (»Darf man das?«) – is an almost unanimous »Yes.« »Tabori, as a Jew, is in this respect privileged,« writes one critic,[37] and a colleague elaborates the point: »One is allowed – if one is called George Tabori, a theatre-man with a faultless biography, who masters like no one else the grotesque overdrawing as a theatrical stylistic device.«[38]

---

34 André Müller: Ich habe mein Lachen verloren. In: Die Zeit, May 6, 1994.
35 Herlinde Kölbl: Jüdische Portraits. Frankfurt/M. 1989, 237.
36 Similar concerns were voiced upon the screening of the prize-winning film »La Vita è Bella« by Roberto Benigni, arguably Europe's most famous comic actor. The film presents the Shoa in a comic vein; it takes place, in part, in a concentration camp. For a report on the film and the problematics involved, see: Daniel Kotzin: A Clown in the Camps. In: The Jerusalem Report, October 26, 1998, 40–45.
37 Paul Kruntorad: Eine Hitler-Farce. In: Frankfurter Rundschau, May 19, 1987.
38 Thomas Rothschild: Hitler in Wien. In: Die deutsche Bühne 7 (1987), 28–30. This view is shared, for instance, by Lothar Sträter: Auf wienerische Art mit Entsetzen

But what about spectators' reactions? It takes three to make a joke, namely the jokester, the butt of the joke, and the listener, and Eric Bentley observes that the need for an audience is no less vital than the need for the joke.[39] I have already mentioned that Tabori's subversive humor is intended to administer an ugly jolt, to have a purgative effect; yet I am doubtful whether the majority of spectators attending *Mein Kampf* experienced this catharsis. I have met spectators perplexed, hesitant, shocked, or unsure of how they are expected to react. I have encountered others who left the theatre »feeling slightly uncomfortable, because it hasn't made you feel at all uncomfortable about its appalling subject.«[40] I have spoken to some who were relieved to discover that a Jewish playwright absolved the majority of the Germans of their collective guilt, those fellow-travellers and bystanders included, while putting the blame – like the so-called »Intentionalists« among historians of the Third Reich – on Hitler, who, on the top of it all, is depicted as a laughable neurotic.

Truly, Tabori's joke stands on a knife's edge in the literal sense.[41] The question then remains open: how many in the audience, in Germany or anywhere else, perceive *Mein Kampf* as Tabori intended it? And, is a response, such as the one he envisioned, at all possible?

Scherz getrieben. In: Badische Neueste Nachrichten, May 12, 1987, and Rainer Weber: Ecce Shlomo. In: Der Spiegel 20 (1987), 273. See also Wend Kässens: Kein
anderer als Tabori kann und darf es sich leisten, jenen millionenfachen Mord der Fa-
schisten als eine böse Groteske zu zeichnen. In: Jörg Gronius/Wend Kässens (Eds.):
Tabori. Frankfurt 1987, 25.

[39] Eric Bentley: The Life of the Drama. London 1965, 232.

[40] Peter Kemp: The Sick Joke. In: The Independent (London), October 6, 1990.

[41] Konrad Paul Ließmann: Die Tragödie als Farce: Anmerkungen zu George Taboris
Mein Kampf. In: Text und Kritik 133 (1997), 85.

List of Contributors

Eitan Bar-Yosef
Department of Foreign Literatures and Linguistics, Ben-Gurion University, Beer Sheva 84105, Israel

Michael Berkowitz
Department of Hebrew & Jewish Studies, University College London, Gower Street, London WC1E 6BT, United Kingdom

Denis Charbit
Department of Political Science, The Open University of Israel, 108 Ravoutski St., Ra'anana 43104, Israel

Anat Feinberg
Hochschule für Jüdische Studien, Friedrichstr. 9, 69117 Heidelberg, Germany

Mark H. Gelber
Department of Foreign Literatures and Linguistics, Ben-Gurion University, Beer Sheva 84105, Israel

Jacob Golomb
Philosophy Department, Hebrew University, Mt. Scopus Campus, Jerusalem 91905, Israel

Bernard Greiner
Deutsches Seminar, Universität Tübingen, Wilhemstraße 50, 72074 Tübingen, Germany

Klaus Hödl
Centrum für Jüdische Studien, Universität Graz, Elizabethstraße 27, 8010 Graz, Austria

Daniel Hoffmann
Koetschaustr. 30, 40474 Duesseldorf, Germany

Jacques Kornberg
  Department of History, University of Toronto, 100 St. George Street, Toronto M5S 3G3, Canada

Vivian Liska
  Faculteit Letteren en Wijsbegeerte, Universiteit Antwerpen (CDE), Universiteitsplain 1, 2610 Wilrijk, Belgium

Na'ama Rokem
  Department of Comparative Literature , Stanford University, Stanford, California 94305-2031, USA

Gershon Shaked, c/o Malka Shaked
  Rehov Tirza 14, Jerusalem 96186, Israel

Frank Stern
  Institut für Zeitgeschichte, Universität Wien, Spitalgasse 2–4, Hof 1, 1090 Wien, Austria

Benno Wagner
  Fachbereich 3 / AL, Sprach-, Literatur- und Medienwissenschaften, Allgemeine Literaturwissenschaft, Universität Siegen, Adolf-Reichwein-Straße 2, 57076 Siegen, Germany

Robert Wistrich
  Department of Jewish History, Hebrew University, Mt. Scopus Campus, Jerusalem 91905, Israel

Index